# *The Meaning of*

# SHAKESPEARE

*Volume I*

By

HAROLD C. GODDARD

THE UNIVERSITY OF CHICAGO PRESS

CHICAGO & LONDON

THE UNIVERSITY OF CHICAGO PRESS, CHICAGO 60637
THE UNIVERSITY OF CHICAGO PRESS, LTD., LONDON

© 1951 by The University of Chicago. All rights reserved.
Published 1951. Paperback edition 1960
Printed in the United States of America
10  09  08  07  06  05  04                    17  18  19  20

ISBN: 0-226-30041-2
LCN: 51-2288


⊗  The paper used in this publication meets the
minimum requirements of the American National
Standard for Information Sciences—Permanence of
Paper for Printed Library Materials, ANSI Z39.48–1992.

*Sweet, sweet, sweet poison for the age's tooth.*

— KING JOHN

*When such a spacious mirror's set before him*
*He needs must see himself.*

— ANTONY AND CLEOPATRA

*The secrets of nature*
*Have not more gift in taciturnity.*

— TROILUS AND CRESSIDA

*Is there any cause in nature that makes these hard*
*hearts?*

— KING LEAR

*How with this rage shall beauty hold a plea*
*Whose action is no stronger than a flower?*

— SONNET 65

# A Word to the Reader

How many a book on Shakespeare has been prefaced with a sort of shame-faced apology for "another book on Shakespeare." Anyone who feels that way should never have produced such a book. For my part, I believe we are nearer the beginning than the end of our understanding of Shakespeare's genius. Poetry forever makes itself over for each generation, and I cannot conceive a time that will not be able to ask with profit what Shakespeare has to say specifically to *it*. Twice within three decades our own time has called on its younger generation to avenge a wrong with the making of which it had nothing to do. For whom, then, if not for us, was *Hamlet* written? To whom, if not to us, did King Lear direct the question, "Is there any cause in nature that makes these hard hearts?" and of what age if not the atomic did Albany make his prediction:

> It will come,
> Humanity must perforce prey on itself,
> Like monsters of the deep.

Ours is a time that would have sent the Greeks to their oracles. We fail at our peril to consult our own.

Nor do I apologize for the length of this book. Maurice Morgann, in the eighteenth century, wrote one of the best books on Shakespeare ever published. When it was done, he was a bit appalled by its length. "The Book is perhaps, as it stands, too bulky for the subject," he remarked, having his quiet joke (it was on Falstaff), "but if the Reader knew how many pressing considerations, as it grew into size, the Author resisted, which yet seemed intitled to be heard, he would the more readily excuse him." Though the evidence may seem against me, I have exercised a like restraint. This book could easily have been several times as long. It is far longer than Morgann's.

But, after all, he was writing of one character; I am compelled to bring in scores.

"Shakespeare deserves to be considered in detail;—a task hitherto unattempted." He does, and Morgann, following his own injunction, was about the first so to consider him. Books by the shelf-full have been written on Shakespeare since the publication of *An Essay on the Dramatic Character of Sir John Falstaff*. Many of them are crowded with specific references and quotations. Yet it is surprising how few of them have considered the poet "in detail" in Morgann's sense, how true his "a task hitherto unattempted" still remains. Any book that considers Shakespeare in detail is bound to be a long book.

*And Shakespeare deserves to be considered as a whole.* I should like to add that dictum to the other. I do not mean merely that all of Shakespeare deserves to be considered. That goes without saying. I mean that his plays and poems deserve to be considered integrally, as chapters, so to speak, of a single work. And there again I do not have in mind just finding passages in *Henry V*, for example, that illuminate *Julius Caesar*, or vice versa. That practice, while valuable, has been long and widely indulged in. I mean treating Shakespeare's works as an organism. No one would dream of pretending to understand the fifth act of *Antony and Cleopatra* without taking the other four into account. If, as I believe, Shakespeare is one, it will be just as useless to try to understand *Antony and Cleopatra* as a whole without catching its relation to, say, *Romeo and Juliet, Troilus and Cressida, Othello,* and *King Lear*. Not to imply that Shakespeare planned or was fully conscious of this deeper unity. The imagination does not work that way. How it does work, Sir Thomas Browne once made clear when he exclaimed: "Now for my life, it is a miracle of thirty years, which to relate were not a History, but a piece of Poetry, and would sound to common ears like a Fable." If we may judge by his works, Shakespeare's life had a like integrity. His inner life at any rate. It must itself have been a work of art. (All this I treat in my chapter, "The Integrity of Shakespeare.")

But to consider Shakespeare as a whole and at the same time to consider him in detail is, to that extent at least, to consider him as a *poet*—for it is the poet who actually achieves that union of the many and the one about which philosophers have dreamed and metaphysicians argued. This book is written out of a conviction that Shakespeare is primarily a poet.

That Shakespeare is primarily a poet ought to be so obvious that even to put the thought in words would be banal. That it is not only not banal but is the thing most necessary to emphasize about him at the present time is a comment on the long ascendency of the historical school of criticism in Shakespeare study. In stressing what Shakespeare meant to the Elizabethan age the historical critics have helped us forget what he might mean to ours. Like the materialists of the nineteenth century, in focusing attention on where things come from they tend to forget where they are going. They tend to forget that poetry means creation, and creation is something that still goes on.

And then there are the theatrical critics—not the theatrical reviewers but the critics whose central interest is dramaturgy. They too have obscured the greater Shakespeare. It is they who are forever insisting that Shakespeare was primarily a playwright, always concerned first of all with the theater, with dramatic construction, stagecraft, acting, scenic effect, and so on. That in his earlier career the theater did nearly "get" him, Shakespeare himself tells us in one of the *Sonnets*. But he plainly implies what his later works prove—that he escaped that fate. Because he mastered the theater, he saw through it.

And so the time seems to have come for a return to Shakespeare the poet,\* for a consideration of his works not merely as poetry in the romantic meaning of that term but as works of the Imagination in the widest and deepest sense: imagination, that language in which all languages are written, that language within which the poet conceals himself as utterly from the crowd and from seekers after pleasure and power as he reveals himself to those rarer individuals who can enter his spirit. The purpose of the poet in this sense is often in direct contradiction with that of the playwright. It may even lead him in the interest of truth to distill

> Sweet, sweet, sweet poison for the age's tooth,

a line which, for our present understanding of him, may be the most important one in all Shakespeare's works. "Behold, I send you forth as sheep in the midst of wolves: be ye therefore wise as serpents, and harmless as doves," said Jesus to his disciples. No one ever followed that advice more effectively than William Shakespeare. Here is a neglected aspect of his works. The world has long since recognized the dove. It has scarcely begun to detect the serpent. (This line of thought I develop in my introductory chapter, "Cadwal and Polydore," and more especially in the chapter, "The Poet-Playwright.")

\* It was after the present work was projected and partly written that Caroline Spurgeon's *Shakespeare's Imagery* appeared. That book, though it is more a catalog and quarry for future critics than a piece of criticism itself, is a milestone in Shakespeare study because it recognizes the fundamental importance of Shakespeare as a poet. Its title, however, is precise and it has more to do with Shakespeare's imagery than with his imagination. Imagery is only the raw material of the imagination. Such works with which I am acquainted as have been inspired by Miss Spurgeon's volume, or as have come out of a similar impulse, impress me as being, like hers, studies of single images or groups of images rather than of the poet's imagination itself. The works of G. Wilson Knight are a partial exception to this statement.

If this book is fortunate enough to find readers, there are bound to be some who, because of its length, will look into it for what it has to say about this or that play as distinguished from those who read all of it. This immediately introduces a double difficulty in a work founded on the belief that Shakespeare's plays are parts of a larger whole. Those who read only about a particular play must expect, therefore, occasional references to other plays which may sound heretical, or passages (only brief ones, I hope) which are even unintelligible apart from the chapters in which those plays are treated. And on the other hand anyone who reads more extensively will forgive, I trust, certain brief repetitions inserted expressly for those who may read a later without having read an earlier chapter.

There will be some to wonder why Dostoevsky is referred to so often in this book. Shakespeare and Dostoevsky were separated by two centuries and a half. Their times, their environments, and apparently their experiences, were widely different, as were the literary mediums they employed. The similarity, in spite of this, of the insight into and the outlook upon life of two geniuses whom not a few would call the world's supreme dramatist and the world's supreme novelist is one of the most impressive phenomena in the history of the human imagination. I have barely scratched the surface of the subject in this volume.

Anyone who has gone on reading Shakespeare for years and then writes a book about him is bound to be at a loss if asked just what he owes to the text itself and his own interpretation of it, what to the commentators, to his friends, or, if he has been a teacher, to his students. The things most indubitably his he is sure of. Beyond that, he cannot be certain. But what difference does it make, if he has made something of his own of them all? He has Shakespeare's royal example for running up debts. He has also his more difficult precedent of using well what he has borrowed rather than trying to repay it in empty acknowledgments. A teacher has no reason to be disturbed when he recognizes an idea of his own in print and realizes that directly or indirectly a former student is responsible for putting it in circulation. If anyone from whom I have inadvertently taken a suggestion should chance to see these pages and feel aggrieved at the lack of a footnote containing his name, let him read the first chapter of *A Pluralistic Universe* where William James inters beyond possible resurrection the practice of embalming every scholarly fly that has fallen into the scholarly amber by dedicating to him the tombstone of a separate footnote. Shakespeare, above everybody, is too big to be owned. Let us give up staking out claims on him.

But if I omit detailed acknowledgments to Shakespearean critics and scholars, there is another deeper kind of indebtedness which I wish not only to acknowledge but to stress: namely, to those recent explorers in the realm of the unconscious among the wisest of whom are Samuel Butler, William James, and Carl G. Jung (not to mention such poetic predecessors of theirs as Blake and Emerson). Those readers who are familiar with the works of these men will understand what I mean and perceive how profound is my debt to them. And no less profound, if less apparent or traceable, have been my obligations in this connection to other figures in world literature from Laotse and the Greek dramatists to Dante and Chaucer. (Chaucer, for example, set me to analyzing dreams long before I had ever heard of Freud.) Psychology in our day has been doing its best to catch up with what is already implicit in the works of such men. Only very ingenuous persons will think that the wise men of the ages did not know of the existence of the unconscious mind because they did not call it by that name or formulate its activities in twentieth-century terms.

*Harold C. Goddard died without naming his book, and the title was given by the publisher.*

# Table of Contents

## Chapter I

# Cadwal and Polydore

Each heart
Hath from the leaves of thy unvalu'd Book
Those Delphick lines with deep impression took.

MILTON, *On Shakespeare*

Shakespeare is like life. There are almost as many ways of taking him as there are ways of living. From the child lost in one of his stories as retold by Charles and Mary Lamb, to the old man turning to his works for fortitude and vision, every age finds in them what it needs. Every new lover of them finds himself, as every generation, from the poet's to our own, has found itself. One by one all the philosophies have been discovered in Shakespeare's works, and he has been charged—both as virtue and weakness—with having no philosophy. The lawyer believes he must have been a lawyer, the musician a musician, the Catholic a Catholic, the Protestant a Protestant. Never was there a more protean genius. Whether his dramas should be taken as plays or as literature has been disputed. But surely they should be taken as both. Acted, or seen on the stage, they disclose things hidden to the reader. Read, they reveal what no actor or theater can convey. And how many ways of reading them there are! Not merely that each fresh voice makes them unique. The lover, the student, the teacher, the scholar, the director, the actor—every one of them finds something that the others miss, until we begin to wonder how many Shakespeares there were. I do not refer to the man Shakespeare, though he too is variously held to have been everything from a shrewd businessman to a dreamer and mystic—or even a myth in the sense that someone else wrote his works under his name.

I refer to the Shakespeare we find in the plays. There at least is the play-wright, the dramatist, the psychologist, the thinker, the humorist, the prophet, and the poet—to name no others. In the face of all this variety it would be interesting to get hold of Shakespeare and ask him how he would prefer to have his plays taken.

As it happens, there is a passage in one of them that may give us a clue as to what his answer to this very question might have been. It is in *Cymbeline*—the scene in which the old man, Belarius, recounts how the king's two sons whom he carried off in their childhood and brought up in the wilds of Wales respond to the tales he is in the habit of telling them. They are as rugged and lovely a pair of boys as the mountains they live among, both of them intelligent, both brimming with vitality. But Shakespeare distinguishes them sharply. The elder, Polydore, formerly Guiderius, is the more objective and active in temperament; the younger, Cadwal, once Arviragus, the more imaginative. They listen in character.

> Jove!

says Belarius of the older boy,

> When on my three-foot stool I sit and tell
> The war-like feats I have done, *his spirits fly out
> Into my story:* say, "Thus mine enemy fell,
> And thus I set my foot on's neck;" even then
> The princely blood flows in his cheek, he sweats,
> Strains his young nerves, and puts himself in posture
> That acts my words.

The reaction of the younger brother, Cadwal, Belarius describes more briefly. He, he says,

> in as like a figure,
> *Strikes life into my speech and shows much more
> His own conceiving.*

Neither youth, in other words, is a mere passive receptacle for the narrative. Each participates in, contributes to it. But how differently! The elder acts it out, spirit and body combining to *be* the story and its hero. The younger re-creates it imaginatively, striking life into it by revealing his individual reaction to it.

Anyone understands the impulse to act out a story. It may be observed in any alert child. It is essentially an impulse toward objectification, realization, an urge to translate the language of words into the language of intonation, gesture, and action in the widest sense. If the story itself is oral, and well told, the vocal part of the translation may be more than begun by the narrator, and, if vividly put, there will be incipient gestures and fire in the eye. But it is left to the actor to translate with his whole body, and *as actor* the closer his rendering to the original the better. His spirits fly out into the story and identify themselves with it.

But translation is rarely creation, and there is a step beyond it. There is nothing that makes a story come to life like linking it with the experience of the moment. We all remember some familiar tale, some proverb or maxim long accepted as true, that one day suddenly lighted up what was happening with such vividness that we realized we had never understood it till that instant. A dead truth had become a living one.

I think of an almost absurd example. It concerns a little boy who might have been Cadwal at an earlier age. He had been gently reprimanded by his aunt for raiding the cookie jar. "What do you suppose the cookie jar would say, if it could talk," she asked him, "when it found all its cookies gone?" "It would say," he answered sweetly, "suffer little children to come unto me, and forbid them not." That is what I call taking the Bible not in vain. The little boy who in an emergency put that pragmatic interpretation on Jesus's words showed "much more his own conceiving" than the meaning their author originally intended. But if Jesus could have overheard, would not his face have lighted up with a smile, and would he not have admitted that this must indeed have been exactly what he had in mind without realizing it?

Extreme examples are the most illuminating. Take one more. Genius is like childhood, and it too can take liberties with Scripture. Jonathan Swift once preached a sermon to the tailors of Dublin on the text, "A remnant shall be saved." Swift knew, as this incident proves, that the function of a bible is to rebuke and inspire the present, not just to record the past. It is not often necessary to wrench a text so far from its original sense as Swift did on this occasion. But better that than that one Dublin tailor should be lost. Most of Jesus' listeners doubtless took his parables just as stories and went on living as before. But a remnant shall be saved.

Granted the extravagance of these examples, they show, nevertheless, how the imagination works and what the nature of poetry is. Poetry is not something that exists in printed words on the page. It is not even something that exists in nature, in sunshine or in moonlight. Nor on the other hand is it something that exists just in the human heart or mind. It is rather the spark that leaps across when something within is brought close to something without, or something without to something within. The poetry *is* the spark. Or, if you will, it is what the spark gives birth to, something as different from either its inner or its outer constituent as water is from the oxygen or the hydrogen that electricity combines.

It is my guess that Shakespeare, when he was a boy, was much like Cadwal and that toward the end of his life he grew more and more like Belarius. If there is anything in this conjecture, it may not be going too far to find in the old man's words an intimation of how Shakespeare would have liked to have his own stories taken. "I like to have them acted," I can imagine him saying. "Whether you are playing them or reading them I like to have your spirits fly out into them, as Polydore's did into the tales of Belarius." But if it came to a choice, who can doubt where Shakespeare's deeper sympathy would lie? And so I hear him adding: "But there is another way of taking my stories that I like even better. I like to have you strike life into my speech by lighting it up with your own experience, as Cadwal did the speech of Belarius. Yes, I love to have my stories taken as dramas, but I love still more to have them taken as poetry."

That at any rate is the way Shakespeare treated the stories of others. He read his Plutarch, his Holinshed, and his Italian tales—and turned them to his own account. In most cases he remained tolerably faithful to the plots, but he put his own interpretation on them and gave his own conception of the characters. And what life he struck into them in doing so! His Greeks and Romans, his Britons and Italians, all became, in one sense, Elizabethan Englishmen, and, in another, what for lack of a better term we can only call "Universal Man."

Do not misunderstand me. Shakespeare was a genius and a writer. We are just common readers. I am not suggesting that we are entitled to take any such freedom with his plays as he took with his sources. But I am suggesting that his attitude toward them does show *in kind* what our attitude toward him should be. He himself, when he is dealing with another genius, Plutarch, preserves a fidelity to his original that he does not exhibit toward writers of a lower order. How much greater should be our reverence, as mere readers, for the supreme genius of Shakespeare! But it should be no merely passive reverence. "A great portrait," says Samuel Butler, "is always more a portrait of the painter than of the painted." With due allowance, what is true of the most gifted painter is true of the humblest reader. It has been true of the greatest critics. The men who have loved Shakespeare best and have kept him most alive have all been Cadwals.

No better criticism of Shakespeare has ever been written than that of Charles Lamb at his best. It is true to Shakespeare—but it is also true to Charles Lamb. And the mystery of it is that the more Lamb there is in it the more there is of Shakespeare.

> To thine own self be true,
> And it must follow, as the night the day,
> Thou canst not then be false to any man.

Shakespeare must have given those words to Polonius at a moment when Polonius was being so false to himself, to show how truth turns to falsehood on the lips of a false man. There are Poloniuses of criticism who are forever telling us to be true to Shakespeare. We should be, but not in their way. No one can be true to Shakespeare until he has first been true to himself.

And the greatest actors, like the greatest critics, have been Cadwals. A good actor is a Polydore—his spirits fly out into the story. Indeed, no acting is even tolerable when this does not take place. But there is rare acting that goes beyond that. "It was something above nature," says Hazlitt of Mrs. Siddons' Lady Macbeth. "It seemed almost as if a being of a superior order had dropped from a higher sphere to awe the world with the majesty of her appearance. . . . She glided on and off the stage like an apparition. To have seen her in that character was an event in every one's life, not to be forgotten." Can anyone doubt that Mrs. Siddons drew from the sleep-walking scene effects that Shakespeare was unaware the text contained? Or that if he had seen her he would have approved?

Chekhov has some wise words on this subject:

"When I was given the part of Anissya in Tolstoy's *Power of Darkness*," says Mme. V. S. Boutov, "Chekhov said to me:

" 'It is a difficult part. How are you going to play it?'

"I said I was afraid of the author, of his greatness.

" 'Never be afraid of an author,' he said, 'an actor is a free artist. You ought to create an image different from the author's. When the two images—the author's and the actor's—fuse into one—then a true artistic work is created.' "

The actor, in other words, should not so much efface himself as come to himself in his role.

How many masters of how many arts have expressed delight when they have found some Cadwal to strike life into their own creations:

"I write to you," says Chopin in one of his letters, "without knowing what my pen is scribbling, for Liszt is at this moment playing my Etudes and he transports me out of my proper senses. I should like to steal from him his way of playing my pieces."

And Chopin was not the only one. "I wish you could have heard Liszt this morning," wrote Schumann to Clara Wieck. "He is most extraordinary. He played some of my compositions—the Novelettes, the Fantasia, the Sonata—in a way that moved me deeply. Many of the details were quite different from the way I conceived them, but always inspired by genius."

Brahms is reported to have taken equal delight in two singers who rendered the end of one of his songs very differently—one with a burst of tone, one soft and sad. Both ways doubtless differed from his own conception.

"We have a great deal of evidence that musical performers have a right to interpret compositions freely," says Serge Koussevitzky. "They hold that right from the composer. Take Bach, for example. In his works we very often find no nuances. Does it mean that Bach intended to have his compositions played without nuances? Positively no. The great Bach leaves that freedom to the performer . . .

"I recall a personal experience with the most outstanding contemporary composer, Jean Sibelius. When I studied his Fourth Symphony for a performance here, I found that the tempo of the last 98 bars of the scherzo was marked twice as slow as the preceding tempo,—and that I could neither feel nor understand. I wrote to Sibelius asking for an explanation, thinking that it was a possible misprint and saying I did not feel that tempo. And Sibelius answered: 'The right tempo is the one that the artist feels.' "

That sentence of Sibelius' says it all. But notice the word *artist!* You and I and the next man are not entitled to read anything we take a fancy to into a symphony or a play. It is only in so far as each of us is an artist that his freedom to interpret a work of art will not degenerate into license. Fortunately, however deeply buried, there is an artist in every man.

> The little Shakspeare in the maiden's heart
> Makes Romeo of a plough-boy on his cárt,

says Emerson. The little Shakespeare is the poet in each of us. Without that Little Shakespeare the Great Shakespeare will remain forever imprisoned in a book.

The history of Shakespearean criticism confirms this statement, demonstrating how only the imagination can apprehend the imagination. That criticism, not counting the Elizabethan, falls into three main periods or divisions. The generalizations I shall make in a few sentences about each of them naturally cannot allow for many exceptions.

The criticism of the first period (often called neoclassic), instead of striking life into Shakespeare's works, sought to subject them to a set of rules and a conception of dramatic art inherited from the past, something that was not at all its "own conceiving." The critics of this age admitted that Shakespeare was a kind of rough genius but contended that he lacked art—which he did, in their sense. They served a purpose in pointing out some of Shakespeare's excesses. But they showed how powerless reason is to grasp imagination.

The romantic period, which followed, was poetic rather than intellectual, and produced, at its best, as good criticism of Shakespeare as has ever been written. But it had the defects of its qualities; and in its lesser writers, in its greatest ones at their worst, and in their later imitators, Shakespearean criticism degenerated into extravagance and fancy—for alongside the man who finds his own soul, and so the soul of everyone, in a work of art, is the man who reads into it his own prejudices and opinions, makes it a point of departure for some sheer invention, or uses it to grind his own axe—all of them fatally different things. As Cicero remarks in *Julius Caesar*,

> men may construe things after their fashion,
> Clean from the purpose of the things themselves.

Decius Brutus does just this sort of violence to the dream of Calphurnia in that very play. He bends it intentionally from the true meaning Calphurnia herself found in it and prostitutes it to the purposes of the conspirators.

In reaction against the vagaries and perversions of the more extreme romantic critics, three types of common-sense, factual, and hardheaded criticism have arisen, which, because they are closely allied, rely heavily on learning, and have emanated largely from the universities, may be conveniently given the name academic—not to imply that the universities have not produced criticism of other kinds. The three main branches of this academic criticism are: the textual, the historical, and the theatrical.

"Let us find out first what Shakespeare really wrote," say the textual critics. "Let us discover how men actually lived and thought in his day," say the historical critics. "Let us never forget that he was a playwright," say the theatrical critics, "that he thought of his works as dramas to be performed by actors before an audience, not as literature to be read, either then, or, much less, centuries later." "Let us get rid of all this subjective business," cry all these critics in unison, "and get back to Shakespeare himself."

*Shakespeare himself!* As if Shakespeare himself were acquainted with any such person, had his own neat theory of Hamlet, or held the same conception of his characters a decade later as on the day they were created. "I must observe that I have often been mistaken," says Chekhov in one of his letters, "and have not always thought what I think now." All free minds say that. Is "Shakespeare's" Hamlet what he thought of him when he finished the play, or what he thought after he had written *King Lear* and *The Tempest?* Be sure that Hamlet's creator was as capable as anybody of finding undetected and surprising things in the Prince of Denmark and could be as amazed afterward at what he had written as Swift was in his old age by *A Tale of a Tub,* or Wagner by the music of *Tristan.* "They come and ask me what idea I meant to embody in *Faust,*" said Goethe, "as if I knew myself, and could inform them." And Bernard Shaw has as good as said that he doesn't pretend to know more about the characters in his own plays than anyone else. . . . "Shakespeare himself"! Which Shakespeare? As well set out on a quest for Kant's *thing in itself*.

"Today," says Koussevitzky in the same passage from which I have already quoted, "we often hear 'musical authorities' declare, when discussing a performance: 'Let music speak for itself.' That up-to-date motto is dangerous, because it paves the way for mediocre performers to come and accurately play over a composition from beginning to end, claiming that they 'let the music speak for itself.' That argument is also not correct because a talented artist, no matter how accurately he follows the markings in the score, renders the composition through his own prism, his own perception of the score, his own temperament and emotion. And the deeper the emotion of the interpreter, the greater and more vivid the performance." The music that speaks for itself plainly inhabits the same mysterious region as "Shakespeare himself."

All this is not said to detract from the substantial and valuable services rendered by the academic critics. Every lover of Shakespeare is indebted to them. But they do not seem to have noticed that in seeking to get rid of "all this subjective business" they have poured out the baby with the bath, Shakespeare himself, namely, in another sense than their own.

To find out first what Shakespeare really wrote sounds eminently sensible. But it is not as objective an inquiry as it seems. Even in determining the text, love is as necessary as learning, for only he who recognizes Shakespeare's *voice* and has penetrated into his spirit is fitted to make the delicate choice among possible readings or to catch the "inspired" emendation. And so it turns out that we must know Shakespeare before we know what he wrote precisely in order to be capable of finding out more nearly what he did write.

Surely, too, it is well to be acquainted with a poet's age. But to read some of the historical critics you would think that only a learned student of Elizabethan society and the Elizabethan stage can pretend to understand Shakespeare. Coleridge was perhaps exaggerating when he declared that "Shakespeare is never coloured by the customs of his age; what appears of contemporary character in him is merely negative; it is just not something else." But he was immensely nearer the truth than the scores of scholars who in the last half-century have created those strange abstractions, "the Elizabethan audience" and "the Elizabethan playgoer." As if the nature of the human imagination, which has scarcely altered in a thousand years, must step aside in deference to "the conventions of the Elizabethan stage"! The whole thing is reduced to absurdity when we begin to hear, as we do, of "Elizabethan ghosts." Shakespeare's lifelong pity for "the fools of time" suggests what he might have thought of this way of approaching his works.

A thoroughgoing historical critic is a man attempting to explain the flower by an exhaustive examination of the soil. It cannot be done. "If anything is humanly certain," says William James, "it is that the great man's society, properly so called, does *not* make him before he can remake it. Physiological forces, with which the social, political, geographical, and to a great extent anthropological conditions have just as much and just as little to do as the condition of the crater of Vesuvius has to do with the flickering of this gas by which I write, are what make him." And Samuel Butler has some no less ringing words to the same effect: "Talk about catching the tone of a vanished society to understand Rembrandt or Giovanni Bellini! It is nonsense—the folds do not thicken in front of these men; we understand them as well as those among whom they went about in the flesh, and perhaps better. Homer and Shakespeare speak to us probably far more effectually than they did to the men of their own time, and most likely we have them at their best."

And of course Shakespeare was a playwright. He tells us, in fact, that like the dyer's hand, his nature just escaped being subdued to what it worked in—to the theater, that is, to acting and to playmaking. Some of those I have called theatrical critics (with no reference to theatrical reviewers), as if sorry that it did escape, do their best to subdue Shakespeare's nature to the theater themselves. But how comes it, if Shakespeare was playwright, or even dramatist, before he was poet, that so many of his references to the stage are slighting or contemptuous; that it is precisely when he makes concessions to theatrical effect, as in *All's Well That Ends Well*, that he is least satisfactory; that the greater his plays become the more they tend to transcend the theater? (No, I have not forgotten *Othello*.) Why did he retire to Stratford at or near the crest of his success? And why in *Cymbeline* does he so manifestly exalt the boy who takes stories as poems above the one who takes them as dramas?

The critics who are continually bringing in the conventions of the Elizabethan stage, insisting above all things on a meticulously accurate text, or forever invoking the spirit of Shakespeare's time, are right and admirable in their reverence for history and fact and in their desire to get rid of "all this subjective business"—right and admirable, that is, up to a certain point. But beyond that point they are just indulging in another kind of subjective business of their own. For the objective business that is the object of their search is neither a whit better nor a whit worse than the subjective business that is the subject of their scorn. The two are extremes that meet. Suppose that in a drop of water an oxygen sect were to appear clamoring for the extinction of all this hydrogen business—or vice versa. It would be a parable of the factual critics. For what they leave out is one of the two constituents of life itself. What they forget is the dual character of the imagination.

Imagination is neither the language of nature nor the language of man, but both at once, the medium of communion between the two—as if the birds, unable to understand the speech of man, and man, unable to understand the songs of birds, yet longing to communicate, were to agree on a tongue made up of sounds they both could comprehend—the voice of running water perhaps or the wind in the trees. Imagination is the *elemental* speech in all senses, the first and the last, of primitive man and of the poets.

When you come into the presence of one of the elements, you never can tell whether it is its spirit or your own that is speaking. Look into a pool of water. There are the sky and the trees. But there, too, is your face at the center—however spiritualized. Call to the rocks and hills. Is it your voice the air brings back? Of course. Yet how strangely amalgamated with the voices of the rocks and hills.

Earth is the grossest of the elements and its power to give back images and echoes is less obvious and immediate than that of water and air. But it too will meet us halfway. By their very names, the creatures of earth, like the constellations in the sky, bear the record of man's imaginative experience with them, all the way from a daisy or aster or blue-eyed grass to some Saddleback or Camelback or Old Man of the Mountain. Our hopes and fears are forever seeking shapes in the external world on which they can project themselves.

> How easy is a bush suppos'd a bear!

as Theseus says in *A Midsummer-Night's Dream*. (Just yesterday I mistook a stump for a brown dog. The resemblance was perfect.)

And so with fire. "You can always see a face in the fire." You can, and the warmer you are within the easier it is to find one—either in the embers on the hearth or in the embers in the west. And more than faces, especially in the sunset. For in a sunset all the elements conspire to one end, and there is nothing with more power to tempt the myth-making faculty in man.

Few things are more certain about Shakespeare than his love of tracing these correspondences between the world without and the world within, particularly in the clouds. Everyone remembers how Hamlet teased Polonius with the camel, the weasel, and the whale. Thousands know by heart the lines of Prospero about the cloud-capped towers. Not so familiar perhaps is the passage in which Antony finds his own unstable nature in "black vesper's pageants":

ANTONY: That which is now a horse, even with a thought
          The rack dislimns, and makes it indistinct,
          As water is in water.

EROS:                              It does, my lord.
ANTONY: My good knave Eros, now thy captain is
        Even such a body. Here I am Antony;
        Yet cannot hold this visible shape.

Poetry, the elemental speech, is like the elements. Its primary function is not to convey thought, but to reflect life. It shows man his soul, as a looking glass does his face. There hangs the mirror on the wall, a definite object, the same for all. Yet whoever looks into it sees not the mirror but himself. We all live in the same world, but what different worlds we see in it and make out of it: Caesar's, Jesus', Machiavelli's, Mozart's—yours and mine.

The oracle remains the type of the purest poetry. Oracles are *ambiguous* (a very different thing from *obscure*). They are uttered, as the world seems to be made, to tempt men to meet them halfway, to find in them one of at least two fatally different meanings. Life or death hangs on how they are taken. "The Lord at Delphi," says Heraclitus, "neither speaks nor conceals, but gives a sign." Dreams have the same Delphic characteristic. So does poetry.

To our age anything Delphic is anathema. We want the definite. As certainly as ours is a time of the expert and the technician, we are living under a dynasty of the intellect, and the aim of the intellect is not to wonder and love and grow wise about life, but to control it. The subservience of so much of our science to invention is the proof of this. We want the facts for the practical use we can make of them. We want the tree for its lumber, not, as Thoreau did, to make an appointment with it as with a friend. We want uranium in order to make an atomic bomb, not for the mysterious quality that gave it its heavenly name. When the intellect speaks, its instrument is a rational prose. The more unmistakable the meaning the better. "Two and two are four." Everybody understands what that means, and it means the same to everybody. But "Become what thou art"; "Know thyself"; "Ye must be born again"; "I should never have sought thee if I had not already found thee"; "The rest is silence": what do they mean? Will any two men ever exactly agree? Such sentences are poetry.

> The Vision of Christ that thou dost see
> Is my Vision's Greatest Enemy ...

writes Blake,

> Thine loves the same world that mine hates,
> Thy Heaven doors are my Hell Gates ...
> Both read the Bible day & night,
> But thou read'st black where I read white.

And two spectators side by side at a play can be as far apart as two readers. "This is the silliest stuff that ever I heard," cries Hippolyta, disgusted by the amount of themselves that the craftsmen, Bottom especially, are injecting into their performance of "Pyramus and Thisbe" in *A Midsummer-Night's Dream.** But Theseus, who is like his creator as certainly as Cadwal and Belarius are, answers her profoundly: "The best in this kind are but shadows, and the worst are no worse, if imagination amend them." "It must be your imagination, then, and not theirs," Hippolyta retorts, wittily but more wisely than she knows.

Hazlitt tells of an experience in crossing the Alps that reads like an allegory of the birth, loss, and recovery of imagination. On the horizon he descried what he thought was Mont Blanc. But his driver assuring him that what he had taken for a mountain was only a cloud, he began chiding himself in secret for his tendency to build theories on a foundation of conjectures and wishes. However, as the day wore on and the cloud maintained the same position, he again mentioned his first idea to his guide. They disputed the point for half a day, Hazlitt goes on to say, and it was not until afternoon, when it suddenly stood right up before them, that the driver acknowledged it to be Mont Blanc. He thought the young man had substituted a bit of vapor for a mountain. But the vapor turned out to be the mountain *as seen by youth.* That is what Keats calls the truth of Imagination.

The reader with a poem before him is like a youth with life before him. In spite of all that the guides and drivers say, he must be faithful *to the text and to himself:* two lions at the gate of his adventure to keep him from wandering off into the desert of custom or the jungle of fancy. This is the answer to those who hold that opening the doors on individual interpretation is opening them on anarchy. If it is, we are to blame. It need not be. We read a poem as we live—at our risk. Though it may take its time about it, the world has a way of bringing up with a sharp jolt the man who attempts to substitute for its facts some private fancy. Fanciful interpretations of literature are doomed to as quick extinction. The text must be as sacred to the reader as his facts are to the scientist. He must discard instantly anything it contradicts. But he must be as ready to strike life into it, from his own experience, as a scientist must be fertile in hypotheses. And this is what the objective school of Shakespearean criticism forgets. How refreshing, when oppressed by the deposit of learning under which it sometimes threatens to bury Shakespeare, to remember a sentence of Emerson's: "A

* Samuel Pepys said of *A Midsummer-Night's Dream* almost exactly what Hippolyta said of the play within it. He pronounced it "the most insipid ridiculous play that ever I saw in my life." But what he saw may have differed widely from Shakespeare.

collector recently bought at public auction, in London, for one hundred and fifty-seven guineas, an autograph of Shakspeare: but for nothing a schoolboy can read *Hamlet*, and can detect secrets of highest concernment yet unpublished therein." What if that should cease to be true! What if someday the heart of Hamlet's mystery should be plucked out and whenever we went to the theater we could count not on seeing a new Hamlet as we do now but on seeing the one original and authentic Hamlet of "Shakespeare himself"! Would we care to attend the theater any longer? How right that Shakespeare's most masterly character should be his most baffling and protean one.

Who has not caught some odd resemblance in an ink blot—to a tree, or a lizard, or a map of Florida? A Swiss psychologist has devised a personality test based on the "reading" of especially receptive ink blots prepared in advance. You tell what you see in the blots and unconsciously you expose your innermost self. The psychologist need not have taken all that trouble. The supreme imaginative literature of the world is a survival of the fittest ink blots of the ages, and nothing reveals a man with more precision than his reaction to it. Anyone who has read poetry with young people over many years knows how they characterize themselves in the ways they take it. "We were saying the other night," a college girl wrote to her mother, "that we probably know the members of our Shakespeare class, deep down, far better than we shall know any class again. You just can't discuss Shakespeare without putting a window in your very soul."

"The color of the object illuminated," says Leonardo da Vinci, "partakes of the color of what illuminates it." In the end, whatever its pretensions, any new book about Shakespeare can be no more than just one other man's experience with him. Yet in so far as its author is true to himself and true to the spirit of Shakespeare (as distinguished from that hypothetical being "Shakespeare himself") he cannot help giving more than an individual interpretation to the poet's works. For on its deeper ancestral layers, from which the imagination emerges, our experience has been the same. In that truth lies the possibility of being as faithful to the text before us as the most exacting scholar but faithful also to something older and more universal than any text. After our long attempt to see Shakespeare in the light of his age, has not the time come to try to see him, not in the light of our age, which is just another abstraction, but in the light of the ages and of the present moment, both of which are realities? "Poetry," says Emerson, "must be as new as foam, and as old as the rock." The foam is the unique experience of the moment, a matter of individual temperament; the rock is the practically unchanging character of the imagination, the accumulated deposit of all human and animal history. Either, without the other, is vain.

So desperate at times appears the condition of our world that it seems as if only a miracle could save us. We forget that in art we have at hand the perpetual possibility of such a miracle. Art is given us to redeem us. All we are in the habit of asking or expecting of it today is that it should please or teach—whereas it ought to captivate us, carry us out of ourselves, make us over into something more nearly in its own image. This transubstantiating power of art is confirmed by all its greatest masters and masterpieces. Homer was a bible to the Hellenic world. Dante composed his *Comedy*, he said, to bring the miserable out of their wretchedness. Beethoven declared that those who listened to his music would be consoled. Dostoevsky wrote *The Brothers Karamazov* to rescue Russia from the bloodshed he saw impending. There are no higher authorities on art than these. But it is not enough that their names should stand like mountain peaks in the distance. We must approach them, or bring them near us, as individuals, that we may begin their ascent. It is not "Shakespeare," but your Shakespeare, my Shakespeare, our Shakespeare, who can save us. "*King Lear* is a miracle," wrote a young woman who had just come under its incomparable spell. "There is nothing in the whole world that is not in this play. It says everything, and if this is the last and final judgment on this world we live in, then it is a miraculous world. This is a miracle play."

*Chapter II*

# The Integrity of Shakespeare

"Shakespeare led a life of allegory: his works are the comments on it."
That sentence of Keats's is by general consent one of the profoundest ever
uttered about Shakespeare. But there is no such general consent as to what
it means. What did Keats have in mind? Something very close, I imagine,
to what Sir Thomas Browne did when he exclaimed: "Now for my life,
it is a miracle of thirty years, which to relate were not a History, but a
piece of Poetry, and would sound to common ears like a Fable." If there
is anything in this conjecture, Keats's sentence implies two things: first,
that Shakespeare's life had the organic character of a work of art; and,
second, that his works are less ends in themselves than a by-product of his
living and hence a kind of unconscious record of his life. If so, they should
be taken not separately but as parts of a whole.

There will be those who will say that this is just the way they have long
been taken. What student is not familiar with the "periods" of Shakespeare's
development: his apprenticeship in the schools of the comedy and history
of his day, his rapid and remarkable cultivation and improvement of those
types, his passage from them to tragicomedy and pure tragedy, and thence,
via plays that achieve a fusion of tragedy and history, to the dramatic ro-
mances that round out his career and bring it to a full close in *The Tempest?*
What is this if not integrity? And if you wish, you can please yourself with
the belief that this development reflects a corresponding one in Shakespeare's life: from youthful high spirits, down through disillusionment into
"the depths," and then, after a struggle, up and out into an ultimate serenity
and peace. Integrity again—if a more conjectural one. Think, too, of the

hundreds of links that scores of critics have pointed out between his plays, not to mention the notes in innumerable editions of them crowded with cross-references and parallel passages. A very superfluity of integrity.

Yet I wonder whether Keats did not have in mind something that goes vastly deeper than all this, something of which these other things are just signs or symptoms.

Anyone with any imagination who has even the most superficial acquaintance with embryology must have been struck by the marvelous way in which complexes of cells group themselves to form an eye that as yet has nothing to see, hands that have nothing to handle, feet that have nowhere to go, and so on. Everything, while contributing to the life of the embryo, seems subordinated to a life of a quite different and higher order yet to come. The embryo has an integrity dictated to it as it were by the future. The meaning of each organ is read back into it by the function it achieves after birth.

Something of the same sort may be observed in the world of dreams. In looking back over the dreams of a considerable period a man may sometimes discover in tiny scraps and fragments, even in single images, meanings to which he was utterly blind at the time. They were parts of a pattern that was being slowly woven. By themselves they were as lacking in significance as the pieces of a jigsaw puzzle before the matching of them has begun. But when assembled each is seen to be a part of a picture, or at least a part of a part of a picture.

The intellect makes a conscious plan in advance. The imagination, like the embryo, makes an unconscious one and discovers what it is in retrospect. "I've got to have a conference with my teacher about the outline of my essay," announced a little girl who was writing her first composition in that form. "Now I should think," she continued with a slight note of disdain in her voice, "that you'd write the essay first and then *find* the outline." The teacher might have personified Intellect, the little girl Imagination. It was in recognition of this principle that Samuel Butler was led to assert that "a man should have any number of little aims about which he should be conscious and for which he should have names, but he should have neither name for, nor consciousness concerning, the main aim of his life." The main aim of a man's life, like the main aim of a work of art, is in the control of the Imagination, formerly known as the Will of God, or the will of the gods. "We who dwell on Earth can do nothing of ourselves," says William Blake; "everything is conducted by Spirits, no less than Digestion or Sleep." But we can draw nearer such spirits when we sense their presence. "No production of the highest kind," says Goethe, "no remarkable discovery, no great thought that bears fruit and has results, is in the power of anyone; but such things are elevated above all earthly control." Yet we can take advantage of a wind we are powerless to create. Shakespeare's works give signs of having been under such higher controls, and Shakespeare himself gives signs of having recognized that fact.

This much at any rate is certain: he was profoundly impressed by the truth that everything contains the seeds of its future. It takes no prophet to predict when an acorn is planted that if anything comes of it it will be an oak. But it does take wisdom and vision to perceive that it is possible to make psychological predictions of the same order. Says Warwick to Henry IV:

> There is a history in all men's lives,
> Figuring the nature of the times deceas'd;
> The which observ'd, a man may prophesy,
> With a near aim, of the main chance of things
> As yet not come to life, which in their seeds
> And weak beginnings lie intreasured.
> Such things become the hatch and brood of time.

The embryo of the event—victory, defeat, love, madness, whatever it may be—inevitably exists before the event itself. What is the art of reading the auspices? Shakespeare came close to answering that question in a classic passage in *Troilus and Cressida* that is possibly unsurpassed in all his works in its importance for an understanding of the poet's own method of observation and creation. It is where Achilles is astounded to discover that Ulysses has penetrated the secret of his love for Polyxena:

> ULYSS.: 'Tis known, Achilles, that you are in love
> With one of Priam's daughters.
> ACHIL.: Ha! known!
> ULYSS.: Is that a wonder?
> The providence that's in a watchful state
> Knows almost every grain of Plutus' gold,
> Finds bottom in the uncomprehensive deeps,
> Keeps place with thought, and almost, like the gods,
> Does thoughts unveil in their dumb cradles.
> There is a mystery—with whom relation
> Durst never meddle—in the soul of state,
> Which hath an operation more divine
> Than breath or pen can give expressure to.

Who can doubt that in just this condition of complete mental tranquillity (this "soul of state") Shakespeare had himself often gazed into the spring of his own imagination and found gold at its bottom—into the world around him and found the future in its cradle, the "future in the instant" as Lady

Macbeth calls it? If we gaze into his early works in the same spirit, we find *his* future there. At his first plays we shall take a glance in succeeding chapters. We may say a word here about the two poems of his youth.

## II

Near the end of *Venus and Adonis*, Venus dedicates five stanzas to a prophecy of the woes in store for lovers because of the death of Adonis. Their lines make a bill of particulars under the general theme,

> The course of true love never did run smooth.

If soon after the year 1590 Shakespeare had had a vision of the love stories he was to write, and had jotted down notes for future use, they might well have taken a form close to these five stanzas. Practically every couplet, line, or half-line contains either a hint or a clear forecast of some future play, character, or situation that he was to employ, sometimes more than one.* Similarly, in the Argument he prefixes to *The Rape of Lucrece* we recognize the dénouement of one of his early plays, *The Taming of the Shrew*,

* 'Since thou art dead, lo! here I prophesy:
Sorrow on love hereafter shall attend;
It shall be waited on with jealousy,
Find sweet beginning, but unsavoury end,
    Ne'er settled equally, but high or low;
    That all love's pleasure shall not match his woe.

'It shall be fickle, false, and full of fraud,
Bud and be blasted in a breathing-while;
The bottom poison, and the top o'erstraw'd
With sweets that shall the truest sight beguile.
    The strongest body shall it make most weak,
    Strike the wise dumb and teach the fool to speak.

'It shall be sparing and too full of riot,
Teaching decrepit age to tread the measures;
The staring ruffian shall it keep in quiet,
Pluck down the rich, enrich the poor with treasures;
    It shall be raging-mad, and silly-mild,
    Make the young old, the old become a child.

'It shall suspect where is no cause of fear;
It shall not fear where it should most mistrust;
It shall be merciful, and too severe,
And most deceiving when it seems most just;
    Perverse it shall be, where it shows most toward,
    Put fear to valour, courage to the coward.

'It shall be cause of war and dire events,
And set dissension 'twixt the son and sire;
Subject and servile to all discontents,
As dry combustious matter is to fire.
    Sith in his prime Death doth my love destroy,
    They that love best their love shall not enjoy.'

and the main instigating incident of one of his latest, *Cymbeline*, and in the poem itself we find much of the story of a third, *Troilus and Cressida*, that came about midway between the other two. These parallelisms are made not less but more interesting by the fact that some of these scenes and situations have other sources of their own.

For sources must not be confused with seeds. Sources, in the scholarly sense, are chiefly soil; whereas seeds are the transubstantiating principle of life itself. It is not the general resemblances that suggest the evolution of a later effect out of an earlier one as distinct from mere repetition. It is the pair or group of passages rather that involve a near-identity of words or imagery, or a musical echo. This is especially true when the earlier is obviously a crude first draft of a later perfect one. Above all, when two earlier effects coalesce to form one later one, or when one earlier one splits up into two or more later ones, we recognize processes familiar biologically in the growth of the embryo and psychologically in the unfolding of a series of dreams.

Numerous foreshadowings of the Tragedies, especially of "the big four," in *The Rape of Lucrece* are of this character. In Tarquin himself, the royal criminal, we catch premonitory glimpses of figures as antithetical as Macbeth and Othello. The most detailed effects of imagery clinch these resemblances.

> Thy sea within a puddle's womb is hears'd,
> And not the puddle in thy sea dispers'd.

What are these words of Lucrece to Tarquin but an inverted and immensely inferior first draft of Macbeth's to himself? —

> Will all great Neptune's ocean wash this blood
> Clean from my hand? No, this my hand will rather
> The multitudinous seas incarnadine,
> Making the green one red.

And

> Fair torch, burn out thy light, and lend it not
> To darken her whose light excelleth thine

is obviously a far-off adumbration of Othello's

> Put out the light, and then put out the light,

even to the point of such a detail as Tarquin's "excelleth" which anticipates Othello's "cunning'st pattern of excelling nature." And, to return to *Venus and Adonis*, in Venus'

> And beauty dead, black chaos comes again,

we have the innermost theme of *Othello* down to Othello's own "chaos is come again," qualified by the one adjective best calculated to link that phrase with the as yet unwritten play about the Moor.

And not only Othello but Iago. In *The Rape of Lucrece*, a dozen years before he was created, is a better characterization of Shakespeare's supreme villain than many critics have been able to achieve with his finished portrait before them:

> Such devils steal effects from lightless hell;
> [Iago] in his fire doth quake with cold,
> And in that cold, hot-burning fire doth dwell;
> These contraries such unity do hold.

Here, too, as I said, is *Troilus and Cressida* in outline (including incidentally the very Hecuba about whom the First Player in *Hamlet* declaims). The lines in which Lucrece states the theme of the story,

> Thy heat of lust, fond Paris, did incur
> This load of wrath that burning Troy doth bear,

anticipate exactly the words of Cassandra into which, with a more terrible brevity, she condenses the identical theme of the play:

> Our firebrand brother, Paris, burns us all.

And at the end of the poem, in Brutus, we have a curious composite forecast of Hamlet, with his antic disposition, Edgar, with his histrionic assumption of madness, and Lear's Fool, with his mixture of professional folly and profound wisdom:

> He with the Romans was esteemed so
> As silly-jeering idiots are with kings,
> For sportive words and uttering foolish things.
> But now he throws that shallow habit by
> Wherein deep policy did him disguise . . .
> "Let my unsounded self, suppos'd a fool,
> Now set thy long-experienc'd wit to school."

Germs of half-a-dozen other plays may be detected in this poem, but it would be tedious if not superfluous to particularize further. Shakespeare himself seems to recognize the nature of the connection between his poems and his later work when he lets Macbeth foresee himself proceeding to the murder of Duncan "with Tarquin's ravishing strides." Over and over *The Rape of Lucrece* looks forward to the Tragedies in just the way in which in this passage *Macbeth* looks back to *The Rape of Lucrece*.

### III

The importance of these two in many ways juvenile poems in Shakespeare's development would be more obvious if we recognized that each of them is an allegory which embodies a truth that Shakespeare never ceased to stress.

*Venus and Adonis* is ostensibly the story of how the goddess of love attempts to lure the boy Adonis to carnal love. On the parabolic level it is one of the most powerful protests ever written against too early initiation into sexual experience. Its essence lies in the question,

> Who plucks the bud before one leaf put forth?

Shakespeare saw that the prolongation of innocence—of "infancy" as the biologists say—is the key to mature strength.

> If springing things be any jot diminish'd,
> They wither in their prime, prove nothing worth . . .
> To grow unto himself was his desire.

Blood upon the flowers is his symbol for what forcibly interferes with this basic right of life, red in the morning his figure for a precocious passion that predicts tempest and wreck later in the day. The poem is practically an equation of lust and force.

Adonis himself is drawn to fit this theme. Both the old myth and his own shining beauty link him with the sun, but with this token of strength he has also the charm and modesty of a young maiden. This was Shakespeare's enunciation of a belief he never abandoned: that ideal young manhood is a union of masculine and feminine qualities. "Men who have the woman in them without being womanized," says George Meredith, "they are the pick of men." Shakespeare would have agreed. From the Young Man of the Sonnets—

> A woman's face with Nature's own hand painted
> Hast thou, the master-mistress of my passion—

through his supreme character, Hamlet, on to a boy like Cadwal, he illustrated over and over his adherence to a conception that goes back via Plato to the *Upanishads*. It has been said that Shakespeare has no heroes. If a hero has to be unadulteratedly masculine, there is point in the observation. Otherwise it is a slander.

And his heroines are the counterparts of his heroes. How fond he was of dressing them up in boys' clothes and giving them boyish traits along with their still dominant girlish ones! Those who explain this tendency by the fact that boys played the parts of women in the Elizabethan theater are confusing cause with occasion and would do well to look a little deeper.

Shakespeare's resourceful heroines are fit companions of his poetical heroes. (The husband of the most feminine of them all greets his wife as "O my fair warrior!") The two types culminate and come together in Ariel, who is so quintessentially both above sex and of both sexes that we do not know what pronoun to use when speaking of "him," and stage directors are at a loss whether to cast a boy or a girl for the role. The imagination, Shakespeare seems to be saying, is an hermaphrodite; in proportion as men and women become imaginative they tend, without losing the dominant characteristics of their own sex, to take on those of the other. Adonis is a far-off prophecy of Ariel.

But note that Venus' masculine behavior is as repulsive as Adonis' maidenly traits are attractive. A mere reversal of the qualities of the sexes on a low plane is as perverted and abhorrent as a harmonizing of them on a higher plane is rare and inspiring.

In *The Rape of Lucrece* the situation in *Venus and Adonis* is inverted. This time it is the woman who is a victim of the lust of man. Allegorically the poem is an extended metaphor asserting the identity of lust and war. As its first line points out, Tarquin comes from the siege of Ardea to the siege of Lucrece, and the imagery in which the author tells the story of the assault is predominantly that of the battlefield. *Rape is miniature war* is what the poem says in so many words. *War is rape on a social scale* is what it implies—offensive war, that is. The story seems to have fixed forever in the poet's imagination the concept of royalty as the ravisher of loveliness, to have set up in his mind a lifelong association of power with sensuality, avarice, and tyranny. With the exception of Henry VI—and I am emphatically *not* forgetting Henry V, ravisher of France—he never gives us a full picture of a good king. The Richards and Henrys, the Edwards and Claudiuses, the Caesars and Macbeths, are, all of them, Tarquins in a generic sense, violators in their several ways of innocence and beauty. All early history is mythical. That the Roman tyranny was ended, or mitigated, by the banishment of the Tarquins may be taken in a symbolic as well as in an historical sense. In this sense Shakespeare seems to have felt from the beginning to the end of his life that what the world needs is a fresh expulsion of the Tarquins. It still does. (Those who in our day incline to exclusively economic theories of war might well take notice.)

## IV

The early plays of Shakespeare—as I shall try to show in their place—have the same seminal character as the poems. But the poems alone are enough to suggest that Shakespeare's development may have been almost as independent of his later environment as the embryo is of the place where the mother happens to reside. But how account in that case, the historical critics will ask, for the way that development kept pace with the changes and even with the fashions of the Elizabethan drama? Why are Shakespeare's ideas in so many instances indistinguishable from what may be called the ideas of his time? But why, then, we may ask in turn, has the world shown no such consuming interest in the other men who followed those same fashions and held those same ideas? Plainly it is something that differentiates Shakespeare from his age, not something that integrates him with it, that is the source of his attraction for us. If I pour water into a cup, a pitcher, a tumbler, and a vase, it will instantly conform in each case to the shape of the vessel into which I pour it. But the cause of the conformity is not to be found in the shape of this or that particular container. It resides rather in the mysterious and unchanging fluidity of the water itself. Genius has something of the same quality. But that is the less interesting half of the story. There are two ways of fitting into one's environment that are as opposite as night and day. To fit into one's age as mud does into a crack, or to be molded by it as putty is under a thumb is one thing; to fit into it and to use it creatively as a seed fits into and uses soil is quite another. The secret of why the germinating seed selects certain ingredients of the soil, while utterly ignoring others, lies in the seed, not in the soil.

There are persons who think they have "explained" a dream when they have linked it to things they saw or did during the previous twenty-four hours. The connections they find are indeed real ones. But the mystery of the dream and the reason it chose those particular fragments of experience out of thousands of possible ones lie not in the fragments themselves but in the imagination of the dreamer. Those who seek to throw light on Shakespeare by linking him with his "day" fall all too easily into this same fallacy. They stop where they should be just beginning.

Shakespeare, as we have seen, had a lifelong pity for "the fools of time." "Minute jacks," "time's flies," "vapours" are a few of the other names he bestowed on those who think life itself changes every time it changes its costume, as it has a habit of doing in little ways every day and in a big way once at least in every generation. His plays are full of this theme. No one, for instance, can forget Hamlet's contempt for the fashionable Osric who had caught so perfectly "the tune of the time." And in the 123d sonnet the poet gives direct utterance to his convictions on this subject once for all. Not a little of what I have called the "academic criticism" of Shakespeare of the last decades is wiped off the slate forever by these fourteen lines:

> No, Time, thou shalt not boast that I do change.
> Thy pyramids built up with newer might
> To me are nothing novel, nothing strange;

They are but dressings of a former sight.
Our dates are brief, and therefore we admire
What thou dost foist upon us that is old,
And rather make them born to our desire
Than think that we before have heard them told.
Thy registers and thee I both defy,
Not wondering at the present nor the past,
For thy records and what we see doth lie,
Made more or less by thy continual haste.
This I do vow and this shall ever be;
I will be true, despite thy scythe and thee.

Only a man with a profound longing for integrity could make that boast. "Shakespeare led a life of allegory: his works are the comments on it."

*Chapter III*

# The Comedy of Errors

*The Comedy of Errors*, it is agreed, is one of Shakespeare's very early plays, possibly his earliest. It is more nearly pure "theater" than anything else he ever wrote except perhaps *The Merry Wives of Windsor*. They are his two plays that have little more to offer the reader after two or three careful perusals. *The Comedy of Errors* especially evokes no sense of the inexhaustibility that characterizes Shakespeare's masterpieces.

And yet it is itself a masterpiece in its own kind. That kind, except for its enveloping action and occasional touches of nature in the main story, is, in spite of its title, farce and not comedy. Few better farces have ever been written, and there is something appropriate in the thought that Shakespeare so early came so close to perfection, even if it was perfection in what is commonly considered an inferior dramatic type. But, as is well known, the credit is not all his. The play is an adaptation from Plautus, and the young Shakespeare had the advantage of standing as it were on the shoulders of his Roman predecessor. However, he quadruples the ingenuity called for in managing the plot by introducing a second pair of twins. Plautus had had but one in *The Menaechmi*.

*The Comedy of Errors* leaves the impression that its author must have possessed this quality of ingenuity above all others. Yet ingenuity—not that he ever lacked it—is one of the last things we associate with the mature Shakespeare. It is an attribute of talent, not of genius.

The action of this play bears the marks of having been planned backward. Its outcome was plainly foreseen and worked up to. One can picture Plautus-Shakespeare making actual puppets or using bits of colored cardboard and moving them about on a table to keep the characters and situations straight—except that a mind endowed with skill of this particular order would probably need no external aids. As we saw in another connection, the intellect makes a plan in advance and works toward its fulfilment, while the imagination, like a living organism, "grows" a plan as it were as it goes along. That of course overemphasizes the contrast. Artistic creation is not quite as unconscious a process as the statement implies, and the intellect is needed to keep the creative impulse in restraint. But for practical purposes we may say that *The Comedy of Errors* is a product of Shakespeare's intellect rather than of his imagination. It was invented rather than created. It came out of the same side of the mind that makes a good chess player or military strategist, a successful practical architect or technically adept composer of contrapuntal music. (If anyone retorts that imagination is just what such activities call for, he is debasing the word from its proper sense when applied to the fine arts.)

We know little about the contemporary reception of *The Comedy of Errors*, but it is easy to fancy its being what we call today a "hit." It gratifies the essential theatrical craving. Why do we love the theater? For various reasons, but for one fundamental one. We live in the midst of a confusing world. We are forever making blunders ourselves and becoming the victims of the blunders of other people. How restful yet exhilarating it would be if for once we could get above it all and from a vantage point watch the blunders going on *below* us. Well, that is just what the theater permits us to do for an hour or two. For a brief interval it enables us to become gods. Stripped of all nonessentials, that, I think, is the ultimate nature of the theatrical *passion*, and that is why in one form or another practically everything that goes on in the theater is based on something misunderstood by some or all of the people on the stage that is at the same time clear to the people who are watching them. The spectator is thrilled to share a confidence of the dramatist at the expense of the actors. Hence the playwright's rule: Never keep a secret from your audience. Here is one explanation of the incessant concern of drama with the theme of appearance versus reality. And herein, too, lies the danger of the theater.

It is inspiring for a man to be put for a few moments in the position of a god. But it is an intoxicating experience, and much of it is as bad for him as a little is good. Too much will inevitably drive him mad. For the theater to be a food and not a drug, this purely theatrical quality must be mixed with and diluted by more terrestrial and substantial ingredients. "Theater" must become drama, and, if possible, poetry.

And there is danger to the playwright as well as to the audience, though of another sort. For the playwright who has once discovered the tricks whereby this theatrical effect is obtained is tempted to rely on them for the success of his invention. *Manufacture a misunderstanding and let the audience in on it* is a cheap but infallible recipe for making a play. It is one of the marks of Shakespeare's greatness that he apparently recognized this from the first and refused to be lured down the road to the easy success that has proved the ruin of thousands of promising young playwrights. He continued to make use of the popular appeal that lies in the ingenious plot and theatrical situation, but he subordinated these things progressively to other ends or transmuted them into something higher. The greatest scenes in his plays, however, like the play scene in *Hamlet*, the temptation scene in *Othello*, the murder and banquet scenes in *Macbeth*, along with their unsurpassed drama and poetry, continue to have in the highest degree this purely theatrical quality.

In proportion as they master them, men grow skeptical of their own professions. When they come to know them, they see through them. Shakespeare lived to see through the theater. He subdued it to himself rather than let it subdue him to itself.

There is one clear sign, even in *The Comedy of Errors*, that its author was not going to rest content with mere theatrical effect achieved by the mechanically made coincidences on which all farce relies. The characters of the play, in the face of the strange occurrences with which they are continually being confronted, keep declaring that they must be dreaming, that things are bewitched, that some sorcerer must be at work behind the scenes. In the aggregate these allusions amount almost to an apology to his audience by the author, an admission that a psychological or metaphysical explanation is demanded to reconcile with reality the unreal conventions of the stage. In that sense not only *A Midsummer-Night's Dream*, but *Macbeth* and *The Tempest* are already implicit in *The Comedy of Errors*.

*Chapter IV*

# The Three Parts of Henry VI

The trilogy on the reign of Henry VI, or at least the first of the three plays, competes with *The Comedy of Errors* for the distinction of being Shakespeare's first dramatic work. Whichever was earliest, no one doubts that all four of them were early, written it may be in the neighborhood of 1591.

After long discussion and disagreement concerning the authorship of the three parts of *Henry VI*, something like critical unanimity seems to be emerging in the belief that Parts II and III were written largely if not entirely by Shakespeare, instead of by Shakespeare and others as was formerly supposed. On the other hand, the present tendency is to hold that Shakespeare had a share, but possibly only a small share, in the play that Maurice Morgann long ago rightly described as "that drum-and-trumpet thing, *The first part of Henry VI*." If he wrote it at all, the marked disparity between its best and its worst passages would seem to indicate that he revised certain parts of it some time after it was originally composed.

But far more important than these plays themselves or the question of their authorship is the fact that at or near the beginning of his dramatic career Shakespeare had his intimate attention drawn to the troubled fifteenth century. That he did may have been a matter of pure theatrical chance. But if so, it was a fortunate chance and one that had a lasting influence on the young dramatist's future, for in the reign of Henry VI he came face to face, probably for the first time, with a subject that continued to enthral him to the end of his days. That subject was nothing other than *chaos*. In the political turmoil of the fifteenth century he encountered chaos itself. Later, in his other Histories and in his Tragedies, he went on to inquire into its causes and effects. Each of the protagonists of his greatest plays,

Brutus, Hamlet, Othello, Macbeth, King Lear, Antony, Cleopatra, Coriolanus, confronts chaos in one form or another. In the brawling factions of
*Henry VI* and the Wars of the Roses there is already a clear forecast of the
"universal wolf" of Ulysses in *Troilus and Cressida*, and at least an intimation of the ominous words of Albany in *King Lear*:

> Humanity must perforce prey on itself,
> Like monsters of the deep.

The political chaos of *Henry VI* is the embryo of the cosmic chaos of *King
Lear*. It would be folly to try to subsume Shakespeare's works under one
head, but, if we were forced to do so, one of the least unsatisfactory ways
would be to say that they are an attempt to answer the question: What is
the cure for chaos?

*I Henry VI* opens, with a note of high irony, on the funeral of Henry V.
Scarcely is the body of the conqueror of France cold in death when the
leaders of church and state begin hurling defiance at each other across his
coffin—as their tawny-coated and blue-coated retainers do a little later in
the streets of London—and right in the middle of a sentence in which the
victor of Agincourt is being compared with Julius Caesar a messenger
enters, followed by another, and then another, announcing the crumbling
of his newly won empire in France. Well may Joan of Arc cry, in what are
perhaps the finest lines and dominating image of the play:

> Glory is like a circle in the water,
> Which never ceaseth to enlarge itself,
> Till by broad spreading it disperse to naught.

Under another aspect, the story is just an interlude between the death of
one "strong" king, Henry V, and the emergence of another, Richard III—
a long succession of ambitions, rivalries, jealousies, treacheries, brawls, battles, crime and treason, of which the superbly done scenes dedicated to Jack
Cade's Rebellion are somehow both a symbol and a reduction to the absurd.
Throughout, with rare exceptions, there is nothing but the subjection of the
public welfare to private ambition and greed. Even a mind less alert than
Shakespeare's would have felt bound to investigate the causes and to trace
the results of such a spectacle.

Here, in the death of Henry V and the sudden loss of France, was an extreme example of nemesis, of "the fall of princes," or at any rate of the
sudden and utter collapse of all that a mighty monarch's life had stood for,
the *débâcle* of an imperialistic dream.

Here, writ large, was the truth that chaos in the state is part and parcel of
chaos in the minds and souls of individuals, that the political problem is,
once and for all, a function of the psychological problem. It is an old truth

that he who ruleth himself is better than he who taketh a city. Shakespeare seems to have sensed very early—what the world at large has still to learn—that he who cannot rule himself is not entitled to rule a city, still less a nation.

Here was a demonstration that tyranny and anarchy, force and the lawless resistance to force, are extremes that meet, each so terrible that its opposite seems like a relief—until it comes. And here, therefore, was the inevitable question: Is history doomed to be nothing but a perpetual oscillation between the two?

Already, even in this play, there is a hint of another way out, a possible escape from the fatal circle. It is found in various little touches, but chiefly in the figure of Henry VI himself.

Whatever one thinks of Henry as a man, no one can deny that his role—except perhaps for a few passages that seem inconsistent with the rest—is a remarkable piece of characterization, so remarkable that one is tempted to think that Shakespeare may have revised it at a later date to bring it more into line and to enhance its contrasts with the roles of Henry's father and grandfather. (His speech on the Simple Life, for instance, seems expressly conceived as a companion piece to that of Henry IV on Sleep and that of Henry V on Ceremony.) However that may be, Henry VI has been the most critically neglected of Shakespeare's kings. Pages have been written about the others for every paragraph about him. There are few characters in Shakespeare the conventional picture of whom stands in greater need of revision, not to say reversal.

Henry, in contrast with his illustrious father, is generally dismissed as a weakling. His political inefficiency and practical unfitness for the crown need no demonstration. But to liken him to Richard II, as has been done over and over, is to misunderstand and underrate him utterly. Richard and Henry were alike in that each came to the throne in his minority and each realized himself most fully through the inner life. But there the resemblance ends. Richard was a dupe of his dreams, a sentimentalist, an actor and self-worshiper, and so, though unintentionally, a liar, a coward and a tyrant—in spite of splendid native gifts. Henry was a simple and sincere, a morally courageous and genuinely religious man and king. He is the only one of Shakespeare's kings whose public and private personalities are identical. As he himself reminds us, he was only nine months old when he came to the throne, and the situation in which he found himself later was not of his making. That he was frequently bewildered by the problems thrust upon him and willing to shed political responsibility is true. But he was childlike—not childish, as Richard was. No other king in Shakespeare had the good of his kingdom so at heart or suffered so keenly at the sufferings of his subjects. When he declares that he would give his life to save them, we do not doubt his word for a second. We get a taste of his quality in such lines as

> What stronger breastplate than a heart untainted!
> Thrice is he arm'd that hath his quarrel just,
> And he but naked, though lock'd up in steel,
> Whose conscience with injustice is corrupted.

Another advocate of the simple life nearer our day, Henry David Thoreau, used the same image to express the same thought: "For an impenetrable shield stand inside yourself." He, too, in the cant of our time, has been dismissed as an "escapist." Henry's unwillingness to seek revenge or to glory over a fallen enemy is another of his virtues that is stressed over and over, and when he declared:

> I'll leave my son my virtuous deeds behind;
> And would my father had left me no more!

he showed more insight into the character of his imperial father than have dozens of the commentators who have condescended to that father's son.

But the most remarkable thing about this childlike and saintly king is that he nearly succeeded in accomplishing what the astute and "practical" men around him were powerless to effect: an understanding between the warring factions of Lancaster and York. Had it not been for that Amazon, Margaret of Lancaster, and that fiend in human shape, the younger Richard of York, he would have. As Richard's brother Edward—later Edward IV—says to Margaret as he looks back:

> Hadst thou been meek, our title still had slept;
> And we, in pity of the gentle king,
> Had slipp'd our claim until another age.

An astounding admission, and the highest tribute to the quiet power of Henry's character. They are possibly the three most significant lines in these plays.

> Strange how such innocence gets its own way,

says a character in one of Robert Frost's poems,

> I shouldn't be surprised if in this world
> It were the force that would at last prevail.

Henry came close to prevailing through just that force. And here is perhaps the first bit of evidence in Shakespeare, evidence that goes on accumulating, that he too had faith that innocence might yet prove to be the force that would overcome the world.

Henry was a shining example of the truth that even in a palace life may be lived well. Of all the deaths with which the History Plays are crowded, Henry's, among the major characters, is far and away the best. His final words of forgiveness to his murderer,

> O, God forgive my sins, and pardon thee!

are a plain echo of the dying words of Christ.

Doubtless Henry was better fitted for the role of saint than of king. But as Plato declares that the perfect state will not be attained until philosophers are kings, so Shakespeare may be intimating that in a happier time than the fifteenth century the ideal ruler may have more of the characteristics of the saint than then seemed feasible. Malcolm, in *Macbeth*, makes a list of the "king-becoming graces":

> justice, verity, temperance, stableness,
> Bounty, perseverance, mercy, lowliness,
> Devotion, patience, courage, fortitude.

It is a startling thought that Henry VI had every one of these virtues. Is there another king in Shakespeare of whom that may be said? What wonder that so untypical a monarch should have elicited from his Amazonian wife the puzzled exclamation on the battlefield:

> What are you made of? you'll nor fight, nor fly.

Henry is the first of a long line of Shakespearean characters who, born to power or having power thrust on them, have a strong distaste for it and a corresponding longing for the simple life. Across Shakespeare's entire dramatic activity Henry VI, the king who longed to be a shepherd, reaches out a hand to Prospero, the Duke who presided over the enchanted isle. Between them are many others of the same type, including the exiled Duke in *As You Like It* and the self-exiled Duke of *Measure for Measure*. Even the misanthropic Timon and the deposed King Lear have bonds of kinship with the rest. The persistence of this type is further testimony to the continuity of Shakespeare's development. This group of characters carries a political implication of especial importance for our day. One of the weakest aspects of democracy as it has so far worked out is that under it the aggressive type that desires power and likes to rule tends to gain power and so does rule—whereas genuine democracy is the art of getting those who are naturally averse to holding power to accept it.

But there is an even subtler truth implicit in Henry's life. He demonstrates—in an almost Chinese fashion—that there is such a thing as being as well as doing, such a thing as doing through being. In this respect Henry is a prophecy, and in a sense a progenitor, of the most saintly character Shakespeare ever created—the divine Desdemona.

*Chapter V*

# Titus Andronicus

All lovers of Shakespeare would be glad to relieve the poet of responsibility for that concentrated brew of blood and horror, *Titus Andronicus*. Though it is ostensibly a Senecan tragedy of revenge, it is not tragedy at all in any proper sense, and, even if it is Shakespeare's, it would be all to the good if commentators were to cease referring to it as his first tragedy.

From an outline of the story one would think that the play itself must be a waking nightmare. But it fails completely to produce any such effect on the modern reader for the reason that its piled-up cruelties and brutalities follow one another with such crudity and rapidity that it produces no conviction of reality, though it doubtless produced more of that conviction in its own day when men were notoriously given to permitting instant way to their passions and impulses.

In spite of wide reluctance to attribute the play to Shakespeare, the evidence that it is his seems decisive. It is on Meres' list and was included in the First Folio by Heminge and Condell. The tradition referred to by Ravenscroft, who himself adapted the play during the Restoration, to the effect that Shakespeare contributed merely a few master-touches to a play written by somebody else, is generally discounted.

And the internal evidence of Shakespeare's authorship is by no means negligible. The play as a whole has a kind of passionate strength and vehemence that may well indicate it was the work of a genius just becoming aware of his capacities. It contains passages of natural beauty that, taken by themselves, are not unlike Shakespeare. Several of its leading figures, notably Titus, Tamora, and Aaron, might be considered rough first drafts of later Shakespearean characters. And there are what look like premonitions of specific lines and phrases that occur in the poet's later works. Of these last the most striking is the memorable couplet:

Wilt thou draw near the nature of the gods?
Draw near them, then, in being merciful,

advice which almost no one in the play, including the speaker, ever follows.

How came the young Shakespeare to indulge in such an orgy of atrocity as the plot of this piece is? The obvious answer is that he probably inherited much of it from an earlier play. But that still leaves us with the question: Why did he choose this story rather than another?

There seem to be two possible reasons, one of which will appeal to most people as much more plausible than the other.

The earlier the date of *Titus* (and nobody knows when it was written), the easier it is to believe that Shakespeare the dramatic apprentice was bent on doing, even more thoroughly and successfully if possible than anyone else had done, what was meeting popular acclaim at the moment in the theatrical world. His early verse shows how capable he was of imitation. As late as *Richard III* he was under the influence of the trend that *Tamburlaine the Great* had started. He seems to be an example of the truth that the poet who is ultimately to prove most original may—as in the case of Keats—begin by a following of current or classic models so close as to seem almost slavish. It would be in keeping with such a tendency for a juvenile Shakespeare to strive in his first theatrical enthusiasm to exceed popular examples of the Senecan tragedy of blood just as in *The Comedy of Errors* he exceeded Plautus in comedy.

Yet, even so, it is hard to account for the immense inferiority of *Titus Andronicus* to *Richard III*, the former a work that retains almost no intrinsic as distinct from historical interest, the latter, in spite of crudities, still an unsurpassed masterpiece in its kind. Either *Titus Andronicus* was written earlier than is generally supposed, or Shakespeare's dramatic genius unfolded with incredible speed.

The second possible way of taking the play, if we could accept it, would resolve this difficulty. This interpretation amounts to much the same as the one already offered, but allows for a more conscious purpose, and even for some humor, in the imitation—as if Shakespeare, however fascinated himself, were astounded by the relish of the public for the tragedy of blood and said to himself: "I'll make an experiment. I'll see how far it is possible to go with this sort of thing. On horror's head I'll let horrors accumulate. I'll write the tragedy of blood to end all tragedies of blood." It would be in keeping with what he was to do in *The Two Gentlemen of Verona* and *The Taming of the Shrew* (if there is anything in my interpretations of those plays) and it would make it easier to reconcile *Titus Andronicus* with the rest of his works. There is blood and there is horror in those plays, but they are always subordinated, as they are not here, to some high poetical end.

*Chapter VI*

# Richard III

*The Tragedy of King Richard III* is one thing if considered as an early play
written in the Marlowe tradition as a sequel to *Henry VI*. It is another and
more impressive one when taken as the climax and conclusion of the eight
English History Plays that begin with *Richard II*—nine if *King John* is included as a sort of overture to the others. Of these nine, five were written
after *Richard III*. Yet one comes to it, when reading them in historical order,
with little sense of incongruity, further testimony to the integral character
of Shakespeare's genius. By itself, the play impresses us especially through
its extraordinary theatrical quality. As the last one in a series, it becomes
predominantly a study in nemesis.

*Richard III*, from beginning to end, is marked by juvenility and genius.
Nothing Shakespeare ever wrote was apparently done with more gusto.
The destructive energy of Richard himself is a measure of the constructive
energy that went into his making. The zest of the poet in fashioning his
villain-hero accounts for our zest in following his machinations. Except toward the end, there is little evidence, as there is in *Macbeth*, that the author
was awed by his own creation. What we feel is a sense of triumph in power,
an exuberance of invention and excess of wit accumulating into a tidal wave
of theatrical effect.

Take the one matter of irony. It is as if the youthful Shakespeare had just
discovered the fun of making words mean two or more contradictory
things at once. He is like a boy with a new toy. Richard fairly exudes expressions that are innocent on the surface and diabolic—no, not underneath,
but on the surface also. For they are so broad and obvious that you **cannot**

miss them. You can almost see Richard wink at the audience and Shakespeare with him as he utters such lines as

'T is death to me to be at enmity.

One searches this play in vain for the subtle ironies of *Macbeth* which can be taken in only at a tenth reading and which no theater audience could conceivably catch. *Richard III* fairly dazzles as a theater piece and even more than *The Comedy of Errors* measures the self-restraint Shakespeare must have exercised, in view of its success, to save himself from prostituting such gifts to popularity.

But in stressing the immaturities of the play there is danger of overstatement. Though it is often closer to melodrama than to tragedy, and has more rhetoric and eloquence than poetry, more breadth than depth of characterization, all through it there are hints and gleams of the highest things (as in Clarence's dream) and its general moral intention and upshot are as sound as those of the later Tragedies. Indeed, a time like our own that has out-Machiavelled Machiavelli has turned into sober realism much in this play that to a reader of forty years ago sounded like sheer invention. The world is forever catching up with Shakespeare—only to fall behind him again.

In Richard we see what results from a union of ambition, intellect, and unlimited faith in force, from a mixture of blood and brains. It is a pity our own age did not take warning from him. The play is a sort of biography of Force, of the tyrannical, or, as we call it, the totalitarian principle. To take its central figure in this titanic, almost allegorical sense makes him the more credible and impressive. The way force, having disposed of its foes, turns on its friends and kind, then on itself ("O! no; alas! I rather hate myself"), has seldom been presented with more parabolic power. The weak, self-indulgent, and lascivious King Edward affords an effective contrast to Richard and permits Shakespeare to imply that violence and lust are brothers.

Historically and politically, the play shows that despotism is the inevitable result of anarchy. Out of the turmoil of the Wars of the Roses a "strong man" was bound to emerge. Ethically, it proves the futility of a moral code that leaves the past, as accumulated in the unconscious, out of account. Psychologically, it renders superfluous most modern treatises on the inferiority complex. It implies all that they say. Though they are not narrated in the play, we cannot help imagining the taunts and insults Richard Crookback must have submitted to as a child and boy because of his broken body. The fantasies of revenge with which he must have answered them are suggested by his mother's description:

Thy school-days frightful, desperate, wild and furious.

He suppressed the love instinct in favor of the power instinct, balanced his sense of inner weakness by a show of outward strength. *Quanto, tanto*. So little within—so big without. Thus he built up his feeling of superiority, his armor of wit and irony, his creed of self-sufficiency: "I am myself alone." But his iron will had its Achilles heel: his superstition. The wife of the man who boasted that he had "neither pity, love, nor fear" declared that she had never enjoyed an hour of peaceful sleep by his side because of his "timorous dreams." He gave the impression of complete self-control because *in the daytime* his will kept his imagination under. The play is the story of how his imagination gradually gets the better of his will. By a master-stroke it is the proposal to make away with the little princes that is made Richard's undoing. This particular touch of genius is to be attributed to history rather than to Shakespeare, but Shakespeare makes the most of it. The death of the two boys is the final strangulation of his soul—of the child within himself. Buckingham, who has hitherto been Richard's willing tool, suddenly confronted with the demand that he become a child-killer, hesitates, and his hesitation precipitates the crisis of the play:

BUCK.:   Give me some little breath, some pause, dear lord,
         Before I positively speak in this.
         I will resolve you herein presently.   (*Exit*)
CATESBY  (*Aside to another*): The king is angry: see, he gnaws his lip.
KING R.  (*Descends from his throne*): I will converse with iron-witted fools
         And unrespective boys: none are for me
         That look into me with considerate eyes.
         High-reaching Buckingham grows circumspect.
         Boy!
PAGE:    My lord!
KING R.: Know'st thou not any whom corrupting gold
         Will tempt unto a close exploit of death?

The gnawing of the lip seems but a trifle, but it is the first indication that Richard's will is slipping, and the stage direction, whether it is Shakespeare's or not, rightly registers that this is the crisis of the play, the descent of Richard from the throne of his self-control. And his intellect, the other of the two pillars on which his power rests, slips at the same time. In his anger, he asks the first person on whom his eye falls—a page!—to find a murderer for him.

The profound transformation in the man is confirmed in the next scene but one. Back in the first act, in a situation seldom surpassed for sheer audacity, Richard woos for his wife the widow of a man he has just murdered, choosing for the occasion of that wooing the funeral of her father-in-law, whom he has also killed. The more impossible the task, the more it appeals to Richard's gigantic pride. And he carries it off successfully. Now, at the end of the play, he attempts something even more incredible. He asks his brother's widow, Queen Elizabeth, mother of the two boys he has just had put out of the way, to give him their sister, her daughter, as his bride. Why should Shakespeare have permitted himself two such preposterous scenes in a single play? Was not one enough? The answer is that the two scenes are not alike—they are precise opposites. In the first, Richard turns a woman around his little finger. In the second, he does the same—apparently. Actually it is the woman who turns him around her finger by pretending to assent when in her heart she is refusing. Scarcely ever is the scene taken in this way. Yet every consideration, moral, psychological, and aesthetic, demands this interpretation. The undoing of this master of irony by such a stroke of irony is so fitting as a measure of the depth of his descent from the throne of his former self-possession and supremacy that, even if it could be proved that Shakespeare never consciously intended anything of the sort, actors and readers would still be justified in so interpreting a scene the text of which offers no obstacle to such a construction. But that Shakespeare did so intend it is all but proved by what follows. Richard, thinking he has accomplished his purpose, kisses the Queen as she goes out and then unbosoms himself in the characteristic line,

Relenting fool, and shallow changing woman!

But instantly, as comment on that line, a messenger enters announcing the appearance on the western coast of Richmond's navy. The formerly imperturbable Richard thereupon falls into a veritable panic. He dispatches messengers without telling them what to say or do, rebukes one for not departing with no orders, and forgets what he told another a moment before. He is utterly rattled. "My mind is chang'd," he weakly apologizes. *That* from the man who just twenty-five lines before had cried:

Relenting fool, and shallow changing woman!

If Shakespeare did not intend that line to flood with illumination the preceding scene with Queen Elizabeth, his genius did. It is a growing habit of his to throw back a sudden light on a scene from the one that follows it.

The most famous line in *Richard III* is the cry on the battlefield,

A horse! a horse! my kingdom for a horse!

with which the King rushes out to his death. Repeated quotation, out of its context, has staled and reduced to a combined banality and jocosity what is perhaps the subtlest and profoundest line in the play. It is the final irony that this master of irony utters, as his last words, a Delphic cry of the undermeaning of which he could have had not the remotest intimation.

To understand that undermeaning we have to go back to the soliloquy into which Richard breaks as he wakes from the dreams in which the ghosts of his former victims have visited him.

> Give me another horse! bind up my wounds!
> Have mercy, Jesu!

The reference to the horse shows that the battle in Richard's nocturnal imagination is a direct preparation for the battle on Bosworth Field. In this soliloquy Shakespeare achieves for a moment the miracle of transforming the melodramatic monster he has created into a genuinely tragic figure who excites our sympathy, and we feel the presence of the future author of *Macbeth*.

> There is no creature loves me,
> And if I die no soul will pity me.

The man who had held himself above all law now finds himself surrounded by thousands of furies crying "Guilty!" The man who had deemed himself self-sufficient now finds himself dependent on human love and pity—and another horse. I shall never forget the mad shiver and sudden twisted glance over the contorted shoulder, the hoarse "Zounds! who's there?" with which Richard Mansfield, at Ratcliff's salutation "My lord!" conveyed the King's sense that this was no human being but a visitant from the infernal world who had entered. What wonder that, when he has partly recovered, the King confesses that

> shadows tonight
> Have struck more terror to the soul of Richard
> Than can the substance of ten thousand soldiers.

He has fortified his waning spirits with wine. But his supreme degradation comes with his declaration:

> Under our tents I'll play the eaves-dropper,
> To hear if any mean to shrink from me.

To such a skulker by night has the former proud king been reduced. This is symbolic as well as literal nemesis. Like all but one of the kings in these History Plays, Richard has failed to come to terms with the nocturnal world—the other side of life—the unconscious. Of that unconscious world, from the myth of Pegasus to the White Horses of *Rosmersholm*, the horse has been a symbol, standing for the living stream of unconscious energy on which consciousness rides. Consciousness must guide it or it will run away with consciousness. The King's final words are a confession that the worldly kingdom, to the attainment of which he has sacrificed everything, is worth less than the few seconds by which another horse might postpone his doom. But, unknown to him, those final words are also the expression of an anguished yet hopeless desire to exchange the hell within himself, the dark world into which he has all his life been forcing down his fears and scruples, for another world, not less deep, of love and pity. Another horse! It was what not Richard alone but every one of Shakespeare's kings in these History Plays, except Henry VI, stood in need of.

In spite of its immaturities, *Richard III* remains one of the most powerful presentations of the idea of nemesis in any literature. It is the same nemesis that was the subject of Greek drama, and, under the name of Compensation, the theme of Emerson's incomparable essay. "There is always some levelling circumstance," says Emerson, "that puts down the overbearing, the strong, the rich, the fortunate, substantially on the same ground with all others. . . . All infractions of love and equity in our social relations are speedily punished. They are punished by fear."

> Bloody thou art, bloody will be thy end,

Richard's mother had predicted. "The bloody dog is dead," are the words with which Richmond greets his end. All through the play Margaret of Lancaster, the Amazonian wife of the saintly Henry VI, is the physical embodiment of this Nemesis. The play is the story of the fulfilment, one by one, of her curses.

The action concludes with the union of Richmond and Elizabeth, the fusion of the Houses of Lancaster and York in the new House of Tudor. And so this group of History Plays of which this is the last has a happy ending. . . . Yet the endings of the majority of them, taken separately, put us on guard. More always remains to be said. So far, if the future be taken into account, there has never been a happy ending in history.

But poetry is more than history. York may be united with Lancaster. The union of the Red Rose and the White is another and more difficult matter. Shakespeare at the time could have realized only partially the symbolic character of his theme. But looking back we can see that all the rest of his works are a study in how the red rose and the white rose may be united. For the red and the white—blood and spirit—are the indispensable ingredients of life. So far, history has been little else than an account of the warfare between them. It is the function of the poet to marry them, to bring peace between them. Shakespeare was at first dimly, then clearly, aware of this function. It must have been some prophetic poetic instinct that led him to choose for his presentation of English history the period of the Wars of the Roses.

## Chapter VII

# The Two Gentlemen of Verona

## I

In no other play of Shakespeare's are there so many premonitions of later ones as in *The Two Gentlemen of Verona*. In this respect it is the opposite and correlative of *Cymbeline*, which contains more echoes of the poet's earlier works than any other. Parts of *The Two Gentlemen* are like a rough draft of *Twelfth Night*. It has marked resemblances to *The Merchant of Venice* and *Romeo and Juliet*. Particular scenes and passages remind us of *The Taming of the Shrew*, *A Midsummer-Night's Dream*, *Much Ado about Nothing*, *Richard II*, *Othello*, and others. And such lines as

> Go, go, be gone, to save your ship from wrack,
> Which cannot perish, having thee aboard,
> Being destin'd to a drier death on shore

look as far forward as *The Tempest*.

In Julia we have the first of a long line of Shakespearean heroines who disguise themselves as boys. This device is an obvious way of producing those misunderstandings which, as we saw in *The Comedy of Errors*, elicit most easily the specifically theatrical emotion. The effect of a girl in disguise was at least doubled on the Elizabethan stage by the fact that the women's parts were played by boys. In *The Two Gentlemen of Verona* one feels the author reveling in this contrivance like a child who has just learned to play hide and seek. In one scene, for instance, we have a boy actor playing the part of a girl, who, disguised as a boy, tells how he disguised himself as a woman in a play. The head swims in the attempt to keep it straight. The young Shakespeare evidently delighted in this artifice of disguise within disguise, as did his audience. But by the time we reach *As You Like It* and Rosalind, he has refined and lifted it from stagecraft into poetry. And when in *Twelfth Night* we find Viola saying

> Disguise, I see, thou art a wickedness,

while she is referring merely to the complications that her impersonation of a boy has brought in the lives of Olivia and the Duke, we can hear the poet hinting in an overtone that mere disguise is too easy a dramatic device and so a sort of artistic wickedness. Already he had given it a psychological-symbolical significance in the Histories, as with Henry V the night before Agincourt, and he was soon to impart new profundities to it in the Tragedies, as in Hamlet's antic disposition and Iago's honesty. In the Comedies it reaches its culmination perhaps in *Cymbeline* and *The Winter's Tale*, where in such figures as Perdita, Hermione, and Imogen it is made to bear the innermost meaning of the play. Even here it still remains good "theater." But it is immensely more.

## II

At bottom, there seem to be just two ways of taking *The Two Gentlemen of Verona*:

1. We may consider it far and away the most juvenile work among the plays whose authorship has never been seriously questioned. There is much to back up this view. The play does reveal a certain skill in plotting, and, as we have just seen, an effective use of disguise, though what is essentially the same situation is so much better exploited in *Twelfth Night* that the handling of it here seems relatively poor and thin. To more than offset its merits, however, the play contains some of the most boring "wit," some of the most amazingly motivated actions, and quite the most incredible ending to be found in Shakespeare. The two heroines, Julia and Silvia, redeem it to a slight extent. Julia especially, who is more individualized than Silvia, is charming in her way, though, even allowing for the wretched specimens of manhood that charming women will fall in love with in real life, it is hard to find any reason except the requirements of the plot for Julia's having considered "divine" such a combined weathercock and cad as Proteus.

But how about Launce? someone will ask. How did such a masterpiece of characterization get into this early play? It is a question that must be confronted, unless we adopt the improbable hypothesis that he is a later interpolation. Launce—or rather Launce-and-his-dog-Crab, for the two are inseparable—is stamped with Shakespeare's genius. He could walk into any play the author ever wrote and not jar us with any sense of immaturity in either conception or execution. Perhaps in this paradox we may find a clue to how Shakespeare wanted his play taken, how so apprentice-like a piece could have been produced so close chronologically to works that so utterly surpass it.

Launce has more sense, humor, and intelligence in his little finger than all the other men in the play have in their so-called brains combined, and it happens that in the course of it he gives his opinion of each of the two gentlemen of Verona. Proteus, his master, he tells us, is "a kind of a knave," and Valentine, the other gentleman, "a notable lubber." Now it happens that the play confirms these judgments to the hilt. Indeed, Proteus' treatment, in succession, of Julia, Valentine, and Silvia makes the name "knave" quite too good for him, as Silvia recognizes when she calls him a "subtle, perjur'd, false, disloyal man," or when she declares that she would rather be eaten by a lion than rescued by such an abject creature. We have his own word for it that he is a sly trickster, and the story proves him to have been not only that but a perfidious friend, a liar, a coward, a slanderer, and a ruffian and would-be ravisher of the woman for whom he had deserted his first love. And this, forsooth, is the man whom his friend Valentine describes as having spent his youth in putting on an "angel-like perfection" of judgment and experience, until

> He is complete in feature and in mind
> With all good grace to grace a gentleman.

Valentine, it is true, is a paragon of virtue compared with such a bounder as Proteus, but his estimate of his friend does little credit to his intelligence and is enough in itself to justify the label "lubber" that Launce puts on him. But if Launce's say-so is not enough, proof is afforded to an almost supernatural degree by the "ladder scene." How any man could act more inanely than Valentine does on that occasion it would be hard to imagine, if we did not have the final incredible scene of the play in which the same man outdoes himself.

Now if Launce had reached the same conclusions about these two gentlemen that the action of the play forces on us independently, it is hard to believe that Shakespeare himself was not in the secret. It sets us wondering just what he meant by his title, *The Two Gentlemen of Verona*, and how far he may have written the play with his tongue in his cheek. If there is anything in this suggestion, we may have to revise our opinion of its juvenility and consider whether some of its apparent flaws are not consciously contrived ironical effects. This is the second of the two possible ways of taking the play.

## III

2. No one who knows Shakespeare can doubt for an instant the high regard in which he held genuinely noble and aristocratic character and

background, nor the ease with which he detected their counterfeits. He had himself been rebuked by one of his "betters" for the effrontery of his own aspirations in histrionic or dramatic art, or both, and had been held up to the public gaze as "an upstart Crow," a "Tyger," "an absolute *Iohannes fac totum*," and one who in his own conceit was "the onely Shake-scene in a countrey." And so it is no strain on the imagination to fancy him saying to himself, as he observed some of the "gentlemen" who frequented the contemporary theaters with their everlasting talk of "love" and "honour": "I will create a compendium of all the fashionable vices, give him a running mate devoid of sense, call the two 'gentlemen,' and palm them off on their English counterparts as the genuine article." What sport!

Make this simple assumption, and most of the crudities and difficulties of the play disappear like mist when the sun comes out. There is much in the piece to support this hypothesis.

Leaving out a minor servant, an innkeeper, and a band of outlaws, there are eight men in the cast. We have taken a look at the two gentlemen themselves and at Launce. The other clown, Speed, though he is intelligence itself compared with the gentlemen of the play, impresses us mainly as a mere trifler and trickster with words. That leaves the two fathers, Antonio and the Duke, and two other gentlemen, Sir Thurio and Sir Eglamour. The fathers are a typical pair of patriarchal tyrants. Proteus' father sums himself up in one line,

> For what I will, I will, and there an end,

and Silvia's father discloses himself in one practice: he keeps his daughter under lock and key at night. Sir Thurio, "a foolish rival to Valentine" for Silvia's hand,

> Vain Thurio, whom my very soul abhors,

as that lady describes him, is a complete nincompoop, a sort of first sketch for Andrew Aguecheek in *Twelfth Night*. In Sir Eglamour, whom Silvia engages to help her escape, we think at first that finally we have come on a truly chivalric figure.

> O Eglamour, thou art a gentleman,

she declares, and, even if she doesn't, we are tempted to stress that "thou." But alas! when the two are met by outlaws, Sir Eglamour abandons the lady to them and runs—at top speed, it is implied. Shakespeare was nothing if not thoroughgoing in this play. If there is anything in this ironic way of taking it, he apparently decided that it should live up to its title and that there should be not one genuine gentleman in it—except Launce, who, by a stroke that seems almost to prove the poet's sarcastic purpose, is chivalric to his dog to the point of Quixotism. Catch that thrust, and you see how delightfully the story of the clowns is integrated with the rest of the play. Launce, the gentleman! Or we might, without stretching it too far, include Speed and have the two gentlemen of Verona!

Compared with their crew of attendant gentlemen in the other sense, the two women are epitomes of virtue and intelligence. This, too, is prophetic of the superiority that Shakespeare almost always gives his heroines over his "heroes" in comedy, and often in tragedy.

If one were to seek a passage brief enough to quote that illustrates the inanity of this play if taken at face value, one might choose the moment when the Duke, Silvia's father, seeks Proteus' aid in forwarding the match between Sir Thurio and his daughter:

DUKE: What might we do to make the girl forget
The love of Valentine, and love Sir Thurio?
PRO.: The best way is to slander Valentine
With falsehood, cowardice, and poor descent,
Three things that women highly hold in hate.
DUKE: Ay, but she'll think that it is spoke in hate.
PRO.: Ay, if his enemy deliver it;
Therefore it must with circumstance be spoken
By one whom she esteemeth as his friend.
DUKE: Then you must undertake to slander him.
PRO.: And that, my lord, I shall be loath to do.
'Tis an ill office for a gentleman,
Especially against his very friend.
DUKE: Where your good word cannot advantage him,
Your slander never can endamage him;
Therefore the office is indifferent,
Being entreated to it by your friend.
PRO.: You have prevail'd, my lord.

It would seem impossible to go beyond that. But Shakespeare does go beyond it—far beyond—in the closing scene of the play. Since it is too long to quote, I will condense and paraphrase its salient points. If the effect is that of parody, I invite anyone who does not remember it to inspect the scene as Shakespeare wrote it and to see whether I have not been faithful to both thought and action. As for the verse, it will be an actual advantage to have that absent for the moment, for "poetry" can conceal a deal of nonsense.

Proteus has rescued Silvia from the band of outlaws, who, he tells her, would have ravished her but for him:

SIL.: I'd rather have been eaten by a lion than rescued by you. You faithless man, you are a counterfeit friend.

PRO.:   What does friendship count for when a man is in love? If you won't respond to gentle words, I'll force you to yield to me.

VAL.   (*Coming forward*): Ruffian! let her go.

PRO.:   Valentine!

VAL.:   Never will I trust you again.

PRO.:   I'm ashamed of myself. Forgive me.

VAL.:   That's all I ask. If that's how you feel, I'll take you back as my friend, and to prove that I mean what I say I hereby resign to you all my claims to Silvia.

JUL.:   Oh, how unhappy I am in that case! (*She faints. Then she comes to and the rings reveal her identity.*)

PRO.:   How? Julia!

JUL.:   Yes. You ought to blush that you made me dress in boy's clothes. But it is better for a woman to change her clothes than for a man to change his mind.

PRO.:   You are right. What did I ever see in Silvia anyway that you do not surpass her in?

VAL.:   Good! Clasp hands on that.

PRO.:   Heaven knows this is what I wanted all along.

    (*Enter Sir Thurio and Duke*)

THU.:   There's Silvia, and she's mine!

VAL.:   Stop, or I'll kill you.

THU.:   Take her, Valentine. I don't care a straw for her. A man is a fool to risk death for a girl who doesn't love him.

DUKE:   Good for you, Valentine! You are a well-born gentleman. [He had shortly before called him a "peasant."] Take my daughter.

Some commentators have tried to explain this psychological hash on the ground that Shakespeare had to have his "happy ending" at any price. Others have tried to squirm out of the absurdity by talk about the Renaissance conception of friendship as transcending love. But the notes of disgust or apology on the part of the critics are too nearly unanimous to escape the inference that nobody likes the ending. Why, then, try to make ourselves think that Shakespeare liked it, except in an ironical sense, any better than we do? The two possibilities are plain. Either this is excellent burlesque of "gentlemanly" manners and morals, or else the young author fooled himself as well as the rest of us by swallowing such silliness because it was sweetened by melodious verse. Take your choice. For myself, I prefer the alternative implying that one of the greatest geniuses of the ages was not quite a fool even as a young man.

The play, taken thus, is not satire in the usual sense. The satirist so hates the custom, institution, or human type he is exposing or deriding that he ceases, like any man in a passion, to see truly. In lashing his victim he lashes himself into blindness. But Shakespeare is like Chaucer. He is so full of humanity, humor, and poetry that it is easy to miss the cutting edge of his condemnation.

If we reread the play in the light of this hypothesis, we see how full it is of hits at the education of the young Renaissance gentleman.

> Home-keeping youth have ever homely wits,

says Valentine. It is about his wisest remark. In view of Launce's homely wit and profound humor one wonders whether all the travel and adventure, the experiences of camp and court, the university training, the music and son-net-writing that were demanded of the cultured young gentlemen of the time were worth the trouble. One of the best strokes of all is the fact that the outlaws pick Valentine as their captain because he is a great linguist!

This interpretation of the play, I believe, both prophesies and is borne out by what Shakespeare did in the rest of his works. From *The Two Gentlemen of Verona* to *The Tempest*, without any deviation, he drew one portrait after another of the fashionable gentleman, either Italian or after the Italian model, and there is no possible mistaking what he thought of them, no matter how good their tailors or how "spacious" they themselves "in the possession of dirt" (as Hamlet remarked of Osric's real estate). Boyet, Don Armado, Gratiano, Tybalt, the Claudio of *Much Ado,* Bertram, Parolles, Sir Andrew Aguecheek, the "popinjay" whom Hotspur scorned, Roderigo, Iachimo: these are just a few of the more striking examples, to whom should be added, in spite of the anachronisms, Rosencrantz and Guildenstern, Osric, Paris (in *Troilus and Cressida*), and even, in some respects, men like Bassanio and Mercutio, not to mention many of the anonymous "gentlemen" and "lords" scattered throughout the plays. Let anyone who doubts trace the word "gentleman" with the help of a con-cordance in the texts of Shakespeare's works as a whole. He will be sur-prised, I think, to find how often the situation or context shows it to be used with ironical intent.

There is a story that Abraham Lincoln, on being told that in England no gentleman ever blacks his own boots, asked in his quiet manner, "Whose boots does he black?" If I am not mistaken, *The Two Gentlemen of Verona,* even more quietly, makes the same point.

## Chapter VIII

# Love's Labour's Lost

*Love's Labour's Lost*, more than any other play of Shakespeare's, even *Troilus and Cressida*, bears the marks of having been written for a special audience, an audience such as would be found not in the public theaters but at court or in the house of some nobleman. Its tone is that of farcical parody of a sort and on a scale that Shakespeare seldom used elsewhere. It is plain that he could count on the intimate acquaintance of his audience with the affectations he was pillorying. Indeed, a great many of its members were probably themselves unconscious embodiments of these affectations. The fact that a number of the characters are stock types from the Italian *Commedia dell'Arte* does not detract from the effect, and Shakespeare imparts to each of them an individual flavor. No pedant such as Holofernes, for instance, ever was before or since on sea or land.

Because of its verbal extravagances, its puns and conceits, its profuse use of rhyme, it was formerly held that *Love's Labour's Lost* was one of the very earliest of Shakespeare's plays. But in so far as the play is satirizing excesses of language, these things are signs not so much of immaturity as of an outgrowing of immaturity, and betray such remarkable knowledge of the social life of the time as to preclude as early a date as was once assigned it. It is a fair conjecture that it may have been written during or immediately after the period in 1593, when the theaters were closed and when the author was presumably busy on his poems or his sonnets or both. The play is packed with topical allusions, many of which would be incomprehensible today without the notes that generations of scholars have accumulated, and the reader suspects the presence of others that never have been and probably never will be uncovered. The dependence of this play upon annotations for anything like full intelligibility only serves to emphasize by contrast the relative independence of Shakespeare's greatest works of these local and temporal factors. Every age has its own brand of wit and wise-cracking. Whoever wishes to know how the wise-cracking of our age will sound a little later may observe how the wise-cracking of this play sounds now. And be certain that Shakespeare was well aware how transient much of it was.

The fact that an actual Biron (Berowne), Longaville, and Dumain figured in the struggle between Henry of Navarre and the Catholic League, and that a historical Princess of France once paid Henry a visit to discuss matters pertaining to Aquitaine, has tempted scholars to seek originals for the characters in this play, to conjecture even that in the "Academe" of Navarre Shakespeare was holding up to ridicule a group headed by Raleigh and supposedly including Marlowe, Chapman, and others who with John Florio thought "it were labour lost to speak of Love" (a possible origin of Shakespeare's title), but who were interested in the new science, especially the new astronomy and the ideas of Copernicus. Much of this, but for one thing, would be of extra-literary interest. That one thing is the fact that Biron in the course of the play proposes an astronomical revolution compared with which the shift from Ptolemy to Copernicus was a minor adjustment. But this concerns the culmination of the play and should be left to the last.

It is a bit odd that this seemingly verbose and somewhat inconsequential work should state its theme with a clarity and brevity unsurpassed by any other the author ever wrote, and that the truth underlying this largely ephemeral piece should be so universal that there is no indication Shakespeare ever deviated from his belief in it to the end of his days.

"What is the end of study?" asks Biron in the opening scene of the play, and from then on the drama is dedicated to answering that question. The answers are mainly negative and consist simply of sorry specimens of what human nature can be perverted into when either or both of those central urges of life toward love and truth go awry, the implication being that, whatever else the end of study may be, it is at any rate not the production of such deformities and sterilities as these.

Faulconbridge in *King John* (written, it may be, not far from the same time as this play) declares that the truthful man must study the ways of deceit for the express purpose of being able to avoid them in practice. *Love's Labour's Lost* implies a corresponding belief on the author's part that he who would master the means of expression must be acquainted with all its exaggerations and perversions, that he who would achieve wit in its old sense of wisdom must know every quirk and turn of "wit" in its degenerate estate, and finally that he who would attain love must be acquainted with "love's" romantic follies.

> How well he's read, to reason against reading!

says the King of Biron. How loving and witty he is at annihilating "love" and "wit," we may say of the author of *Love's Labour's Lost*. He beats at their own game the people he is making fun of. Only a lover and master of language who was at the same time something of a skeptic about it could have exposed the linguistic manias of his day so devastatingly and at the same time so merrily and genially. And have done the same for its learning and its "love."

What, then, is the end of study?

For one thing, as the fate of Navarre's Academe makes plain, it is not "philosophy" in the sense of a cloistered cultivation of the intellect and pursuit of truth for its own sake in a spot secluded from the world and from women. Nor is it "love" in its romantic sense sheltered from life's suffering and reality—"love" with all its ritual and manners, its form and style, its fads and foibles, its "wit" and repartee, its masks and costumes, its rhyming and sonneteering, its language of

> Taffeta phrases, silken terms precise,
> Three-pil'd hyperboles, spruce affectation,
> Figures pedantical.

These things are but summer flies that blow their worshipers full of ostentation, as they did Boyet—Boyet who picked up wit as pigeons do peas, Boyet the ladies' man, forerunner of Osric, who kissed his hand away in courtesy. Neither is the end of education erudition, the barren learning that transformed the pedant Holofernes into a walking dictionary of synonyms; nor slavery to authority and the past, the bondage that never let the sycophantic curate Nathaniel utter an idea or opinion without backing it up with an "as the Father saith." Nor, at the other extreme, is it subservience to fashion and the present, such as made the swashbuckling Don Adriano de Armado a mint of fire-new phrases emitting a "smoke of rhetoric."

What is the matter with these creatures, one and all? The trouble is that they have either divorced their heads from their hearts or their hearts from their heads. And so, as foil for them and as sun and center of his play, Shakespeare creates one of the most attractive figures he has given birth to up to this time: Biron, a man who in his delightful blend of poetry, humor, skepticism, and common sense reminds us of no one so much as his maker. Biron has precisely Shakespeare's capacity to taste without swallowing, to dally with the tempter until he is intimately acquainted with him, only in the end to resist the temptation. Biron never really believed in the Academe of Navarre. He subscribed reluctantly to its ridiculous terms only because he knew in his heart that it would be bound to disintegrate before it was fairly founded. In Biron we catch a glimpse of Shakespeare as it were in the very act of shaking off some of his juvenile extravagances and resolving on a greater simplicity. Henceforth, says Biron, I'll renounce ornate language and my wooing shall be

> In russet yeas and honest kersey noes.

But he stubs his toe, or his tongue, in the very next couplet:

> And, to begin, wench,—so God help me, la!—
> My love to thee is sound, sans crack or flaw.

> Sans 'sans,' I pray you,

retorts the keen and critical Rosaline.* I'm a sick man, the crestfallen Biron admits, but I'll get over it by degrees. It is like Shakespeare's own confession.

If our enthusiasm for Biron seem excessive, it is perhaps because we are reading back into one speech of his things which it prophesies in the later Shakespeare. That speech, of course, is his tirade on education and women's eyes. Nearly all commentators have seen that this speech is the key to the play. Not so many have perceived what is more important, that, like the Bastard's speech on Commodity in *King John*, it is one of the keys to Shakespeare. So superior is it to all but a few other lines in the play that it is a temptation to think it was added to, or expanded from, the original text at the time when, according to the Quarto of 1598, that text was "newly corrected and augmented" for presentation before the Queen "this last Christmas." The fact that the speech as it stands contains obvious repetitions lends a certain credibility to the view that it underwent revision and that the compositor failed to cut out some passages marked for deletion.

In the frivolous context of this farcical play it is easy to pass over or dismiss as just so much more romantic nonsense Biron's contention that women's eyes are the true academes. We do so at our peril. Viewing it retrospectively in the light of the part that woman's love plays in Shakespeare's later masterpieces, and more concretely in the light of the speeches on the human eye of Achilles and Ulysses in *Troilus and Cressida*, we begin to see what it means, how seriously Shakespeare as well as Biron intended it. "What loving astronomer has ever fathomed the ethereal depths of the eye?" What ages of purification the human spirit had to undergo before

---

* That "sans 'sans,' I pray you," lets us see precisely what Shakespeare thought of the last line of Jaques' famous Seven Ages of Man:
  "Sans teeth, sans eyes, sans taste, sans everything."

it was possible for Henry David Thoreau to write that sentence! Anyone thinks he understands it, but few probably even begin to. Shakespeare, through Biron, shows that he would have understood Thoreau. Indeed, at bottom, he is saying the same thing, even down to the same metaphor.

> For when would you, my lord, or you, or you,
> Have found the ground of study's excellence
> Without the beauty of a woman's face?
> From women's eyes this doctrine I derive:
> They are the ground, the books, the academes
> From whence doth spring the true Promethean fire . . .
> For where is any author in the world
> Teaches such beauty as a woman's eye?
> Learning is but an adjunct to ourself,
> And where we are our learning likewise is:
> Then when ourselves we see in ladies' eyes,
> Do we not likewise see our learning there? . . .
> Other slow arts entirely keep the brain,
> And therefore, finding barren practisers,
> Scarce show a harvest of their heavy toil;
> But love, first learned in a lady's eyes,
> Lives not alone immured in the brain,
> But, with the motion of all elements,
> Courses as swift as thought in every power,
> And gives to every power a double power,
> Above their functions and their offices.

Here we have ideas that stem from what is at the same time the most ancient and the most seminal and prophetic doctrine of love and the sexes to which human thought has given birth. The *Upanishads* tell us that man, originally one, fell two, became man and woman. Ever since then the two sexes have sought reunion. "He who understands the masculine," says Laotse, "and keeps to the feminine shall become the whole world's channel. Eternal wisdom shall not depart from him and he shall return to the state of an infant." The Greeks, Plato especially, took up this idea that human nature is hermaphroditic, and from them it passed into Western thought and has been expressed and re-expressed in countless forms down the centuries. When Benjamin Franklin observed jocularly: "A single man . . . is an incomplete animal. He resembles the odd Half of a pair of Scissors," he was probably unaware of the venerable religious lineage of his remark. Thoreau, on the contrary, undoubtedly knew he was echoing ancestral voices when he wrote: "Man is continually saying to woman, Why will you not be more wise? Woman is continually saying to man, Why will you not be more loving? It is not in their wills to be wise or to be loving; but unless each is both wise and loving, there can be neither wisdom nor love." There, expressed with an oracular compactness that surpasses Biron, is the belief on which *Love's Labour's Lost* is founded, the doctrine that mental and spiritual, like physical, procreation is bisexual. An idea or a feeling, if it is to live and survive, must have two parents. The sterility of most of the so-called ideas and feelings in this play comes from the fact that they are not begotten through any intercourse of heart and mind. Wit, the intellect, is masculine and by itself is barren. And the same is true of learning. In Biron's phrase they "entirely keep the brain." Each must be married to the feminine principle to be found in women's eyes "from whence doth spring the true Promethean fire." This fire enkindles the whole man, gives to every power a double power

> Above their functions and their offices,

a new seeing to the eye, a new hearing to the ear, a new sensitiveness to every faculty. And once more we are reminded of Thoreau:

> I hearing get, who had but ears,
> And sight, who had but eyes before;
> I moments live, who lived but years,
> And truth discern, who knew but learning's lore,

and still more of John Donne and those lines of his which possibly come as near an ultimate expression of this conception as anything equally brief ever written:

> We understood
> Her by her sight; her pure and eloquent blood
> Spoke in her cheeks, and so distinctly wrought
> That one might almost say, her body thought.

This is indeed the wedding of blood and spirit, a prophecy of the ultimate miracle, the complete union of soul and body, a miracle forecast on a tiny scale whenever the heart turns wit into humor or knowledge into wisdom.

Seldom has a seemingly romantic and artificial play had a more realistic and unartificial conclusion than *Love's Labour's Lost*. Its denouement is as satisfying as that of *The Two Gentlemen of Verona*, unless taken ironically, is unsatisfying. At the end the honors pass from Biron to the Princess and Rosaline, who, with an appropriate feminine practicality and concreteness, subject his lofty theories to the test of life. As a trial of his fidelity, the Princess sentences the King, if he still wishes to win her, to a year in a hermitage far from the pleasures of the world. And Rosaline orders Biron to jest a twelvemonth in a hospital in an attempt to make the sick smile at his wit. "Impossible!" cries Biron. But Rosaline sticks to her guns:

> Why, that's the way to choke a gibing spirit . . .
> A jest's prosperity lies in the ear
> Of him that hears it, never in the tongue
> Of him that makes it.

If the sick, for all their groans, will listen to your idle scorn, she declares, continue it; otherwise, if you would have me, renounce it forever. Shakespeare leaves to our imaginations the sixth act of this play. But somehow we have faith in Biron.

The two songs at the very end, of Spring and Winter, echo the same theme. In Spring life is easy, but the Cuckoo is the bird of infidelity; in Winter it is hard, but the Owl is the bird of wisdom. Of how much in Shakespeare is this prophetic.

What a warning to scholars and commentators *Love's Labour's Lost* is! If the truth that it teaches is applicable to its author's own works (including this one), their secret will never be revealed to mere erudition or learning on the one hand nor to mere romantic glorification on the other. And, above all, those academic elucidations of them that aspire to be purely objective and scorn the introduction of any personal element in their interpretation come under its specific condemnation of sterility. A play's prosperity, we might almost say, paralleling the words of Rosaline,

> A play's prosperity lies in the ear
> Of him that hears it, never in the pen
> Of him that writes it.

*Chapter IX*

# The Poet-Playwright

## I

Compared with many poets, Shakespeare was a master from the beginning. Compared with what he became, he had his apprenticeship. Here, near the end of that period, is a natural place to pause and glance back. When we do, it seems as if his genius and the obstacles that beset it were conspiring to one end.

The love of watching or taking part in a dramatic performance may doubtless be traced, both biologically and psychologically, to the mimetic instinct of the child and to the sense of freedom and omnipotence that play imparts. Historically, in Greece, it has been attributed by Nietzsche to the double identification of chorus and audience with a god, Dionysus. The theater has wandered far from its religious origins, but its function remains the same. As *The Comedy of Errors* reveals, it is a place of illusion. Whatever other ends it serves, its basic purpose is to transform the spectator into a god in the sense of allowing him for an hour or two to look down from above, in comedy on the very errors and blunders he himself commits, and in tragedy on the sufferings he is compelled to undergo in real life. It lets him exult in the fact that he is not being that fool or that victim he sees below him, and take pride in identifying himself with that hero. To bring this about there must be all sorts of mistakes and misunderstandings among the puppets on the stage. And the easiest way of creating these is through disguise and the mistaken identity to which disguise gives rise. Just as the child begins his play by pretending he is someone else, dressing up in imagination if not in fact, so the playwright has no safer way of beginning his play than by introducing the same ingredient. Here the playwright's and the actor's arts are one. For what is acting but being someone else than yourself, and so disguise? (Hence the importance of costume.) It is interesting that the word "hypocrite" is just Greek for "one who plays a part on the stage," a dissembler. In achieving his end, so long as he maintains the illusion of life, playwright or actor may depart to any degree from life itself, may invent with utter license. The playwright especially is almost compelled to impart to his work a high degree of "form," if I may use that word for a moment in an inferior sense.

The temptation to surrender to a pleasing illusion is an almost irresistible one. Hence the appeal of the theater to the young and inexperienced, and hence its evil influence when unmitigated. Those who give in to it, as millions of movie fans do in our day, are destined to remain children, not in the sense of keeping their innocence but in the sense of staying content with pretense, of never growing up. Harmless or even helpful as this kind of illusion may be for occasional purposes of relaxation and escape, only the weak-minded can be satisfied with it as a steady diet. Even Shakespeare confessed that the theater nearly "got" him. Fortunately, at the same time that he came under its spell, he came under the spell of something diametrically different. He felt the attraction of history. He was the author of *The Comedy of Errors;* but he was also the author of *Henry VI.* It may have been history that saved him from the theater.

How can a man be both playwright and historian? The world and the stage: how shall they be reconciled? Here is an antinomy: the theater with its dedication to illusion, history with its reverence for fact. *The Comedy of Errors* and *King Henry VI, Parts I, II,* and *III*—even a dull brain could not fail to get the contrast—the neat, symmetrical, ingenious, un-lifelike elegance and unity of Plautine comedy, and the sprawling chaos and reality of the Wars of the Roses. But it is the mark of a brain that is *not* dull that it will not rest content with an antithesis but will seek a synthesis on a higher plane:

> These contraries such unity do hold,

a line (from *Lucrece*) that shows how early Shakespeare had felt and understood that urge. Even *The Comedy of Errors* is not all ingenuity, nor *Henry VI* all formlessness. From the outset Shakespeare must have perceived that history, on the stage, must have more form than it is generally given in the old chronicles, and that intricate plots and thrilling situations in the theater must have real people, like those in history, to give them body and vitality. Here was the basis for a genuine fusion, a fruitful marriage. It is a commonplace of criticism that in the main Shakespeare gave the first decade of his dramatic activity to the exploring and mastering, side by side, of comedy and history. But there is little evidence that he was interested, as scholars are, in dramatic types for their own sakes. Life is not neatly divided into categories with no crossing the lines between them, and dramatic art, to be true to life, cannot be either. There is plenty of evidence that that is precisely what Shakespeare came to think. Everyone remembers how he poked fun through the mouth of Polonius at dramatic classification ("pastoral-comical, historical-pastoral, tragical-historical, tragical-comical-historical-pastoral"). This does not mean that there is no meaning in these distinctions or that Shakespeare was not interested in what underlies them. What he was exploring in those years before 1600 was not just comedy and history but the two great realms of fact and illusion between "the pass and fell-incensed points" of which man's destiny lies: life as it is, and life simplified and remodeled nearer to the heart's desire. If history saved Shakespeare from the theater, the theater saved Shakespeare from history.

*Richard III* records a young man's attempt to unite history and the theater. But it was a forced marriage (a tour de force in more senses than one), and the theatrical partner so predominated that it was not a genuine or lasting union. The pendulum swung in the opposite direction in *King John* and *Richard II* and it was not until *Henry IV* that the synthesis was achieved. The fact that *Henry IV* is probably Shakespeare's greatest History Play, and that Falstaff is certainly his greatest comic character, shows the fusion that was to take place—though he went even further in *King Lear*, and especially in *Antony and Cleopatra* where history, comedy, and tragedy are chemically united and the distinctions among dramatic types obliterated.

## II

Meanwhile, Shakespeare was finding subtler and less drastic ways than those employed in *Richard III* of bridging the gap between the theater and life. After an initial outburst of delight at his discovery of the ease with which "errors" may be invented for the stage, he realized the artistic "wickedness" of the crasser forms of disguise. It was too much like amusing or scaring a child with a mask or a jack-in-the-box. In seeking a refinement of these primitive devices all he had to do was to look around him. Disguise is no monopoly of the stage. Life is full of it. Disguise, indeed, is the very link he was seeking between the realm of illusion and the domain of fact. If the stage is a world where every kind of pretense and its exposure are fascinating to the onlooker, the world no less is a stage whereon men and women assume a thousand psychological disguises that make the tricks of the popular play crude in comparison. "We begin low with coarse masks," says Emerson, "and rise to the most subtle and beautiful. . . . Life will show you masks that are worth all your carnivals." There is the dramatic biography of William Shakespeare in two sentences.

Shakespeare began low with coarse masks. Plays like *The Two Gentlemen of Verona* and *Love's Labour's Lost* are full of literal cloaks and dominoes. But even so early these stage devices are beginning to be emblems and metaphors of what is everywhere. What is the face but a mask to conceal the man behind it?

> There's no art
> To find the mind's construction in the face.

What is social position, what are offices, titles, dignities, degrees, but mantles in which men wrap themselves to hide, from themselves even more than from others, the banality of their lives?

> O place and greatness! millions of false eyes
> Are stuck upon thee.

What is a human life but a role a man enacts, as different from his hidden self as the role of an actor is from his part in ordinary life? What are words but means of disguising thought? What is life itself but a play for which most of the players are miscast, a masquerade at which only a few of the rarest and most heroic, or of the most brutal and cynical, ever unmask? As these last four adjectives imply, to all these statements there are exceptions. But the point is that they are exceptions.

Clothes! that is a metaphor that sums it up, and from *The Comedy of Errors* to *The Tempest* there is not a more persistent metaphor in Shakespeare. Being versus seeming! that is the theme which underlies it all, and there is not a more persistent theme in Shakespeare's plays. To go no further back, from the "All that glisters is not gold" of *The Merchant of Venice*, through Hamlet's

> Seems, madam! Nay, it is; I know not 'seems,'

and Iago's

> When devils will the blackest sins put on,
> They do suggest at first with heavenly shows,

to Caliban's
> What a thrice-double ass
> Was I, to take this drunkard for a god,
> And worship this dull fool!

Shakespeare found it unendingly meet to set it down that one may smile and smile and be a villain.

> O, what may man within him hide,
> Though angel on the outward side!

He condenses his idea of complete regeneration, through the mouth of Posthumus in *Cymbeline*, into the words,

> To shame the guise o' the world, I will begin
> The fashion, less without and more within,

and his remedy for the conquest of Death itself, in the poem that comes closer than anything else in his works to being an expression of his own religious creed, the 146th sonnet, is:

> Within be fed, without be rich no more.

Now words as well as actions are the medium of drama, and because words are the garments of thought, they are indispensable instruments for obtaining and maintaining the effect of duality in life and on the stage. Like clothes, they are used oftener to conceal than to express. "Words, words, words," says Hamlet, condensing his contempt for them into three words. And Hamlet's creator implies a not very different reaction through the great taciturn characters of his maturity, the mute tribute of this master of words to the virtue of dispensing with them.

Shakespeare is saturated with the idea of their hypocrisy. An anthology from his works could be made on this subject.

CLOWN: To see this age! A sentence is but a cheveril glove to a good wit: how quickly the wrong side may be turned outward!

VIOLA: Nay, that's certain: they that dally nicely with words may quickly make them wanton. . . .

CLOWN: . . . indeed, words are very rascals . . . so false, I am loath to prove reason with them.

This protean character of words is the basis of Shakespeare's inveterate love of puns and irony. Puns are the farce and comedy of words, irony their tragedy, both being the product of that faculty in virtue of which they can say two things at once, one to the superficial, the other to the interior, intelligence. But what is that but disguise on the verbal level? Like the life out of which it has grown and which it seeks to express, language is dual.

### III

And here lay a third danger that threatened Shakespeare, the danger that besets anyone who grows too conscious of this duality there is in everything. I once knew a little boy who in the very midst of an outburst of temper would stop dead, remark in a tone of completest detachment, as if he were stating the title of a picture, "Boy — crying," and instantly resume his tempest of weeping. It is a perfect example of the spectator, or critic, that resides in each of us. This critic is invaluable. He permits us to see things for a moment as they are from the outside. But the man who lets this bystander develop unduly runs a fatal risk, the risk of becoming detached from life, the risk of superiority, of pride. It was Lucifer, the angel of light, who fell. He who looks down as from above on the pettinesses and hypocrisies of life may escape them, but in doing so he may cut himself off from nothing less than life itself. He may have the satisfaction of perpetual attendance at the theater of existence but he will never have a part of his own in the play. At the worst he will become a satirist or cynic; at the best a philosopher. (Better go on "crying" than to lift one's self as mere spectator above all the knocks and bumps.) The theater and history saved Shakespeare from history and the theater. What saved him from philosophy?

To that perhaps the only answer is, his humility and his warm heart—a sympathy that told him he must do more than observe and analyze foolish and weak men, that he must come down and enter into them.

> Such a price
> The Gods exact for song:
> To become what we sing.

Luckily for himself, and for us, Shakespeare could confess in one of his *Sonnets:*

> in my nature reigned
> All frailties that besiege all kinds of blood.

He had the dramatic instinct, as we say. And so—if we may beg the question and at the same time give it its best answer—what saved Shakespeare from philosophy was that he was born a poet. The poet is both above life and in the midst of it at once. Hence the superiority of poetry to both history and philosophy, as Aristotle saw. A handsome admission from a philosopher!

But the thinker in Shakespeare did not succumb to the poet without a struggle. Shakespeare had such intellect that the temptation to become a satirist, to surrender to the bastard type of poetry that satire is, must have been terrific. There must have come a moment when, like his own Beatrice, he said, "Contempt, farewell!" That was a supreme moment. Even after it the foe arose to smite him. But *he* smote *it.*

Here, however, we are getting ahead of ourselves, and long before Shakespeare won this battle he had a more immediate one to win as a practical man of the theater. So long as this duality of things of which we have said so much, with its attendant errors and deceptions of act and word, is kept obvious, as in the villainy and irony of Richard III, the dressing-up of Julia as a boy in *The Two Gentlemen*, or the maskings and unmaskings of the lovers in *Love's Labour's Lost*, it is so much grist to the playwright's mill. But the minute it begins to grow subtle, to involve the finer hues and shades, to become imaginative, quite the opposite is true. For the demands of drama and poetry are not identical.

## IV

Drama is the most democratic of the arts in the sense that a play must have a wide and almost immediate appeal to a large number of people of ordinary intelligence if it is to have success enough in the theater to permit the author to go on writing plays. The playwright must be nothing if not lucid. As we have seen, he must keep no secrets if he is to feed that specifically theatrical emotion which resides in the sense of omniscience. If a play's action is not plain and its characters are not easily grasped, it will obviously soon close its run. There is no going back and rereading in the theater.

Poetry, on the contrary, is an aristocratic art. The poet is bound to please himself and the gods rather than the public—to tell the truth regardless of its popularity, to seek the buried treasure of life itself. In that sense he cannot help having a secret, and, even if he would, he cannot share it with the populace. When the moment of inspiration passes, he may not even comprehend it fully himself.

What wonder, if this is so, that, among innumerable playwrights and many poets, there have been so few poet-playwrights. The poet-playwright is a contradiction in terms. Yet a poet-playwright is exactly what the young Shakespeare was.

Plainly, if this paradoxical being is to survive, he must practice a little deception himself. And it is not just his audience that he must fool. If he must please the public, he must also placate the powers-that-be. If the crowd does not want the truth lest it disturb its animal contentment, those in authority do not want it lest it undermine their power. Between the upper millstone of the powerful and the nether millstone of the crowd the lot of the poet-playwright is not an easy one. No wonder that in the situation he resorts to a practice life had already evolved to deal with this problem long before there was either poetry or theaters.

Almost from the beginning the biological device of protective coloration is testimony to the necessity of deception for the survival of all but the dominant types of life. Force rules—if not in its crude form, then in some of its protean disguises—and where force rules, truth must either undergo martyrdom, be silent,* or speak a language its enemy cannot understand.

* "That truth should be silent I had almost forgot." Enobarbus in *Antony and Cleopatra*.

A few saints and heroes have always taken the first way. The common people generally the second. The poets the third—not always, but more often than not. They have ever delighted in palming off on the oppressor as harmless what from his own point of view, if he only knew, is deadly poison. Oppressors seldom understand humor and never understand poetry. If they did, they would not be oppressors. The powerful suppress the protests of the rebel and stifle the cries of the distressed. But even the Nazis did not ban the music of Beethoven. Poetry might be defined as the speech that tyrants do not understand.* If there were no other reasons for it, this would be enough to explain the Delphic character of so much of the world's art, including its folklore, its fables and fairy tales. Think, for instance, of the revolutionary implications of the story of Cinderella!

Shakespeare, in his early days, created no more true-blue character than the Bastard, Philip Faulconbridge, in *King John*. Over and over Faulconbridge gives the impression of seeing things eye to eye with his creator. His great speech on expediency, for example, is vouched for as Shakespearean doctrine by several of the Sonnets. Now it happens that Faulconbridge gives utterance to the precise belief of which we have been speaking: that the man who seeks the truth must know the ways of deceit. I can never, when I read the lines, escape the conviction that they come straight from Shakespeare's heart. At any rate, they express his practice.

> And not alone in habit and device,
> Exterior form, outward accoutrement,
> But from the inward motion to deliver
> Sweet, sweet, sweet poison for the age's tooth;
> Which, though I will not practise to deceive,
> Yet, to avoid deceit, I mean to learn.

Sweet poison! What a sanction it is for the belief that this poet-playwright, too, said to himself: "I will give them, apparently, exactly what they want. But all the while it shall actually be something as different from their ordinary diet, and more divine, as poison is different from food, and more diabolic." No one who would understand Shakespeare can afford to forget that

> Sweet, sweet, sweet poison for the age's tooth.

There is a letter of the musician-playwright, Richard Wagner, that confirms all this in the most extraordinary fashion. "My child," he writes, "this *Tristan* is getting frightful. This last act! I am afraid the opera will be for-

---

* An example of a deliberately ingenious outwitting of the authorities by genius is found in the way in which Robert Schumann concealed the theme of the *Marseillaise* in *Faschingsschwank aus Wien*.

bidden—if the whole thing is not to become a burlesque through bad production. Only mediocre production can save me. Too good would make people crazy. I cannot imagine it otherwise. I have been driven as far as this." How close Shakespeare may have come to getting into trouble over *Richard II* nobody knows. Not that he had any revolutionary purpose in writing the play, or even a polemic one. He was interested in life and character, not in political abstractions. But what can be more revolutionary than that? There were plenty of dangerous implications in the play for anyone who wanted to find them there. The partisans of Essex, at any rate, thought it pertinent enough to the times to have it performed at the Globe the afternoon before their uprising, and Queen Elizabeth felt uneasy enough to remark to the keeper of the Tower, "I am Richard II, know ye not that?" The play, or the special performance of it, was adduced as evidence against Essex at his trial, and Shakespeare knew what it was to have the very heart of his drama cut out by the censor in all editions of the play published during the Queen's lifetime. The next time he tried a kindred theme, in *Julius Caesar*, he was more circumspect—and subtle.

"Only a mediocre production can save me." How often the author of *King Lear* may have thought just that! Many people seem to have the notion that Shakespeare gave specific explanations and directions to the actors in his plays, even coaching them perhaps in their parts, so that, if theatrical tradition had not been broken by the closing of the playhouses during the Puritan ascendancy, we would know just how all of them should be acted. The idea reveals a curious misunderstanding of genius. Imagine Shakespeare "explaining" Falstaff, Hamlet, or Cleopatra! Why trouble to create such characters if he had a formula for them? Only the character itself can explain itself.* Suppose an actress capable of acting Desdemona should appear—something I am certain never did or never could occur. Would not the play become unendurable? The sensitive ones in the audience would swarm across the footlights to rescue her from Iago and Othello. "Too good would make people crazy." Wagner is exactly right. And so the poet has not only the crowd and the police to beware of; he must stop short of allowing inspired acting to drive the poets in his audience mad. Blessed are the mediocre productions of Shakespeare, for they shall be saved—from the censor.

"Behold, I send you forth as sheep in the midst of wolves," said Jesus to his disciples. Poets in this world are always that. And the greatest of them draw just the inference, for themselves, that Jesus did: "Be ye therefore wise as serpents, and harmless as doves." No better brief statement of the

---

* All other comments, including those of the author and of all the commentators, including this one, can give only glimpses.

principle of psychological camouflage was ever made, and no poet was in this sense ever more harmless than Shakespeare. So utter was his harmlessness that it has been mistaken for mere neutrality. Those who take it so have recognized the dove but have failed to perceive the serpent.

## V

Nor is protective coloration confined to the animal and human worlds. Mythology confirms biology in asserting that disguise is intrinsic in life. From Zeus down, the divinities (as well as the devils) always have hidden and always will hide themselves in human form when they would communicate with humanity. How else could they communicate? Homer did not think it a disgrace to let Athena appear to Telemachus in lowliest human guise. Apollo became a shepherd to Admetus. Jesus—the simple believer holds—may knock at your door any night as a tired wayfarer seeking shelter. It is the universal tradition of the gods.

And therefore it is the universal tradition of the poets. Shakespeare is full of it. If his kings and dukes, his priests and prelates—most of them—pass themselves off under the insignia of office for more than they are, if his knaves and villains disguise themselves for sinful or criminal purposes, so not a few of his daughters of dukes and kings, and here and there his men of high estate, pass themselves off for less than they are; and over and over there are those of low degree whose nobility is hidden by their humble station. This contra-disguise, as it might be called, plays a quantitatively smaller but a spiritually more significant part in life than disguise itself. Shakespeare, like all poets, became a specialist in seeking out rarity of character concealed under plain habiliments or deep humility.

> For still the task of genius is
> To mask a god in weeds.

Timon of Athens rescued humanity from the indictment of universal depravity by proclaiming

> One honest man—mistake me not—but one;
> No more, I pray,—and he's a steward.

King Lear's best friends were a fool and a servant (who was an earl in disguise). And it was Desdemona, not Iago, who said,

> I do beguile
> The thing I am by seeming otherwise,

though Iago of course, if not in the same words, said the same thing. The angels disguise themselves as well as the devils, the heroes as well as the hypocrites. It was as a mark of her favor that Athena shed a deep mist about Odysseus. Dostoevsky's Prince Myshkin was known as an idiot. The Prince of Denmark sought to pass himself off as a madman. "Valor in the dark is my Maker's code." So Emily Dickinson sums it up—in almost exactly the same terms in which Shakespeare sums it up in his 94th sonnet:

> They rightly do inherit heaven's graces.

Who are they who rightly inherit the grace of heaven? They, Shakespeare says,

> That do not do the thing they most do show.

## VI

I have enumerated a few of the diverse urges that impel the poet-playwright toward duality; at their root, the mimetic instinct and the nature of play, with the sense of freedom, of omnipotence and omniscience they impart. Deriving from this, the character of acting, which in its essence is "hypocrisy" and disguise, and of the theatrical emotion of the spectator which resides in the illusion of being lifted above life. The law of protective coloration. The double role of every man as individual soul and fool of time—and so of social imposter. In consequence of this, the "masquerade" of human life, which it is the business of the dramatist to portray. The ambiguity of language. And finally—the first as well as the last—the tradition of mythology and the universal practice of the gods.

When so many things point in the same direction, it cannot be coincidence. There must be something *there*. What is it in this case? What underlies all this duality?

Nothing less, surely, than the dual nature of the human mind, conscious and unconscious, and the character of the instrument that seeks to integrate that duality, the imagination. For the imagination is neither consciousness nor unconsciousness, but both at once. It is on earth, but its roots go down into the underworld and its branches reach up toward the sky where birds from above hover over and alight on them. Its function as mediator between the two sides of the mind can best be seen in the single image or symbol (the better word, to avoid confusion with "image" in another sense), the unit that with other such units makes up the alphabet of the imagination, and from which its vocabulary, and ultimately its poetry, is derived.

A symbol is a physical object or entity which because of long, often immemorial, immersion in human experience has taken on its color, acquired undertones and overtones of thought and feeling that link it with other things and give it a significance beyond itself (by derivation, συμβάλλειν, to throw with or compare). A symbol is immensely more than a concept, or complex of concepts. It is as much sensation, feeling, and impulse as it is idea. It is bound up with our fears and hopes, our memories and our aspirations. It is generally self-contradictory. Dawn, for example, stands for beginning, youth, hope, but also for the transient, the uncertain, the unrealized. Autumn suggests harvest and consummation, but also the end of growth and the approach of death. This ambivalent character of symbols, especially of the most ancient ones, is a clear mark of their roots in the unconscious, as are the troop of associations that cluster around them with their attractions and repulsions, their power to point to the past and future, to tug unmercifully at the heart. But their unsurpassed ability to clarify, illuminate, and indicate the way, reveals just as intimate a relation to consciousness. Take, for example, the four elements.

Water is this transparent fluid in which I dip my hand. It is the gentle rain, and the flood. It is what quenches thirst, and what drowns. It is the ocean and the brook, the Eternal Depths and the Stream of Life. . . . Earth is this planet on which I stand, and this handful of soil. It is the garden, and the avalanche. It is life, and death; the Mother from which we all come, the Grave into which we all go. . . . Air is this impalpable substance with which I am surrounded. The soft breeze, and the hurricane. The Sky above, the Breath within. It is Spirit, both good and bad, the Invisible One. But its effects are visible enough. . . . Fire is the sun, and this flame on the hearth. It is what warms, and what burns. It is the candle that lights, the star that guides, the conflagration that consumes. It is love and hate, Heaven and Hell.

From the four elements we might go on to the four seasons, Spring, Summer, Autumn, Winter, or the four points of the compass, North, South, East, and West, and find an antinomy in each. Or we might pick any of a hundred other ancient symbols at random: light—that illuminates, but blinds; night—that brings rest, but brings fear; a road—that penetrates the wilderness, but becomes the beaten track; a rainbow—that is a bridge, but a bridge no man may cross; a bridge itself—that connects, but divides. And so on, and so on.

Such contradictions are calculated to drive a rational mind mad. But they are the very stuff of the imagination. The vocabulary of the imagination consists of hundreds, if not thousands, of such self-contradictory images. If a single one of them can have such polar range, what must poetry, that is a web and complex of them, have? Not only will the "meaning" of it change, chameleon-like, with the context, vary with the uniqueness of the individual experiencing it—it will awaken echoes in the sensitive mind from the remotest past of the race and open vistas on its future. Such iridescence is not only beyond definition, it is beyond comprehension. Even a brief sentence of the commonest words can illustrate this Delphic character of the imagination. "Call no man happy until he is dead." Is that the last word in pessimism, the last word in optimism, or merely a warning against pride? It all depends. "The good die young." Is that just a statement of fact, fierce cynicism, or profound faith in life? Again, it can be any of the three. "How little things count!" Three, four, maybe more, separate philosophies of life according to the stress and intonation of these four words. And yet there are people who say that Shakespeare always means "just what he says"! Lady Macbeth's famous "We fail!" is enough in itself to put that doctrine out of court. He who thinks that to find over- and undermeanings in Shakespeare's plays is to take unwarranted liberties with them is like a man who holds that the word "spring" must refer only to a particular period of the year and could not possibly mean birth, or youth, or hope. He is a man who has never associated anything with anything else. He is a man without metaphors. And such a man is no man at all, let alone a poet.

## VII

Much of the older criticism, especially that of the romantic period, emphasized the accomplishment of Shakespeare as a poet. Recent criticism has tended to remind us constantly that he was a man of the theater. I have offered reasons to suggest that he must be seen as both simultaneously if he is to be understood—though in which capacity he is acting as master and in which as servant should never be obscured.

Just as he was emerging from his apprentice period, Shakespeare, if his practice means anything, was beginning to realize fully the paradox of the poet-playwright and the duality of the world that it was his business to depict. This, rather than its interest as a matter of speculation, is the justification of the stress that we have given the subject here. It certainly was not chance that led Shakespeare to produce at just this time three plays that in three different ways share a common theme: being versus seeming, shadow and substance, appearance and reality, all three emphasizing the contrast between the superficial and the essential, between what is without and what is within. One of them, *The Taming of the Shrew*, parts of which have sometimes been attributed to another hand, seems to straddle, as it were, the period that was passing and the one that was coming. Its more farcical scenes could be contemporary with *The Comedy of Errors*; at its best it compares with *Much Ado about Nothing*. The other two, *A Midsummer-Night's Dream* and *The Merchant of Venice*, are masterpieces without apology.

## Chapter X

# The Taming of the Shrew

### I

*Richard III* proves that *double-entendre* was a passion of the youthful Shakespeare, and both *The Two Gentlemen of Verona* and *Love's Labour's Lost* illustrate the fact that he was fond of under- and overmeanings he could not have expected his audience as a whole to get. But it is *The Taming of the Shrew* that is possibly the most striking example among his early works of his love of so contriving a play that it should mean, to those who might choose to take it so, the precise opposite of what he knew it would mean to the multitude. For surely the most psychologically sound as well as the most delightful way of taking *The Taming of the Shrew* is the topsy-turvy one. Kate, in that case, is no shrew at all except in the most superficial sense. Bianca, on the other hand, is just what her sister is supposed to be. And the play ends with the prospect that Kate is going to be more nearly the tamer than the tamed, Petruchio more nearly the tamed than the tamer, though his wife naturally will keep the true situation under cover. So taken, the play is an early version of *What Every Woman Knows*—what every woman knows being, of course, that the woman can lord it over the man so long as she allows him to think he is lording it over her. This interpretation has the advantage of bringing the play into line with all the other Comedies in which Shakespeare gives a distinct edge to his heroine. Otherwise it is an unaccountable exception and regresses to the wholly un-Shakespearean doctrine of male superiority, a view which there is not the slightest evidence elsewhere Shakespeare ever held.

## II

We must never for a moment allow ourselves to forget that *The Taming of the Shrew* is a play within a play, an interlude put on by a company of strolling players at the house of a great lord for the gulling of Christopher Sly, the drunken tinker, and thereby for the double entertainment of the audience. For the sake of throwing the picture into strong relief against the frame—as in a different sense in the case of *The Murder of Gonzago* in *Hamlet*—the play within the play is given a simplification and exaggeration that bring its main plot to the edge of farce, while its minor plot, the story of Bianca's wooers, goes quite over that edge. But, even allowing for this, the psychology of the Katharine-Petruchio plot is remarkably realistic. It is even "modern" in its psychoanalytical implications. It is based on the familiar situation of the favorite child. Baptista is a family tyrant and Bianca is his favorite daughter. She has to the casual eye all the outer marks of modesty and sweetness, but to a discerning one all the inner marks of a spoiled pet, remade, if not originally made, in her father's image. One line is enough to give us her measure. When in the wager scene at the end her husband tells her that her failure to come at his entreaty has cost him a hundred crowns,

> The more fool you for laying on my duty,

she blurts out. What a light that casts back over her previous "sweetness" before she has caught her man! The rest of her role amply supports this interpretation, as do the hundreds of Biancas—who are not as white as they are painted—in real life.

Apart from the irony and the effective contrast so obtained, there is everything to indicate that Kate's shrewishness is superficial, not ingrained or congenital. It is the inevitable result of her father's gross partiality toward her sister and neglect of herself, plus the repercussions that his attitude has produced on Bianca and almost everyone else in the region. Kate has heard herself blamed, and her sister praised at her expense, to a point where even a worm would turn. And Kate is no worm. If her sister is a spoiled child, Kate is a cross child who is starved for love. She craves it as a man in a desert craves water, without understanding, as he does, what is the matter. And though we have to allow for the obvious exaggeration of farce in his extreme antics, Petruchio's procedure at bottom shows insight, understanding, and even love. Those actors who equip him with a whip miss Shakespeare's man entirely. In principle, if not in the rougher details, he employs just the right method in the circumstances, and the end amply justifies his means.

It is obvious that his boast at the outset of purely mercenary motives for marrying is partly just big talk—at any rate the dowry soon becomes quite subsidiary to Kate herself and the game of taming her. In retrospect it seems to have been something like love at first sight on both sides, though not recognized as such at the time. Whatever we think of Petruchio's pranks in the scenes where farce and comedy get mixed, there is no quarreling with his instinctive sense of how in general Kate ought to be handled. When a small child is irritable and cross, the thing to do is not to reason, still less to pity or pamper, or even to be just kind and understanding in the ordinary sense. The thing to do is to take the child captive. A vigorous body and will, combined with good humor and a love that is not expressed in words but that makes itself felt by a sort of magnetic communication, will sweep the child off his feet, carry him away, and transform him almost miraculously back into his natural self. Anyone who does not know that knows mighty little about children. This is precisely what Petruchio does to Kate (and what Shakespeare does to his audience in this play). She is dying for affection. He keeps calling her his sweet and lovely Kate. What if he is ironical to begin with! The words just of themselves are manna to her soul, and her intuition tells her that, whether he knows it or not, he really means them. And indeed Kate is lovely and sweet by nature. (She is worth a bale of Biancas.) What girl would not like to be told, as Petruchio tells her, that she sings as sweetly as a nightingale and has a countenance like morning roses washed with dew? She knows by a perfectly sound instinct that he could never have thought up such lovely similes to be sarcastic with if he considered her nothing but a shrew. There is a poet within him that her beauty has elicited. What wonder that she weeps when the poet fails to appear for the wedding! It is not just humiliation. It is disappointed love.

And Kate is intelligent too. She is a shrewd "shrew." You can put your finger on the very moment when it dawns on her that if she will just fall in with her husband's absurdest whim, accept his maddest perversion of the truth as truth, she can take the wind completely out of his sails, deprive his weapon of its power, even turn it against him—tame him in his own humor. Not that she really wants to tame him, for she loves him dearly, as the delightful little scene in the street so amply proves, where he begs a kiss, begs, be it noted, not demands. She is shy for fear they may be overseen, but finally relents and consents.

KATH.: Husband, let's follow, to see the end of this ado.
PET.: First kiss me, Kate, and we will.
KATH.: What! in the midst of the street?
PET.: What! art thou ashamed of me?
KATH.: No, sir, God forbid; but ashamed to kiss.

PET.: Why, then let's home again. Come, sirrah, let's away.
KATH.: Nay, I will give thee a kiss; now pray thee, love, stay.
PET.: Is not this well? Come, my sweet Kate.
Better once than never, for never too late.

How this little scene is to be fitted into the traditional interpretation of the play it is hard to see.

Everything leads up to Kate's long lecture at the end on the duty of wives to their lords. What fun she has reading it to those two other women who do not know what every woman knows! How intolerable it would be if she and Shakespeare really meant it (as if Shakespeare could ever have meant it!), though there is a deeper sense in which they both do mean it, a sense that ties the speech to Biron's on the complementary natures of man and woman. The self-styled advanced thinkers of our day, who have been for obliterating all distinctions between the sexes and leveling them to a dead equality, are just lacking enough in humor to think Kate's speech the most retrograde nonsense, as indeed it would be if it were the utterance of a cowering slave.

Though actresses in the past have edged in the direction of this interpretation of Kate, a triumph still remains for one who will go the whole distance and find in her a clear first draft and frank anticipation of Beatrice. Petruchio, too, must be made fine and bold, not just rough and bold, or crude and bold. And as for Bianca, you can pick up a dozen of her in the first high school you happen on, any one of whom could act her to perfection by just being herself.

*The Taming of the Shrew*, by slighting certain things like the tamer's begging for a kiss, is undeniably susceptible of the traditional rowdy interpretation whereby Petruchio becomes a caveman and Kate a termagant. It has been so acted down the years and there is little doubt that it was so acted in Shakespeare's time. Poets are under no obligation to spoil the popular success of their plays by revealing their secrets, even to stage directors. But unless *The Taming of the Shrew* is frankly taken as sheer farce, the primitive interpretation of it is utterly offensive to our sensibilities, saved only by its wit from being as brutal a spectacle as a bearbaiting. Indeed, the analogy that dominated the Elizabethan mind throughout must have been that of the taming of the female hawk. If, then, without distortion, the text is susceptible of another construction that both satisfies us better and at the same time deepens the psychological complexity and truth of the main characters, what, pray, is the authority of tradition that shall prevent our adopting it? If I find a key that fits a treasure chest and am about to open it, but am suddenly confronted with indisputable evidence that it is a key to an entirely different chest several hundred years old, I may defer to the authenticity of the historical documents that have proved the fact, but what a fool I would be not to go ahead in spite of them and open the chest! A work of art exists for what it says to us, not for what it said to the people of its "own" day, nor even necessarily for what it said, consciously, to its author. A work of art is an autonomous entity. So long as we do no violence to it, we may fit it to our own experience in any way we wish.

## III

But, as it happens, there is something quite specific in this particular case to indicate the author is giving us not just general but quite express leave to take his play in a subterranean sense. This clue, if I may call it that, is found in the "Induction."

In a mathematical proportion, if three of the terms are known, the fourth unknown one $(x)$ can easily be determined. Thus, if $(a/b) = (c/x)$, it follows that $x = (bc/a)$. The poet often proceeds from the known to the unknown by a similar procedure, but unlike the mathematician he does not meticulously put the $x$ on one side and carefully label the other side of the equation "answer." He supplies the data rather and leaves it to the reader to figure out or not, as he chooses, what follows from them. This was plainly the method Shakespeare used in relating the story of Christopher Sly to the story of Petruchio.

It is generally agreed that the Induction to *The Taming of the Shrew* is one of the most masterly bits of writing to be found anywhere in Shakespeare's earlier works. Much as the authorship of the play has been debated, no one, so far as I recall, has ever questioned the authorship of the Induction. Shakespeare evidently bestowed on it a care that indicates the importance it had in his eyes. In *The Taming of a Shrew* (whose relation to *The Taming of the Shrew* has recently been widely discussed) the purpose of the Induction with reference to the play itself is made perfectly clear by a return to Sly at the end after the play within the play is over. Christopher Sly, the drunken tinker, has a wife who is a shrew. In the play that is acted before him he watches the successful subjugation of another woman to the will of her husband, and at the end of the performance we see him starting off for home to try out on his own wife the knowledge he has just acquired. Whatever part, if any, Shakespeare had in the earlier play, why did he spoil a good point in the later one by not completing its framework, by failing to return to Sly at the end of the Petruchio play? All sorts of explanations for the artistic lapse have been conjured up, the most popular being that the last leaf of the manuscript, in which he did so return, was somehow lost or that the scene was left to the improvisation of the actors and so was never reduced to writing. But surely the editors of the *Folio* would have been aware of this and could have supplied at least a stage direction to clear things up!

I wonder if the explanation of the enigma is not a simpler and more characteristic one: that Shakespeare saw his chance for a slyer and profounder relation between the Induction and the play than in the earlier version of the story.

In the Induction to *The Taming of the Shrew*, Christopher Sly the tinker, drunk with ale, is persuaded that he is a great lord who has been the victim of an unfortunate lunacy. Petruchio, in the play which Sly witnesses (when he is not asleep), is likewise persuaded that he is a great lord—over his wife. Sly is obviously in for a rude awakening when he discovers that he is nothing but a tinker after all. Now Petruchio is a bit intoxicated himself—who can deny it?—whether with pride, love, or avarice, or some mixture of the three. Is it possible that he too is in for an awakening? Or, if Kate does not let it come to that, that *we* at least are supposed to see that he is not as great a lord over his wife as he imagined? The Induction and the play, taken together, do not allow us to evade these questions. Can anyone be so naïve as to fancy that Shakespeare did not contrive his Induction for the express purpose of forcing them on us? Either the cases of Sly and Petruchio are alike or they are diametrically opposite. Can there be much doubt which was intended by a poet who is so given to pointing out analogies between lovers and drunkards, between lovers and lunatics? Here surely is reason enough for Shakespeare not to show us Sly at the end when he no longer thinks himself a lord. It would be altogether too much like explaining the joke, like solving the equation and labeling the result ANSWER. Shakespeare wants us to find things for ourselves. And in this case in particular: why explain what is as clear, when you see it, as was Poe's Purloined Letter, which was skilfully concealed precisely because it was in such plain sight all the time?

There are two little touches in the first twenty-five lines of the Induction that seem to clinch this finally, if it needs any clinching. The Lord and his huntsmen come in from hunting. They are talking of the hounds and their performances:

LORD:      Saw'st thou not, boy, how Silver made it good
                  At the hedge-corner, in the coldest fault?
                  I would not lose the dog for twenty pound.
FIRST HUNT.:  Why, Bellman is as good as he, my lord;
                  He cried upon it at the merest loss,
                  And twice today pick'd out the dullest scent:
                  Trust me, I take him for the better dog.

Why, in what looks like a purely atmospheric passage, this double emphasis on the power to pick up a dull or cold scent? Why if not as a hint to spectators and readers to keep alert for something they might easily miss?

*Chapter XI*

# A Midsummer-Night's Dream

*A Midsummer-Night's Dream* is one of the lightest and in many respects the most purely playful of Shakespeare's plays. Yet it is surpassed by few if any of his early works in its importance for an understanding of the unfolding of his genius. It is characteristic of its author that he should have chosen this fanciful dream-play through which to announce for the first time in overt and unmistakable fashion the conviction that underlies every one of his supreme Tragedies: that this world of sense in which we live is but the surface of a vaster unseen world by which the actions of men are affected or overruled. He had already in *The Comedy of Errors* hinted at a witchcraft at work behind events. But that at the moment seemed little more than the author's apology for the amount of coincidence in his plot. Now he begins to explore the causes of coincidence. Not until the end of his career, in *The Tempest*, was he to treat this theme with such directness, not even in *Macbeth*. It may be objected that this is taking a mere dream or fantasy quite too seriously. It is of course possible to hold that in *A Midsummer-Night's Dream* Shakespeare is not so much giving utterance to convictions of his own as recording a folklore which itself carries certain metaphysical implications. There is doubtless some truth in this view—how much it is hard to tell. But it makes little difference. For the implications, in the latter case, were the seeds of the convictions, and our mistake, if any, is merely that of finding the oak in the acorn. The congruity, in spite of their differences, of *A Midsummer-Night's Dream* with *The Tempest* is one of the most striking demonstrations of the continuity and integrity of Shakespeare's genius that his works afford.

There are two passages, as distinct from incidents, in *A Midsummer-Night's Dream* that perhaps above all others embody its central theme.

Each enhances the other. One of them, Theseus' well-known speech on the imagination at the beginning of Act V, has always been accorded due importance. The other, oddly, though almost as universally praised, has generally been looked on as a kind of digression, a purple patch that justifies itself by its own beauty rather than through any particular pertinence to the rest of the play. The lines have been widely and deservedly acclaimed for their sound. But their euphony is only one aspect of their miraculous quality. The passage is the one in the first scene of Act IV where Theseus and Hippolyta, just as the dogs are about to be released for the hunt, speak of the music of the hounds in words that by some magic catch and echo that very music itself:

THE.: My love shall hear the music of my hounds.
　　　Uncouple in the western valley; let them go:
　　　Dispatch, I say, and find the forester.
　　　We will, fair queen, up to the mountain's top,
　　　And mark the musical confusion
　　　Of hounds and echo in conjunction.
HIP.: I was with Hercules and Cadmus once,
　　　When in a wood of Crete they bay'd the bear
　　　With hounds of Sparta: never did I hear
　　　Such gallant chiding; for, besides the groves,
　　　The skies, the fountains, every region near
　　　Seem'd all one mutual cry. I never heard
　　　So musical a discord, such sweet thunder.
THE.: My hounds are bred out of the Spartan kind,
　　　So flew'd, so sanded; and their heads are hung
　　　With ears that sweep away the morning dew;
　　　Crook-knee'd, and dew-lapp'd like Thessalian bulls;
　　　Slow in pursuit, but match'd in mouth like bells,
　　　Each under each. A cry more tuneable
　　　Was never holla'd to, nor cheer'd with horn,
　　　In Crete, in Sparta, nor in Thessaly:
　　　Judge, when you hear.

This a digression! On the contrary it is as nearly perfect a metaphor as could be conceived for *A Midsummer-Night's Dream* itself and for the incomparable counterpoint with which its own confusions and discords are melted into the "sweet thunder" of a single musical effect. How can British fairies and Athenian nobility be mingled with decency in the same play? As easily as the "confusion" of hounds and echoes can make "conjunction." How can the crossings and bewilderments of the four lovers lead to their happy reunion at the end? As easily as discord can contribute to harmony in music. How can the foolish and awkward pranks of the

rustics adorn the wedding celebration of a great duke? As easily, to turn
things the other way around, as a fairy dream can enter the head of an ass
or as animals who are like bulls can emit sounds that are like bells—as easily
as thunder can be sweet.

The very incongruities, anachronisms, contradictions, and impossible juxtapositions of *A Midsummer-Night's Dream*, and the triumphant manner
in which the poet reduces them to a harmony, are what more than anything
else make this play a masterpiece. The hounds are symbols of the hunt, and
so of death. But their voices are transmuted by distance, in the ear of the
listener, to symbols of harmony and life. The hunt is called off; the will
of the cruel father is overborne; a triple wedding is substituted for it:

> Our purpos'd hunting shall be set aside.
> Away with us to Athens: three and three,
> We'll hold a feast in great solemnity.

We might discover the whole history of humanity, past and future, in those
lines.

It is right here that the passage about the hounds links with Theseus'
speech on the imagination. The Duke, in words too well known to need
quotation, tells of the power of this faculty, whether in the lunatic, the
lover, or the poet, to create something out of nothing. The poet alone, however, has power to capture this "airy nothing" and anchor it, as it were,
to reality, even as Shakespeare gives actuality to fairies in this very play.
Yet Theseus is suspicious of the "tricks" of imagination, conscious of its
illusory quality. He hints that it must be brought to the test of "cool reason." Strictly, what Theseus is talking about is not imagination at all in its
proper sense, but fantasy. Hippolyta catches just this distinction and for
once seems wiser than her lover. She holds that the miracles of love are
even greater than those of fancy, and because the same miracle takes place
at the same time in more than one mind she believes that they testify to
something solid and lasting that emerges from this "airy nothing." Theseus
had called this faculty more strange than true. Hippolyta holds it both
strange and true:

> But all the story of the night told over,
> And all their minds transfigur'd so together,
> More witnesseth than fancy's images,
> And grows to something of great constancy,
> But, howsoever, strange and admirable.

In practice Theseus agrees with this exactly, as is shown later in the same
scene when he insists on hearing the play that the craftsmen have prepared.
The master of revels, Philostrate, protests against its selection:

A MIDSUMMER-NIGHT'S DREAM

```
PHIL.:                          in all the play
         There is not one word apt, one player fitted.
                   . . . No, my noble lord,
         It is not for you. I have heard it over,
         And it is nothing, nothing in the world. . . .
THE.:                       I will hear that play;
         For never anything can be amiss,
         When simpleness and duty tender it. . . .
HIP.:    He says they can do nothing in this kind.
THE.:    The kinder we, to give them thanks for nothing.
```

That four-times reiterated "nothing" is Shakespeare's way of sending our
minds back to the "airy nothing" of Theseus' earlier speech which, he then
said and now proves, imagination has power to turn into something actual.
It is Hippolyta this time who fails.

> This is the silliest stuff that ever I heard,*

she protests as the play proceeds. Appropriately, now that it is a question
of art, Theseus turns out to be wiser than she, as she was wiser than he when
it was a question of love. "The best in this kind are but shadows," he
reminds her, "and the worst are no worse, if imagination amend them."
At last, Theseus is using "imagination" in its proper sense, and in his words
we seem to catch the very accent and secret of the poet's own tolerance
and sympathy.

Shakespeare, in this play and elsewhere, was only too well aware how
frail imagination can appear in the face of ineluctable fact. "The course of
true love never did run smooth." "So quick bright things come to confusion."

> These things seem small and undistinguishable,
> Like far-off mountains turned into clouds.

What, indeed, is more insubstantial than a midsummer-night's dream? And
yet from about this time, if not from the beginning, he never lost faith in
"bright things," in the power of the imagination to transmute the lead of
life into its own gold. More and more, if with some ebbings, some descents
into the valleys, this faith grew in him, in Hippolyta's words, to "something
of great constancy." Is it any wonder, after the miracle that Imagination
had performed through him in this very play?

*A Midsummer-Night's Dream* is a kind of fugue with four voices

> match'd in mouth like bells,
> Each under each.

* Just what Samuel Pepys said of *A Midsummer-Night's Dream* itself, "The most
insipid ridiculous play that ever I saw."

{ 77 }

There are the fairies. There are the lovers. There are the rustics. There is the court. What metaphysical as well as social gulfs divide them! But Imagination bridges them all. Imagination makes them all one.

And the play has four voices in another and profounder sense.

*A Midsummer-Night's Dream* is itself, as its title says, a dream. Its action occurs mostly at night. Its atmosphere is that of moonlight and shadows. Its characters are forever falling asleep and dreaming. And at the end Puck invites the audience to believe that as they have been sitting there they have nodded and slumbered and that all that has passed before them has been a vision.

But as the other part of its title suggests, *A Midsummer-Night's Dream* is not only a dream, it is "play" in the quite literal sense of that term, a piece pervaded with the atmosphere of innocent idleness and joy befitting a midsummer night. It is not merely a play; it is the spirit of play in its essence. From the pranks of Puck and the frolics of the fairies, through the hide-and-seek of the lovers in the wood and the rehearsals of the rustics, on to the wedding festivities of the court and the final presentation of the masque of Pyramus and Thisbe, the tone of the piece is that of love-in-idleness, of activity for the sheer fun of it and for its own sake.

And because *A Midsummer-Night's Dream* is permeated with this spirit of doing things just for the love of doing them or for the love of the one for whom they are done, because the drama opens and closes on the wedding note and what comes between is just an interweaving of love stories, the piece may be said to be not only *dream* from end to end, and *play* from end to end, but also *love* from end to end.

And finally *A Midsummer-Night's Dream* is *art* from end to end—not just a work of art itself, which of course it is, but dedicated in good measure to the theme of art and made up of many little works of art of varying degrees of merit: its innumerable songs, its perpetual references to music, its rehearsal and presentation of the story of Pyramus and Thisbe, to say nothing of its many quotable passages, which, like the one about the hounds, the one about the superiority of silence to eloquence, the one about true love, the one about the mermaid on the dolphin's back, when lifted from their context seem like poems or pictures complete in themselves, whatever subtler values they may have in relation to the whole.

Dream, play, love, art. Surely it is no coincidence that these four "subjects" which are here interwoven with such consummate polyphony represent the four main aspects under which Imagination reveals itself in human life. Dream: what is that but a name for the world out of which man emerges into conscious life, the world of the unconscious as we have a habit of calling it today? Play: the instrument by which the child instinctively repeats the experience of the race and so by rehearsal prepares himself for the drama of life. Love: a revelation to each of the sexes that it is but a fragment of Another, which, by combined truth and illusion, seems at first concentrated in a person of the opposite sex. Art: the dream become conscious of itself, play grown to an adult estate, love freed of its illusion and transferred to wider and higher than personal ends. Dream, play, love, art: these four. Is there a fifth?

The fifth perhaps is what we finally have in this play, a union of the other four, Imagination in its quintessence—not just dream, nor play, nor love, nor art, but something above and beyond them all. With the attainment of it, the first becomes last, dream comes full circle as Vision, an immediate conscious apprehension of an invisible world, or, if you will, transubstantiation of the world of sense into something beyond itself.*

The example of Bottom and his transformation will serve to bring these un-Shakespearean abstractions back to the concrete. To the average reader, Puck and Bottom are probably the most memorable characters in the play, Bottom especially. This instinct is right. Bottom is as much the master-character here as Launce is in *The Two Gentlemen of Verona*. Bottom symbolizes the earthy, the ponderous, the slow, in contrast with Puck, who is all that is quick, light, and aerial. Bottom is substance, the real in the common acceptation of that term. If Puck is the apex, Bottom is the base without whose four-square foundation the pyramid of life would topple over. He is the antithesis of the thesis of the play, the ballast that keeps the elfin bark of it from capsizing. He is literally what goes to the bottom. Like all heavy things he is content with his place in life, but his egotism is the unconscious selfishness of a child, both a sense and a consequence of his own individuality, not greed but pride in the good significance of that word. His realistic conception of stagecraft is in character. To Puck, Bottom is an ass. Yet Titania falls in love with him, ass's head and all.

> And I will purge thy mortal grossness so
> That thou shalt like an airy spirit go,

she promises. And she keeps her promise by sending him Bottom's dream.

The moment when Bottom awakens from this dream is the supreme moment of the play.† There is nothing more wonderful in the poet's early

---

* I refrain from using the word Religion for this ultimate phase of the Imagination. A word so contaminated with theological, ecclesiastic, and moral considerations can lead only to confusion. If the word were only uncontaminated, it might be a near synonym for Vision as I use it.

† "I have had a most rare vision. I have had a dream, past the wit of man to say what dream it was. Man is but an ass, if he go about to expound this dream. Methought I was—there is no man can tell what. Methought I was,—and methought I had,—but man is but a patch'd fool, if he will offer to say what methought I had. The eye of man

works and few things more wonderful in any of them. For what Shakespeare has caught here in perfection is the original miracle of the Imagination, the awakening of spiritual life in the animal man. Bottom is an ass. If Bottom can be redeemed, matter itself and man in all his materiality can be redeemed also. Democracy becomes possible. Nothing less than this is what this incident implies. Yet when it is acted, so far as my experience in the theater goes, this divine insight is reduced to nothing but an occasion for roars of laughter. Laughter of course there should be, but laughter shot through with a beauty and pathos close to tears. Only an actor of genius could do justice to it. Bottom himself best indicates its quality when he declares that the dream deserves to be *sung* at the conclusion of a play and that it should be called Bottom's dream "because it hath no bottom." It is the same thought that Thoreau expounds when he shows why men persist in believing in bottomless ponds. For a moment in this scene, however far over the horizon, we sense the Shakespeare who was to describe the death of Falstaff, compose *King Lear*, and create Caliban.

Indeed, *A Midsummer-Night's Dream* as a whole is prophetic, in one respect at least, as is no other of the earlier plays, of the course the poet's genius was to take. There are few more fruitful ways of regarding his works than to think of them as an account of the warfare between Imagination and Chaos—or, if you will, between Imagination and the World—the story of the multifarious attempts of the divine faculty in man to ignore, to escape, to outwit, to surmount, to combat, to subdue, to forgive, to convert, to redeem, to transmute into its own substance, as the case may be, the powers of disorder that possess the world. Taken retrospectively, *A Midsummer-Night's Dream* seems like the argument of this story, like an overture to the vast musical composition which the poet's later masterpieces make up, like a seed from which the Shakespearean flower developed and unfolded.

---

hath not heard, the ear of man hath not seen, man's hand is not able to taste, his tongue to conceive, nor his heart to report, what my dream was. I will get Peter Quince to write a ballad of this dream. It shall be called 'Bottom's Dream,' because it hath no bottom; and I will sing it in the latter end of a play, before the Duke; peradventure, to make it the more gracious, I shall sing it at her death."

*Chapter XII*

# The Merchant of Venice

## I

The anti-Semitism of the twentieth century lends a fresh interest to *The Merchant of Venice*. It raises anew the old question: How could one of the most tolerant spirits of all time have written a play that is centered around, and seems to many to accept, one of the most degraded prejudices of the ages? "About 1594," says a recent critic of high standing, "public sentiment in England was roused to an outbreak of traditional Jew-baiting; and for good and evil, Shakespeare the man was like his fellows. He planned a *Merchant of Venice* to let the Jew dog have it, and thereby to gratify his own patriotic pride of race." "The bond story," says another contemporary commentator, "has an anti-Semitic edge, and in recent years many secondary schools have wisely removed the play from the curriculum. . . . Shakespeare simply accepts the Jews as a notoriously bad lot. . . . I do not see how a Jew can read *The Merchant of Venice* without pain and indignation." And others express themselves to the same effect.

Not all, of course, go that far. There have been many to point out that Shylock is by no means a monster. He has traits that humanize him and excite our sympathy. But few who vindicate Shakespeare do so in a bold or ringing tone. They are timid, or qualified, or even apologetic. The thought of how the Elizabethan crowd at any rate must have taken Shylock makes them shudder. And beyond doubt, whatever the poet intended, most of his audience must have made the Jew an object of ridicule or contempt, or both. Is there danger that modern schoolboys will do the same?

"Shakespeare is a great psychologist," said Goethe, "and whatever can be known of the heart of man may be found in his plays." If it has come

to the point where a masterpiece of this great psychologist has to be removed from the schools because of the bad passions it may arouse, it would
seem to be time to re-examine that oft-examined masterpiece once more.

## II

However it may be now, there was a time when anyone who had been
through high school knew that *The Merchant of Venice* is an interweaving
of three strands commonly known as the casket story, the bond story, and
the ring story. The teacher in those days always pointed out the skill with
which Shakespeare had made three plots into one, but generally left out the
much more important fact that the three stories, as the poet uses them,
become variations on a single theme.

The casket story obviously stresses the contrast between what is within
and what is without. So, however, if less obviously, do the other two. The
bond story is built about the distinction between the letter and the spirit
of the law. But what are letter and spirit if not what is without and what is
within? And the ring story turns on the difference between the outer form
and the inner essence of a promise. When Bassanio rewards the Young Doctor of Laws with Portia's ring, he is keeping the spirit of his vow to her
as certainly as he would have been breaking it if he had kept the ring on his
finger. In the circumstances literal fidelity would have been actual faithlessness.

Yet in spite of this thematic unity (into which the love story of Lorenzo
and Jessica can also be fitted) we find one of the keenest of recent critics
asking: "What in the name of all dramatic propriety and economy are the
casket scenes doing? They are quite irrelevant to the plot, and . . . for the
characterization of Bassanio, a positive nuisance. . . . They are a mere piece
of adornment. And the answer to that 'why' is no doubt just that Shakespeare knew that they were effective episodes, and that no audience with
the colour of the scenes in their eyes and the beauty of his verse in their
ears was going to trouble its heads that they were no more than episodes.
Shakespeare was writing for audiences and not for dramatic critics."

Of course Shakespeare the playwright was writing for audiences. But
how about Shakespeare the poet?

Drama, as we have said, must make a wide and immediate appeal to a large
number of people of ordinary intelligence. The playwright must make his
plots plain, his characters easily grasped, his ideas familiar. The public does
not want the truth. It wants confirmation of its prejudices. That is why the
plays of mere playwrights have immediate success but seldom survive.

What the poet is seeking, on the other hand, is the secret of life, and,
even if he would, he cannot share with a crowd in a theater, through the

distorting medium of actors who are far from sharing his genius, such gleams of it as may have been revealed to him. He can share it only with the few, and with them mostly in solitude.

A poet-playwright, then, is a contradiction in terms. But a poet-playwright is exactly what Shakespeare is. And so his greater plays are one thing as drama and another as poetry, one thing on the outside, another within. Ostensibly, *The Merchant of Venice* is the story of the friendship of an unselfish Venetian merchant for a charming young gentleman who is in love with a beautiful heiress; of the noble sacrifice that the friend is on the point of making when nearly brought to disaster by a vile Jew; of the transformation of the lovely lady into lawyer and logician just in the nick of time and her administration to the villain of a dose of his own medicine. Was ever a play more compact with popular appeal? But what if, all the while, underneath and overhead, it were something as different from all this as the contents of the three caskets are from their outward appearance? It would be in keeping. What if the author is putting to the test, not just the suitors of Portia, but other characters as well, even, possibly, every reader or spectator of his play? It would be like him.

The seductive atmosphere of the play lends immediate credence to such an hypothesis. The critic quoted believes that the playwright was counting on it to hypnotize his audience into not noticing irrelevancies. It may be that he was also counting on it for profounder and more legitimate reasons.

The social world of Venice and more especially of Belmont centers around pleasure. It is a golden world—a gilded world we might better say. It is a world of luxury and leisure, of idle talk and frivolity, of music and romance. It has the appearance of genuine grace and culture. Except for a few scenes, the average production of *The Merchant of Venice* leaves an impression of bright costumes, witty conversations, gay or dreamy melody, and romantic love. Gold is the symbol of this world of pleasure. But what is under this careless ease? On what does it rest for foundation? The answer is—on money. Or, if you will, on the trade and commerce that bring the money, and on the inheritance that passes it along. Now this world of trade and commerce, as it happens, does not resemble very closely the world that its profits purchase. Its chief symbol in the play is silver, which in the form of money is the "pale and common drudge 'tween man and man." When the Prince of Arragon opens the silver casket, he finds, within, the portrait of a blinking idiot and verses telling him that he is a fool who has embraced a shadow in mistake for substance.

But there is something even worse than money under the surface of this social world. Exclusiveness—and the hypocrisy exclusiveness always involves, the pretense that that which is excluded is somehow less real than that which excludes. When the Prince of Morocco opens the golden casket he finds not a fool's head, as Arragon finds, but a Death's head—so much deadlier than money is the moral degradation that money so often brings. "All that glisters is not gold."

Dimly, in varying degrees, these Venetians and Belmontese reveal an uneasiness, a vague discontent, an unexplained sense of something wrong. This note, significantly, is sounded in the very first words of four or five of the leading characters.

> In sooth, I know not why I am so sad,

says Antonio in the first line of the play. "By my troth, Nerissa, my little body is aweary of this great world," are Portia's first words. "Our house is hell," Jessica announces in her opening speech. And we wonder what cruelty her father has been guilty of, until she goes on to explain that the hell she refers to is tediousness. Melancholy, weariness, tedium—the reiteration of the note cannot be coincidence. And the other characters confirm the conjecture. Over and over they give the sense of attempting to fill every chink of time with distraction or amusement, often just words, to prevent their thinking. Bassanio makes his bow with a greeting to Salanio and Salarino:

> Good signiors both, when shall we laugh? say when?

and Gratiano (after a reference to Antonio's morose appearance, from which he takes his cue) begins:

> Let me play the fool!
> With mirth and laughter let old wrinkles come,
> And let my liver rather heat with wine
> Than my heart cool with mortifying groans.

Gratiano's cure for care is merriment and torrents of talk. He is not the only one in Venice who "speaks an infinite deal of nothing." Launcelot Gobbo, the "witsnapper," is merely a parody and reduction to the absurd of the loquaciousness that infects the main plot as well as the comic relief. Lorenzo condemns as fools those of higher station who, like Launcelot, "for a tricksy word defy the matter," and then proceeds in his very next speech to defy it in the same way. We can feel Shakespeare himself wearying of "wit"—the verbal gold that conceals paucity of thought—and it would scarcely be far-fetched to find a prophecy of his great taciturn characters, like Cordelia and Virgilia, in the declaration: "How every fool can play upon the word! I think the best grace of wit will shortly turn into silence, and discourse grow commendable in none only but parrots."

What is the trouble with these people and what are they trying to hide?

Why should the beautiful Portia, with all her adorers, be bored? Nerissa, who under her habit as waiting-maid has much wisdom, hits the nail on the head in *her* first speech in answer to Portia's: "For aught I see, they are as sick that surfeit with too much as they that starve with nothing." What these people are trying to elude is their own souls, or, as we say today, the Unconscious.

Now Shylock is a representative of both of the things of which we have been speaking: of money, because he is himself a moneylender, and of exclusion, because he is the excluded thing. Therefore the Venetian world makes him their scapegoat. They project on him what they have dismissed from their own consciousness as too disturbing. They hate him because he reminds them of their own unconfessed evil qualities. Down the ages this has been the main explanation of racial hatred and persecution, of the mistreatment of servant by master. Our unconsciousness is our foreign land. Hence we see in the foreigner what is actually the "foreign" part of ourselves.

Grasp this, and instantly a dozen things in the play fall into place, and nearly every character in it is seen to be one thing on the outside and another underneath—so inherent, so little mere adornment, is the casket theme. It ramifies into a hundred details and into every corner of the play.

## III

Bassanio is a good example to begin with. He fools the average reader and, especially if the play is conventionally cast and handsomely mounted, the average spectator, as completely as the dashing movie star does the matinee girl. Is he not in love with the rich heroine?

Bassanio admits that he has posed as wealthier than he is and has mortgaged his estate

> By something showing a more swelling port
> Than my faint means would grant continuance.

And Antonio abets the deception. As a youth, says Bassanio, when I lost one arrow, I shot another in the same direction and often retrieved both. So now. Lend me a little more to make love to a lady who has inherited a fortune (and who has beauty and virtue) and with good luck I will repay you (out of her wealth) both your new loan and your old ones:

> I have a mind presages me such thrift.

This is not exactly in the key of *Romeo and Juliet*.

If this seem an ungracious way of putting it, note that Bassanio himself describes it as a "plot" to get clear of his debts. But when the young spendthrift is handsome, we forgive him much. In watching the development of the love affair it is easy to forget its inception. And yet, when Bassanio stands in front of the golden casket, clad in the rich raiment that Antonio's (i.e., Shylock's) gold has presumably bought, and addresses it,

> Therefore, thou gaudy gold,
> Hard food for Midas, I will none of thee,

we feel that if Shakespeare did not intend the irony it got in in spite of him. No, gold, I'll have none of thee, Bassanio declares (whether he knows it or not), except a bit from Antonio-Shylock to start me going, and a bit from a certain lady "richly left" whose dowry shall repay the debts of my youth and provide for my future. Beyond that, none.

> *Who chooseth me must give and hazard all he hath.*

It is almost cruel to recall the inscription on the casket Bassanio picked in the light of what he *received* from Shylock and of what he let Antonio *risk* in his behalf.

If it be objected that this is subjecting a fairy tale to the tests of realistic literature, the answer is that it is not the first time that a fairy tale has been a fascinating invention on the surface and the hardest fact and soundest wisdom underneath. Ample justice has been done by his admirers to Bassanio's virtues. It is the economic aspect of his career that has been understressed. Like a number of others in this play the source of whose income will not always bear inspection, like most of us in fact, he was not averse to receiving what he had not exactly earned. Bassanio is the golden casket. He gained what many men desire: a wealthy wife.

## IV

Antonio's case is a bit subtler than Bassanio's but even more illuminating. Why is Antonio sad?

Shakespeare devotes a good share of the opening scene of the play to a discussion of that question.

> In sooth, I know not why I am so sad.
> It wearies me; you say it wearies you;
> But how I caught it, found it, or came by it,
> What stuff 'tis made of, whereof it is born,
> I am to learn;
> And such a want-wit sadness makes of me,
> That I have much ado to know myself.

Salanio and Salarino confirm his changed appearance and suggest that he is anxious over his argosies. But Antonio brushes that aside. His ventures are not in one bottom trusted nor all his wealth committed to the present enterprise:

Therefore, my merchandise makes me not sad.

He denies, too, the charge that he is in love. So Salarino, baffled, concludes that it is a matter of temperament. Antonio was just born that way. But this explains nothing and his altered looks give it the lie.

Commentators have commonly either side-stepped the problem or explained Antonio's melancholy as a presentiment of the loss of his friend Bassanio through marriage. That may have accentuated it at the moment, but Antonio has had barely a hint of what is coming when the play opens, while his depression has all the marks of something older and deeper. It is scarcely too much to say that he is a sick man. Later, at the trial, when the opportunity of sacrificing himself is presented, his sadness becomes almost suicidal:

> I am a tainted wether of the flock,
> Meetest for death. The weakest kind of fruit
> Drops earliest to the ground; and so let me.
> You cannot better be employ'd, Bassanio,
> Than to live still, and write mine epitaph.

Only something fundamental can explain such a sentimental welcome to death. The opening of the play is an interrogation three times underscored as to Antonio's sadness.

Later, a similar question is propounded about another emotion of another character: Shylock and his thirst for revenge. Now Shylock is a brainier man than Antonio, and his diagnosis of his own case throws light on Antonio's. The Jew gives a number of reasons for his hatred. Because Antonio brings down the rate of usury in Venice. Because he hates the Jews. Because he rails on Shylock in public. Because he is a hypocrite. Because he is a Christian. Because he has thwarted the Jew's bargains. Because he has heated his enemies. Because he has cooled his friends. And so on, and so on. An adequate collection of motives, one would say. Yet not one of them, or all together, sufficient to account for his passion. They are rationalizations, like Iago's reasons for his plot against Othello, or Raskolnikov's for his murder of the old woman in *Crime and Punishment*. And Shylock comes finally to recognize that fact. In the court scene when the Duke asks his reason for his mad insistence on the pound of flesh, Shylock says he can and will give no reason other than "a certain loathing I bear Antonio." A certain loathing! It matches exactly the certain sadness of Antonio.

But it matches another emotion of Antonio's even more closely. If Shylock loathes Antonio, Antonio has a no less savage detestation of Shylock. His hatred is as "boundless" as was Juliet's love. It appears to be the one passion that like a spasm mars his gentle disposition, as a sudden squall will ruffle the surface of a placid lake.

> A kinder gentleman treads not the earth,

says Salarino, and so Antonio impresses us except in this one relation. When Shylock complains,

> Fair sir, you spat on me on Wednesday last;
> You spurn'd me such a day; another time
> You call'd me dog,

we might think it the hallucination of a half-maddened mind. But does Antonio deny the charge? On the contrary he confirms it:

> I am as like to call thee so again,
> To spit on thee again, to spurn thee too.

That from this paragon of kindliness! It is not enough to say that in those days everybody hated the Jews, for that leaves unexplained why the gentlest and mildest man in the play is the fiercest Jew-baiter of them all. As far as the record goes, he outdoes even the crude and taunting Gratiano. Oh, but Shylock is a usurer, it will be said, while Antonio is so noble that the mere mention of interest is abhorrent to him. Why, then, does not Antonio state his objection to it like a rational being instead of arguing with kicks and saliva? Why is he so heated, as well as so noble?

Unless all signs fail, Antonio, like Shylock, is a victim of forces from far below the threshold of consciousness. What are they?

Shakespeare is careful to leave no doubt on this point, but, appropriately, he buries the evidence a bit beneath the surface: Antonio abhors Shylock because he catches his own reflection in his face.

"What! Antonio like Shylock!" it will be said. "The idea is preposterous. No two men could be more unlike." They are, in many respects. But extremes meet, and in one respect they are akin. It is Antonio's unconscious protest against this humiliating truth that is the secret of his antipathy. "Wilt thou whip thine own faults in other men?" cries Timon of Athens. Shakespeare understood the principle, and he illustrates it here.

The contrast between Shylock and Antonio is apparently nowhere more marked than in the attitude of the two men toward money. Shylock is a usurer. So strong is Antonio's distaste for usury that he lends money without interest. But where does the money come from that permits such generosity? From his argosies, of course, his trade. For, after all, to what has Antonio dedicated his life? Not indeed to usury. But certainly to money-making, to profits. And profits, under analysis, are often only "usury" in a more respectable form. Appearance and reality again.

Shakespeare seizes one of the most exciting moments of the play (when the dramatic tension is so high that nobody will notice) to drive home this truth, the instant when Portia, disguised as a Young Doctor of Laws, enters the courtroom.

> Which is the merchant here and which the Jew?

she inquires in almost her first words. All she wants, of course, is to have defendant and plaintiff identified. But the Shakespearean overmeaning is unmistakable. Merchant and Jew! Noble trader of Venice and despicable money-changer, at what poles they appear to stand! Yet—which is which? (Editors who punctuate the line

> Which is the merchant here? And which the Jew?

miss the point.)

Nor is the distinction between merchant and moneylender the only one, the poet implies, that may be difficult at times to draw. As if to prepare us for Portia's Delphic line, Shakespeare has Gratiano anticipate it in cruder form with respect to Gentile and Jew. Jessica, in boy's clothes, is about to elope with Lorenzo:

> I will make fast the doors, and gild myself
> With some more ducats, and be with you straight.
> *(Exit above)*

That "gild," with its clear allusion to the golden casket, not to mention the familiar symbolism of the descent from above, gives us in one word the moral measure of this girl who crowns her deception and desertion of her father by robbing him. As the young thief comes down, Gratiano cries in delighted approval,

> Now, by my hood, a Gentile, and no Jew.

Gratiano is thinking of the fascinating boldness of this saucy boy-girl. She's too good to be a Jew, he says, she's one of us. But Shakespeare has not forgotten the stolen ducats. That unusual oath, "by my hood," is enough to suggest that there is something under cover here. Is it her dashing air or her hard heart that entitles Jessica to the name of Gentile? The poet does not say. But he clearly asks. Plainly Jew and Gentile are not to him separate species with distinct virtues and vices. Morocco makes a like point when he says his blood will be found as red as that of the fairest blonde from the north. And Shylock, when he asks, "If you prick us, do we not bleed?" Under the skin, all men are brothers.

And here an interesting fact should be recorded. On July 22, 1598, James Roberts entered in the Stationers' Register *The Marchaunt of Venyce or otherwise called the Jewe of Venyce.* Here is testimony that already in Shakespeare's own day the public was puzzled by the title of the play and had substituted for, or added to, the author's another title more expressive of what seemed to be its leading interest and central figure. The world did not have to wait for Kean and Irving to discover its "hero." Yet the poet knew what he was about when he named it.

> Which is the merchant here and which the Jew?

The public needed two titles. Shakespeare is content with two-in-one.

Now Shylock, with his incisive mind, grasps very early this resemblance of Antonio's vocation to his own. Apparently it first strikes him with full force on the occasion when Antonio backs Bassanio's request for a loan. Knowing of old the merchant's antipathy to interest, Shylock is astonished:

> Methought you said you neither lend nor borrow
> Upon advantage.

Antonio admits it is not his habit.

> When Jacob graz'd his uncle Laban's sheep,

Shylock begins. Jacob? What has Jacob to do with it?

> And what of him? Did he take interest?

Antonio inquires.

> No; not take interest; not, as you would say,
> Directly interest.

That "directly"! It is necessary to get the tone as well as the word. The sarcasm of it is the point. There are more ways than one of taking interest, it says. There are many tricks of the trade, many ways of thriving, as Jacob knew in the old days. *And as certain others know nowadays.* But Antonio, quite unaware in his self-righteousness of the fact that he is himself the target, thinks the story Shylock goes on to tell of how Jacob increased his wages by a sly device is told to justify the taking of interest, whereas what the Jew is saying, if a bit less bluntly, is: Look a bit closer, Antonio, and you will see that your profits amount to the same thing as my interest. We are in the same boat.

Antonio, though unaware that he is hit, does scent some danger lurking in the story and insists on a distinction essential to his self-respect:

> This was a venture, sir, that Jacob serv'd for;
> A thing not in his power to bring to pass,
> But sway'd and fashion'd by the hand of heaven,

and, still puzzled over the point of Shylock's illustration, he adds:

Was this inserted to make interest good?
Or is your gold and silver ewes and rams?

"I cannot tell," answers Shylock, "I make it breed as fast."

"Your example turns against you, Shylock!" is what Antonio implies. Rams and ewes are very different from silver and gold. It is right and proper that they should multiply, but it is against nature for barren metal to. Antonio's speech is an example of how a man may say one thing with his tongue and quite another with his soul. It is the word "venture" that gives him away. The very term he had applied to his own argosies ("My ventures are not in one bottom trusted")! It is these and not Jacob's lambs that are really troubling him, and his "sway'd and fashion'd" confirms the conjecture, the one an allusion to the winds of heaven as certainly as the other is to the hand of heaven. But this unconscious introduction of the argosies into the argument, by way of self-defense, is fatal to Antonio's contention. For when it comes to generation, cargoes generally resemble gold and silver far more nearly than they do ewes and rams. In so far as they do, Aristotle's famous argument against interest proves to be equally cogent against profits. Antonio and Shylock are still in the same boat.

But Antonio, blind as ever, turns to his friend and says:

> Mark you this, Bassanio,
> The devil can cite Scripture for his purpose.
> An evil soul, producing holy witness,
> Is like a villain with a smiling cheek,
> A goodly apple rotten at the heart.
> O, what a goodly outside falsehood hath!

Considering Antonio's reputation for virtue (what are the smiling villain and goodly apple but the golden casket?), the speech is a moral boomerang if there ever was one. He very conveniently forgets that he no more produced the treasures with which his argosies are loaded than Shylock did his ducats—treasures which he himself boasts a few speeches further on will bring in within two months "thrice three times the value of this bond." Antonio's business is thriving. Usury? God forbid! "Not, as *you* would say, directly interest."

This does not mean that Antonio is a hypocrite. Far from it. Who does not know an Antonio—a man too good for money-making who has dedicated his life to money-making? Antonio was created for nobler things. And so he suffers from that homesickness of the soul that ultimately attacks everyone who "consecrates" his life to something below his spiritual level. Moreover, Antonio is a bachelor, and his "fie, fie!" in answer to Salanio's bantering suggestion that he is in love may hint at some long-nourished disappointment of the affections. Antonio has never married, and he is not the man to have had clandestine affairs. So he has invested in gentle friendship emotions that nature intended should blossom into love. But however tender and loyal, it is a slightly sentimental friendship, far from being an equivalent of love. Both it and the argosies are at bottom opiates. Those who drown themselves in business or other work in order to forget what refuses to be forgotten are generally characterized by a quiet melancholy interrupted occasionally by spells of irritation or sudden spasms of passion directed at some person or thing that, if analyzed, is found to be a symbol of the error that has spoiled their lives.

> Therefore, my merchandise makes me not sad.

By his very denial Antonio unwittingly diagnoses his ailment correctly. This surely is the solution of the opening conundrum of the play, and anger at himself, not a conventional anti-Semitism of which Antonio could not conceivably be guilty, is the cause of his fierce and irrational outbursts against Shylock. Antonio is the silver casket. He got as much as he deserved: material success and a suicidal melancholy.

## V

Why did Shylock offer Antonio a loan of three thousand ducats without interest?

On our answer to that crucial question, it is scarcely too much to say, our conception of the Jew and our interpretation of the play will hinge.

The superficial reader or auditor will think this is complicating what is a simple matter. He has probably heard the outcome of the bond story before he ever picks up the book or enters the theater, or, if not, is the willing victim of an actor who has. Where, he will ask, is there any problem? Shylock is a villain. He is out from the first for bloody revenge. Doesn't he say so, in an aside, the moment Antonio enters his presence?

> If I can catch him once upon the hip,
> I will feed fat the ancient grudge I bear him.

What could be plainer than that? The Jew foresees (as does the actor of his part) that Antonio will not be able to pay on the appointed day, and so, slyly and cruelly, traps the merchant into signing the bloody bond under the pretense that he is joking.

Unfortunately the text contradicts in a dozen places this easy assumption that the Jew is a sort of super-Iago. (We will mention some of them presently.) But apart from this, the idea that as intelligent a man as Shylock could have deliberately counted on the bankruptcy of as rich a man as Antonio, with argosies on seven seas, is preposterous. And if anyone would cite to the contrary his speech about land-rats and water-rats, waters, winds, and rocks, the answer is that that is the merest daydreaming, the sheerest wishful thinking. The bond, whatever else it is, is more of the same. It does indeed reveal a hidden desire on Shylock's part to tear out Antonio's heart, but that is a power-fantasy pure and simple. It is like a child's "I'll kill you!" Such things are at the opposite pole from deliberate plans for murder, even judicial murder.

Shylock's offer to take no interest for his loan was obviously as unexpected to him as it was to Bassanio and Antonio. Just thirty-six lines before he makes it he was considering the rate he should charge:

> Three thousand ducats; 'tis a good round sum.
> Three months from twelve; then, let me see; the rate—

Then comes the well-known speech beginning

> Signior Antonio, many a time and oft
> In the Rialto you have rated me . . .

(a significant pun, by the way, on the word "rate"). "You spat upon me, kicked me, called me dog," is the gist of what he says, "and for these courtesies you now expect me to lend you money?"

"No!" cries Antonio, stung by the justice of Shylock's irony, "I want no courtesy or kindness. Friends take no interest from friends. Let this transaction be one between enemies, so that, if I forfeit, you can exact the penalty with a better conscience, and so that I" (he does not say it, but who can doubt that he thinks it?) "may retain my right to spit on you."

How to the heart Antonio is hit is revealed by the stage direction which Shakespeare, as so often, skilfully inserts in the text.

> Why, look you, how you storm!

cries Shylock. Antonio's anger is as good as a confession, but, clad in the pride of race and virtue, he does not realize it. How the tables are now turned, how the relation between the two is reversed! Hitherto, Antonio has always been the superior, Shylock the inferior. It is not just that the borrower, being the beggar, is always below the lender. That is a trifle here. The significant thing is that the man who loses his temper is below the man who keeps his self-control. A small man meets anger with anger. A big man meets it with augmented patience and self-restraint. Does Shylock show himself great or small in the situation? And if great, is it genuine greatness of heart, or only the counterfeit greatness of intelligent self-interest?

It is just here that he makes his offer to forget the past, to supply Antonio's wants, as a friend would, without interest. What is back of this obviously unpremeditated and apparently uncharacteristic move on the Jew's part? Is it

1. Fawning?—a sudden realization that he must hold on to Antonio at any price lest in his anger he turn on his heel and depart.

2. Shrewdness?—a calculated attempt to buy off this rich merchant's insults.

3. Thirst for moral revenge?—a move to humiliate his enemy by putting him under obligation to him.

4. Protective coloration?—the instinctive reaction of the animal to delude the pursuer, accompanied, presumably, with an unconscious desire to kill.

5. Bait?—a deliberate device to tempt his foe, when off guard, into signing the bloody bond. Or, finally,

6. Just what it purports to be?—a sincere wish to wipe out the past and be friends.

Shylock is not a *unanimous* man. (Who is?) There are several Shylocks pulling Shylock simultaneously in several directions and (except No. 5) there may be at least a touch of every one of these motives activating him at the moment. Even in the normal man, instinct, reason, and imagination are at cross-purposes. How much more in this torn victim of Gentile insolence! Hence we must discriminate scrupulously between what happens in Shylock's conscious from what happens in his unconscious mind. His capacity to rationalize was shown in his account of his motives for hating Antonio. The tendency will be bound to manifest itself in the present situation.

The reaction to Antonio's anger of the shrewd, intelligent, logical Shylock is least open to question. (Not to imply that he formulated it precisely in his own mind.) Here the man who had always treated him like a cur has approached him as a human being. But, stung by his sarcasm, his foe threatens to revert to his old insults or break off negotiations entirely. This must be prevented at any cost. Friends, Antonio says, never lend at interest. Instantly the Jew sees his opening. His enemy has supplied it! Here is the chance of chances to humble him by compelling him to do just what he does not want to do, accept a loan, namely, on an outward basis of friendship. Such a loan would be heaping coals of fire on his head in the most savage sense of that ferocious metaphor. Here would be revenge at its sweetest, in its most exquisite, prolonged, and intellectual form. What could any interest be, even the most extortionate, compared with this?

But lest this sudden reversal of a lifetime practice be suspect, and its motive exposed, it must be covered with the pretense of a jest. Hence the improvisation of the "merry bond" with the extravagant penalty in case of forfeiture. And to back this up with a more plausible reason, Shylock adds:

> I say,
> To buy his favour I extend this friendship.

But surely this is an afterthought. The interest Shylock will lose will be more than offset by the elimination of Antonio's interference with the Jew's other bargaining, to say nothing of the buying-off of his insults. But this is something thrown in, as it were, a secondary consideration, not the main motive, so much stronger in Shylock is hatred than avarice. And we think the more highly of him for that fact, to the extent that revenge is a spiritual, avarice a material evil.

Somewhat on this order must have been the response of the moneylender Shylock to Antonio's outburst. But what forces moved beneath the surface of this moneylender's mind?

Shakespeare is at pains to make plain the noble potentialities of Shylock, however much his nature may have been warped by the sufferings and persecutions he has undergone and by the character of the vocation he has followed. His vices are not so much vices as perverted virtues. His pride of race in a base sense is pride of race in a high sense inverted, his answer to the world's scorn. His love of sobriety and good order is a degeneration of his religion. His domestic "tyranny"—which it is easy to exaggerate—a vitiated love of family and home. His outward servility, a depraved patience. His ferocity, a thwarted self-respect. Even his avarice is partly a providence imposed by the insecurity of his lot. There is a repressed Shylock.

Now repression inevitably produces a condition of high tension between the conscious and the unconscious, with sudden unpredictable incursions of the latter into the former attended by a rapid alternation of polar states of mind. Dostoevsky is the unsurpassed expositor of this mental condition. What reader of that book, for instance, will not remember the old man in *The Insulted and Injured* who in secret covers with kisses the locket containing the picture of his adored but wayward daughter, but who later, when no longer alone, hurls it on the ground, stamps on it, and curses the one whose image it holds, only to fall sobbing like a child—again clasping and kissing the object he has just been trampling underfoot; or the poverty-stricken captain, father of Ilusha, in *The Brothers Karamazov*, who, when offered money after the insult he has received, is at one instant in a heaven of ecstasy at the thought of the happiness it will buy and at the next is crumpling the notes in his fist and then treading them into the dirt; or Dmitri Karamazov in the same book (more injured by neglect in childhood than by insult) who, when the perfect opportunity to kill his father comes, has actually lifted the weapon to strike the blow when his hand is suddenly stayed by an angelic impulse? Such, declares Dostoevsky in character after character, in book after book, is the psychology of the insulted and injured. Now if ever a man was insulted and injured it is Shylock. When we find him, then, acting in the exact pattern of his Dostoevskian counterparts, it is as if Shakespeare were confirming Dostoevsky, and Dostoevsky Shakespeare. Only very ingenuous persons will think that these two supreme students of the human mind, because they do not express themselves in scientific nomenclature or in the language of the twentieth century, must have been ignorant of truths that psychology is only now beginning to formulate.

Shylock has tried to fuse the usurer with the father of Jessica—but in vain. They will no more mix than oil and water. Troubled dreams about his money bags are proof of this—symptoms of struggle in a divided nature. And so the two Shylocks exist side by side, now the one, now the other asserting sovereignty. The reiterated cry "My daughter! O my ducats!" which the next moment becomes "My ducats, and my daughter!" is an example of this ambivalent state of the man's mind. It is a mark of the near-balance between outraged love and avarice, though it is not without significance that the daughter—the first time at least—is mentioned first. It is the same with the turquoise that he had of Leah when he was a bachelor. First, it is the jewel as a memento of romance, then as a valuable material possession. But there is a still more revealing instance. "Would she were hearsed at my foot and the ducats in her coffin!" That tormented cry is usually taken as meaning, "I would give my daughter's life to get my ducats back." And doubtless that is what Shylock thinks he is saying. But note that it is not Jessica dead and the ducats locked up in his vault. The ducats are in the coffin too! Plainly an unconscious wish to bury his own miserliness. Shylock is ripe for a better life. It takes a Shakespeare to give a touch like that.

Such passages shed an intense light on the offer to Antonio of a loan without interest, followed instantly by the stipulation of the bloodthirsty bond (passed off as a jest). The pattern is identical. When we read the passage for the first time, or see the incident on the stage, we are too excited by the situation and the suspense to look beneath the surface. We are taking the play as drama and consider each scene separately as it comes or as interpreted by an actor who is probably thinking more of its effect on the audience than of the truth of its psychology. But when, later, we read it as poetry, and take the parts in the light of the whole, we see how perfectly the Jew's words and actions here cohere with the rest of his role.

Let us analyze the incident a bit further.

Shylock, the despised usurer, is on the point of lending Antonio, the great merchant, three thousand ducats, presumably at a high rate of interest, when he is suddenly confronted by a storm of anger from a man humiliated by the necessity of borrowing from a Jew (whom he has been in the habit of insulting) and stung by the Jew's recognition of the highly ironical nature of the situation. The merchant's loss of temper brings an inversion of everything. The inferior is suddenly the superior—in all senses. As certainly as when a wheel revolves and what was a moment before at the bottom is now at the top, so certainly what was deep down in Shylock is bound to come to the surface. But what is deep down in Shylock is precisely his goodness. How often the finer Shylock must have dreamed of a different kind of life, of being received into the fellowship of the commercial princes of Venice, treated as a human being, even as an equal. And now suddenly the beginning of that dream comes true. One of the greatest of Venetian merchants does come to him, without insults, asking a favor. How can the Jew's imagination fail, for a moment at least, to round out the pattern of the old daydream? Whatever the moneylender feels, or fancies he feels, what the dreamer within Shylock experiences is an impulse to be friendl

> SHY.: I would be friends with you and have your love,
> Forget the shames that you have stain'd me with,
> Supply your present wants, and take no doit
> Of usance for my moneys, and you'll not hear me.
> This is kind I offer.
> BASS.: This were kindness.
> SHY.:                 This kindness will I show.

Bassanio's words show that there was no obvious irony in Shylock's tone nor conspicuous fawning in his manner. Only gross distortion could impart to the Jew's lines the accent of Iago, an accent they would have to carry if Shylock were a deliberate villain. On the contrary, little as he may recognize it himself, here is the instinctive reaction of the nobler Shylock. But, precisely as with all the analogous Dostoevskian characters, the good impulse is followed instantly by its polar opposite. The wheel goes on revolving. The highest gives place to the lowest. When the window is opened to the angel, the devils promptly rush in at the unguarded back door. The daydream of kindness is followed by the daydream of killing. As the imaginative Shylock pictured himself coming to the aid of a friend, so the primitive Shylock dreams of shedding the blood of an enemy. In the first fantasy the heart of one man goes out to unite with the heart of the other. In the second the hand of the one would tear out the heart of the other. The perfect chiasmus stamps the two as products of the unconscious. Such a diametrical contradiction is one of its almost infallible marks.

Anyone should be able to corroborate this psychology. Who, in love or hatred, has not let his deepest feeling or conviction escape in a word or look only to try the next instant, in shame or fear, to pass the slip off as a jest? So ashamed, and then so terrified, is the conscious Shylock, first at the friendliness, then at the ferocity, of the uncomprehended impulses within him. When we say what we think we do not mean, we may mean it to the *n*th degree. So the two Shylocks, between them, mean both the friendliness and the ferocity.

The opposite hypothesis—that the offer of no interest is a snare and the bond a deliberate trap—breaks down completely for another reason. If Shylock were that sort of plotter, however much he might have tried not to show it, he would have leaped with the eagerness of a villain at the first news that Antonio's argosies had miscarried. But, as several discerning critics have pointed out, he does nothing of the sort. When Salarino asks him if he has not heard of Antonio's loss at sea, he does not cry even to himself, "Ah, now I have him on the hip!" but only "There I have another bad match," the noun revealing that his mind is still on his daughter, and it is Salarino himself who has to recall the pound of flesh and ask him of what possible use it can be to him. Shylock's reply is scarcely what Salarino was fishing for. Instead of an anticipatory daydream of blood, it is precisely the famous speech, "I am a Jew. Hath not a Jew eyes? . . ." which, more than any other in his role, wrings sympathy even from those who elsewhere grudge him a particle of it.

So, too, a moment later, when Tubal mentions Antonio's ill luck. Shylock takes the news joyfully, to be sure, but casually, in fact almost absent-mindedly, his "in Genoa?" showing that his confused thoughts are still in the place where his fellow-Jew has been trying to trace his daughter. Tubal has to keep whipping his thoughts back to Antonio and the impending forfeiture. Indeed, if Tubal had been trying deliberately to forge a link in Shylock's mind between the infidelity of his daughter and the forfeiture of the bond he could not have proceeded more skilfully. He is trying. He does forge it. Jessica–Antonio; Jessica–Antonio; Jessica–Antonio: back and forth from the one to the other Tubal yanks Shylock's mind. Yet the utmost he can extort from it concerning Antonio is "I'll torture him"—not kill him. And when in his very next speech Shylock cries, with regard to the ring his daughter has exchanged for a monkey, "Thou torturest me, Tubal," the echoed word shows that if he lives to torture Antonio it will be because Jessica and Tubal have tortured him. If ever a man egged on revenge it is this other Jew. Indeed it is he rather than Shylock who is acting the role of "Shylock" in this scene, by which of course I mean the Shylock of popular conception. That Shylock needs no one to instigate him. But Shakespeare's Shylock, strangely, does. Those who find a bloodthirsty Jew in this play are right. But they have picked the wrong man.

TUB.: But Antonio is certainly undone.
SHY.: Nay, that's true, that's very true. Go, Tubal, fee me an officer; bespeak him a fortnight before. I will have the heart of him, if he forfeit; for, were he out of Venice, I can make what merchandise I will.

"Were he out of Venice"! Here is the proof that, even at this late hour, Shylock is thinking of tearing out Antonio's heart in a metaphorical sense only and has no idea of literal bloodshed. Just five words. But what a difference they make!

It must be something else, then, that turns the Jew from a desire to be rid of Antonio's presence in Venice to the idea of demanding the literal pound of flesh, a desire that only a madman could entertain. Salanio's description of Shylock in the streets gives us the clue:

> I never heard a passion so confus'd,
> So strange, outrageous, and so variable,
> As the dog Jew did utter in the streets . . .

There are scarcely three more illuminating lines in the play, little as their speaker is aware of the light he is shedding. Plainly this proud man, displaying his inmost heart to all beholders (like Katerina Ivanovna in *Crime and Punishment* coming out in public to die), has been driven to the verge of madness. The combined infidelity and thievery of his own child, culminating in her elopement with a Christian, are what have done it. Tubal and Salarino, as we have seen, precisely when the Jew was in the most suggestible state, implant in his mind what amounts to posthypnotic directions to demand the literal fulfilment of his bond. And no one knows what the street urchins contribute to the same end. But it is the daughter who first releases the flood of despair that helps these later seeds to germinate. Salanio foresees what may come of such passion:

> Let good Antonio look he keep his day,
> Or he shall pay for this.

He is still picturing the distracted creature he saw in the streets, and it suddenly comes over him that that creature is a different one from the man he has formerly known as Shylock, a more ferocious creature that, unlike the other, might stop at nothing. And he does nothing to make him stop. On the contrary, the next time they meet we hear him lashing the Jew's despair on toward madness by intentionally misunderstanding him.

SHY.:    My own flesh and blood to rebel!
SALAN.:    Out upon it, old carrion! rebels it at these years?
SHY.:    I say my daughter is my flesh and blood.

That "flesh and blood," fitting so exactly the penalty prescribed in the bond, reveals in a flash how much the dereliction of the daughter has to do with the final bloodthirsty intention of the father. Everything, we might almost say.

And we must not forget that Bassanio and Antonio have connived in the elopement of Jessica. Yet the tormented Shylock, pursued by jeering boys, has not even then become fully conscious of his own murderous impulses, for the scene with Tubal, with its "were he out of Venice," comes after that. It is not until he runs on Antonio with the jailer that the Jew, enraged perhaps at seeing his enemy at large, threatens him directly:

> Thou call'dst me dog before thou hadst a cause,
> But, since I am a dog, beware my fangs.

At last Shylock recognizes that the animal within him is gaining ascendancy. "You called me dog. I'll take you at your word, and myself at your own estimate." His repetitions betoken his irrational state:

> I'll have my bond; speak not against my bond:
> I have sworn an oath that I will have my bond . . .
> I'll have my bond; I will not hear thee speak.
> I'll have my bond, and therefore speak no more. . . .
> I'll have no speaking; I will have my bond.

It is as if the revengeful Shylock were afraid that even one reasonable word from Antonio might revive the natural instincts of the kinder Shylock now so near extinction. The repeated "I'll have no speaking" measures the tremendous inner resistance the Jew has had to overcome before he could surrender and become unmitigatedly bad.

What was the nature of this resistance that at last seems to be breaking down? Obviously it was a desire to be just the opposite of what he now feels himself becoming. Though he was rendered coldhearted by his vocation, made cruel by the insults that had been heaped upon him by everybody from the respectable Antonio to the very children in the streets, driven to desperation by his daughter, there is nothing to indicate that Shylock was congenitally coldhearted, cruel, or desperate. On the contrary, it is clear that he had it in him, however deep down, to be humane, kindly, and patient, and his offer to Antonio of a loan without interest seems to have been a supreme effort of this submerged Shylock to come to the surface. If so, here is the supreme irony of this ironical play. If so, for a moment at least, the Jew was the Christian. The symbolism confirms the psychology: Shylock was the leaden casket with the spiritual gold within.

## VI

The moment this fact is grasped the court scene becomes something quite different from what it seems to be. It is still a trial scene, but it is Portia who is on trial. Or, better, it is a casket scene in which she is subjected to the same test to which she has submitted her suitors. Can she detect hidden gold under a leaden exterior?

Concerning Portia's own exterior the poet leaves us in no doubt. To the eye she is nothing if not golden, and she does nothing if she does not shine. The praise showered on her within the play itself has been echoed by thousands of readers and spectators and the continued appeal of her role to actresses is proof of the fascination she never fails to exercise. No one can deny her brilliance or her charm, or could wish to detract from them. (If I do not linger on them here, it is because ample justice has been done to them so often.) Yet Portia, too, like so many of the others in this play, is not precisely all she seems to be. Indeed, what girl of her years, with her wealth, wit, and beauty, could be the object of such universal adulation and come through unscathed? In her uprush of joy when Bassanio chooses the right casket there is, it is true, an accent of the humility that fresh love always bestows, and she speaks of herself as "an unlesson'd girl, unschool'd, unpractis'd." There the child Portia once was is speaking, but it is a note that is sounded scarcely anywhere else in her role. The woman that child has grown into, on the contrary, is the darling of a sophisticated society which has nurtured in her anything but unself-consciousness. Indeed, it seems to be as natural to her as to a queen or princess to take herself unblushingly at the estimate this society places on her.

> *Who chooseth me shall gain what many men desire.*
> Why, that's the lady: all the world desires her;
> From the four corners of the earth they come . . .

says Morocco. And tacitly Portia assents to that interpretation of the inscription on the golden casket. She mocks half a dozen of her suitors unmercifully in the first scene in which we see her, and it never seems to occur to her that any man who could would not choose her. Yet it is not easy to imagine Hamlet choosing her, or Othello, or Coriolanus. (Nor Shakespeare himself, I feel like adding.)

> *Who chooseth me shall get as much as he deserves.*
> I will assume desert,

says Arragon. Portia, likewise, quietly assumes that she somehow deserves the attention and sacrifices of these crowding suitors. Perhaps she does. Yet we cannot help wishing she did not know it, though we scarcely blame her for thinking what everyone around her thinks.

But if Portia is willing to let her suitors take any risk in her pursuit in the spirit of the third inscription,

> *Who chooseth me must give and hazard all he hath,*

there is nothing to indicate that life has ever called on her to sacrifice even a small part of all she has, and when the man of her choice attains her, though she modestly wishes that for his sake she were a thousand times more fair, she also wishes significantly that she were ten thousand times more rich. Bassanio pronounces her

> nothing undervalu'd
> To Cato's daughter, Brutus' Portia.

But it is hard to think Shakespeare would have thought the comparison a happy one. Both Portias were good women. But, granted that, how could they be more different? If it is a question of the poet's later heroines, another comes to mind. When the Prince of Morocco goes out after having chosen the wrong casket, Portia dismisses him and innumerable other un-inspected suitors with the line:

> Let all of his complexion choose me so.

Who is judging now by the outside? And we remember Desdemona's

> I saw Othello's visage in his mind.

In view of her father's scheme for selecting her husband, no one will blame Portia for giving Bassanio several hints on the choice of the right casket. Because of her declared intention not to be forsworn, we give her the benefit of the doubt and assume the hints were unconscious ones.* Indeed, the fact that she uses the word "hazard" (from the inscription on the leaden casket), not only before Bassanio chooses but before Morocco and Arragon do, all but proves that the suspense and peril of the choice fas-cinate her at the moment hardly less than her passion for Bassanio. She is not the only girl who has been excited by the adventure of getting married, as well as by being in love with her future husband. Contrast her with Juliet, who did give and hazard all she had for love, and you feel the difference.

---

* Who selected the song that is sung while Bassanio meditates we shall never know. It of course gives away the secret. And in that connection there is a point I have never happened to see noted. The verses inside the golden casket begin with a rhyme on long *o* (gold); those inside the silver casket on a rhyme on short *i* (this). The song sung while Bassanio is making up his mind begins with a rhyme on short *e* (bred). But *bred* (as someone has pointed out) is a full rhyme with *lead!*

This is not to suggest that Portia ought to have been a Juliet, or a Desdemona, and still less that Shakespeare should have made her anything other than she is. Given his sources, it is easy to see why Portia had to be just what she is.

The casket motif, the court scene, and the ring incident taken together comprise a good share of the story. Each of them is intrinsically spectacular, histrionic, or theatrical—or all three in one. Each is a kind of play within a play, with Portia at the center or at one focus. The casket scenes are little symbolic pageants; the court scene is drama on the surface and tragedy underneath; the ring incident is a one-act comedy complete in itself. What sort of heroine does all this demand? Obviously one with the temperament of an actress, not averse to continual limelight. Portia is exactly that.

When she hears that the man who helped her lover woo and win her is in trouble, her character and the contingency fit each other like hand and glove. Why not impersonate a Young Doctor of Laws and come to Antonio's rescue? It is typical of her that at first she takes the "whole device," as she calls it, as a kind of prank. Her imagination overflows with pictures of the opportunities for acting that her own and Nerissa's disguise as young men will offer, of the innocent lies they will tell, the fun they will have, the fools they will make of their husbands. The tragic situation of Antonio seems at the moment the last thing in her mind, or the responsibility of Bassanio for the plight of his friend. The fact that she is to have the leading role in a play in real life eclipses everything else. There is more than a bit of the stage-struck girl in Portia.

And so when the curtain rises on Act IV, Shakespeare the playwright and his actress-heroine, between them, are equipped to give us one of the tensest and most theatrically effective scenes he had conceived up to this time. What Shakespeare the poet gives us, however, and what it means to Portia the woman, is something rather different.

## VII

When Shylock enters the courtroom he is in a more rational if not less determined state than when we last saw him. He is no longer unwilling to listen, and the moderate, almost kindly words of the Duke,

> We all expect a gentle answer, Jew,

lead us to hope that even at the eleventh hour he may relent.

Shylock's answer to the Duke is one of the most remarkable evidences of Shakespeare's overt interest in psychological problems in any of the earlier plays. The passage is sufficient in itself to refute the idea that it is "modernizing" to detect such an interest on his part. Naturally Shylock does not talk about complexes, compulsions, and unconscious urges, but he recognizes the irrational fear of pigs and cats in the concrete for what it is, a symbol of something deeper that is disturbing the victim. He senses in himself the working of similar forces too tremendous for definition, too powerful to oppose even though he feels them driving him—*against his will and to his shame*, he implies—to commit the very offense that has been committed against him. Imagine Richard III or Iago speaking in that vein! If this be "villainy," it is of another species. Here is the main theme of the play in its profoundest implication. For what is the relation of what is conscious to what is unconscious if not the relation of what is on the surface to what is underneath? Thus Shylock himself—and through him Shakespeare—hands us the key: to open the casket of this play we must look beneath *its* surface, must probe the unconscious minds of its characters.

> You'll ask me why I rather choose to have
> A weight of carrion flesh than to receive
> Three thousand ducats. I'll not answer that;
> But say it is my humour. Is it answer'd?
> What if my house be troubled with a rat
> And I be pleas'd to give ten thousand ducats
> To have it ban'd? What, are you answer'd yet?
> Some men there are love not a gaping pig;
> Some, that are mad if they behold a cat;
> And others, when the bagpipe sings i' the nose,
> Cannot contain their urine: for affection,
> Mistress of passion, sways it to the mood
> Of what it likes or loathes. Now, for your answer:
> As there is no firm reason to be render'd
> Why he cannot abide a gaping pig;
> Why he, a harmless necessary cat;
> Why he, a wauling bagpipe; but of force
> Must yield to such inevitable shame
> As to offend, himself being offended;
> So can I give no reason, nor I will not,
> More than a lodg'd hate and a certain loathing
> I bear Antonio, that I follow thus
> A losing suit against him. Are you answer'd?

(Note, especially, that "losing suit"!)

Antonio recognizes the futility of opposing Shylock's passion with reason. You might as well argue with a wolf, he says, tell the tide not to come in, or command the pines not to sway in the wind. The metaphors reveal his intuition that what he is dealing with is not ordinary human feeling within Shylock but elemental forces from without that have swept in and taken possession of him. And Gratiano suggests that the soul of a wolf has infused itself with the Jew's. Shylock's hatred does have a primitive quality. But Gratiano did not need to go back to the wolves, or even to Pythagoras, to account for it. It is elemental in character because it comes out of something vaster than the individual wrongs Shylock has suffered: the injustice suffered by his ancestors over the generations. As Hazlitt finely remarks: "He seems the depositary of the vengeance of his race." It is this that gives him that touch of sublimity that all his fierceness cannot efface. The bloody Margaret of *Henry VI*, when she becomes the suffering Margaret of *Richard III*, is endowed with something of the same tragic quality. If this man is to be moved, it must be by forces as far above reason as those that now animate him are below it.

And then Portia enters.

## VIII

The introduction and identifications over, Portia, as the Young Doctor of Laws, says to Shylock:

> Of a strange nature is the suit you follow;
> Yet in such rule that the Venetian law
> Cannot impugn you as you do proceed.

This bears the mark of preparation, if not of rehearsal. It seems a strange way of beginning, like a partial prejudgment of the case in Shylock's favor. But his hopes must be raised at the outset to make his ultimate downfall the more dramatic. "Do you confess the bond?" she asks Antonio. "I do," he replies.

> Then must the Jew be merciful.

Portia, as she says this, is apparently still addressing Antonio. It would have been more courteous if, instead of speaking of him in the third person, she had turned directly to Shylock and said, "Then must you be merciful." But she makes a worse slip than that: the word *must*. Instantly Shylock seizes on it, pouring all his sarcasm into the offending verb:

> On what compulsion "*must*" I? Tell me that.

Portia is caught! You can fairly see her wheel about to face not so much the Jew as the unanswerable question the Jew has asked. He is right—she sees it: "must" and "mercy" have nothing to do with each other; no law, moral or judicial, can force a man to be merciful.

For a second, the question must have thrown Portia off balance. This was not an anticipated moment in the role of the Young Doctor. But forgetting the part she is playing, she rises to the occasion superbly. The truth from

Shylock elicits the truth from her. Instead of trying to brush the Jew aside or hide behind some casuistry or technicality, she frankly sustains his exception:

> The quality of mercy is not strain'd. . . .

"I was wrong, Shylock," she confesses in effect. "You are right"; mercy is a matter of grace, not of constraint:

> It droppeth as the gentle rain from heaven
> Upon the place beneath. . . .

Shylock, then, supplied not only the cue, but, we might almost say, the first line of Portia's most memorable utterance.

In all Shakespeare—unless it be Hamlet with "To be or not to be"—there is scarcely another character more identified in the world's mind with a single speech than Portia with her words on mercy. And the world is right. They have a "quality" different from anything else in her role. They are no prepared words of the Young Doctor she is impersonating, but her own, as unexpected as was Shylock's disconcerting question. Something deep down in him draws them from something deep down—or shall we say high up?—in her. They are the spiritual gold hidden not beneath lead but beneath the "gold" of her superficial life, her reward for meeting Shylock's objection with sincerity rather than with evasion.

A hush falls over the courtroom as she speaks them (as it does over the audience when *The Merchant of Venice* is performed). Even the Jew is moved. Who can doubt it? Who can doubt that for a moment at least he is drawn back from the brink of madness and logic on which he stands? Here is the celestial visitant—the Portia God made—sent expressly to exorcise the demonic powers that possess him. Only an insensible clod could fail to feel its presence. And Shylock is no insensible clod. Can even he show mercy? Will a miracle happen? It is the supreme moment. The actor who misses it misses everything.

And then, incredibly, it is Portia who fails Shylock, not Shylock Portia. The same thing happens to her that happened to him at that other supreme moment when he offered Antonio the loan without interest. Her antipodal self emerges. In the twinkling of an eye, the angel reverts to the Doctor of Laws. "So quick bright things come to confusion." Whether the actress in Portia is intoxicated by the sound of her own voice* and the effect it is producing, or whether she feels the great triumph she has rehearsed being

---

* "It is a sad but sure truth that every time you speak of a fine purpose, especially if with eloquence and to the admiration of bystanders, there is the less chance of your ever making a fact of it in your own poor life."—CARLYLE, quoted in John Buchan's *Pilgrim's Way* (Boston, 1940), p. 136.

stolen from her if Shylock relents, or both, at any rate, pushing aside the divine Portia and her divine opportunity, the Young Doctor resumes his role. His "therefore, Jew" gives an inkling of what is coming. You can hear, even in the printed text, the change of voice, as Portia sinks from compassion to legality:

> I have spoke thus much
> To mitigate the justice of thy plea,
> Which if thou follow, this strict court of Venice
> Must needs give sentence 'gainst the merchant there.

It would be unbelievable if the words were not there. "You should show mercy," the Young Doctor says in effect, "but if you don't, this court will be compelled to decide in your favor." It is as if a mother, having entreated her son to desist from some wrong line of conduct and feeling she had almost won, were to conclude: "I hope you won't do it, but, if you insist, I shall have to let you, since your father told you you could." It is like a postscript that undoes the letter. Thus Portia the lover of mercy is deposed by Portia the actress that the latter may have the rest of her play. And the hesitating Shylock, pushed back to the precipice, naturally has nothing to say but

> My deeds upon my head! I crave the law,
> The penalty and forfeit of my bond.

The rest of the scene is an overwhelming confirmation of Portia's willingness to sacrifice the human to the theatrical, a somewhat different kind of sacrifice from that referred to in the inscription on the leaden casket. If there was any temptation that Shakespeare understood, it must have been this one. It was his own temptation. And, as he tells us in the *Sonnets*, he nearly succumbed to it:

> And almost thence my nature is subdu'd
> To what it works in, like the dyer's hand.

Portia's *was* subdued.

## IX

The skill with which from this point she stages and acts her play proves her a consummate playwright, director, and actress—three in one. She wrings the last drop of possible suspense from every step in the mounting excitement. She stretches every nerve to the breaking point, arranges every contrast, climax, and reversal with the nicest sense for maximum effect, doing nothing too soon or too late, holding back her "Tarry a little" until Shylock is on the very verge of triumph, even whetting his knife perhaps. It is she who says to Antonio, "Therefore lay bare your bosom." It is she who asks if there is a balance ready to weigh the flesh, a surgeon to stay the blood. And she actually allows Antonio to undergo his last agony, to utter, uninterrupted, his final farewell.

It is at this point that the shallow Bassanio reveals an unsuspected depth in his nature by declaring, with a ring of sincerity we cannot doubt, that he would sacrifice everything, including his life and his wife, to save his friend.

*Who chooseth me must give and hazard all he hath.*

It is now, not when he stood before it, that Bassanio proves worthy of the leaden casket. Called on to make good his word, he doubtless would not have had the strength. But that does not prove that he does not mean what he says at the moment. And at that moment all Portia can do to help him is to turn into a jest—which she and Nerissa are alone in a position to understand—the most heart-felt and noble words her lover ever uttered.

> POR.: Your wife would give you little thanks for that,
> If she were by to hear you make the offer.

This light answer, in the presence of what to Antonio and Bassanio is the very shadow of death, measures her insensibility to anything but the play she is presenting, the role she is enacting.

From this jest, in answer to the Jew's insistence, she turns without a word of transition to grant Shylock his sentence:

> A pound of that same merchant's flesh is thine.
> The court awards it, and the law doth give it . . .
> And you must cut this flesh from off his breast.
> The law allows it, and the court awards it.

It is apparently all over with Antonio. The Jew lifts his knife. But once more appearances are deceitful. With a "tarry a little" this mistress of the psychological moment plays in succession, one, two, three, the cards she has been keeping back for precisely this moment. Now the Jew is caught in his own trap, now he gets a taste of his own logic, a dose of his own medicine. Now there is no more talk of mercy, but justice pure and simple, an eye for an eye:

> POR.:          as thou urgest justice, be assur'd
> Thou shalt have justice, more than thou desir'st.

Seeing his prey about to elude him, Shylock is now willing to accept the offer of three times the amount of his bond, and Bassanio actually produces the money. He is willing to settle on those terms. But not Portia:

> The Jew shall have all justice; soft! no haste:
> He shall have nothing but the penalty.

Shylock reduces his demand: he will be satisfied with just his principal. Again Bassanio has the money ready. But Portia is adamant:

> He shall have merely justice, and his bond.

When the Jew pleads again for his bare principal, she repeats:

> Thou shalt have nothing but the forfeiture,

and as he moves to leave the courtroom, she halts him with a

> Tarry, Jew:
> The law hath yet another hold on you.

All this repetition seems enough to make the point clear. But that the "beauty" of the nemesis may be lost on no one in the courtroom (nor on the dullest auditor when *The Merchant of Venice* is performed) Shakespeare has the gibing Gratiano on the spot to rub in the justice of the retribution: "O learned judge!" "O upright judge!" "A second Daniel, a Daniel, Jew!" "A second Daniel!" over and over. Emily Dickinson has spoken of "the mob within the heart." Gratiano is the voice of that mob, and he sees to it that a thrill of vicarious revenge runs down the spine of every person in the theater. So exultant are we at seeing the biter bit.

Why are we blind to the ignominy of identifying ourselves with the most brutal and vulgar character in the play? Obviously because there is a cruel streak in all of us that is willing to purchase excitement at any price. And excitement exorcises judgment. Only when we are free of the gregarious influences that dominate us in an audience does the question occur: What possessed Portia to torture not only Antonio but her own husband with such superfluous suspense? She knew what was coming. Why didn't she let it come at once? Why didn't she invoke immediately the law prescribing a penalty for any alien plotting against the life of any citizen of Venice instead of waiting until she had put those she supposedly loved upon the rack? The only possible answer is that she wanted a spectacle, a dramatic triumph with herself at the center. The psychology is identical with that which led the boy Kolya in *The Brothers Karamazov* to torture his sick little friend Ilusha by holding back the news that his lost dog was found, merely in order to enjoy the triumph of restoring him to his chum at the last moment in the presence of an audience. In that case the result was fatal. The child died from the excitement.

To all this it is easy to imagine what those will say who hold that Shakespeare was first the playwright and only incidentally poet and psychologist. "Why, but this is just a play!" they will exclaim, half-amused, half-contemptuous, "and a comedy at that! Portia! It isn't Portia who contrives the postponement. It is Shakespeare. Where would his play have been if his heroine had cut things short or failed to act exactly as she did?" Where indeed? Which is precisely why the poet made her the sort of woman who would have acted under the given conditions exactly as she did act. That was his business: not to find or devise situations exciting in the theater (any third-rate playwright can do that) but to discover what sort of men and women would behave in the often extraordinary ways in which they are represented as behaving in such situations in the stories he inherited and selected for dramatization.

## X

"Logic is like the sword," says Samuel Butler, "—those who appeal to it shall perish by it." Never was the truth of that maxim more clearly illustrated than by Shylock's fate. His insistence that his bond be taken literally is countered by Portia's insistence that it be taken even more literally—and Shylock "perishes." He who had been so bent on defending the majesty of the law now finds himself in its clutches, half his goods forfeit to Antonio, the other half to the state, and his life itself in peril.

And so Portia is given a second chance. She is to be tested again. She has had her legal and judicial triumph. Now it is over will she show to her victim that quality which at her own divine moment she told us "is an attribute to God himself"? The Jew is about to get his deserts. Will Portia forget her doctrine that mercy is mercy precisely because it is not deserved? The Jew is about to receive justice. Will she remember that our prayers for mercy should teach us to do the deeds of mercy and that in the course of justice none of us will see salvation? Alas! she will forget, she will not remember. Like Shylock, but in a subtler sense, she who has appealed to logic "perishes" by it.

Up to this point she has been forward enough in arrogating to herself the function of judge. But now, instead of showing compassion herself or entreating the Duke to, she motions Shylock to his knees:

> Down therefore and beg mercy of the Duke.

"Mercy"! This beggar's mercy, though it goes under the same name, has not the remotest resemblance to that quality that drops like the gentle rain from heaven. Ironically it is the Duke who proves truer to the true Portia than Portia herself.

> DUKE: That thou shalt see the difference of our spirits,
>      I pardon thee thy life before thou ask it.

And he suggests that the forfeit of half of Shylock's property to the state may be commuted to a fine.

> Ay, for the state; not for Antonio,

Portia quickly interposes, as if afraid that the Duke is going to be too merciful, going to let her victim off too leniently. Here, as always, the aftermath of too much "theatrical" emotion is a coldness of heart that is like lead. The tone in which Portia has objected is reflected in the hopelessness of Shylock's next words:

> Nay, take my life and all! Pardon not that!
> You take my house when you do take the prop
> That doth sustain my house. You take my life
> When you do take the means whereby I live.

Portia next asks Antonio what "mercy" he can render. And even the man whom Shylock would have killed seems more disposed than Portia to mitigate the severity of his penalty: he is willing to forgo the half of Shylock's goods if the Duke will permit him the use of the other half for life with the stipulation that it go to Lorenzo (and so to Jessica) at his death. But with two provisos: that all the Jew dies possessed of also go to Lorenzo-Jessica and that

> He presently become a Christian.

Doubtless the Elizabethan crowd, like the crowd in every generation since including our own, thought that this was letting Shylock off easily, that this *was* showing mercy to him. Crowds do not know that mercy is wholehearted and has nothing to do with halves or other fractions. Nor do crowds know that you cannot make a Christian by court decree. Antonio's last demand quite undoes any tinge of mercy in his earlier concessions.

Even Shylock, as we have seen, had in him at least a grain of spiritual gold, of genuine Christian spirit. Only a bit of it perhaps. Seeds do not need to be big. Suppose that Portia and Antonio, following the lead of the seemingly willing Duke, had watered this tiny seed with that quality that blesses him who gives as well as him who takes, had overwhelmed Shylock with the grace of forgiveness! What then? The miracle, it is true, might not have taken place. Yet it might have. But instead, as if in imitation of the Jew's own cruelty, they whet their knives of law and logic, of reason and justice, and proceed to cut out their victim's heart. (That that is what it amounts to is proved by the heartbroken words,

> I pray you give me leave to go from hence.
> I am not well.)

Shylock's conviction that Christianity and revenge are synonyms is confirmed. "If a Christian wrong a Jew, what should his sufferance be by Christian example? Why, revenge." The unforgettable speech from which that comes, together with Portia's on mercy, and Lorenzo's on the harmony of heaven, make up the spiritual argument of the play. Shylock asserts that a Jew is a man. Portia declares that man's duty to man is mercy—which comes from heaven. Lorenzo points to heaven but laments that the materialism of life insulates man from its harmonies. A celestial syllogism that puts to shame the logic of the courtroom.

That Shakespeare planned his play from the outset to enforce the irony of Portia's failure to be true to her inner self in the trial scene is susceptible of something as near proof as such things can ever be. As in the case of Hamlet's

A little more than kin, and less than kind,

the poet, over and over, makes the introduction of a leading character seemingly casual, actually significant. Portia enters *The Merchant of Venice* with the remark that she is aweary of the world. Nerissa replies with that wise little speech about the illness of those that surfeit with too much (an observation that takes on deeper meaning in the retrospect after we realize that at the core what is the trouble with Portia and her society is boredom). "Good sentences and well pronounced," says Portia, revealing in those last two words more than she knows. "They would be better if well followed," Nerissa pertinently retorts. Whereupon Portia, as if gifted with insight into her own future, takes up Nerissa's theme:

If to do were as easy as to know what were good to do, chapels had been churches, and poor men's cottages princes' palaces. It is a good divine that follows his own instructions: I can easier teach twenty what were good to be done, than be one of the twenty to follow mine own teaching.

If that is not a specific preparation for the speech on mercy and what follows it, what in the name of coincidence is it? The words on mercy were good sentences, well pronounced. And far more than that. But for Portia they remained just words in the sense that they did not teach her to do the deeds of mercy. So, a few seconds after we see her for the first time, does Shakespeare let her pass judgment in advance on the most critical act of her life. For a moment, at the crisis in the courtroom, she seems about to become the leaden casket with the spiritual gold within. But the temptation to gain what many men desire—admiration and praise—is too strong for her and she reverts to her worldly self. Portia is the golden casket.

## XI

The last act of *The Merchant of Venice* is often accounted a mere epilogue, a device whereby Shakespeare dissipates the tension aroused by the long court scene of Act IV. It does dissipate it, but the idea that it is a mere afterpiece is superficial.

To begin with, the moonlight and the music take up the central theme and continue the symbolism. At night what was concealed within by day is often revealed, and under the spell of sweet sounds what is savage in man is tamed, for "music for the time doth change his nature." It is not chance that in the first hundred lines and a little more of this scene (at which point the music ceases) Portia, Nerissa, Lorenzo, and even Jessica utter words that might well have been out of their reach by day or under other conditions. Lorenzo's incomparable lines on the harmony of heaven seem, in particular, too beautiful for the man who called Jessica "wise" and "true" at the very time when she was robbing her father. But under the influence of love and moonlight this may be his rare moment. Over and over Shakespeare lets an unsuspected depth in his characters come out at night. However that may be, the passage lends a sort of metaphysical sanction to the casket metaphor. Moonlight opens the leaden casket of material reality and lets us see

how the floor of heaven
Is thick inlaid with patines of bright gold.

But the garden by moonlight is only a glimpse, a prelude, or rather an interlude, and with the return of the husbands and Antonio, the poetry and romance largely disappear, the levity is resumed, the banter, the punning, the sexual allusions, including some very frank ones on Portia's part, until the secret of the impersonations is revealed and everything is straightened out. What a picture it is of the speed with which so-called happy people rush back to the idle pleasures of life after a brief compulsory contact with reality. Privilege was forced for a moment to face the Excluded. It makes haste to erase the impression as quickly and completely as it can. Similarly, for theatergoers, the fifth act erases any earlier painful impressions. The story came out all right after all! Nothing need cloud the gaiety of the after-theater supper.

In spite of this fifth act, there has been much discussion of the dissonance which the Shylock story introduces into what is otherwise a light and diverting play, much quoting of authorities on the question of what is, and what is not, permissible in a comedy. There is nothing to indicate that Shakespeare's imagination ever allowed itself to be shackled by such prescriptions or definitions. Indeed in this case, as so often, I think he gives us a direct hint how his drama should be taken.

Those who stress the matter of construction have often pointed out that the playwright meticulously prepares for a scene in this play that he never presents—the masque at which Lorenzo was to make Jessica his torchbearer. After whetting our appetites, the whole matter is dismissed in one line (with an explanatory second line) when Antonio announces:

No masque to-night: the wind is come about;
Bassanio presently will go aboard.

Just so the winds of life are forever coming about and calling off life's revels at the last moment. In that sense no comedy is true to life in which the seeds of tragedy are not concealed. Every performance of *The Merchant of Venice* might well be heralded with the cry: *No comedy tonight. The winds are come about.* And so the scene Shakespeare prepared for and left out is not left out after all. Those who think the playwright showed slipshod craftsmanship here should look a bit deeper at the poet's intention.

## XII

The authority of imaginative literature resides in the fact that its masterpieces, whenever or wherever written, confirm one another. Anyone who doubts that the overtones and undertones of *The Merchant of Venice* were intended by their author, anyone who doubts that Shylock might have been transformed if Portia had been true to herself, should read Chekhov's *Rothschild's Fiddle*. Here is another story written around the same economic theme. Here is the same contrast of inner and outer, the same two major characters, the Christian money-maker and the despised Jew, the same hatred of the Jew by the Christian because he is an unconscious symbol of his own wasted life—but with the other ending: mercy, forgiveness, spiritual transformation, even a hint of immortality. Though the chances against it are as great as in Shakespeare's play, the miracle does take place, a double miracle, in both Christian and Jew. "The gods are to each other not unknown." Not the only case where Shakespeare and Chekhov agree.

Such harmony is in immortal souls.

Shakespeare could not have used Chekhov's ending. His work is a play to be presented before a crowd, not just a story to be read by individuals—and the crowd demands the obvious. It is (ostensibly) a comedy—and the crowd demands a happy ending. But the conclusion of a poem, unlike the conclusion of a play, is not always to be found at the end. And in this sense the conclusions of the English and Russian versions of this theme are at one.

It is the crowning virtue of a work of art, as it is of a man, that it should be an example of its own doctrine, an incarnation of its own main symbol. A poem about fire ought to burn. A poem about a brook ought to flow. A poem about childhood ought not just to tell about children but ought to be like a child itself, as are the best of Blake's *Songs of Innocence*. *Rothschild's Fiddle* and *The Merchant of Venice* both meet this test. *Rothschild's Fiddle*, as its title indicates, is a story about money and music. Or, better, about death and music, for, just as in *The Merchant of Venice*, money and death are equated. A coffin and a violin are its focal symbols. But they are more than that. The story is itself a coffin within which the author compels each reader to lie down, either to be buried within it (if he is one thing) or (if he is another) to be awakened and lifted out of it by strains of music. In precisely the same sense *The Merchant of Venice* is a casket. In fashioning it its author proceeded like the Maker of all things: he put the muddy vesture of decay—that is, the gilt and glitter—on the outside where no one can miss it and left the heavenly harmony in the overtones for those to hear who can. If this be deception, it is divine deception.

The metaphor that underlies and unifies *The Merchant of Venice* is that of alchemy, the art of transforming the base into the precious, lead into gold. Everything in it comes back to that. Only the symbols are employed in a double sense, one worldly and one spiritual. By a kind of illuminating confusion, gold is lead and lead is gold, the base precious and the precious base. Portia had a chance to effect the great transformation—and failed. But she is not the only one. Gold, silver, and lead in one, the play subjects every reader or spectator to a test, or, shall we say, offers every reader or spectator the same opportunity Portia had. Choose—it says—at your peril. This play anti-Semitic? Why, yes, if you find it so. Shakespeare certainly leaves you free, if you wish, to pick the golden casket. But you may thereby be revealing more of yourself than of his play.

And what is true of an individual is true of an age. Poetry forever makes itself over for each generation. *The Merchant of Venice* seems expressly written for a time like our own when everywhere the volcano of race hatred seems ready to erupt. But even when we see this we may still be taking it too narrowly. Its pertinence for us is no more confined to the racial aspect than are our hatreds and exclusions. What inspired Shakespeare to introduce into this gay entertainment, with all its frivolity and wedding bells, prototypes of those two giants of the twentieth century, Trade and Finance (each so different at heart from its own estimation of itself), to let them look in each other's eyes, and behold—their own reflections?

Which is the merchant here and which the Jew?

How came he to inject so incongruously into it that haunting figure that has grown steadily more tragic with the years until it has thrown his supposed comedy quite out of focus? More sinned against than sinning, this villain-victim now strikes us as more nearly the protagonist, a far-off forerunner of King Lear himself. Beside him, the gentleman-hero of the piece shrinks to a mere fashion-plate, and his sad-eyed friend to a mere shadow. It is as if, between the passing darkness of feudalism and the oncoming darkness of capitalism, the sun broke forth briefly and let the poet store up truth for the future. When the Old Corruption goes, there is always such a glimpse of clear sky before the New Corruption assumes the throne. Not that Shakespeare was interested in economic evolution or foresaw its course. Poetic prophecy does not work in that way. Goethe reveals its secret rather when he says: "If a man grasp the particular vividly he also grasps the general without being aware of it at the time, or he may make the discovery long afterward." It is in this sense that Shakespeare wrote *The Merchant of Venice* for us even more than for his own age. Its characters are around us everywhere. Its problems still confront us—on an enormously enlarged scale.

At a time like our own when economic problems sometimes threaten to eclipse all others, their relation to moral and spiritual problems gets forgotten. But to divorce the two is to leave both insoluble. *The Merchant of Venice* not only does not make this error itself, it corrects it for us. It offers precisely the wisdom that we need, a wisdom that goes deeper than the doctrine of any economic school or sect. Shylock made his money by usury, Antonio his by trade, Portia got hers by inheritance, Bassanio by borrowing and then by marriage, Jessica by theft and later by judicial decree. The interplay of their lives makes enthralling drama. But to those not content to stop with the story it propounds questions that have a strangely contemporary ring: How are these various modes of acquiring and holding property related? Are they as unlike as they seem? And, coming closer home: Am I myself possibly, thanks to one or more of them, living in a golden world?

Those who might be compelled to answer "yes" to this last question will generally be protected from asking it. Some instinct of self-preservation— or fear of death—will keep them from seeking where they might discover, could they understand them, grounds sounder, in their opinion, than its supposed anti-Semitism for withdrawing *The Merchant of Venice* from the schools.

"There are certain current expressions and blasphemous modes of viewing things," says Thoreau, "as when we say 'he is doing a good business' more profane than cursing and swearing. There is death and sin in such words. Let not the children hear them." The author of *The Merchant of Venice*, I suspect, would have understood and agreed. He knew what he was doing when he named his play and when he made its merchant the victim of a melancholia so intense it verged on the suicidal.

"God won't ask us whether we succeeded in business."

## Chapter XIII

# Romeo and Juliet

### I

One word has dominated the criticism of *Romeo and Juliet:* "star-cross'd."

> From forth the fatal loins of these two foes,

says the Prologue-Chorus,

> A pair of star-cross'd lovers take their life.

"Star-cross'd" backed by "fatal" has pretty much surrendered this drama to the astrologers. "In this play," says one such interpreter, "simply the Fates have taken this young pair and played a cruel game against them with loaded dice, unaided by any evil in men." That is merely an extreme expression of the widely held view that makes *Romeo and Juliet*, in contrast with all Shakespeare's later tragedies, a tragedy of accident rather than of character and on that account a less profound and less universal work. That this play betrays signs of immaturity and lacks some of the marks of mastery that are common to the other tragedies may readily be granted. But that its inferiority is due to the predominance of accident over character ought not to be conceded without convincing demonstration. The burden of proof is certainly on those who assert it, for nowhere else does Shakespeare show any tendency to believe in fate in this sense. The integrity of his mind makes it highly unlikely that in just one instance he would have let the plot of the story he was dramatizing warp his convictions about freedom.

The theme of *Romeo and Juliet* is love and violence and their interactions. In it these two mightiest of mighty opposites meet each other squarely

—and one wins. And yet the other wins. This theme in itself makes *Romeo and Juliet* an astrological play in the sense that it is concerned throughout with Venus and Mars, with love and "war," and with little else. Nothing ever written perhaps presents more simply what results from the conjunction of these two "planets." But that does not make it a fatalistic drama. It all depends on what you mean by "stars." If by stars you mean the material heavenly bodies exercising from birth a predestined and inescapable occult influence on man, Romeo and Juliet were no more star-crossed than any lovers, even though their story was more unusual and dramatic. But if by stars you mean—as the deepest wisdom of the ages, ancient and modern, does—a psychological projection on the planets and constellations of the unconsciousness of man, which in turn is the accumulated experience of the race, then Romeo and Juliet and all the other characters of the play are star-crossed as every human being is who is passionately alive.

> In tragic life, God wot,
> No villain need be! Passions spin the plot,
> We are betrayed by what is false within.

The "villain" need not be a conspicuous incarnation of evil like Richard III or Iago; the "hero" himself may be the "villain" by being a conspicuous incarnation of weakness as was another Richard or a Troilus. Or the "villain" may consist in a certain chemical interplay of the passions of two or more characters. To seek a special "tragic flaw" in either Romeo or Juliet is foolish and futile. From pride down, we all have flaws enough to make of every life and of life itself a perpetual and universal tragedy. Altering his source to make the point unmistakable, Shakespeare is at pains to show that, however much the feud between Capulets and Montagues had to do with it incidentally, the tragedy of this play flowed immediately from another cause entirely. But of that in its place. Enough now if we have raised a suspicion that the "star-cross'd" of the Prologue should be taken in something other than a literal sense, or, better, attributed to the Chorus, not to the poet. The two are far from being the same.*

In retrospect, Shakespeare's plays, which in one sense culminate in *King Lear* and in another in *The Tempest*, are seen to deal over and over with the same underlying subject that dominates the Greek drama: the relation of the generations. *Romeo and Juliet*, as the first play of its author in which this subject is central, assumes a profound seminal as well as intrinsic interest on that account. It points immediately in this respect to *Henry IV* and *Hamlet*, and ultimately to *King Lear* and *The Tempest*.

This theme of "the fathers" is merely another way of expressing the

* See the discussion of the Choruses of *Henry V* on this point.

theme of "the stars." For the fathers are the stars and the stars are the fathers in the sense that the fathers stand for the accumulated experience of the past, for tradition, for authority, and hence for the two most potent forces that mold and so impart "destiny" to the child's life. Those forces, of course, are heredity and training, which between them create that impalpable mental environment, inner and outer, that is even more potent than either of them alone. The hatred of the hostile houses in *Romeo and Juliet* is an inheritance that every member of these families is born into as truly as he is born with the name Capulet or Montague. Their younger generations have no more choice in the matter than they have choice of the language they will grow up to speak. They suck in the venom with their milk. "So is the will of a living daughter curbed by the will of a dead father," as Portia puts it in *The Merchant of Venice*. The daughter may be a son and the father may be living, but the principle is the same. Thus the fathers cast the horoscopes of the children in advance—and are in that sense their stars. If astrology is itself, as it is, a kind of primitive and unconscious psychology, then the identity of the stars and the fathers becomes even more pronounced.

Now there is just one agency powerful enough in youth to defy and cut across this domination of the generations, and that is love. Love also is a "star" but in another and more celestial sense. Romeo, of the Montagues, after a sentimental and unrequited languishing after one Rosaline, falls in love at first sight with Juliet, of the Capulets, and instantly the instilled enmity of generations is dissipated like mist by morning sunshine, and the love that embraces Juliet embraces everything that Juliet touches or that touches her.

> My bounty is as boundless as the sea,
> My love as deep; the more I give to thee,
> The more I have, for both are infinite.

The words—music, imagery, and thought uniting to make them as wonderful as any ever uttered about love—are Juliet's, but Romeo's love is as deep—almost. It is love's merit, not his, that his enemies suddenly become glorified with the radiance of the medium through which he now sees everything. Hostility simply has nothing to breathe in such a transcendental atmosphere. It is through this effect of their love on both lovers, and the poetry in which they spontaneously embody it, that Shakespeare convinces us it is no mere infatuation, but love indeed in its divine sense. Passion it is, of course, but that contaminated term has in our day become helpless to express it. Purity would be the perfect word for it if the world had not forgotten that purity is simply Greek for fire.

## II

Shakespeare sees to it that we shall not mistake this white flame of Romeo's love, or Juliet's, for anything lower by opposing to the lovers two of the impurest characters he ever created, Mercutio and the Nurse. And yet, in spite of them, it has often been so mistaken. Mercutio and the Nurse are masterpieces of characterization so irresistible that many are tempted to let them arrogate to themselves as virtue what is really the creative merit of their maker. They are a highly vital pair, brimming with life and fire—but fire in a less heavenly sense than the one just mentioned. Juliet, at the most critical moment of her life, sums up the Nurse to all eternity in one word. When, in her darkest hour, this woman who has acted as mother to her from birth goes back on her completely, in a flash of revelation the girl sees what she is, and, reversing in one second the feeling of a lifetime, calls her a fiend ("most wicked fiend"). She could not have chosen a more accurate term, for the Nurse is playing at the moment precisely the part of the devil in a morality play. And Juliet's "ancient damnation" is an equally succinct description of her sin. What more ancient damnation is there than sensuality—and all the other sins it brings in its train? Those who dismiss the Nurse as just a coarse old woman whose loquacity makes us laugh fail hopelessly to plumb the depth of her depravity. It was the Nurse's desertion of her that drove Juliet to Friar Laurence and the desperate expedient of the sleeping potion. Her cowardice was a link in the chain that led to Juliet's death.

The Nurse has sometimes been compared with Falstaff—perhaps the poet's first comic character who clearly surpassed her. Any resemblance between them is superficial, for they are far apart as the poles. Falstaff was at home in low places but the sun of his imagination always accompanied him as a sort of disinfectant. The Nurse had no imagination in any proper sense. No sensualist—certainly no old sensualist—ever has. Falstaff loved Hal. What the Nurse's "love" for Juliet amounted to is revealed when she advises her to make the best of a bad situation and take Paris (bigamy and all). The man she formerly likened to a toad suddenly becomes superior to an eagle.

> Go, counsellor,

cries Juliet, repudiating her Satan without an instant's hesitation,

> Thou and my bosom henceforth shall be twain.

It is the rejection of the Nurse. But unlike Falstaff, when he is rejected, she carries not one spark of our sympathy or pity with her, and a pathetic account of her death, as of his, would be unthinkable. We scorn her as utterly as Juliet does.

## III

The contrast between Friar Laurence and the Nurse even the most casual reader or spectator could scarcely miss. The difference between the spiritual adviser of Romeo and the worldly confidant of Juliet speaks for itself. The resemblance of Mercutio to the Nurse is more easily overlooked, together with the analogy between the part he plays in Romeo's life and the part she plays in Juliet's. Yet it is scarcely too much to say that the entire play is built around that resemblance and that analogy.

The indications abound that Shakespeare created these two to go together. To begin with, they hate each other on instinct, as two rival talkers generally do, showing how akin they are under the skin. "A gentleman, nurse," says Romeo of Mercutio, "that loves to hear himself talk, and will speak more in a minute than he will stand to in a month." The cap which Romeo thus quite innocently hands the Nurse fits her so perfectly that she immediately puts it on in two speeches about Mercutio which are typical examples of *her* love of hearing herself talk and of saying things *she* is powerless to stand by:

An a' speak any thing against me, I'll take him down, an 'a were lustier than he is, and twenty such Jacks; and if I cannot, I'll find those that shall. Scurvy knave! I am none of his flirt-gills; I am none of his skains-mates. (*Turning to* PETER, *her man*) And thou must stand by too, and suffer every knave to use me at his pleasure! . . . Now, afore God, I am so vexed, that every part about me quivers. Scurvy knave!

That last, and the tone of the whole, show that there was a genuinely vicious element in the Nurse under her superficial good nature, as there invariably is in an old sensualist; and I do not believe it is exceeding the warrant of the text to say that the rest of the speech in which she warns Romeo against gross behavior toward her young gentlewoman—quite in the manner of Polonius and Laertes warning Ophelia against Hamlet— proves that in her heart she would have been delighted to have him corrupt her provided she could have shared the secret and been the go-between. "A bawd, a bawd, a bawd!" is Mercutio's succinct description of her.

But, as usual, when a man curses someone else, he characterizes himself. In what sense Mercutio is a bawd appears only too soon. In the meantime what a pity it is that he is killed off so early in the action as to allow no full and final encounter between these two fountains of loquacity! "Nay, an there were two such, we should have none shortly." Mercutio himself says it in another connection, but it applies perfectly to this incomparable pair. Their roles are crowded with parallelisms even down to what seem like the most trivial details. "We'll to dinner thither," says Mercutio, for example, parting from Romeo in Act II, scene 4. "Go, I'll to dinner," says the Nurse on leaving Juliet at the end of scene 5. A tiny touch. But they are just the two who would be certain never to miss a meal. In Shakespeare even such trifles have significance.

The fact is that Mercutio and the Nurse are simply youth and old age of the same type. He is aimed at the same goal she has nearly attained. He would have become the same sort of old man that she is old woman, just as she was undoubtedly the same sort of young girl that he is young man. They both think of nothing but sex—except when they are so busy eating or quarreling that they can think of nothing. (I haven't forgotten Queen Mab; I'll come to her presently.) Mercutio cannot so much as look at the clock without a bawdy thought. So permeated is his language with indecency that most of it passes unnoticed not only by the innocent reader but by all not schooled in Elizabethan smut. Even on our own unsqueamish stage an unabridged form of his role in its twentieth-century equivalent would not be tolerated. Why does Shakespeare place the extreme example of this man's soiled fantasies precisely before the balcony scene? Why but to stress the complete freedom from sensuality of Romeo's passion? Place Mercutio's dirtiest words, as Shakespeare does, right beside Romeo's apostrophe to his "bright angel" and all the rest of that scene where the lyricism of young love reaches one of its loftiest pinnacles in all poetry—and what remains to be said for Mercutio? Nothing—except that he is Mercutio. His youth, the hot weather, the southern temperament, the fashion among Italian gentlemen of the day, are unavailing pleas; not only Romeo, but Benvolio, had those things to contend with also. And they escaped. Mercury is close to the sun. But it was the material sun, Sol, not the god, Helios, that Mercutio was close to. Beyond dispute, this man had vitality, wit, and personal magnetism. But personal magnetism combined with sexuality and pugnacity is one of the most dangerous mixtures that can exist. The unqualified laudation that Mercutio has frequently received, and the suggestion that Shakespeare had to kill him off lest he quite set the play's titular hero in the shade, are the best proof of the truth of that statement. Those who are themselves seduced by Mercutio are not likely to be good judges of him. It may be retorted that Mercutio is nearly always a success on the stage, while Romeo is likely to be insipid. The answer to that is that while Mercutios are relatively common, Romeos are excessively rare. If Romeo proves insipid, he has been wrongly cast or badly acted.

"But how about Queen Mab?" it will be asked. The famous description of her has been widely held to be quite out of character and has been set down as an outburst of poetry from the author put arbitrarily in Mercutio's mouth. But the judgment "out of character" should always be a last resort.

Undoubtedly the lines, if properly his, do reveal an unsuspected side of Mercutio. The prankish delicacy of some of them stands out in pleasing contrast with his grosser aspects. The psychology of this is sound. The finer side of a sensualist is suppressed and is bound to come out, if at all, incidentally, in just such a digression as this seems to be. Shakespeare can be trusted not to leave such things out. Few passages in his plays, however, have been more praised for the wrong reasons. The account of Queen Mab is supposed to prove Mercutio's imagination: under his pugnacity there was a poet. It would be nearer the truth, I think, to guess that Shakespeare put it in as an example of what poetry is popularly held to be and is not. The lines on Queen Mab are indeed delightful. But imagination in any proper sense they are not. They are sheer fancy. Moreover, Mercutio's anatomy and philosophy of dreams prove that he knows nothing of their genuine import. He dubs them

> the children of an idle brain,
> Begot of nothing but vain fantasy.

Perhaps his are—the Queen Mab lines would seem to indicate as much. Romeo, on the other hand, holds that dreamers "dream things true," and gives a definition of them that for combined brevity and beauty would be hard to better. They are "love's shadows." And not only from what we can infer about his untold dream on this occasion, but from all the dreams and premonitions of both Romeo and Juliet throughout the play, they come from a fountain of wisdom somewhere beyond time. Primitives distinguish between "big" and "little" dreams. (Aeschylus makes the same distinction in *Prometheus Bound*.) Mercutio, with his aldermen and gnats and coach-makers and sweetmeats and parsons and drums and ambuscadoes, may tell us a little about the littlest of little dreams. He thinks that dreamers are still in their day world at night. Both Romeo and Juliet know that there are dreams that come from as far below the surface of that world as was that prophetic tomb at the bottom of which she saw him "as one dead" at their last parting. Finally, how characteristic of Mercutio that he should make Queen Mab a midwife and blemish his description of her by turning her into a "hag" whose function is to bring an end to maidenhood. Is this another link between Mercutio and the Nurse? Is Shakespeare here preparing the way for his intimation that she would be quite capable of assisting in Juliet's corruption? It might well be. When Shakespeare writes a speech that seems to be out of character, it generally, as in this case, deserves the closest scrutiny.

And there is another justification of the Queen Mab passage. Romeo and Juliet not only utter poetry; they are poetry. The loveliest comment on

Juliet I ever heard expressed this to perfection. It was made by a girl only a little older than Juliet herself. When Friar Laurence recommends philosophy to Romeo as comfort in banishment, Romeo replies:

> Hang up philosophy!
> Unless philosophy can make a Juliet . . .
> It helps not, it prevails not. Talk no more.

"Philosophy can't," the girl observed, "but poetry can—and it did!" Over against the poetry of Juliet, Shakespeare was bound, by the demands of contrast on which all art rests, to offer in the course of his play examples of poetry in various verbal, counterfeit, or adulterate estates.

> This precious book of love, this unbound lover,
> To beautify him, only lacks a cover.

That is Lady Capulet on the prospective bridegroom, Paris. It would have taken the play's booby prize for "poetry" if Capulet himself had not outdone it in his address to the weeping Juliet:

> How now! a conduit, girl? What, still in tears?
> Evermore showering? In one little body
> Thou counterfeit'st a bark, a sea, a wind;
> For still thy eyes, which I may call the sea,
> Do ebb and flow with tears; the bark thy body is,
> Sailing in this salt flood; the winds, thy sighs;
> Who, raging with thy tears, and they with them,
> Without a sudden calm, will overset
> Thy tempest-tossed body.

It is almost as if Shakespeare were saying in so many words: That is how poetry is not written. Yet, a little later, when the sight of his daughter, dead as all suppose, shakes even this egotist into a second of sincerity, he can say:

> Death lies on her like an untimely frost
> Upon the sweetest flower of all the field.

There is poetry, deep down, even in Capulet. But the instant passes and he is again talking about death as his son-in-law—and all the rest. The Nurse's vain repetitions in this scene are further proof that she is a heathen. Her O-lamentable-day's only stress the lack of one syllable of genuine grief or love such as Juliet's father shows. These examples all go to show what Shakespeare is up to in the Queen Mab speech. It shines, and even seems profound, beside the utterances of the Capulets and the Nurse. But it fades, and grows superficial, beside Juliet's and Romeo's. It is one more shade of what passes for poetry but is not.

## IV

The crisis of *Romeo and Juliet*, so far as Romeo is concerned, is the scene (just after the secret marriage of the two lovers) in which Mercutio and Tybalt are slain and Romeo banished. It is only two hundred lines long. Of these two hundred lines, some forty are introduction and sixty epilogue to the main action. As for the other hundred that come between, it may be doubted whether Shakespeare to the end of his career ever wrote another hundred that surpassed them in the rapidity, inevitability, and psychologic truth of the succession of events that they comprise. There are few things in dramatic literature to match them. And yet I think they are generally misunderstood. The scene is usually taken as the extreme precipitation in the play of the Capulet-Montague feud; whereas Shakespeare goes out of his way to prove that at most the feud is merely the occasion of the quarrel. Its cause he places squarely in the temperament and character of Mercutio, and Mercutio, it is only too easy to forget, is neither a Capulet nor a Montague, but a kinsman of the Prince who rules Verona, and, as such, is under special obligation to preserve a neutral attitude between the two houses.

This will sound to some like mitigating the guilt of Tybalt. But Tybalt has enough to answer for without making him responsible for Mercutio's sins.

The nephew of Lady Capulet is as dour a son of pugnacity as Mercutio is a dashing one:

> What, drawn, and talk of peace! I hate the word,
> As I hate hell.

These words—almost the first he speaks in the play—give Tybalt's measure. "More than prince of cats," Mercutio calls him, which is elevated to "king of cats" in the scene in which he mounts the throne of violence. (It is a comment on the Nurse's insight into human nature that she speaks of this fashionable desperado as "O courteous Tybalt! honest gentleman!") Mercutio's contempt for Tybalt is increased by the latter's affectation of the latest form in fencing: "He fights as you sing prick-song, keeps time, distance, and proportion. . . . The pox of such antic, lisping, affecting fantasticoes; these new tuners of accents!" Yet but a moment later, in an exchange of quips with Romeo, we find Mercutio doing with his wit just what he has scorned Tybalt for doing with his sword. For all their differences, as far as fighting goes Mercutio and Tybalt are two of a kind and by the former's rule are predestined to extinction: "an there were two such, we should have none shortly, for one would kill the other." When one kills the other, there is not one left, but none. That is the arithmetic of it. The **encounter** is not long postponed.

Tybalt is outraged when he discovers that a Montague has invaded the Capulet mansion on the occasion of the ball when Romeo first sees Juliet. But for his uncle he would assail the intruder on the spot:

> Patience perforce with wilful choler meeting
> Makes my flesh tremble* in their different greeting.
> I will withdraw; but this intrusion shall
> Now seeming sweet convert to bitter gall.

He is speaking of the clash between patience and provocation in himself. But he might be prophesying his meeting with Romeo. As the third act opens, he is hunting his man.

Tybalt is not the only one who is seeking trouble. The first forty lines of the crisis scene are specifically devised to show that Mercutio was out to have a fight under any and all circumstances and at any price. As well ask a small boy and a firecracker to keep apart as Mercutio and a quarrel. Sensuality and pugnacity are the poles of his nature. In the latter respect he is a sort of Mediterranean Hotspur, his frank southern animality taking the place of the idealistic "honour" of his northern counterpart. He is as fiery in a literal as Romeo is in a poetic sense.

The scene is a public place. Enter Mercutio and Benvolio. Benvolio knows his friend:

> I pray thee, good Mercutio, let's retire.
> The day is hot, the Capulets abroad,
> And, if we meet, we shall not 'scape a brawl,
> For now, these hot days, is the mad blood stirring.

Mercutio retorts with a description of the cool-tempered Benvolio that makes him out an inveterate hothead:

Thou! why, thou wilt quarrel with a man that hath a hair more, or a hair less, in his beard, than thou hast. Thou wilt quarrel with a man for cracking nuts, having no other reason but because thou hast hazel eyes. What eye but such an eye would spy out such a quarrel? Thy head is as full of quarrels as an egg is full of meat, and yet thy head hath been beaten as addle as an egg for quarrelling. Thou hast quarrelled with a man for coughing in the street, because he hath wakened thy dog that hath lain asleep in the sun. Didst thou not fall out with a tailor for wearing his new doublet before Easter? with another, for tying his new shoes with old riband?

This, the cautious and temperate Benvolio! As Mercutio knows, it is nothing of the sort. It is an ironic description of himself. It is he, not his friend, who will make a quarrel out of anything—out of nothing, rather, and give it

---

* *Nurse* (II, iv, 172): "Now, afore God, I am so vexed that every part about me quivers." Another revealing analogy.

a local habitation and a name, as a poet does with the creatures of his imagination. Mercutio is pugnacity in its pure creative state. At the risk of the Prince's anger, he makes his friend Romeo's cause his own and roams the streets in the hope of encountering some Capulet with whom to pick a quarrel. The feud is only a pretext. If it hadn't been that, it would have been something else. The Chorus may talk about "stars," but in this case Mars does not revolve in the skies on the other side of the Earth from Venus, but resides on earth right under the jerkin of this particular impulsive youth, Mercutio. Or if this "fate" be a god rather than a planet, then Mercutio has opened his heart and his home to him with unrestrained hospitality. So Romeo is indeed "star-cross'd" in having Mercutio for a friend.

Mercutio has no sooner finished his topsy-turvy portrait of Benvolio than Tybalt and his gang come in to reveal which of the two the description fits. Tybalt is searching for Romeo, to whom he has just sent a challenge, and recognizing Romeo's friends begs "a word with one of you." He wishes, presumably, to ask where Romeo is. But Mercutio, bent on provocation, retorts, "make it a word and a blow." Benvolio tries in vain to intervene. Just as things are getting critical, Romeo enters, and Tybalt turns from Mercutio to the man he is really seeking:

> Romeo, the love I bear thee can afford
> No better term than this,—thou art a villain.

Here is the most direct and galling of insults. Here are Mercutio, Benvolio, and the rest waiting to see how Romeo will take it. The temperature is blistering in all senses. And what does Romeo say?

> Tybalt, the reason that I have to love thee
> Doth much excuse the appertaining rage
> To such a greeting; villain am I none;
> Therefore farewell; I see thou know'st me not.

We who are in the secret know that "the reason" is Juliet and that his love for her is capable of wrapping all Capulets in its miraculous mantle, even "the king of cats."

But Tybalt is intent on a fight and will not be put off by kindness however sincere or deep. "Boy," he comes back insolently,

> this shall not excuse the injuries
> That thou hast done me; therefore turn and draw.

Romeo, however, is in the power of something that makes him impervious to insults:

> I do protest I never injur'd thee,
> But love thee better than thou canst devise
> Till thou shalt know the reason of my love;
> And so, good Capulet,—which name I tender
> As dearly as my own,—be satisfied.

The world has long since decided what to think of a man who lets himself be called a villain without retaliating. Romeo, to put it in one word, proves himself, according to the world's code, a mollycoddle. And indeed a mollycoddle might act exactly as Romeo appears to. But if Romeo is a mollycoddle, then Jesus was a fool to talk about loving one's enemies, for Romeo, if anyone ever did, is doing just that at this moment. And Juliet was demented to talk about love being boundless and infinite, for here Romeo is about to prove that faith precisely true. Those who think that Jesus, and Juliet, and Romeo were fools will have plenty of backing. The "fathers" will be on their side. They will have the authority of the ages and the crowd. Only a philosopher or two, a few lovers, saints, and poets will be against them. The others will echo the

> O calm, dishonourable, vile submission!

with which Mercutio draws his rapier and begins hurling insults at Tybalt that make Tybalt's own seem tame:

MER.: Tybalt, you rat-catcher, will you walk?
TYB.: What wouldst thou have with me?
MER.: Good king of cats, nothing but one of your nine lives.

And Mercutio threatens to stick him before he can draw if he does not do so instantly. What can Tybalt do but draw? "I am for you," he cries, as he does so.

Such, however, is the power of Romeo's love that even now he attempts to prevent the duel:

> Gentle Mercutio, put thy rapier up.

But Mercutio pays no attention and the two go to it. If ever a quarrel scene defined the central offender and laid the responsibility at one man's door, this is the scene and Mercutio is the man. It takes two to make a quarrel. Romeo, the Montague, will not fight. Tybalt, the Capulet, cannot fight if Romeo will not. With Mercutio Tybalt has no quarrel. The poet takes pains to make that explicit in a startling way. "Peace be with you, sir," are the words Tybalt addresses to Mercutio when Romeo first enters. *That* from the man who once cried,

> peace! I hate the word,
As I hate hell.

Now we see why Shakespeare had him say it. It was in preparation for this scene. Thus he lets one word exonerate Tybalt of the responsibility for what ensues between himself and Mercutio.

And now, condensed into the fractional part of a second, comes the crisis in Romeo's life. Not later, when he decides to kill Tybalt, but now. Now is the moment when two totally different universes wait as it were on the turning of a hand. There is nothing of its kind to surpass it in all Shakespeare, not even in *Hamlet* or *King Lear*, not, one is tempted to think, in all the drama of the world. Here, if anywhere, Shakespeare shows that the fate we attribute to the stars lies in our own souls.

> Our remedies oft in ourselves do lie,
> Which we ascribe to heaven: the fated sky
> Gives us free scope.

Romeo had free scope. For, if we are free to choose between two compulsions, we are in so far free. Romeo was free to act under the compulsion of force or under the compulsion of love—under the compulsion of the stars, that is, in either of two opposite senses. Granted that the temptation to surrender to the former was at the moment immeasurably great, the power of the latter, if Juliet spoke true, was greater yet:

> My bounty is as boundless as the sea,
> My love as deep; the more I give to thee,
> The more I have, for both are *infinite*.

Everything that has just preceded shows that the real Romeo wanted to have utter faith in Juliet's faith. "Genius trusts its faintest intimation," says Emerson, "against the testimony of all history." But Romeo, whose intimations were not faint but strong, falls back on the testimony of all history that only force can overcome force. He descends from the level of love to the level of violence and attempts to part the fighters with his sword.

> Draw, Benvolio; beat down their weapons.
> Gentlemen, for shame, forbear this outrage!
> Tybalt, Mercutio, the prince expressly hath
> Forbidden bandying in Verona streets.
> Hold, Tybalt! good Mercutio!

Here, if anywhere, the distinction between drama and poetry becomes clear. Drama is a portrayal of human passions eventuating in acts. Poetry is a picture of life in its essence. On the level of drama, we are with Romeo absolutely. His purpose is noble, his act endearingly impulsive. We echo that purpose and identify ourselves with that act. In the theater we do, I mean, and under the aspect of time. But how different under the aspect of eternity! There the scene is a symbolic picture of life itself, of faith surrendering to force, of love trying to gain its end by violence—only to discover, as it soon does, and as we do too, that what it has attained instead is death. A noble motive never yet saved a man from the consequences of an unwise act, and Romeo's own words to Mercutio as he draws his sword are an unconscious confession in advance of his mistake. Having put aside his faith in Juliet's faith, his appeal is in the name of law rather than of love: "The prince expressly hath forbidden." That, and his "good Mercutio," reveal a divided soul. And it is that divided soul, in a last instant of hesitation, that causes an awkward or uncoördinated motion as he interferes and gives the cowardly Tybalt his chance to make a deadly thrust at Mercutio under Romeo's arm. If Romeo had only let those two firebrands fight it out, both might have lost blood with a cooling effect on their heated tempers, or, if it had gone to a finish, both might have been killed, as they ultimately were anyway, or, more likely, Mercutio would have killed Tybalt. ("An there were two such, we should have none shortly, for one would kill the other.") In any of these events, the feud between the two houses would not have been involved. As it is, the moment of freedom passes, and the rest is fate.

The fallen Mercutio reveals his most appealing side in his good humor at death. But why his reiterated "A plague o' both your houses"? He is one more character in Shakespeare who "doth protest too much." Four times he repeats it, or three and a half to be exact. How ironical of Mercutio to attribute his death to the Capulet-Montague feud, when the Capulet who killed him had plainly been reluctant to fight with him, and the chief Montague present had begged and begged him to desist. That "plague o' both your houses" is Mercutio's unwitting confession that his own intolerable pugnacity, not the feud at all, is responsible. And if that be true, how much that has been written about this tragedy must be retracted.

What follows puts a final confirmation on Romeo's error in trying to part the duelists by force. With Mercutio dead as a direct result of his interference, what can Romeo say? We heard him fall from love to an appeal to law and order while the fight was on. Now it is over, he descends even lower as he bemoans his "reputation stain'd with Tybalt's slander." Reputation! Iago's word.

> O sweet Juliet,
> Thy beauty hath made me effeminate
> And in my temper soften'd valour's steel!

Were ever words more tragically inverted? That fire should soften metal must have seemed a miracle to the man who first witnessed it. How much greater the miracle whereby beauty melts violence into love! That is the miracle that was on the verge of occurring in *Romeo and Juliet.*

Instead, Benvolio enters to announce Mercutio's death. Whereat Romeo, throwing the responsibility of his own mistake on destiny, exclaims:

> This day's black fate on more days doth depend;
> This but begins the woe others must end.

Could words convey more clearly the fact that the crisis has passed? Freedom has had its instant. The consequences are now in control.

Tybalt re-enters. Does Romeo now remember that his love for Juliet makes every Capulet sacred? Does he recall his last words to her as he left the orchard at dawn?—

> Sleep dwell upon thine eyes, peace in thy breast!
> Would I were sleep and peace, so sweet to rest!

Does he now use his sword merely to prevent bloodshed?

> Away to heaven, respective lenity,

he cries, implying without realizing it the infernal character of his decision,

> And fire-ey'd fury be my conduct now!

Fury! Shakespeare's invariable word for animal passion in man gone mad. And in that fury Romeo's willingness to forgive is devoured like a flower in a furnace:

> Now, Tybalt, take the villain back again
> That late thou gav'st me; for Mercutio's soul
> Is but a little way above our heads,
> Staying for thine to keep him company.
> Either thou, or I, or both, must go with him.

The spirit of Mercutio does indeed enter Romeo's body, and though it is Tybalt who is to go with the slain man literally, it is Romeo who goes with him in the sense that he accepts his code and obeys his ghost. Drawing his rapier, he sends Tybalt to instant death—to the immense gratification of practically everyone in the audience, so prone are we in the theater to surrender to the ancestral emotions. How many a mother, suspecting the evil influence of some companion on her small son, has put her arms about him in a desperate gesture of protection. Yet that same mother will attend a performance of *Romeo and Juliet*, and, seduced by the crowd, will applaud Romeo's capitulation to the spirit of Mercutio to the echo. So frail is the tenderness of the mothers in the face of the force of the fathers.

In this respect the scene is like the court scene in *The Merchant of Venice* when we gloat over Shylock's discomfiture. Here, as there, not only our cooler judgment when we are alone but all the higher implications of the tragedy call for a reversal of our reaction when with the crowd. In this calmer retrospect, we perceive that between his hero's entrance and exit in this scene Shakespeare has given us three Romeos, or, if you will, one Romeo in three universes. First we see him possessed by love and a spirit of universal forgiveness. From this he falls, first to reason and an appeal to law, then to violence—but violence in a negative or "preventive" sense. Finally, following Mercutio's death, he passes under the control of passion and fury, abetted by "honour," and thence to vengeance and offensive violence. In astrological terms, he moves from Venus, through the Earth, to Mars. It is as if Dante's *Divine Comedy* were compressed into eighty lines and presented in reverse—Romeo in an inverted "pilgrimage" passing from Paradise, through Purgatory, to the Inferno.

This way of taking the scene acquits Romeo of doing "wrong," unless we may be said to do wrong whenever we fail to live up to our highest selves. Love is a realm beyond good and evil. Under the aspect of time, of common sense, possibly even of reason and morality, certainly of "honour," Romeo's conduct in the swift succession of events that ended in Tybalt's death was unexceptionable. What else could he have done? But under the aspect of eternity, which is poetry's aspect, it was less than that. We cannot blame a man because he does not perform a miracle. But when he offers proof of his power, and the very next moment has the opportunity to perform one, and does not, the failure is tragic. Such was the "failure" of Romeo. And he himself admits it in so many words. Death, like love, lifts us for a moment above time. Just before he drinks the poison, catching sight of the body of Tybalt in the Capulet vault, Romeo cries, "Forgive me, cousin." Why should he ask forgiveness for what he did in honor, if honor be the guide to what is right?

Romeo as an honorable man avenges his friend. But in proving himself a man in this sense, he proves himself less than the perfect lover. "Give all to love," says Emerson:

> Give all to love . . .
> 'Tis a brave master;
> Let it have scope:
> Follow it utterly,
> Hope beyond hope . . .
> Heartily know,
> When half-gods go,
> The gods arrive.

Juliet's love had bestowed on Romeo power to bring down a god, to pass even beyond the biblical seventy times seven to what Emily Brontë calls the "first of the seventy-first." But he did not. The play is usually explained as a tragedy of the excess of love. On the contrary it is the tragedy of a deficiency of it. Romeo did not "follow it utterly," did not give quite "all" to love.

## V

Romeo's mental condition following the death of Tybalt is proof of the treason he has committed against his own soul. Up to this point in the scene, as we saw, Shakespeare has given us three Romeos. Now he gives us a fourth: the man rooted to the spot at the sight of what he has done. The citizens have heard the tumult and are coming. "Stand not amaz'd," cries Benvolio—and it is a case where one poet's words seem to have been written to illuminate another's. Wordsworth's lines are like a mental stage direction for the dazed Romeo:

> Action is transitory—a step, a blow,
> The motion of a muscle—this way or that—
> 'Tis done; and in the after-vacancy
> We wonder at ourselves like men betrayed:
> Suffering is permanent, obscure and dark,
> And has the nature of infinity.

"O! I am Fortune's fool," cries Romeo. "Love's not Time's fool," says Shakespeare, as if commenting on this very scene, in that confession of his own faith, the 116th sonnet:

> O, no! it is an ever-fixed mark,
> That looks on tempests and is never shaken;
> It is the star to every wandering bark,
> Whose worth's unknown, although his height be taken.

*There* is an astrology at the opposite pole from that of the Chorus to this play. Romeo's love looked on a tempest—and it was shaken. He apparently has just strength enough left to escape and seek refuge in Friar Laurence's cell, where, at the word of his banishment, we find him on the floor,

> Taking the measure of an unmade grave,

in a fit of that suicidal despair that so often treads on the heels of "fury." It is not remorse for having killed Tybalt that accounts for his condition, nor even vexation with himself for having spoiled his own marriage, but shame for having betrayed Juliet's faith in the boundlessness of love.

Meanwhile, at the scene of the duels, citizens have gathered, followed by the Prince with Capulets and Montagues. Lady Capulet, probably the weakest character in the play, is the first to demand more blood as a solution of the problem:

> Prince, as thou art true,
> For blood of ours, shed blood of Montague.

But the Prince asks first for a report of what happened.

> Benvolio, who began this bloody fray?

Benvolio mars what is otherwise a remarkably accurate account of the affair by failing utterly to mention Mercutio's part in instigating the first duel, placing the entire blame on Tybalt.

> He is a kinsman to the Montague,

cries Lady Capulet,

> Affection makes him false; he speaks not true.
> Some twenty of them fought in this black strife,
> And all those twenty could but kill one life.

Her sense of reality and character are on a level with her courage.

In Capulet's orchard, the Nurse brings to Juliet the rope ladder by which her husband is to reach her chamber—and with it the news of Tybalt's death and Romeo's banishment.

> O serpent heart, hid with a flowering face!
> Did ever dragon keep so fair a cave?

cries Juliet,

> O nature, what hadst thou to do in hell,
> When thou didst bower the spirit of a fiend
> In mortal paradise of such sweet flesh?

Even in the exaggeration of her anguish, Juliet diagnoses what has happened precisely as Shakespeare does: a fiend—the spirit of Mercutio—has taken possession of her lover-husband's body. Contrast her insight at such a moment with the Nurse's drivellings:

> There's no trust,
> No faith, no honesty in men; all perjur'd,
> All forsworn, all naught, all dissemblers.
> Ah, where's my man?

A fair sample of how well her inane generalizations survive the test of a concrete need.

Back in Friar Laurence's cell, the stunned Romeo is like a drunken man vaguely coming to himself after a debauch. When he draws his sword to make away with himself, the Friar restrains him not by his hand,* as Romeo had once sought to restrain Mercutio at a similarly critical moment, but by the force of his words:

> Hold thy desperate hand!
> Art thou a man?

And he seeks to sting him back to manhood by comparing his tears to those of a woman and his fury to that of a beast.

> Thou hast amaz'd me. . . .
> Why rail'st thou on thy birth, the heaven, and earth?
> Since birth, and heaven, and earth, all three do meet
> In thee at once, which thou at once wouldst lose.

No nonsense about "star-cross'd lovers" for Friar Laurence. Shakespeare, like Dante before him and Milton after him, knew where the stars are, knew that heaven and hell, and even earth, are located within the human soul. Romeo is the "skilless soldier" who sets afire the powder in his own flask.

## VI

Juliet too in her despair can think of death. But with what relative calmness and in what a different key! The contrast between the two lovers at this stage is a measure of the respectively innocent and guilty states of their souls.

Their meeting at night is left to our imagination, but their parting at dawn is Shakespeare's imagination functioning at its highest lyrical intensity, with interwoven symbols of nightingale and lark, darkness and light, death and love. Then follow in swift succession the mother's announcement of her daughter's impending marriage with Paris, Juliet's ringing repudiation of the idea, the rejection of her, in order, by her father, her mother, and the Nurse—the first brutal, the second supine, the third Satanic. And then, with an instantaneousness that can only be called divine, Juliet's rejection of the Nurse. In a matter of seconds the child has become a woman. This is the second crisis of the drama, Juliet's, which, with Romeo's, gives the play its shape as certainly as its two foci determine the shape of an ellipse. If ever two crises were symmetrical, and opposite, these are.

Romeo, in a public place, lured insensibly through the influence of Mercutio to the use of force, falls, and as a direct result of his fall, kills Tybalt.

---

* The actor may easily make a mistake here and spoil Shakespeare's point.

Juliet, in her chamber, deserted by father and mother and enticed to faithlessness by the Nurse, child as she is, never wavers for an instant, puts her tempter behind her, and consents as the price of her fidelity to be "buried" alive. Can anyone imagine that Shakespeare did not intend this contrast, did not build up his detailed parallelism between Mercutio and the Nurse to effect it? Romeo, as we said, does not give quite "all" for love. But Juliet does. She performs her miracle and receives supernatural strength as her reward. He fails to perform his and is afflicted with weakness. But eventually her spirit triumphs in him. Had it done so at first, the tragedy would have been averted. Here again the heroine transcends the hero. And yet Romeo had Friar Laurence as adviser while Juliet was brought up by the Nurse! The profounder the truth, the more quietly Shakespeare has a habit of uttering it. It is as if he were saying here that innocence comes from below the sources of pollution and can run the fountain clear.

To describe as "supernatural" the strength that enables Juliet "without fear or doubt" to undergo the ordeal of the sleeping potion and the burial vault does not seem excessive:

> Give me, give me! O! tell me not of fear!

Long before—in the text, not in time—when she had wondered how Romeo had scaled the orchard wall below her balcony, he had said:

> With love's light wings did I o'erperch these walls;
> For stony limits cannot hold love out,
> And what love can do that dares love attempt.

Juliet is now about to prove the truth of his words, in a sense Romeo never dreamed of, "in that dim monument where Tybalt lies." The hour comes, and after facing the terrors her imagination conjures up, Juliet goes through her "dismal scene" alone, is found "dead," and following a scene that anticipates but reverses *Hamlet* in that a wedding is turned into a funeral, is placed in the Capulet vault in accordance with Friar Laurence's desperate plan. But after force has had its instant way, fate in the guise of fear usually has its protracted way, and to oppose it is like trying to stay an avalanche with your hand.

## VII

The pestilence prevents the Friar's messenger from reaching Romeo. Instead, word is brought to him that Juliet is dead, and, armed with a drug of an apothecary who defies the law against selling poison, he ends his banishment to Mantua and starts back to Verona to seek beside Juliet the eternal banishment of death. The fury with which he threatens his companion Balthasar, on dismissing him when they reach the churchyard, if he should return to pry, reveals Romeo's mood:

> By heaven, I will tear thee joint by joint
> And strew this hungry churchyard with thy limbs.
> The time and my intents are savage-wild,
> More fierce and more inexorable far
> Than empty tigers or the roaring sea.

And when he encounters and slays Paris, the contrast between his death and that of Mercutio, or even Tybalt, shows that we are dealing here not so much with the act of a free agent choosing his course in the present as with the now fatal consequences of an act in the past, of an agent then free but now no longer so. Paris is little more than the branch of a tree that Romeo pushes aside—and his death affects us almost as little. It is all like a dream, or madness. Finding the sleeping—as he supposes the dead—Juliet, Romeo pours out his soul in words which, though incomparable as poetry, err in placing on the innocent heavens the responsibility for his own venial but fatal choice:

> O, here
> Will I set up my everlasting rest,
> And shake the yoke of inauspicious stars
> From this world-wearied flesh.

And then, by one of those strokes that, it sometimes seems, only Shakespeare could achieve, the poet makes Romeo revert to and round out, in parting from Juliet forever, the same metaphor he had used when she first gazed down on him from her balcony and he had tried to give expression to the scope and range of his love. How magically, placed side by side, the two passages fit together, how tragically they sum up the story:

> I am no pilot; yet, wert thou as far
> As that vast shore wash'd with the farthest sea,
> I would adventure for such merchandise.

> Come, bitter conduct, come, unsavoury guide!
> Thou desperate pilot, now at once run on
> The dashing rocks thy sea-sick weary bark!
> Here's to my love! (*Drinks.*) O true apothecary!
> Thy drugs are quick. Thus with a kiss I die. (*Dies.*)

*Enter Friar Laurence*—a moment too late. That fear is with him Shakespeare shows by another echo. "Wisely and slow; they stumble that run fast," the Friar had warned Romeo on dismissing him after his first confession of his love for Juliet, and now he says:

> How oft to-night
> Have my old feet stumbled at graves! . . .
> . . . Fear comes upon me.

He discovers the dead Romeo. Just then Juliet awakes. But at the same moment he hears a noise. The watch is coming! He cannot be found here.

> Come, go, good Juliet, I dare no longer stay,

and when she refuses to follow, he deserts her. With a glance into the empty cup in Romeo's hand and a kiss on the lips that she hopes keep poison for her own—anticipating touches at the deaths of both Hamlet and Cleopatra—she snatches Romeo's dagger and kills herself.

Why did Shakespeare, after building up so noble a character as Friar Laurence, permit him to abandon Juliet at so fatal a moment? Why add *his* name to the so different ones of Capulet, Lady Capulet, and the Nurse, no matter how much better the excuse for his desertion of her? For two reasons, I think: first, to show how far the infection of fear extends that Romeo's use of force had created. "Here is a friar, that trembles, sighs, and weeps," says the Third Watchman, and Laurence himself confesses, when he tells his story,

> But then a noise did scare me from the tomb.

And then, to show that Juliet, abandoned *even by religion*, must fall back for courage finally on love alone.

The pestilence plays a crucial part toward the end of the action. It is a symbol. Whatever literal epidemic there may have been in the region, it is plain that fear is the real pestilence that pervades the play. It is fear of the code of honor, not fate, that drives Romeo to seek vengeance on Tybalt. It is fear of the plague, not accident, that leads to the miscarriage of Friar Laurence's message to Romeo. It is fear of poverty, not the chance of his being at hand at the moment, that lets the apothecary sell the poison. It is fear of the part he is playing, not age, that makes Friar Laurence's old feet stumble and brings him to the tomb just a few seconds too late to prevent Romeo's death. It is fear of being found at such a spot at such a time, not coincidence, that lets him desert Juliet at last just when he does. Fear, fear, fear, fear, fear. Fear is the evil "star" that crosses the lovers. And fear resides not in the skies but in the human heart.

## VIII

The tragedy ends in the reconciliation of the two houses, compensation, it is generally held, for the deaths of the two lovers. Doubtless the feud was not renewed in its former form. But much superfluous sentiment has been spent on this ending. Is it not folly to suppose that Capulet or Lady Capulet was spiritually transformed by Juliet's death? And as for Montague, the statue of her in pure gold that he promised to erect in Verona is proof in itself how incapable he was of understanding her spirit and how that spirit alone, and not monuments or gold, can bring an end to feuds. (Lady Montague, who died of a broken heart, was far and away the finest of the four parents.) Shakespeare's happy endings are, almost without exception, suspect. Or rather they are to be found, if at all, elsewhere than in the last scene and final speeches, and are "happy" in a quite untheatrical sense.

Cynics are fond of saying that if Romeo and Juliet had lived their love would not have "lasted." Of course it wouldn't—in the cynic's sense. You can no more ask such love to last than you can ask April to last, or an apple blossom. Yet April and apple blossoms do last and have results that bear no resemblance to what they come from—results such as apples and October—and so does such love. Romeo, in his last words, referred to the phenomenon known as "a lightning before death." Here is that lightning, and here, if it have one, is the happy ending of *Romeo and Juliet*:

> ROM.: If I may trust the flattering truth of sleep,
> My dreams presage some joyful news at hand.
> My bosom's lord sits lightly in his throne,
> And all this day an unaccustom'd spirit
> Lifts me above the ground with cheerful thoughts.
> I dreamt my lady came and found me dead—
> Strange dream, that gives a dead man leave to think!—
> And breath'd such life with kisses in my lips,
> That I reviv'd and was an emperor.
> Ah me! how sweet is love itself possess'd,
> When but love's shadows are so rich in joy!

*Enter Balthasar*—with news of Juliet's death.

Dreams go by contraries, they say, and this seems to be an example. But is it?

*Chapter XIV*

# King John

*King John* has generally been relegated to a place among Shakespeare's relatively minor works. It is a mere chronicle, it is said, just an inconsequence of events. It lacks the organized unity of a work of art. It is a play at which the author "perhaps pegged away," a recent commentator suggests, "when he did not feel in the right mood" for *Richard II*, on which he may have been working at the same time.

Granted that *King John* is not among Shakespeare's masterpieces, these judgments do the play an injustice. It has a clear leading idea, marked unity, and such excellent characterization as to put quite out of court the supposition that the poet took a perfunctory interest in it. It is built around a theme that Shakespeare never thereafter lost sight of. That theme is close to the heart of nearly all the other History Plays, both English and Roman; it is essential to *Hamlet*; it culminates in *King Lear*; it echoes through *The Tempest*. This is not the place to back up these assertions in detail. But if there is truth in them, *King John* is another extraordinarily seminal work.

The plan of *King John* is simplicity itself. It is centered around a devastating contrast. In the title role is John himself, about the unkingliest king Shakespeare ever created. The fact is, John has never grown up. He is mentally dominated by his ambitious mother. When he hears that a foreign foe has landed in force on his shores, he cries out:

> Where is my mother's care,
> That such an army could be drawn in France,
> And she not hear of it?

He is like a bewildered child in the night. And when a moment later he is told that his mother is dead, his repeated exclamation, "What! mother dead!

... My mother dead!" illuminates him like a flash of lightning. We pity him. Yet it is under that same mother's influence that he has become a liar and a coward. "Weakness possesseth me." "Within me is a hell." Those words at the end, though spoken more of his physical than his moral condition, are his own last judgment on himself. They sum him up with justice.

How could a drama be written about such a cipher? It couldn't. And so, quite re-creating a figure he found in his source, Shakespeare puts over against John as upright, downright, forthright a hero as he ever depicted, Philip Faulconbridge. Faulconbridge is everything John is not: truthful, faithful, courageous, humorous, without personal ambition, utterly loyal to his sovereign and to England. He is direct and picturesque in speech to the point of genius. He lacks, if you will, some of the transcendental virtues, but, within his limits, he is a man. "Look at them!" Shakespeare seems to say as he places them side by side, "a man is greater than a king!" But there is another kind of king, and in that sense Faulconbridge is king of *King John*. That is the irony of the title. That is the key to the play. And to make the pill the bitterer to the feudally minded, this king is a bastard. He hasn't even the ordinary title of son. His title is the truth. As the clown was the natural gentleman in *The Two Gentlemen of Verona*, so the bastard is the natural king in *King John*. Here, too, if in quite different senses of the terms, master and man have exchanged places. If ever a play brought the mere name of king, the mere institution of royalty, into disrepute, it is this one. But in behalf of no shallow equalitarianism. For, after all, Faulconbridge has royal blood in his veins. Thoreau once remarked that the life of a great man is the severest satire. The Bastard shows exactly what he meant. But how quietly Shakespeare makes his point.

The fact that Faulconbridge was illegitimate doubtless first suggested the ironic antithesis between him and John. And this antithesis in turn brought the impulse to compose the variations that run through every scene and ramify into every corner of the drama, imparting to it its high degree of unity.

An illegitimate son is likely to react to his birth in one or the other of two opposite ways. "I am a bastard," he may argue. "I was born outside the law. Therefore, I am entitled to revenge myself for the wrong committed against me by setting all law and social conformity at naught whenever it is to my advantage to do so." Don John in *Much Ado about Nothing*, Thersites in *Troilus and Cressida*, and Edmund in *King Lear* are studies in this type. But on the other hand the illegitimate child may reason: "I am a natural son. Instead of becoming a victim of the customs and conventions that reduce most men to slavery, I will be free—true to the best impulses life has implanted in my heart. I will be a son of nature." That was Faulconbridge's reaction. It was the easier for him doubtless because he suspected he was the son of Richard the Lionhearted. When he rejects the Faulconbridge name and inheritance and declares,

> I am I, howe'er I was begot,

he shows where he stands on the question with which so much of the play is concerned: which is better, the truth without worldly possessions and position, or worldly possessions and position without the truth? His attitude toward his mother in this matter defines another abysmal difference between himself and the King. John is like a little boy tied to his mother's apron strings. The Bastard dares his mother to reveal his father's name and elicits the truth from her by his very audacity. Thus the first act, which would otherwise be a mere prologue or almost a separate little piece in one act, is perfectly integrated with the rest of the play.

But it is not just John who is foil to Faulconbridge. The play is filled with weaklings, timeservers, turncoats, and traitors. The Bastard's name for the god, or rather the devil, that these worldlings worship is Commodity. There are few if any more important passages in the early works of Shakespeare than the lines at the end of Act II of this play in which the Bastard pays his respects to the God of This World to whom all but a few rare characters bow down. Shakespeare's profound agreement with his hero in regard to this object of man's adoration is proved by two of his greatest sonnets, the 123d and 124th, on Time and Policy, which are nothing but the Bastard's soliloquy in another key, or two other keys.

To the Elizabethans, Machiavelli was the father of this god, Commodity. But he is descended from human nature itself. No synonym quite expresses the wealth of meaning that the Bastard compresses into the word. Its derivation suggests a falling-in with, or a taking-up with, the fashion, practice, or advantage of the moment to the neglect of deeper or eternal concerns. The Commodity-server, in Shakespeare's favorite phrase, is the fool of time. Worldliness, compliance, compromise, policy, diplomacy, casuistry, expediency, opportunism: they all are somehow comprehended under the one name. Commodity is intimately related to Langland's Lady Meed, to Bunyan's Worldly Wiseman, to William James's "bitch-goddess, Success." Some of its other names are Mammon, the Main Chance, and The Band-Wagon.

> Commodity, the bias of the world;
> The world, who of itself is peized well,
> Made to run even upon even ground,
> Till this advantage, this vile-drawing bias,
> This sway of motion, this Commodity,

> Makes it take head from all indifferency,
> From all direction, purpose, course, intent.

Broker, break-vow, purpose-changer, bawd, cheat, devil, gentleman: Faulconbridge cannot find names strong enough or bad enough to characterize it. Yet he has the modesty and sense of humor to fear that he himself may not be strong enough to resist the wiles of the very tempter he is condemning. So he ironically winds up his diatribe with the couplet:

> Since kings break faith upon Commodity,
> Gain, be my lord, for I will worship thee.

This is, of course, the last thing on earth he intends to do or, as the event proves, ever does. But his irony makes dupes of many readers. Indeed, one of the acutest of recent commentators remarks that Faulconbridge "is essentially a crude person, the successful opportunist and materialist, as one sees from his 'commodity' speech (II, i, 561) with its characteristic ending, 'Gain, be my lord, for I will worship thee.'" That is getting the Bastard as completely upside down as it would be to call Iago honest or Desdemona a hypocrite.

There are some earlier words of this man that supply the key to his attitude. They come just after he has been made Sir Richard by the King. After some delightful jocosities about the snobberies his new rank will entitle him to practice, his tone suddenly alters and he adds:

> And not alone in habit and device,
> Exterior form, outward accoutrement,
> But from the inward motion to deliver
> Sweet, sweet, sweet poison for the age's tooth;
> Which, though I will not practise to deceive,
> Yet, to avoid deceit, I mean to learn.

In more biblical language, what he is saying is that he intends to live in the world, but, so far as he can, to keep himself unspotted by it. Somehow (if I may repeat what certainly deserves repeating)* I cannot escape the conviction that those words come as directly from Shakespeare's own heart as from the Bastard's, that he too meant to deliver

> Sweet, sweet, sweet poison for the age's tooth.

And so the Bastard's dedication of himself to the worship of Gain is found to be a sort of inverted hypocrisy.

There is nothing inverted about the hypocrisy of the genuine worshipers of Commodity in the play. King John is too weak a man to be the perfect

* See p. 62.

representative of this Devil. That honor falls to Cardinal Pandulph, the papal legate, arch power-politician of the play, one of the first and one of the worst of the corrupt ecclesiastics of whom there are so many in Shakespeare's works. He is a perfect preview of some of the totalitarians of our time. The contrast between him and the Bastard is if anything even more striking than that between the Bastard and John. If ever the style was the man, and if ever two styles were at opposite poles, it is the style of the Cardinal and the style of the Bastard. Neither can utter a line without characterizing himself. A long quotation is needed to give the full flavor of Pandulph's casuistry and verbosity, but these devious and cacophonous sentences from one of his endless, sinuous speeches will have to suffice:

> The better act of purposes mistook
> Is to mistake again; though indirect,
> Yet indirection thereby grows direct,
> And falsehood falsehood cures, as fire cools fire
> Within the scorched veins of one new-burn'd.
> It is religion that doth make vows kept;
> But thou hast sworn against religion
> By what thou swear'st, against the thing thou swear'st,
> And mak'st an oath the surety for thy truth
> Against an oath: the truth thou art unsure
> To swear, swears only not to be forsworn;
> Else what a mockery should it be to swear!
> But thou dost swear only to be forsworn;
> And most forsworn, to keep what thou dost swear.

"Zounds!" we are tempted to cry with the Bastard (as he put it on another occasion),

> 'Zounds! I was never so bethump'd with words
> Since I first call'd my brother's father dad,

lines which may serve as a good example of *his* style: always vernacular, and never a polysyllable where a monosyllable will serve as well.

Interesting as he is, to analyze Pandulph in detail would be superfluous. It is enough to say that he anticipates and rolls into one two of Shakespeare's most famous characters: Polonius and Iago. Iago and Polonius! could there be a more dreadful mixture? Pandulph's profession is turning not only every weakness and slip, but every virtue of other men to his advantage.

> 'Tis wonderful
> What may be wrought out of their discontent.

The gusto of that needs but another turn of the screw to transform it into Iago's

> So will I turn her virtue into pitch,
> And out of her own goodness make the net
> That shall enmesh them all.

And the cynicism of

> How green you are and fresh in this old world!

has the exact accent of Shakespeare's supreme villain when talking with Roderigo. Similarly, the voice, as well as the mental and moral attitude, of Polonius can be caught in

> though indirect,
> Yet indirection thereby grows direct,

down even to the very words:

> By indirections find directions out.

Almost literally Pandulph may be said to have "split" into Polonius and Iago. It is a good example of what I have called the embryological character of Shakespeare's early works.

Shakespeare carries his central theme into still other parts of his play. The mainspring of *King John* is the rivalry of two jealous women—mothers ambitious for their sons—Elinor for John, who holds the English throne, and Constance for Arthur, who is legitimate heir to it, being the son of John's deceased older brother Geffrey. The poet sharpens the difference between these two women into one more of the high contrasts in which the play abounds. Elinor is a power-politician in her own right, and her ambition is selfish and worldly, not primarily maternal. The completeness with which she has crushed her son's individuality is proof of this. The ambition of Constance, on the other hand, is maternal, the woman's hero-worship of her son. Extravagant as it is, and sentimental or even touched with madness as her grief becomes at Arthur's death, it is human and forgivable, whereas Elinor's machinations are cold and deliberate. Once more, Nature with all her faults looks lovely compared with Commodity.

In addition to the Bastard and the Mother, there is a third representative of Nature in the play, the Child. In spite of a number of conceits that mar his role (touches that a few years later the poet would not have been guilty of), Arthur is one of the most effective portrayals of childhood Shakespeare ever achieved, and the scene in which his innocence and trust overcome

Hubert's temptation to do a dastardly deed for the King, who wants Arthur put out of the way, is the emotional climax of the play. Unlike practically all its other characters, who are on the side either of Commodity or of Truth, Hubert trembles for a moment on the brink of the World and then, under the child's influence, turns his back on temptation and is saved. It is a tribute to the Bastard's psychological insight that he accepts Hubert's protestations of innocence in the face of the most damning circumstantial evidence of his guilt.

Emergencies winnow the weak from the strong. At the end of the play, when the French invade England, John, who since Arthur's death by accident has been in a panic, resigns all power to the Bastard:

> Have thou the ordering of this present time,

and the latter, almost single-handed, holds the enemy in check until Nature, ever impartial in such conflicts, has her say. The sea swallows half the English force and all the French supplies. Pandulph brings an overture of peace from the French.

> The Cardinal Pandulph is within at rest,
> Who half an hour since came from the Dauphin,

is the way the announcement is made. That nap of the Cardinal's tells us as nothing else could of the pressure he has brought to bear on the previously recalcitrant Lewis and of the assurance he has of its results. The Bastard is wary enough to keep on a war footing while the peace is being arranged.

Meanwhile, King John, poisoned by a monk, has come to an ignominious end. Yet in his last speeches a kind of despairing poetry breaks from him that is a measure perhaps of what nature in vain intended him to be. His last words are "confounded royalty."

It was the Elizabethan custom to give the final lines of a play to the man of highest rank. In breaking that custom and putting the last words of *King John* into the mouth of the Bastard rather than of Prince Henry, who, save for his formal coronation, is now King Henry III, Shakespeare clinches the fact that the Bastard is the king of the play. And in the speech itself, particularly in its last line, and most particularly in its last word, he confirms its main theme: Truth or Commodity. Few, if any, of Shakespeare's plays have a finer ending. It is like the note of a trumpet:

> Come the three corners of the world in arms,
> And we shall shock them. Naught shall make us rue,
> If England to itself do rest but true.

Shakespeare has often been criticized for omitting all reference in this play to what historians and political scientists consider the main event of John's reign: the granting of Magna Carta. Yet how trivial the exaction of that compact from John was compared with the everlasting conflict between Truth and Commodity that Shakespeare records so powerfully in this drama. Perhaps education will some day revert to a perception of what was so like an axiom to Shakespeare: that psychology goes deeper than politics and that a knowledge of man himself must precede any fruitful consideration of the institutions he has created.

*Chapter XV*

# Richard II

I

Nobody knows whether *King John* or *Richard II* was written first. It is more natural to suppose that Shakespeare went on from *Richard II* to *Henry IV*, which is a continuation of the same story, than back to *King John*, whose connection with the later chronicle plays is thematic rather than historical. He may possibly have been working on the two pieces at the same time. At any rate they are built on the same contrast of a weak king with a strong man. But the effect is entirely different. Richard, though weak, is no nonentity like John, but a man of unusual, though perverted, gifts. And Henry Bolingbroke, though strong, is not loyal and true like the Bastard, but selfish and calculating, as cold as Faulconbridge is warm, as hard as he is human. No one could conceivably prefer John to Faulconbridge. But anyone with a distaste for a combination of worldliness and intelligence will prefer even the sentimental Richard, with all his sins, to the shrewd Henry with all his success. The naïve reader, encountering this play for the first time, is inclined to give Henry the benefit of the doubt and think that he came back to England from his banishment merely to recover his inheritance, not with his eye on the crown. But no one can believe that for a second when he reads the rest of the story. The four plays of which this is the first make a single work of art in four parts, and should be so taken.

The character of Richard II is the most minute and extended, and in many ways the most subtle piece of psychological analysis that Shakespeare had made up to this time. It is a study in fantasy. Over and over, critics have spoken of Richard's imagination. But it is not imagination that he possesses; it is only the raw material of imagination. All young men with a poetical gift pass into a stage when they are hypnotized by words. They have not yet grasped the relation between verbal symbols and life. Many never pass out of that stage. Shakespeare's two long poems, and passages in his other early works, show the affluence of his fancy. He was threatened by its very abundance. In a sense Shakespeare may be said to have faced this danger in Richard II and subdued it. His portrayal may well have meant a kind of catharsis for the poet. Many readers detect a kinship between Richard and his creator, as they do between Richard and Hamlet. His love of words and his gift of figurative expression are undoubtedly a main source of this impression. Before *Richard II*, Shakespeare himself occasionally confused imagination with "imagination." After *Richard II*, he seldom or never did.

## II

All through the play it is implied that Richard's personal appearance is attractive but a bit effeminate. His wife speaks of him as her "fair rose." He was a rose potentially. But he was blasted in the bud—blasted by royalty, we might say, for he was as hopelessly miscast for the role of king as a maiden of fifteen would be for the part of Lady Macbeth or a lame man of eighty for that of Ariel. Richard II did his best. But as Samuel Butler once remarked: "What does a fish's best amount to out of water?"

"Woe to the land when the king is a child," cried Richard's contemporary Langland, quoting Ecclesiastes, in *Piers the Plowman*. Richard came to the throne at the age of ten. What more natural for a child who knows he is to inherit a throne than to play at being king, or for a sensitive and poetic youth who wears a crown—while others govern in his name—to go on conceiving life as a brilliant spectacle of which he is the center? And, once it is ingrained, how easy to maintain this attitude beyond the time when most men shed their illusions. There is nothing in the text of Shakespeare's play to prove that this was the basis of Richard's weakness, and it is not permissible to go beyond the text in the elucidation of a character. Nevertheless, the fact remains that Shakespeare's Richard was just the sort of man that this kind of childhood might have produced. He went on playing king until he was deposed. Right here lies the difference between Richard and Henry VI, two who have often been loosely coupled as "weak kings." Henry had the sense to realize his limitations, to stand on the sidelines as it were and let his simplicity, honesty, bravery, and piety have what effect they could; whereas Richard fooled himself into thinking he was born to be a king and made a mess of the kingdom and himself, the mess a man always makes when he accepts a role for which he does not know that he is not fitted.

Shakespeare was to show many men in a like position before he was done. So this first detailed analysis of one of this type is of quite special interest.

## III

Henry, Duke of Hereford, surnamed Bolingbroke, son of John of Gaunt, and later King Henry IV, accuses Thomas Mowbray, Duke of Norfolk, of murdering the Duke of Gloucester, uncle of both Richard and Henry, and challenges him to a duel. Richard, in words that sound pacific and Christian, begs the two men to forget and forgive. But they refuse to be reconciled and on the appointed day are about to begin combat when the King throws down his warder, calls off the duel, and banishes both men from the kingdom, Bolingbroke for a decade, Mowbray for life, though a little later he reduces the former's sentence by four years.

Thus Richard averts violence and acts, apparently, as a friend of peace. But examine the matter and the exact opposite turns out to be the fact. Here was the moment when the destiny of England for a century or more was being decided, and Shakespeare makes clear that hypocrisy, lying, and fear can be worse enemies of peace even than bloodshed. For Richard was himself not guiltless in the matter of Gloucester's death, the ostensible occasion of the quarrel. His show of impartiality, therefore, was pure sham. It was fear, not love of peace, that led him to call off the duel in an attempt to solve an ugly problem by the easy device of pushing it out of sight. There were both bad conscience and bad judgment in the discrepancy between the two sentences, and when he cut the lesser one from ten years to six what looked like mercy was a sense of guilt. By this bit of cowardice Richard not only sealed his own doom, but initiated that century of feuds and quarrels which culminated in the Wars of the Roses.

> O, when the king did throw his warder down,
> His own life hung upon the staff he threw;
> Then threw he down himself and all their lives
> That by indictment and by dint of sword
> Have since miscarried under Bolingbroke.

So, many years later (in *II Henry IV*), cries the young Mowbray, son of the man Richard had banished. And even then the national chaos was nearer its beginning than its end. In so far as things historical have any beginning, it was in the murder of Gloucester and the resulting fears and lies of Richard that the young Shakespeare found the answer to the question that the three Henry VI plays had inevitably propounded: How had these things come to be?

"The evil that men do lives after them." Anyone will assent to the proposition in abstract form—and be little impressed. But demonstrated as it is in these History Plays in dozens of scenes extending over thousands of lines with all the particulars presented, the abstraction becomes an overwhelming reality. With the aftermath of the moment in mind it is interesting to examine the words Richard speaks to the two dukes after he has called off their duel:

> Draw near,
> And list what with our council we have done.
> For that our kingdom's earth should not be soil'd
> With that dear blood which it hath fostered;
> And for our eyes do hate the dire aspect
> Of civil wounds plough'd up with neighbours' sword;
> And for we think the eagle-winged pride
> Of sky-aspiring and ambitious thoughts,
> With rival-hating envy, set on you
> To wake our peace, which in our country's cradle
> Draws the sweet infant breath of gentle sleep;
> Which so rous'd up with boist'rous untun'd drums,
> With harsh-resounding trumpets' dreadful bray,
> And grating shock of wrathful iron arms,
> Might from our quiet confines fright fair peace
> And make us wade even in our kindred's blood;
> Therefore, we banish you our territories:
> You, cousin Hereford, upon pain of life,
> Till twice five summers have enrich'd our fields
> Shall not regreet our fair dominions,
> But tread the stranger paths of banishment.

What a denunciation of war! What an appeal for peace! ... And not one word of it sincere! The tortuously long sentence, the involved construction, the piled-up relative clauses, the pronouns with ambiguous antecedents, the excess of hyphenated adjectives, all go to show how a poetically gifted but mentally dishonest and frightened man expresses himself when he opens his mouth and lets what will come come. Examine the speech, and it falls to pieces like the pack of—words that it is.

The central figure is that of Peace, an infant, asleep in its cradle, England. But why should a professed lover of tranquility like Richard wish to keep peace asleep? Obviously, when peace sleeps, war and domestic turmoil have their chance. Don't awaken peace, says Richard, lest she frighten out of our land ... and to our logical consternation we discover that what this aroused infant peace is to scare into exile is, of all things, peace itself!

> To wake our peace ...
> Which ...
> Might from our quiet confines fright fair peace.

Subject and object the same! The verbiage between almost conceals that fact. It is amusing to behold scholars with more linguistic learning than psychological insight laboring, with contortions almost equal to Richard's, to bring some sense and logic into what Shakespeare only too plainly made senseless and logicless on purpose. If rhetoric is the art of saying nothing finely, Richard proves himself an arch-rhetorician. He himself speaks a little later of adders that lurk under flowers. So do cowardice and injustice lurk under Richard's flowery words, as appears a moment later in his banishment of Bolingbroke and Mowbray. It is fear of John of Gaunt, possessor of unpleasant secrets, that leads him to mitigate the sentence of his son. But he compensates in the next scene for this act of "mercy" by praying God to put it in the mind of the old man's physician

> To help him to his grave immediately,

while he, Richard, confiscates his property. So close do violent thoughts follow "pitiful" ones.

Compared with such a man, an honest fighter like Faulconbridge is an angel of peace. And so Richard's senseless speech about the infant Peace in its cradle makes sense after all. But it is Shakespeare's sense, not Richard's. The King's predicate, because of the verbal meanderings that lay between, forgot its subject. But Shakespeare takes Richard's rhetoric—falsehood, cowardice, mixed metaphors, bad grammar and all—and turns it into truth from the gods themselves. "Peace" will indeed frighten peace out of England. It did for a century on this occasion. It did in our own day when an English leader in a difficult position thought he had purchased "peace in our time" by a similar act of fear.

IV

The problem Richard turns his back on by the device of banishment returns to plague him when Henry, while Richard is in Ireland, comes home with powerful forces and claims the inheritance which the King has stolen from his father, Gaunt. Shakespeare converts Richard's reaction to this situation into a ruthless reduction to the absurd of the doctrine of the divine right of kings. There is another doctrine of divine right in which the poet believes with all his heart. But the feudal doctrine in its debased form he so riddles with scorn in this play that not a shred is left of it.

The feudal doctrine in its undebased form conceived of God as a Heavenly Father from whom humanity derives life as nature does from the sun. But in practice this conception quickly reverted to the patriarchal idea of

{ 152 }

the Father as absolute monarch, who exacts servile submission. Richard falls back on a sentimentalized perversion of this conception when menaced by Bolingbroke. He acts like a small boy who, bullied by a big one, takes refuge in his mother's arms and threatens his enemy with what his father will do to him. So exactly is it that that one can't help thinking Shakespeare had that very analogy in mind. On reaching his native soil Richard is dissolved in tears. He stoops down to kiss his mother earth and calls on its spiders, toads, and adders to bring death to his foes. The very stones, he prophesies, will rise like soldiers to put down rebellion.

The Bishop of Carlisle, one of Shakespeare's few high churchmen of high character, punctures this egoistic fatalism at a stroke:

> Fear not, my lord: that power that made you king
> Hath power to keep you king in spite of all.
> The means that heaven yields must be embrac'd,
> And not neglected; else, if heaven would,
> And we will not, heaven's offer we refuse,
> The proffer'd means of succour and redress.

Cromwell's "Trust God and keep your powder dry," and another Poor Richard's "God helps those who help themselves," come to mind. But the Bishop has made no dent in the emotional armor of the young king. Having sentimentalized earth as mother, he proceeds to sentimentalize heaven as father. God becomes a sort of combined Celestial Recruiting Officer and Commander-in-Chief who will do the fighting for him with an army of angels:

> For every man that Bolingbroke hath press'd
> To lift shrewd steel against our golden crown,
> God for his Richard hath in heavenly pay
> A glorious angel; then, if angels fight,
> Weak men must fall, for heaven still guards the right.

Richard, of course, stresses "men" in that last line in contrast with "angels," having Bolingbroke and himself in mind. But Shakespeare, in an overtone, stresses "weak," and thereby prophesies this weak man's fall. It is a perfect example of an effect that cannot be attained in the theater, for the actor naturally must speak the line as Richard would have. But the imagination of the reader can hear the line in both ways simultaneously. "A pen has so many inflections," says Emily Dickinson, "a voice but one."

The long passage* from which these five lines are taken is as absurd a

---

* I append it here for any who may not remember it:
> "Discomfortable cousin! know'st thou not
> That when the searching eye of heaven is hid
> Behind the globe, and lights the lower world,

philosophy of war as the one about the infant asleep in its cradle was of peace. It is a sort of effeminate inversion of Napoleon's "God fights on the side of the strongest battalions." Richard's emotional ups and downs in the scene that follows betoken his neurotic condition. When he finally faces Henry, and the armies of stones and angels on which he had depended do not appear, he is in the situation of Blake's "little boy lost" whose father turns out to be a vapor. So, drowning himself in an orgy of self-pity, Richard proceeds to uncrown himself. For that is what it amounts to. Northumberland comes to summon him to a conference with Bolingbroke:

> NORTH.: My lord, in the base court he doth attend
> To speak with you; may it please you to come down.
> K. RICH.: Down, down I come; like glist'ring Phaethon,
> Wanting the manage of unruly jades.
> In the base court? Base court, where kings grow base,
> To come at traitors' calls and do them grace.
> In the base court? Come down? Down, court! down, king!
> For night-owls shriek where mounting larks should sing.

*Undone by a pun* might be a succinct description of what happens. And the stage direction, confirming the symbolism, is *Exeunt from above*.

The King's consent to come down is the crisis of the play, exactly as Richard III's descent from the throne was in a very different situation. The interpretations confirm each other. (Shakespeare is forever giving this symbolic implication to his upper and lower stages.) Bolingbroke, with

> Then thieves and robbers range abroad unseen
> In murders and in outrage, boldly here;
> But when from under this terrestrial ball
> He fires the proud tops of the eastern pines
> And darts his light through every guilty hole,
> Then murders, treasons, and detested sins,
> The cloak of night being pluck'd from off their backs,
> Stand bare and naked, trembling at themselves?
> So when this thief, this traitor, Bolingbroke,
> Who all this while hath revell'd in the night
> Whilst we were wand'ring with the antipodes,
> Shall see us rising in our throne, the east,
> His treasons will sit blushing in his face,
> Not able to endure the sight of day,
> But, self-affrighted, tremble at his sin.
> Not all the water in the rough rude sea
> Can wash the balm from an anointed king;
> The breath of worldly men cannot depose
> The deputy elected by the Lord.
> For every man that Bolingbroke hath press'd
> To lift shrewd steel against our golden crown,
> God for his Richard hath in heavenly pay
> A glorious angel; then, if angels fight,
> Weak men must fall, for heaven still guards the right."

mock humility, falls on his knees before the King, but Richard, with the word "base" still ringing in his ears, begs him, in tones of sentimental sarcasm, to rise:

> Fair cousin, you debase your princely knee
> To make the base earth proud with kissing it . . .
> Up, cousin, up; your heart is up, I know,
> Thus high at least, although your knee be low.

Obviously Richard touches his crown to indicate the level of his cousin's aspiration.

> My gracious lord, I come but for mine own,

protests Henry.

Richard instantly puts the worst construction on this ambiguous utterance:

> Your own is yours, and I am yours, and all.

It is the abjectest of surrenders. Yet, even after it, Bolingbroke can say, though still enigmatically:

> So far be mine, my most redoubted lord,
> As my true service shall deserve your love.

But one thing remains to complete Richard's ignominy. Having begun his abdication with a pun, he ends it with a rhetorical question:

> What you will have, I'll give, and willing too;
> For do we must what force will have us do.
> Set on towards London, cousin, is it so?

(London of course meaning the Tower.)

Bol.: Yea, my good lord.
K. Rich.:                    Then I must not say no.

Though Bolingbroke was bent on getting the crown in the end, if Richard had not practically placed it on his head he might very well have asked no more at the moment than the restitution of his inheritance. There is nothing more provocative of violence than the dread of violence. The shrinking victim evokes a devil in the victor. The more Richard cowers, the more Henry tightens the screws. It is a vivid demonstration of the truth that fear and force are poles of a single entity. If a whirlwind meets a vacuum it naturally rushes into it. So force, into fear. Fear is as creative as faith. It brings into being what it imagines. The evil that stained the life of Henry IV from this day on was in no small measure of Richard's making.

## V

The fourth act, like the first, opens with a quarrel. This one is over the responsibility for Gloucester's death. But Henry, not Richard, is now arbitrator and he handles the situation very differently. York brings word that the "plume-pluck'd" King adopts Bolingbroke as his heir, and the latter is about to ascend the throne when the Bishop of Carlisle stands up in protest. Even thieves, he points out, are allowed to be present when they are judged. Will you dethrone a king in his own absence? He calls Henry what he is, a traitor. If he is crowned, prophesies Carlisle,

> Peace shall go sleep with Turks and infidels,

and he foresees, as in a vision, the chaos which the Wars of the Roses were soon to bring to England. The courage and directness of his utterance inevitably bring to mind the indirectness and cowardice of Pandulph, in *King John.* As that Cardinal's chicaneries were crowned with worldly success, so this Bishop's courage is rewarded with instant arrest for treason. Such is the relation of usurpers to the truth.

But Carlisle has at least convinced Henry that Richard must go through a more formal and public abdication. The theft must be legalized. So the deposed King is summoned, and in a spectacular scene (which had the distinction of being cut out of all editions of the play published in Elizabeth's lifetime) he degrades himself with all the elaboration of simile, metaphor, and symbol that was to be expected from a king whom nature intended to be a poet. The skill with which Shakespeare uses the figures of fire and water all through the play here comes to a climax. Because he was king and because of his personal beauty, Richard has been identified with fire and the sun. Bolingbroke, with mock humility, accepts the role of water. He knows what generally happens when those elements encounter:

> Methinks King Richard and myself should meet
> With no less terror than the elements
> Of fire and water, when their thundering shock
> At meeting tears the cloudy cheeks of heaven.
> Be he the fire, I'll be the yielding water.

That was earlier. Now, with Richard's tears, the metaphors begin to shift.

> Are you contented to resign the crown?

asks Henry.

> Ay, no; no, ay,

answers the wavering Richard, summing himself up in four words. But his hesitation is purely histrionic.

Now mark me, how I will undo myself,

he cries, and proceeds to do so:

> With mine own tears I wash away my balm,
> With mine own hands I give away my crown . . .
> Though some of you with Pilate wash your hands
> Showing an outward pity; yet you Pilates
> Have here deliver'd me to my sour cross,
> And water cannot wash away your sin. . . .
> Mine eyes are full of tears, I cannot see;
> And yet salt water blinds them not so much
> But they can see a sort of traitors here. . . .
> O that I were a mockery king of snow,
> Standing before the sun of Bolingbroke,
> To melt myself away in water-drops!

Fire and water have exchanged places. He who, as king, thought of himself almost as God, now, as martyr, identifies himself with Christ. He calls for a mirror. It is the best symbol in the play for this Narcissus-King. The mirror is brought and he gazes at the face that once made beholders blink as at the sun. In rage he shatters the glass against the ground:

> How soon my sorrow hath destroy'd my face.

> The shadow of your sorrow hath destroy'd
> The shadow of your face,

says Henry. Richard has been indeed a shadow-king. A moment later he is on his way to the Tower.

## VI

With Richard's deposition our sympathy shifts. Now he is underdog. Now we see the Queen's "fair rose" wither, hear of the dust and rubbish that a fickle populace cast from windows on his head after roaring applause at the sight of his successor. But it is not just pity that we feel. Our respect for Richard rises also, for, uncrowned, he is free to be a man instead of a king. (The theme of *King John* again.) He learns through suffering, and though much of what he says is still vitiated by self-pity, he foresees, like Carlisle, the trouble in store for England and the house of Lancaster. His prophecy, beginning

> Northumberland, thou ladder wherewithal
> The mounting Bolingbroke ascends my throne,

was soon to be fulfilled.

In the last act, before the catastrophe, Shakespeare inserts a little tragi-comedy in which three members of the York family and the new king are actors. Such a diversion of interest so near the end looks questionable. But Shakespeare's digressions are anything but digressions. York, Richard's uncle and Henry's, regent during Richard's absence in Ireland, has given his pledge in Parliament for the fealty to the new king of his son, Aumerle, who is suspect because of his friendship for Richard and his part in the Duke of Gloucester's death. When York discovers that Aumerle has entered a conspiracy to kill the King, he dashes off, followed by his wife in frantic protest, to expose the villain and demand his death. He finds him on his knees before Henry asking pardon. The immediate motives of the four actors in this little drama are plain enough. But behind each is a deeper fear or sense of guilt for which he is compensating. Back of Aumerle's concern for his life is his part in Gloucester's death. Back of the Duchess's mother-love is a dread that her husband thinks her unfaithful. Back of York's regard for his pledged word is his treachery to Richard when he was regent. "Fear, and not love, begets his penitence," he cries to the King. He might have been speaking of himself. He has projected his own sense of guilt on his son and demands for him the penalty he will not admit he himself deserves. But it is the King's conduct that is most interesting. Why does he pardon the man who has conspired against his life? It is not mercy. It is an attempted purchase of indulgence in advance for the murder of Richard, against whose life he is conspiring, precisely as his sparing of Carlisle's life is a begging of indulgence after that deed. These scenes are a series of unconscious confessions, variations on the same theme of fear and the compensation for fear of which Richard's own life is one long embodiment. Shakespeare composes like a musician. There is more than meets the ear at a first hearing. He is here exhibiting in action precisely those hidden impulses that modern psychology is now attempting to analyze and formulate.

## VII

Richard, taken, ominously, not to the Tower as announced but to the dungeon of Pomfret castle, soliloquizes on this very theme of compensation:

> I have been studying how I may compare
> This prison where I live unto the world. . . .

It is as if Hamlet were being born under our very eyes—one of the Hamlets, that is, the Jaques-Hamlet. And when music penetrates Richard's cell there are even premonitions of *King Lear*:

> This music mads me; let it sound no more;
> For though it have holp madmen to their wits,
> In me it seems it will make wise men mad.

Richard is in a dreamy, meditative, yet subtly irritated frame of mind. But the philosophizing mood (again precisely as with Hamlet) is followed by the lightning bolt of passion in which the scene ends: Richard kills two of the attendants of the man who has come to murder him before their master can strike him down. In this one flash of action Shakespeare recapitulates and condenses the meaning of the play.

> The lion dying thrusteth forth his paw,
> And wounds the earth, if nothing else, with rage
> To be o'erpower'd.

Such was his Queen's reproach to Richard for his weakness, when she parted from him for the last time. She would have applauded his translation of her analogy into action at his death. Does Shakespeare?

The plain implication of the play up to this point has been that a sentimental pacifism is nothing but violence in disguise and is likely to be converted into it at a moment's notice. The death scene of Richard is a stunning translation of that truth into act. How little trust Richard placed in non-resistance and divine aid is revealed, first, when he strikes his keeper:

> The devil take Henry of Lancaster, and thee!
> Patience is stale, and I am weary of it,

and, again, a moment later, when he kills the two attendants, crying to one of them as he strikes him down:

> Go thou, and fill another room in hell.

"O, God forgive my sins, and pardon thee!" were the words with which Henry VI took leave of his murderer and the world.

Strangely, Richard's ultimate act has often been admired as bravery, a final burst of courage from a coward. It is nothing of the sort. We die as we have lived. It is just the reflex action of a man without self-control in the presence of death, as little willed as the galvanic twitching of a frog's leg. It is a fury of desperation pure and simple, a particularly ignominious and ironic end for a king who pretended to believe that everything from stones to angels would come to his rescue in the hour of need.

But if Shakespeare condemned Richard's version of divine right, he had just as little use for Henry's doctrine of the strong man. Where that doctrine leads, the rest of the History Plays reveal.

Is there no other way? Is there nothing between the feudal idea and the revolutionary practice that sought to replace it?

Yes, in a little scene that seems utterly incidental, Shakespeare characteristically drops a hint. Between the doctrine of legitimacy and the belief that he who can seize and hold power is entitled to it, there appears to be no resting place except in something resembling what we now call democracy. In a poetic rather than in a strictly political sense there are intimations of democracy in this seemingly casual scene.

A gardener and his two servants discuss the impending changes in the state, while Richard's Queen overhears them from the shadows of neighboring trees. The three are clearly put in to contrast with the murderer and his two assistants in the final scene. Gardeners and murderers—agents of life and death.

> O, what pity is it,

says the Head Gardener, of Richard,

> That he had not so trimm'd and dress'd his land
> As we this garden! . . .
> Had he done so, himself had borne the crown,
> Which waste of idle hours hath quite thrown down.

England is compared in so many words to a sea-walled garden, and political and social analogies are found for all the horticultural activities: for the tender care of the gardener himself, the fertilizing, the weeding, the pruning, the killing of insects. Inordinate ambition in particular must be restrained:

> All must be even in our government.

The good gardener, by submitting himself to the creative forces of nature, but checking them where they grow excessive or unfruitful, becomes a creator himself. A good ruler, it is intimated, is like a good gardener, participating in the fructifying activities of his kingdom instead of merely standing off and watching them, interfering with them, or expecting them to intervene in his behalf in an emergency. Here, in a metaphor, is suggested an everlasting divine right of kings and men alike. It comes from simple workers with imagination enough to extend their own experience and vocation into a political analogy. This is a faith that Shakespeare never abandoned. It is central in *Cymbeline*, for instance, one of his latest plays. Whoever would understand Shakespeare's political philosophy may well meditate on the life of Richard II and on the reasons why, where he failed, his gardeners succeeded.

*Chapter XVI*

# Henry IV

I

The two parts of *King Henry IV* are really a single drama in ten acts. Indeed the best things in Part II are invisible when it stands by itself, more proof, if any were needed, that Shakespeare did not think in purely theatrical terms, for staging the two parts as one play must always have been impracticable, and the second part has seldom been produced in our day.

The richness and complexity of this double drama may be seen in the fact that any one of three men may with reason be regarded as its central figure. If we think of it as a continuation of the story of Henry Bolingbroke who deposed and murdered Richard II, then King Henry IV, as the title implies, is the protagonist. If we conceive it as background and preface to *Henry V*, Prince Hal is central. But if we just give ourselves to it spontaneously as the spectator or naïve reader does, the chances are that the comic element will overbalance the historical. Sir John runs away with us as some critics think he did with the author. In that case these are "the Falstaff plays," and Falstaff himself the most important as he certainly is the most captivating figure in them. By stretching a point we might even find a fourth "hero": there have been productions of Part I in which Hotspur has outshone the other three. But that must have been a chance of casting, or miscasting.

II

In *Richard II* Shakespeare interred the doctrine of the divine right of kings. In *Henry IV* he tries out what can be said for the opposing theory. The twentieth century has fought two wars at enormous cost of life and treasure to avert the threat of the "strong" man. It is a pity that it could not have paid more attention in advance to Shakespeare's analysis and annihilation of this type and theory in his History Plays, particularly to the story of King Henry IV. Richard III was a "strong man" melodramatically represented. Pandulph, arch-power-politician of *King John*, was another, done closer to life. But compared with Henry IV either of these was a stage Machiavel with the label "Villain" on his sleeve. Henry, whatever he became, was natively neither cruel nor tyrannical, but a man of intelligence and insight and not devoid of a sense of justice. His story for that reason approximates tragedy.

The hypocrite has always been a favorite subject of satire. Henry IV is one of the most subtly drawn and effective hypocrites in literature, in no small measure because the author keeps his portrayal free of any satirical note. But not of any ironical note. Richard II had done Henry an injustice in banishing him and confiscating his inheritance. Coming back, the exile discovers that the opportunity to right his personal wrongs coincides with the chance to rid his native land of a weak king. So he finds himself ascending the throne almost before he knows it. Or so at least he protests later.

> Though then, God knows, I had no such intent,
> But that necessity so bow'd the state
> That I and greatness were compell'd to kiss.

"Necessity, the tyrant's plea." As previously in *The Rape of Lucrece*, as later in *Macbeth*, as so often in all literature from Aeschylus to Dostoevsky, opportunity is here made the mother of crime. And the punishment, though delayed outwardly, inwardly is immediate. It comes in the form of fear. Confirming a change that had long been in incubation, on the day when Henry deposed Richard he became a double man, one thing to the world, another to his own conscience. Force gives birth to fear. Fear gives birth to lies. And fear and lies together give birth to more force. Richard, symbol of Henry's own unjust act, had to be put out of the way. From the moment Henry gave the hint that ended in Richard's death to the moment of his own death at the end of *II Henry IV*, his life became a continuous embodiment of the strange law whereby we come to resemble what we fear. The basis of that law is plain. What we are afraid of we keep in mind. What we keep in mind we grow like unto.

Already at the conclusion of the play that bears Richard's name that nemesis had begun to work. Near its beginning Richard banished two men, Henry and Mowbray, who were symbols of his own fear and guilt. He wanted them out of his sight. At the end of the same play Henry does the same thing. He banishes Carlisle and Exton. He wants them out of his sight

—Carlisle because he is a symbol of truth and loyalty to Richard, Exton because he has been his instrument in Richard's murder.

Shakespeare dramatizes these ideas with impressive brevity and power. Unknown to Henry, the coffin containing Richard's body is at the door. It is as if the victim's ghost rises then and there from the dead and as if Henry, sensing its nearness, spares Carlisle's life in hope of indulgence. But to grant the Bishop a full pardon is beyond his power, for he could not endure the perpetual accusation and conviction of his presence. So he tells him to

> Choose out some secret place, some reverend room,

in which to spend the rest of his life. (It is like a prophecy of the Jerusalem Chamber in which Henry's own life was to end.) At that moment Exton enters, "*with Attendants bearing a coffin*," and announces:

> Great king, within this coffin I present
> Thy buried fear.

By "buried fear" Exton of course means "the body of the man you feared." But the future reads into those three words another and more fearful meaning. It was indeed a buried fear, a fear buried deep in Henry's breast, that that coffin contained, a fear that was to shape every act and almost every thought of that "great king" henceforth. The spirit of the man who had once banished him and whom he had deposed enters his body and deposes and banishes his own spirit. When Henry bids Exton

> With Cain go wander through the shades of night,

it is to his own soul that, unawares, he issues that order. The later soliloquy on sleep shows through what shades of night that soul was destined to wander. From the moment he mentions the name of Cain, Henry's story is the story of the buried Richard within him:

> Lords, I protest, my soul is full of woe,
> That blood should sprinkle me to make me grow.

We do not need to wait for *Hamlet* to know that Henry "doth protest too much." It is not a protest but a confession. And to compensate for his crime in the eyes of the world, he decrees

> a voyage to the Holy Land,
> To wash this blood off from my guilty hand.

### III

*I Henry IV* opens with a proclamation of peace and a definite proposal of the promised crusade to the sepulcher of Christ:

> To chase these pagans in those holy fields
> Over whose acres walk'd those blessed feet
> Which fourteen hundred years ago were nail'd
> For our advantage on the bitter cross.

It must have seemed to the pagans an odd way of instituting peace. But pagans of course did not count as human beings to Henry. There sounds, however, a note of something like genuine contrition in the reference to Christ. Yet, on his deathbed, Henry was to confess explicitly that this crusade was a purely political move to distract attention from civil unrest!

For the usual thing had happened. The men who helped Henry to the throne (the Percys) grew envious of the power they did not share and of his friendship:

> The king will always think him in our debt,
> And think we think ourselves unsatisfied,
> Till he hath found a time to pay us home.

This suspicion, reciprocated, led to acts on both sides that put foundations under it with the result that Henry's reign, where it was not open war, was incessant dissension.

Henry has no sooner declared the end of "civil butchery" in the opening speech of the play than a messenger from Wales enters announcing a thousand men "butcher'd" by the wild and irregular Glendower. And on the heels of this, news from Scotland: Hotspur has met and defeated the Scots. Ten thousand of them slain, and prisoners taken. But their captor refuses to hand them over to the King! This must be looked into. The pilgrimage to Jerusalem must be postponed.

A bit later the King confronts the Percys: father, son, and uncle. He declares that he has been too forbearing in the past, "smooth as oil, soft as young down," and implies that from now on he will demand the respect due him. Worcester bids him remember who helped him to his throne. To which the King retorts:

> Worcester, get thee gone; for I do see
> Danger and disobedience in thine eye.

The ghost of Richard again! Henry solving a problem by pushing it out of sight, doing to his enemy exactly what Richard did to him! The "buried fear" is stirring in its grave.

And the King's self-control is in for an even more severe jolt. Hotspur refuses to give up his prisoners unless his brother-in-law, Mortimer, who has been captured by the Welshman Glendower, shall be ransomed. At the mention of Mortimer something seems to explode inside the King:

> Let me not hear you speak of Mortimer;
> Send me your prisoners with the speediest means
> Or you shall hear in such a kind from me
> As will displease you.

Can this be Henry? The tone, so unlike him, shows that the name of Mortimer has touched something at the very foundation of his nature. When the King, in high dudgeon, has gone out, Worcester explains. Mortimer is legal heir to the throne: so by right, and so proclaimed by Richard. Of what avail to have had Richard murdered if his title transmigrated into a living man?

This is news to Hotspur. Mortimer! With the diabolic insight of a small boy who has hit on a scheme for teasing his sister, he dances about in an ecstasy and cries:

> I will find him when he lies asleep,
> And in his ear I'll holla "Mortimer!"
> Nay,
> I'll have a starling shall be taught to speak
> Nothing but "Mortimer," and give it him,
> To keep his anger still in motion.

Henry stands revealed to him for the hypocrite he is: a "vile politician," a "fawning greyhound," a "king of smiles."

Forthwith the three Percys hatch a plot to unite under themselves the Scots, the Welsh, and the Archbishop of York and, with Mortimer as the cutting edge, to defy the King. I said that three men, or even four, contend for the primacy in this play. And now we have a fifth. Mortimer is on the stage in only one scene. But he is the play's mainspring as certainly as is the Ghost in *Hamlet*. Shakespeare grew more and more fond of quietly suggesting the immense dramatic importance of figures partly or wholly behind the action, of making the absent present.*

## IV

These Percys, who having made a king now plan to unmake him, are an interesting group. They take up, both singly and together, the theme that

* Shakespeare may have gotten the hint for this technique from painting. Note this stanza from the description of the picture of the Siege of Troy in *The Rape of Lucrece*:

> "For much imaginary work was there;
> Conceit deceitful, so compact, so kind,
> That for Achilles' image stood his spear,
> Gripp'd in an armed hand; himself, behind,
> Was left unseen, save to the eye of mind:
>   A hand, a foot, a face, a leg, a head,
>   Stood for the whole to be imagined."

Richard II introduced and Henry IV continued, and play their variations on it, the theme of fear and lies—and the violence to which they inevitably give rise. Shakespeare seems as bent on getting together every known type of duplicity, counterfeit, and deceit in this play as a boy is on collecting every kind of bird's egg.

The elder Henry, Earl of Northumberland, the main factor in Boling-broke's elevation to the throne, is remembered as the man who in the abdication scene kicked Richard when he was down. Confirming the old proverb about the bully, he is the archcoward of *Henry IV*. He ruins the cause of the rebellion against the King by his fears, his delays, his faking of illness, his running away. While his son is fighting and dying at Shrewsbury, he lies "crafty-sick" in his castle. When his party rallies after its defeat, he starts north for Scotland.

Thomas Percy, Henry's brother, Earl of Worcester, is hardly more attractive. He is a sour, dour, suspicious, and jealous man, envious himself and therefore counting on and helping to create envy in Henry. His concealment from Hotspur of the King's offer of peace before the battle of Shrewsbury is characteristic of him. If his brother is the coward, he is the liar.

And finally there is the younger Henry, "the Hotspur of the North; he that kills me some six or seven dozen of Scots at a breakfast, washes his hands, and says to his wife, 'Fie upon this quiet life! I want work.'" The colorful Hotspur at any rate, it will be said, is in another world from his father and uncle. In one sense he is indeed their utter antithesis. But in another he is more like them than he seems. One cannot help loving Hotspur for his blunt honesty. It seems almost his central quality. And yet his very honesty is based on a lie, a degenerate form of the medieval conception of "honour." The fact that Hotspur talks so incessantly and extravagantly about "honour" shows that he distrusts his own faith in it. He is another who "doth protest too much." This fact is clinched by his uneasy sleep, which his wife reveals. He fights all night long in his dreams. We are reminded of Richard III's "timorous dreams," which *his* wife reveals. Far as the noble Hotspur is from the villainous Richard, the psychology is the same. It is fear begotten by falsehood.

The undegenerate chivalric conception of honor was a lofty one. Under it trial by battle, and war, became religious affairs. Courage and morale were given a religious ground. God was in the right arm of the man whose cause was righteous, and to win under his sanction was to cover oneself with glory, the glory of God himself. But the line between war for God's sake and war for war's sake can become a very thin one to one who enjoys fighting. It does in Hotspur's case. He rationalizes his inborn pugnacity into a creed. War to him is the natural state of man, the noble as well as the royal occupation. It is what art for art's sake is to the artist. He is the extreme antitype of that "certain lord," that "popinjay," who, fresh as a bridegroom, accosted him, when he was breathless and faint from fighting, with the declaration

> that it was great pity, so it was,
> This villanous saltpetre should be digg'd
> Out of the bowels of the harmless earth,
> Which many a good tall fellow had destroy'd
> So cowardly; and but for these vile guns,
> He would himself have been a soldier.

Militarism and pacifism have always had a strange family resemblance, and Hotspur and his popinjay are equally deluded. To put Hotspur beside that other picturesque talker and valiant fighter, Faulconbridge, is to put the "idealism" of war beside its realism, to the immense disadvantage of the former.

But we must be fair to Hotspur. There are plenty of echoes in him of the great tradition from which he comes. When he hears that his father has failed them on the eve of battle, and cries,

> It lends a lustre and more great opinion,
> A larger dare to our great enterprise,

he anticipates the Winston Churchill of 1940. Even finer is his

> the time of life is short;
> To spend that shortness basely were too long.

And when he bids them on the field of Shrewsbury

> Sound all the lofty instruments of war,
> And by that music let us all embrace,

it is as intoxicating as fife and drum to a small boy. But that is the trouble. Hotspur intoxicates himself with "honour," and when "the morning after" comes he is capable of saying, for example, that he would have Prince Hal poisoned with a pot of ale if he weren't afraid that it would please the King, his father. When honor has come to that pass, it is ready to be debunked. Falstaff is on the horizon. When the play is done, there is about as much left of "honour" as there was of the divine right of kings at the end of *Richard II*. In fact the sentimental Richard and the pugnacious Hotspur are closer to each other than they look. They are both the victims of words.

## V

And this brings us to the fourth and last of the Henrys in what are sometimes appropriately called these "Henry" plays: Henry, Prince of Wales, *alias* Harry, *alias* Hal, companion of Falstaff and heir apparent to the throne. His father first introduces us to him in the last act of *Richard II* when he asks,

> Can no man tell me of my unthrifty son?

and goes on to confess the low resorts that he haunts with a crew of dissolute companions, even the robberies he commits in their company. So at least the reports have it that have come to him. And Hotspur, who has recently talked with the Prince, more than confirms them. He tells specifically of Hal's intention to burlesque the spirit of chivalry in the spirit of the brothel.

With this glimpse of the heir to the throne added to what we have seen of the other three Henrys, the political pattern of these plays becomes clear. Henry IV, by deposing his legitimate sovereign, Richard, has committed himself to the best-man theory of kingship, which, in practice, is equivalent to the strong-man theory. Between himself and Richard, in his own opinion and in that of many others, there could be no question of relative merit. But here is Hotspur, the incarnation of valor (and brother-in-law incidentally of Mortimer, legal heir to the throne). And here is his own good-for-nothing son. What about the succession in this case, on the King's own theory?

Plainly Henry's revised version of the divine right of kings is in for trouble. He is caught in his own trap. And the nemesis is personal as well as political. "What the father hath hid cometh out in the son," says Nietzsche, "and often have I found the son a father's revealed secret." There was never a better illustration of this truth. In his concentration on power the elder Henry has suppressed both the playful and the passionate tendencies of his nature.

> My blood hath been too cold and temperate.

What he has kept under comes out in Hal, who leads a life of abandon under the tutelage of Falstaff. We are told little of the early life of the King. But what he says of his son is sufficient:

> Most subject is the fattest soil to weeds;
> And he, the noble image of my youth,
> Is overspread with them: therefore my grief
> Stretches itself beyond the hour of death.

Evidently Henry had had his fling too. His "grief" is partly unconscious envy—regret for his own lost youth, like that of that other hypocrite, Polonius, when he sent his son to Paris. But the important point is that the King recognizes his earlier self in his son.

Though it comes later, it is Henry's great soliloquy on sleep that confirms all this.* It is the nocturnal part of a man that receives what he puts behind his back or under his feet in the daytime. In the apostrophe to sleep this victim of insomnia reveals the unrealized half of his soul. The lines have been called out of character. They are Shakespeare the poet, we are told, running away with Shakespeare the dramatist; Henry was incapable of anything so imaginative. On the contrary, the soliloquy is a measure of the amount of imagination that must be repressed before nature will permit one of her own creatures to be transformed into a worldling. It defines the distance Henry has travelled from innocence, and, in contrast with his diurnal aspect, the thickness of the mask that rank imposes.

> The king hath many marching in his coats,

cries Hotspur at Shrewsbury, referring to the counterfeit "kings" sent into the battle line in royal costume to lessen the chances of the real King's death. The device is a symbol of the man—as he became. The soliloquy on sleep tells us what he might have become.

When it is a question of the Prince, his father is honest and intelligent enough to perceive that he is himself trying to eat his cake and have it. The doctrine of the strong man and the doctrine of hereditary succession,

---

* I append the speech here:
"How many thousand of my poorest subjects
Are at this hour asleep! O sleep, O gentle sleep,
Nature's soft nurse, how have I frighted thee
That thou no more wilt weigh my eyelids down
And steep my senses in forgetfulness?
Why rather, sleep, liest thou in smoky cribs,
Upon uneasy pallets stretching thee,
And hush'd with buzzing night-flies to thy slumber,
Than in the perfum'd chambers of the great
Under the canopies of costly state,
And lull'd with sound of sweetest melody?
O thou dull god, why liest thou with the vile
In loathsome beds, and leav'st the kingly couch
A watch-case or a common 'larum-bell?
Wilt thou upon the high and giddy mast
Seal up the ship-boy's eyes, and rock his brains
In cradle of the rude imperious surge
And in the visitation of the winds,
Who take the ruffian billows by the top,
Curling their monstrous heads and hanging them
With deaf'ning clamour in the slippery clouds,
That, with the hurly, death itself awakes?
Canst thou, O partial sleep, give thy repose
To the wet sea-boy in an hour so rude,
And in the calmest and most stillest night,
With all appliances and means to boot,
Deny it to a king? Then happy low, lie down!
Uneasy lies the head that wears a crown."

he sees, do not cohere when the son is unworthy of the father. He catches the deadly parallel between the unkingly Richard and his own unkingly son and puts it in so many words to Hal:

> For all the world
> As thou art to this hour was Richard then
> When I from France set foot at Ravenspurgh,
> And even as I was then is Percy now.
> Now, by my sceptre and my soul to boot,
> He hath more worthy interest to the state
> Than thou the shadow of succession.

As Henry was to Richard, so is Hotspur now to Hal. There it is in a sentence. Hal gets the point and promises to be more himself in the future—at Hotspur's expense. The latter has been busy storing up glorious deeds all his life. Now Hal will make him exchange those deeds for his own "indignities."

> This, in the name of God, I promise here....
> And I will die a hundred thousand deaths
> Ere break the smallest parcel of this vow.

To which boast his delighted father replies:

> A hundred thousand rebels die in this.

The Prodigal Son has returned and the Father has forgiven him! So at any rate it seems to those who make this play a fresh version of the biblical story. It is temptingly simple. But it leaves several things out of account.

To begin with, long before the Prince made to his father the promise to reform, he made it to himself. Left alone at the end of the scene in which we first see him, he breaks out into the memorable words which, though they have been quoted so often, must be quoted once more:

> I know you all, and will awhile uphold
> The unyok'd humour of your idleness:
> Yet herein will I imitate the sun,
> Who doth permit the base contagious clouds
> To smother up his beauty from the world,
> That, when he please again to be himself,
> Being wanted, he may be more wonder'd at,
> By breaking through the foul and ugly mists
> Of vapours that did seem to strangle him.
> If all the year were playing holidays,
> To sport would be as tedious as to work;
> But when they seldom come, they wish'd for come,

And nothing pleaseth but rare accidents.
So, when this loose behaviour I throw off
And pay the debt I never promised,
By how much better than my word I am,
By so much shall I falsify men's hopes;
And like bright metal on a sullen ground,
My reformation, glittering o'er my fault,
Shall show more goodly and attract more eyes
Than that which hath no foil to set it off.
I'll so offend, to make offence a skill;
Redeeming time when men think least I will.

On top of our first glimpse of the carefree Hal, these lines come with a painful shock, casting both backward and forward, as they do, a shadow of insincerity. At a first reading or witnessing of the play the soliloquy is soon forgotten. But when we return to the text, there it is! So all this unaffected fun was not unaffected after all. Affected, according to Hal, is precisely what it was, put on for a purpose—only perhaps, deep down, it was just the other way around, perhaps it was the fun that was unaffected and it was the desire to make a dramatic impression on the world that was put on.

The speech just doesn't cohere with the Hal we love, his admirers protest. It is out of character. It is Shakespeare speaking, not Henry. And in support of them, the historical critics point out that the poet was merely following a familiar Elizabethan convention of tipping off the audience that they might be in the secret. It is odd, however, if it is just Shakespeare, that he made the speech so long and detailed and chose to base it on a metaphor that was forever running through Henry's mind. The playwright could have given the necessary information in a quarter of the space.

It is true that the soliloquy is unlike Hal. Yet there is not a speech in the role more strictly in character. How can that be? It can be for the simple reason that it is not Hal, primarily, who makes the speech at all. The Prince makes it. There are two Henrys. This is no quibble; it is the inmost heart of the matter. We saw that there were two elder Henrys. The King who had Richard murdered bears little resemblance to the man who utters the soliloquy on sleep. There are two younger Henrys who resemble each other just as little. If we need authority for what page after page of the play drives home, we have it in Falstaff, who makes just this distinction:

PRINCE:     Darest thou be as good as thy word now?
FALSTAFF: Why, Hal, thou knowest, as thou art but man, I dare; but as thou
              art Prince, I fear thee as I fear the roaring of the lion's whelp.

Hal and the Prince: we shall never get anything straight about this story if we confuse them or fail to mark the differences, the connections, and the interplay of the two. Talk about the Prodigal Son! There is indeed more than a touch of him in Hal; but in the deliberately and coldly ambitious Prince not a spark. In him the Prodigal was reformed before he ever came into existence.

The Henry who is the Prince is, appropriately, like the Henry who is the King, the son like the father. And Shakespeare takes the utmost pains to point this out. The theme of the famous soliloquy is the function of the foil. The Prince says he will imitate the sun and suddenly appear from behind clouds at the theatrical moment to dazzle all beholders. Well, turn to that heart-to-heart talk between the King and his heir that ends in the latter's promise to amend his ways, and straight from the father's mouth we have the son's philosophy. The elder Henry tells how in earlier days he kept himself from the public gaze and dressed himself in humility in contrast with Richard, so that

> By being seldom seen, I could not stir
> But like a comet I was wonder'd at;
> That men would tell their children, "This is he";
> Others would say, "Where, which is Bolingbroke?"

Whereas Richard (and Hal of course catches the point)

> Grew a companion to the common streets . . .
> So when he had occasion to be seen,
> He was but as the cuckoo is in June,
> Heard, not regarded; seen, but with such eyes
> As, sick and blunted with community,
> Afford no extraordinary gaze,
> Such as is bent on sun-like majesty
> When it shines seldom in admiring eyes.

Not only the Prince's idea. His very metaphor! The young man has already bettered his adviser in advance. His opening soliloquy was nothing but a variation on his father's theme: the uses of contrast. But the father kept himself rare, it will be said, while the son made himself common, acting like Richard instead of following his father's example. That was indeed the ground of the King's complaint. But he got the truth there exactly upside down. He did not see that his son was acting far more like himself than he was like Richard. The Prince was doing precisely what his father had done, only in a wilier way. The King had kept himself literally hidden and then suddenly appeared. The Prince was keeping himself figuratively hidden by his wild ways in order to emerge all at once as a self-disciplined king. As between the two, who can question which was the more dramatic and effective? But we like neither father nor son for his tricks, no matter how well contrived or brilliantly executed. The better the worse, in fact, in both cases. "A great act has no subordinate mean ones," says Thoreau. In view of the elder Henry's abortive attempt to disprove this truth, we wonder whether the younger Henry will have better success.

Yet even after hearing his confession that his escapades are a political experiment in which his heart is not enlisted, we go on to the tavern scenes with unaffected delight. Hal seems to throw himself into them with a zest that gives the lie to the idea that he is holding anything back. Like ourselves, he seems to have forgotten his own words and plunges into the fun for its own sake quite in Falstaff's spirit. Not only does he appear to, he does— Hal does, that is. But the Prince is there in the background and occasionally intrudes. Then Hal will return and only the alertest sense can detect the Prince's presence. This is in accord with common experience. Who has not found himself so changed today from what he was yesterday that he could easily believe that other fellow was another man? He was. These vaunted modern discoveries about dual and multiple personalities are not discoveries at all. Shakespeare understood all about them in the concrete. I have quoted Falstaff. Let me quote a more recent and not less profound psychologist, **Dostoevsky.**

The second chapter of Dostoevsky's *The Devils* (wrongly called in English *The Possessed*) is entitled "Prince Harry." In it we are given an account of the youth of Nikolay Vsyevolodovitch Stavrogin. Utterly neglected by his father, Nikolay is initiated at his mother's request into the military life, just as some higher aspirations are being awakened in him by his tutor. Soon strange rumors come home. The young man has suddenly taken to riotous living. He is indulging in all sorts of outrageous conduct. His mother is naturally alarmed. But the tutor reassures her. It is only the first effervescence of a too richly endowed nature. The storm will subside. It is "like the youth of Prince Harry, who caroused with Falstaff, Poins, and Mrs. Quickly, as described by Shakespeare." The mother listens eagerly and asks the tutor to explain his theory. She even, in the words of the author, "took up Shakespeare herself and with great attention read the immortal chronicle. But it did not comfort her, and indeed she did not find the resemblance very striking." Neither may we, though we do not have the excuse of mother love to blind us. The resemblance is there just the same: the same charm, the same neglect, the same plunge into dissipation, the same outrageous pranks, the same contact with military life, the same impossibility of reconciling what seem like two different men. "I had expected to see a dirty ragamuffin, sodden with drink and debauchery," says the narrator of

Nikolay's story. "He was, on the contrary, the most elegant gentleman I had ever met." One anecdote in particular clinches the parallelism. Leaning down to whisper something to the Governor of the province, Nikolay, on one occasion, suddenly takes his ear between his teeth. The exact, if exaggerated, counterpart of Hal's striking the Chief Justice.

Henry IV gives us an analysis of his son's temperament in advising Hal's brother how to handle him. It would fit Nikolay nearly as well.

> blunt not his love,
> Nor lose the good advantage of his grace
> By seeming cold or careless of his will;
> For he is gracious, if he be observ'd:
> He hath a tear for pity and a hand
> Open as day for melting charity;
> Yet notwithstanding, being incens'd, he's flint,
> As humorous as winter, and as sudden
> As flaws congealed in the spring of day.
> His temper, therefore, must be well observ'd:
> Chide him for faults, and do it reverently,
> When you perceive his blood inclin'd to mirth;
> But, being moody, give him line and scope,
> Till that his passions, like a whale on ground,
> Confound themselves with working.

What in Henry's case is deep variation in mood amounts in Nikolay's to a pathological split in personality. If Nikolay's place in the world had been more comparable with Henry's, their histories might have been more alike than they were. Even so, the violence and tragedy that came from this division within the soul of Stavrogin are a profounder comment than any criticism could be on the gradual fading of the carefree Hal and the slow emergence of the formidable victor of Agincourt. Dostoevsky understood Shakespeare better than did either the tutor or the mother in his novel. His chapter title "Prince Harry" was no mistake.

But now comes the most remarkable fact: Falstaff diagnoses Hal precisely as Dostoevsky does Stavrogin! "Dost thou hear, Hal?" he cries, just after the ominous "knocking from within" which proves to be the Sheriff. "Dost thou hear, Hal? never call a true piece of gold a counterfeit: thou art essentially mad without seeming so." "Mad" appears to be just about the last word to apply to the self-controlled and cold-blooded Henry. He certainly does not seem mad. But that is precisely what Falstaff says. "Oh, but Falstaff was only joking!" it will be objected. Of course he was; but it is the very genius of Falstaff to utter truth in jest. There is madness and madness.

The moment we follow Falstaff's lead and cease thinking of Henry as Henry and conceive him as Hal-and-the-Prince we see how right Shakespeare was to build this play on an alternation of "tavern" scenes and political-military ones. Instead of being just chronicle play relieved by comedy (as historians of the drama are bound to see it), what we have is a genuine integration, both psychological and dramatic, the alternating character of the scenes corresponding to the two sides of a dual personality.

## VI

And now we come to the third candidate for the role of "hero" in these plays.

Who at this late date can hope to say a fresh word about Falstaff? Long since, his admirers and detractors have drained language dry in their efforts to characterize him, to give expression to their fascination or detestation. Glutton, drunkard, coward, liar, lecher, boaster, cheat, thief, rogue, ruffian, villain are a few of the terms that have been used to describe a man whom others find the very incarnation of charm, one of the liberators of the human spirit, the greatest comic figure in the history of literature. "A besotted and disgusting old wretch," Bernard Shaw calls him. And isn't he?—this man who held up unprotected travelers for pastime, betrayed innocence in the person of his page, cheated a trusting and hard-working hostess, borrowed a thousand pounds from an old friend with no intention of repaying it, abused his commission by taking cash in lieu of military service, and insinuated his way into the graces of the heir apparent with an eye to later favor. And yet after three centuries there the old sinner sits, more invulnerable and full of smiles than ever, his sagging paunch shaking like a jelly, dodging or receiving full on, unperturbed, the missiles his enemies hurl at him. Which is he? A colossus of sack, sensuality, and sweat—or a wit and humorist so great that he can be compared only with his creator, a figure, to use one of Shakespeare's own great phrases, livelier than life? One might think there were two Falstaffs.

The trouble with the "besotted and disgusting old wretch" theory is that Shakespeare has given us that old wretch exactly, and he is another man: the Falstaff of *The Merry Wives of Windsor*. The disparagers of Falstaff generally make him out a mixture, in varying proportions, of this other Falstaff, Sir Toby Belch, and Parolles, each of whom was an incalculably inferior person. But to assert that Falstaff is another man is not saying that he does not have many or even all of the vices of the "old wretch" for whom his defamers mistake him. Salt is not sodium, but that is not saying that sodium is not a component of salt. The truth is that there *are* two Falstaffs, just as there are two Henrys, the Immoral Falstaff and the Immortal

Falstaff, and the dissension about the man comes from a failure to recognize that fact. That the two could inhabit one body would not be believed if Shakespeare had not proved that they could. That may be one reason why he made it so huge.

Curiously, there is no more convincing testimony to this double nature of the man than that offered by those who are most persistent in pointing out his depravity. In the very process of committing the old sinner to perdition they reveal that they have been unable to resist his seductiveness. Professor Stoll, for instance, dedicates twenty-six sections of a long and learned essay to the annihilation of the Falstaff that his congenital lovers love. And then he begins his twenty-seventh and last section with the words: "And yet people like Falstaff"! And before his first paragraph is done, all his previous labor is obliterated as we find him asserting that Falstaff is "supremely poetic" (even his most ardent admirers would hardly venture that "supremely") and that "his is in many ways the most marvellous prose ever penned." (It is, but how did the old sot, we wonder, ever acquire it?) Before his next paragraph is over, Stoll has called Falstaff "the very spirit of comradeship," "the king of companions," and "the prince of good fellows." "We, too, after all, like Prince Hal and Mrs. Quickly," he goes on, "take to a man because of his charm, if it be big enough, not because of his virtue; and as for Falstaff, we are bewitched with the rogue's company." (A Falstaff idolater could scarcely ask for more than that.) "Under the spell of his presence and speech," Stoll concludes, we should forget, as she does, the wrong he has done Mrs. Quickly, "did we not stop to think."

"Stop to think"! One may determine the orbit of the moon, or make an atomic bomb, by stopping to think, but when since the beginning of time did one man ever get at the secret of another by means of the intellect? It is all right to stop to think after we have taken a character to our hearts, but to do so before we have is fatal. Dr. Johnson stopped to think about Falstaff and as a result he decided that "he has nothing in him that can be esteemed." A child would be ashamed of such a judgment. But a child would never be guilty of it. "As for *Henry IV*," wrote one of the most imaginatively gifted young women I have ever known, "I love it. And I must have an utterly vulgar nature, for I simply adore Falstaff. He is perfectly delightful—not a fault in his nature, and the Prince is a DEVIL to reject him." That young woman evidently did not "stop to think." When she does, she will moderate that "not a fault in his nature," for that is the function of thinking—to hold our imagination within bounds and cut down its excrescences. Meanwhile, Falstaff has captured her, and she has captured Falstaff, for, as Blake said, enthusiastic admiration is the first principle of knowledge, and the last. Those who think about Falstaff before they fall in love with him may say some just things about him but they will never enter into his secret. "Would I were with him, wheresome'er he is, either in heaven or in hell!" Those words of poor Bardolph on hearing the account of Falstaff's death remain the highest tribute he ever did or ever could receive. In their stark sincerity they are worthy (irreverent as the suggestion will seem to some) to be put beside Dante's sublime incarnation of the same idea in the Paolo and Francesca incident in *The Inferno*, or even beside the words addressed to the thief who repented on the cross.

The scholars have attempted to explain Falstaff by tracing his origins. He has been found, variously, to have developed from the Devil of the miracle plays, the Vice of the morality plays, the boasting soldier of Plautine comedy, and so on. Now roots, up to a certain point, are interesting, but it takes the sun to make them grow and to illuminate the flower. And I think in this case we can find both roots and sun without going outside Shakespeare. If so, it is one of the most striking confirmations to be found of the embryological nature of his development.

If I were seeking the embryo of Falstaff in Shakespeare's imagination, I should consider the claims of Bottom—of Bottom and another character in *A Midsummer-Night's Dream*. "What!" it will be said, "the dull realistic Bottom and the lively witty Falstaff? They are nearer opposites." But embryos, it must be remembered, seldom resemble what they are destined to develop into. Bottom, like the physical Falstaff at least, is compact of the heaviness, the materiality, the reality of earth; and the ass's head that Puck bestows on him is abundantly deserved, not only in special reference to his brains but in its general implication of animality. But instead of letting himself be humiliated by it, Bottom sings, and Titania, Queen of the Fairies, her eyes anointed by the magic flower, awakening, mistakes him for an angel, and taking him in her arms, lulls him to sleep. The obvious meaning of the incident of course is that love is blind. Look at the asinine thing an infatuated woman will fall in love with! But whoever stops there, though he may have gotten the fun, has missed the beauty. The moment when Bottom emerges from his dream, as we pointed out when discussing *A Midsummer-Night's Dream*, is Shakespeare at one of his pinnacles. By a stroke of genius he turns a purely farcical incident into nothing less than a parable of the Awakening of Imagination within Gross Matter. It is the poet's way of saying that even within the head of this foolish plebeian weaver a divine light can be kindled. Bottom is conscious of transcendent things when he comes to himself. A creation has taken place within him. He struggles, in vain, to express it, and, in his very failure, succeeds:

God's my life! . . . I have had a most rare vision. I have had a dream, past the wit of man to say what dream it was. Man is but an ass, if he go about to expound this dream. Methought I was—there is no man can tell what. Methought I was,— and methought I had,—but man is but a patch'd fool, if he will offer to say what methought I had. The eye of man hath not heard, the ear of man hath not seen, man's hand is not able to taste, his tongue to conceive, nor his heart to report, what my dream was. I will get Peter Quince to write a ballad of this dream. It shall be called "Bottom's Dream," because it hath no bottom.

The dreamer may still be Bottom. But the dream itself is Puck. For one moment the two are one. Ass or angel? Perhaps Titania was not so deluded after all.

Do not misunderstand me. I am not suggesting that Shakespeare ever consciously connected Puck and Bottom with Falstaff in his own mind. But having achieved this inconceivable integration of the two, how easily his genius would be tempted to repeat the miracle on a grander scale: to create a perfect mountain of flesh and show how the same wonder could occur within it, not momentarily, but, humanly speaking, perpetually. That at any rate is what Falstaff is: Imagination conquering matter, spirit subduing flesh. Bottom was a weaver—a weaver of threads. "I would I were a weaver," Falstaff once exclaimed. He was a weaver—a weaver of spells. Here, if ever, is the embryology of the imagination. "Man is but a patch'd fool, if he will offer to say. . . ." Who cannot catch the very accent of Falstaff in that?

> I'll put a girdle round about the earth
> In forty minutes.

It might have been said of Falstaff's wit. His Bottom-like body is continually being dragged down, but his Puck-like spirit can hide in a thimble or pass through a keyhole as nimbly as any fairy's. What wonder that this contradictory being—as deminatured as a satyr or a mermaid—who is forever repeating within himself the original miracle of creation, has taken on the proportions of a mythological figure. He seems at times more like a god than a man. His very solidity is solar, his rotundity cosmic. To estimate the refining power we must know the grossness of what is to be refined. To be astounded by what lifts we must know the weight of what is to be lifted. Falstaff is levitation overcoming gravitation. At his wittiest and most aerial, he is Ariel tossing the terrestrial globe in the air as if it were a ball. And yet— as we must never forget—he is also that fat old sinner fast asleep and snoring behind the arras. The sins, in fact, are the very things that make the miracle astonishing, as the chains and ropes do a Houdini's escape.

To grasp Falstaff thus *sub specie aeternitatis* we must see him, as Titania did Bottom, with our imagination, not with our senses. And that is why we shall never see Falstaff on the stage. On the stage there the monster of flesh stands—made, we know, mainly of pillows—with all his sheer material bulk and greasy beefiness, a palpable candidate for perdition. It takes rare acting to rescue him from being physically repulsive. And as for the miracle—it just refuses to happen in a theater. It would take a child to melt this too too solid flesh into spirit. It would take Falstaff himself to act Falstaff. But in a book! On the stage of our imagination! That is another matter. There the miracle can occur—and does for thousands of readers. Falstaff is a touchstone to tell whether the juice of the magic flower has been squeezed into our eyes. If it has not, we will see only his animality. To the vulgar, Falstaff will be forever just vulgar.

The problem of Falstaff himself cannot be separated from the problem of the fascination he exercises over us. Critics have long since put their fingers on the negative side of that secret. Half his charm resides in the fact that he is what we long to be and are not: *free*. Hence our delight in projecting on him our frustrated longing for emancipation. It is right here that those who do not like Falstaff score a cheap victory over those who do. The latter, say the former, are repressed or sedentary souls who go on a vicarious spree in the presence of one who commits all the sins they would like to commit but do not dare to. Like some of Falstaff's own hypotheses, the idea has an air of plausibility. But it involves a pitifully superficial view of Falstaff—as if his essence lay in his love of sack! No! it is for liberation from what all men want to be rid of, not just the bloodless few, that Falstaff stands: liberation from the tyranny of things as they are. Falstaff is immortal because he is a symbol of the supremacy of imagination over fact. He forecasts man's final victory over Fate itself. Facts stand in our way. Facts melt before Falstaff like ice before a summer sun—dissolve in the *aqua regia* of his resourcefulness and wit. He realizes the age-old dream of all men: to awaken in the morning and to know that no master, no employer, no bodily need or sense of duty calls, no fear or obstacle stands in the way—only a fresh beckoning day that is wholly ours.

But we have all awakened that way on rare occasions without becoming Falstaffs. Some men often do. An untrammeled day is not enough; we must have something to fill it with—besides lying in bed. Freedom is only the negative side of Falstaff. Possessing it, he perpetually does something creative with it. It is not enough for him to be the sworn enemy of facts. Any lazy man or fool is that. He is the sworn enemy of the factual spirit itself, of whatever is dull, inert, banal. Facts merely exist—and so do most men. Falstaff lives. And where he is, life becomes bright, active, enthralling.

Who has not been a member of some listless group on whom time has been hanging heavy when in the twinkling of an eye a newcomer has altered the face of everything as utterly as the sun, breaking through clouds, transforms the surface of a gray lake? Boredom is banished. Gaiety is restored. The most apathetic member of the company is laughing and alert and will shortly be contributing his share to the flow of good spirits. What has done it? At bottom, of course, the mysterious fluid of an infectious personality. But so far as it can be analyzed, some tall tale or personal adventure wherein a grain of fact has been worked up with a pound of fiction, some impudent assumption about the host or absurd charge against somebody present rendered plausible by a precarious resemblance to the truth. Always *something made out of nothing*, with power, when added to the facts, to get the better of them. Never an unadulterated lie, but always some monstrous perversion, some scandalous interpretation, of what actually happened. An invention, yes, but an invention attached to reality by a thread of truth—the slenderer the better, so long as it does not break. What is Falstaff but an aggrandized, universalized, individualized version of this familiar phenomenon? He makes life again worth living.

And so, whether we approach Falstaff from the mythological or the psychological angle, we reach the same goal.

But alas! we have been neglecting the other Falstaff, the old sot. Unluckily—or perhaps luckily—there is another side to the story. Having fallen in love with Falstaff, we may now "stop to think" about him without compunction. And on examining more closely this symbol of man's supremacy over nature we perceive that he is not invulnerable. He has his Achilles heel. I do not refer to his love of Hal. That is his Achilles heel in another and lovelier sense. I refer to a tiny fact, two tiny facts, that he forgets and that we would like to: the fact that his imagination is stimulated by immense potations of sack and that his victories are purchased, if necessary, at the price of an utter disregard for the rights of others. We do not remember this until we stop to think. And we do not want to stop to think. We want to identify ourselves with the Immortal Falstaff. Yet there the Immoral Falstaff is all the while. And he must be reckoned with. Shakespeare was too much of a realist to leave him out.

The Greeks incarnated in their god Dionysus the paradox of wine, its combined power to inspire and degrade. *The Bacchae* of Euripides is the profoundest treatment of this theme in Hellenic if not in any literature. "No one can hate drunkenness more than I do," says Samuel Butler, "but I am confident the human intellect owes its superiority over that of the lower animals in great measure to the stimulus which alcohol has given to imagination—imagination being little else than another name for illusion."* "The sway of alcohol over mankind," says William James, "is unquestionably due to its power to stimulate the mystical faculties of human nature [the imagination, that is, in its quintessence], usually crushed to earth by the cold facts and dry criticisms of the sober hour. Sobriety diminishes, discriminates, and says no; drunkenness expands, unites, and says yes. It is in fact the great exciter of the *Yes* function in man . . . it is part of the deeper mystery and tragedy of life that whiffs and gleams of something that we immediately recognize as excellent should be vouchsafed to so many of us only in the fleeting earlier phases of what in its totality is so degrading a poisoning."

James's contrast between the earlier and the later phases of alcoholic intoxication inevitably suggests the degeneration that Falstaff undergoes in the second part of *Henry IV*. That degeneration is an actual one, though several recent critics have tended to exaggerate it. Dover Wilson thinks that Shakespeare is deliberately trying to make us fall out of love with Falstaff so that we may accept with good grace his rejection by the new king. If so, for many readers he did not succeed very well. (Of that in its place.)

It is significant that we never see Falstaff drunk. His wit still scintillates practically unabated throughout the second part of the play, though some critics seem set on not admitting it. He is in top form, for instance, in his interview with the Chief Justice, and, to pick a single example from many, the reply he gives to John of Lancaster's reproach,

> When everything is ended, then you come,

is one of his pinnacles: "Do you think me a swallow, an arrow, or a bullet?" No, the degeneration of Falstaff is not so much in his wit or even in his imagination as in his moral sensibility. The company he keeps grows more continuously low, and his treatment of Shallow and of his recruits shows an increasing hardness of heart. Shakespeare inserts too many little realistic touches to let us take these scenes as pure farce, and while no one in his senses would want to turn this aspect of the play into a temperance tract it seems at times like an almost scientifically faithful account of the effect of an excess of alcohol on the moral nature. In view of what Shakespeare was at this time on the verge of saying about drunkenness in *Hamlet* and of what he was to say about it later in *Othello, Antony and Cleopatra*, and *The Tempest*, it is certain that he was profoundly interested in the subject;

---

* It is usually presumptuous to disagree with Samuel Butler's use of words. But if he had substituted "mind" for "intellect" in the foregoing quotation I think he would have been nearer the mark. And only the unwary reader will think that by "illusion" Butler means the same thing as delusion or lie.

and it is not far-fetched to suppose that he had in the back of his mind in portraying the "degeneration" of Falstaff the nemesis that awaits the artificially stimulated mind. If so, the fat knight is Shakespeare's contribution, in a different key, to the same problem that is treated in *The Bacchae*, and his conclusions are close to those at which Euripides arrives.

## VII

And then there is *The Merry Wives of Windsor*. (Here appears to be the right place for a brief interlude on that play.) Criticism has been much concerned over the connection, if any, between the Falstaff of *The Merry Wives* and the Falstaff of *Henry IV*—with something like a consensus that with the exception of a few dying sparks of the original one this is another man. Yet one link between the two Falstaffs cannot be denied: with respect to wit and resourcefulness they are exact opposites. The Falstaff we admire is an incarnation of readiness; this one of helplessness. Nothing is too much for the former. Anything is too much for the latter. They are, respectively, presence and absence of mind. Such an utter antithesis is itself a connection. Shakespeare must have meant something by it.

Nearly everyone is acquainted with the tradition that *The Merry Wives of Windsor* was written in a fortnight at the command of Queen Elizabeth, who wished to see the fat man in love. Shakespeare does appear to have "tossed off" this sparkling farce-comedy, his one play of purely contemporary life and of almost pure prose, and, along with *The Comedy of Errors*, his most inconsequential and merely theatrical one. Several hypotheses, or some combination of them, may account for the Falstaff of this play.

Poets, as distinct from poets laureate, do not like commissions. It would be quite like Shakespeare, ordered by the Queen to write another play about Falstaff, to have his playful revenge by writing one about another man entirely, under the same name. That was precisely the sort of thing that Chaucer did when commanded by another Queen to write a *Legend of Good Women*. It is fun to make a fool of royalty. Then, too, the conditions under which the play was written, if the tradition is true, practically compelled it to keep close to farce. And farce is the very atmosphere in which parody thrives. This Falstaff is a kind of parody of the other one. But the closer Shakespeare gets to farce, fancy, or nonsense, as he proves over and over, the more certain he is to have some serious underintention. On that principle, what better place than *The Merry Wives of Windsor* in which to insert an oblique comment on the Falstaff of *Henry IV?* Be that as it may, the Falstaff of this play is, as we said, an almost perfect picture, in exaggerated form and in a farcical key, of the Immoral Falstaff of the other plays, the old wretch of Bernard Shaw. Only the light tone of the piece keeps him from being "besotted and disgusting" also. Critics have seriously tried to determine at what spot chronologically this play should be inserted in the Henry series. Such an attempt betrays a curious ignorance of the ways of the imagination. But, after all due discount for the farce and fooling, the Falstaff of *The Merry Wives* looks like pretty good natural history of the latter end of an "old soak." From him it is a relief to get back, after our interlude, to the Immortal Falstaff, who, however entangled with the Immoral Falstaff, as the soul is with the body, breathes another and more transcendental air.

## VIII

Is there any activity of man that involves the same factors that we find present in this Falstaff: complete freedom, an all-consuming zest for life, an utter subjugation of facts to imagination, and an entire absence of moral responsibility? Obviously there is. That activity is play.

Except for that little item of moral responsibility, "play" expresses as nearly as one word can the highest conception of life we are capable of forming: life for its own sake, life as it looks in the morning to a boy with

> no more behind
> But such a day to-morrow as to-day,
> And to be boy eternal,

life for the fun of it, as against life for what you can get out of it—or whom you can knock out of it. "Play" says what the word "peace" tries to say and doesn't. "Play" brings down to the level of everyone's understanding what "imagination" conveys to more sophisticated minds. For the element of imagination is indispensable to true play. Play is not sport. The confusion of the two is a major tragedy of our time. A crowd of fifteen-year-old schoolboys "playing" football on a back lot are indulging in sport. They are rarely playing. The one who is playing is the child of five, all alone, pretending that a dirty rag doll is the rich mother of a dozen infants—invisible to the naked eye. Even boys playing war, if they are harmonious and happy, are conducting an experiment in peace. Play is the erection of an illusion into a reality. It is not an escape from life. It is the realization of life in something like its fulness. What it *is* an escape from is the boredom and friction of existence. Like poetry, to which it is the prelude, it stands for a converting or winning-over of facts on a basis of friendship, the dissolving of them in a spirit of love, in contrast with science (at least the science of our day), which, somewhat illogically, stands first for a recognition of the absolute autonomy of facts and then for their impressment and subjection to human demands by a kind of military conquest.

Now Falstaff goes through life playing. He coins everything he encounters into play, often even into *a* play. He would rather have the joke on himself and make the imaginative most of it than to have it on the other fellow and let the fun stop there. Whenever he seems to be taken in because he does not realize the situation, it is safer to assume that he does realize it but keeps quiet because the imaginative possibilities are greater in that case.

Watching him, we who in dead earnest have been attending to business or doing what we are pleased to call our duty suddenly realize what we have been missing. "The object of a man's life," says Robert Henri, "should be to play as a little child plays." If that is so we have missed the object of life, while Falstaff has attained it, or at least not missed it completely, as we have. It is his glory that, like Peter Pan, he never grew up, and that glory is the greater because he is an old man. As his immense size and weight were utilized by Shakespeare as a foil for the lightness of his spirit, so his age is used to stress its youthfulness. "You that are old," he says to the Chief Justice, who has been berating him for misleading the Prince, "consider not the capacities of us that are young." The Chief Justice replies that Falstaff is in every part "blasted with antiquity," his belly increasing in size, his voice broken, "and will you yet call yourself young? Fie, fie, fie, Sir John!" Falstaff retorts that as for his belly, he was born with a round one; as for his voice, he has lost it hollaing and singing of anthems; and as for his age, he is old only in judgment and understanding. Though the Lord Chief Justice has all the facts on his side, Falstaff has the victory. There has seldom been a more delicious interview.

As this scene suggests, the right way to take the Falstaff whom we love is to take him as a child. Mrs. Quickly did that in her immortal account of his death: he went away, she said, "an it had been any christom child." To call him a liar and let it go at that is like being the hardheaded father of a poetic little son who punishes him for falsehood when he has only been relating genuine imaginative experiences—as Blake's father thrashed him for saying he had seen angels in a tree. And to call him a coward and let it go at *that* is being no profounder.

But if it is the glory of the Immortal Falstaff that he remained a child, it is the shame of the Immoral Falstaff that he never became a man—for it is a child's duty to become a man no less than it is a man's duty to become a child. Falstaff detoured manhood instead of passing through it into a higher childhood. He is like the character in *The Pilgrim's Progress* who tried to steal into Paradise by climbing over the wall near its entrance instead of passing through the wicket gate and undergoing the trials that it is the lot of man to endure. He wanted the victory without paying the price. He wanted to be an individual regardless of the social consequences, to persist in the prerogatives of youth without undertaking the responsibilities of maturity. But if his virtues are those of a child rather than those of a man, that does not prevent him from being immensely superior to those in these plays who possess the virtues of neither man nor child, or from giving us gleams of a life beyond good and evil.

Dover Wilson* would have us take *Henry IV* as a morality play wherein a madcap prince grows up into an ideal king. Falstaff is the devil who tempts the Prince to Riot. Hotspur and especially the Lord Chief Justice are the good angels representing Chivalry and Justice or the Rule of Law. It is a struggle between Vanity and Government for the possession of the Royal Prodigal.

The scheme is superbly simple and as moral as a Sunday-school lesson. But it calmly leaves the Immortal Falstaff quite out of account! If Falstaff were indeed just the immoral creature that in part he admittedly is, Wilson's parable would be more plausible, though even then the words he picks to characterize Falstaff are singularly unfortunate. "Vanity" by derivation means emptiness or absence of substance, and "riot" quarrelsomeness. Imagine calling even the Immoral Falstaff empty or lacking in substance— or quarrelsome! He had his vices but they were not these. For either vanity or riot there is not a single good word to be said. To equate Falstaff with them is to assert that not a single good word can be said for him—a preposterous proposition. Wit, humor, laughter, good-fellowship, insatiable zest for life: are these vanity or does Falstaff *not* embody them? That is the dilemma in which Mr. Wilson puts himself. And as for the Lord Chief Justice, he is indeed an admirable man; a more incorruptible one in high position is not to be found in Shakespeare. But if the poet had intended to assign him any such crucial role as Mr. Wilson thinks, he certainly would have presented him more fully and would have hesitated to let Falstaff make him look so foolish. For the Chief Justice's sense of justice was better developed than his sense of humor. And even justice is not all.

*Henry IV* does have a certain resemblance to a morality play. The two, however, between whom the younger Henry stands and who are in a sense contending for the possession of his soul are not Falstaff and the Chief Justice, but Falstaff and the King. It is between Falstaff and the Father—to use that word in its generic sense—that Henry finds himself.

Now in the abstract this is indeed Youth between Revelry and Responsibility. But the abstract has nothing to do with it. Where Henry really stands is between this particular companion, Falstaff, and this particular father and king, Henry IV. Of the two, which was the better man?

Concede the utmost—that is, take Falstaff at his worst. He was a drunk-

* Following Professor R. A. Law.

ard, a glutton, a profligate, a thief, even a liar if you insist, but withal a fundamentally honest man. He had two sides like a coin, but he was not a counterfeit. And Henry? He was a king, a man of "honour," of brains and ability, of good intentions, but withal a "vile politician" and respectable hypocrite. He *was* a counterfeit. Which, if it comes to the choice, is the better influence on a young man? Shakespeare, for one, gives no evidence of having an iota of doubt.

But if even Falstaff at his worst comes off better than Henry, how about Falstaff at his best? In that case, what we have is Youth standing between Imagination and Authority, between Freedom and Force, between Play and War. My insistence that Falstaff is a double man, and that the abstract has nothing to do with it, will acquit me of implying that this is the whole of the story. But it is a highly suggestive part of it.

The opposite of war is not "peace" in the debased sense in which we are in the habit of using the latter word. Peace ought to mean far more, but what it has come to mean on our lips is just the absence of war. The opposite of war is creative activity, play in its loftier implications. All through these dramas the finer Falstaff symbolizes the opposite of force. When anything military enters his presence, it instantly looks ridiculous and begins to shrink. Many methods have been proposed for getting rid of war. Falstaff's is one of the simplest: laugh it out of existence. For war is almost as foolish as it is criminal. "Laugh it out of existence"? If only we could! Which is the equivalent of saying: if only more of us were like Falstaff! These plays should be required reading in all military academies. Even the "cannon-fodder" scenes of Falstaff with his recruits have their serious implications and anticipate our present convictions on the uneugenic nature of war.

How far did Shakespeare sympathize with Falstaff's attitude in this matter? No one is entitled to say. But much further, I am inclined to think, than he would have had his audience suspect or than the world since his time has been willing to admit. For consider the conditions under which Falstaff finds himself:

Henry has dethroned and murdered the rightful king of England. The Percys have helped him to obtain the crown, but a mutual sense of guilt engenders distrust between the two parties, and the Percys decide to dethrone the dethroner. Falstaff is summoned to take part in his defense. "Life is given but once." Why should Falstaff risk his one life on earth, which he is enjoying as not one man in a hundred million does, to support or to oppose the cause of either of two equally selfish and equally damnable seekers after power and glory? What good would the sacrifice of his life accomplish comparable to the boon that he confers daily and hourly on the world, to say nothing of himself, by merely being? This is no case of tyranny on one side and democracy on the other, with the liberty or slavery of a world at stake. This is a strictly dynastic quarrel. When two gangs of gunmen begin shooting it out on the streets of a great city, the discreet citizen will step behind a post or into a doorway. The analogy may not be an exact one, but it enables us to understand Falstaff's point of view. And there is plenty of Shakespearean warrant for it.

> See the coast clear'd, and then we will depart,

says the Mayor of London when caught, in *I Henry VI*, between similar brawling factions,

> Good God! these nobles should such stomachs bear;
> I myself fight not once in forty year.

And Mercutio's "A plague o' both your houses!" comes to mind. Shakespeare meant more by that phrase than the dying man who coined it could have comprehended.

"But how about Falstaff's honor?" it will be asked. "Thou owest God a death," says the Prince to him before the battle of Shrewsbury. " 'Tis not due yet," Falstaff answers as Hal goes out,

> I would be loath to pay him before his day. What need I be so forward with him that calls not on me? Well, 'tis no matter; honour pricks me on. Yea, but how if honour prick me off when I came on? how then? Can honour set to a leg? No. Or an arm? No. Or take away the grief of a wound? No. Honour hath no skill in surgery, then? No. What is honour? A word. What is in that word honour? What is that honour? Air; a trim reckoning! Who hath it? He that died o' Wednesday. Doth he feel it? No. Doth he hear it? No. 'Tis insensible, then? Yea, to the dead. But will it not live with the living? No. Why? Detraction will not suffer it. Therefore I'll none of it. Honour is a mere scutcheon: and so ends my catechism.

"You must be honorable to talk of honor," says a character in *A Raw Youth*, "or, if not, all you say is a lie." The word "honor," as that sentence of Dostoevsky's shows, is still an honorable word. It can still mean, and could in Shakespeare's day, the integrity of the soul before God. The Chief Justice had honor in that sense. But "honour" in its decayed feudal sense of glory, fame, even reputation, as page after page of these Chronicle Plays records, had outlived its usefulness and the time had come to expose its hollowness. The soul, lifted up, declared Saint Teresa (who died in 1582), sees in the word "honor" "nothing more than an immense lie of which the world remains a victim. . . . She laughs when she sees grave persons, persons of orison, caring for points of honor for which she now feels profoundest contempt. . . . With what friendship we would all treat each other if our interest in honor and in money could but disappear from the earth! For my own part, I feel as if it would be a remedy for all our ills."

Saint Teresa and Sir John Falstaff! an odd pair to find in agreement—about honor if not about money. In the saint's case no ambiguity is attached to the doctrine that honor is a lie. In the sinner's, there remains something equivocal and double-edged. Here, if ever, the two Falstaffs meet. The grosser Falstaff is himself a parasite and a dishonorable man, and coming from him the speech is the creed of Commodity and the height of irony. But that does not prevent the man who loved Hal and babbled of green fields at his death from revealing in the same words, as clearly as Saint Teresa, that life was given for something greater than glory or than the gain that can be gotten out of it.

"Give me life," cries Falstaff on the field of Shrewsbury. "Die all, die merrily," cries Hotspur. That is the gist of it. The Prince killed Hotspur in the battle, and Falstaff, with one of his most inspired lies, claimed the deed as his own. But Falstaff's lies, scrutinized, often turn out to be truth in disguise. So here. Falstaff, not Prince Henry, did kill Hotspur. He ended the outworn conception of honor for which Hotspur stood. The Prince killed his body, but Falstaff killed his soul—or rather what passed for his soul.

The dying Hotspur himself sees the truth. The verdict of his final breath is that life is "time's fool" and he himself dust. And the Prince, gazing down at his dead victim, sees it too, if only for a moment.

> Ill-weav'd ambition, how much art thou shrunk!
> When that this body did contain a spirit,
> A kingdom for it was too small a bound,

he exclaims, and, turning, he catches sight of another body from which life has also apparently departed:

> What, old acquaintance! could not all this flesh
> Keep in a little life? Poor Jack, farewell!
> I could have better spar'd a better man.

But nobody was ever more mistaken on this subject of life and flesh than was Henry on this occasion, as the shamming Falstaff proves a moment later, when the Prince goes out, by rising from the dead. " 'Sblood," he cries,

'twas time to counterfeit, or that hot termagant Scot had paid me scot and lot too. Counterfeit? I lie, I am no counterfeit. To die is to be a counterfeit; for he is but the counterfeit of a man who hath not the life of a man; but to counterfeit dying, when a man thereby liveth, is to be no counterfeit, but the true and perfect image of life indeed. The better part of valour is discretion.

> I fear thou art another counterfeit,

Douglas had cried, coming on Henry IV on the field of Shrewsbury,

> Another king! they grow like Hydra's heads.
> I am the Douglas, fatal to all those
> That wear those colours on them. What art thou,
> That counterfeit'st the person of a king?

The literal reference of course is to the knights, disguised to represent the King, that Henry had sent into the battle to divert the enemy from his own person. "The better part of valour is discretion." This, and that repeated word "counterfeit," is Shakespeare's sign that he intends the contrast, and the deeper unconscious meaning of Douglas'

> What art thou,
> That counterfeit'st the person of a king?

(a king, notice, not the king) is just one more of the poet's judgments upon Henry. For all his "discretion," the Douglas would have killed this counterfeit king who tries to save his skin by the death of others if the Prince had not come to his rescue in the nick of time.

But that was earlier in the battle. At the point we had reached the Prince comes back with his brother John and discovers the "dead" Falstaff staggering along with the dead Hotspur on his back—a symbolic picture if there ever was one.

> Did you not tell me this fat man was dead?

cries Lancaster.

> I did; I saw him dead,
> Breathless and bleeding on the ground,

replies Henry. He has underrated the vitality of the Imagination, and even now thinks he sees a ghost:

> Art thou alive?
> Or is it fantasy that plays upon our eyesight?
> I prithee, speak; we will not trust our eyes
> Without our ears. Thou art not what thou seem'st.

"No: that's certain," retorts Falstaff, "I am not a double man." And to prove it, he throws down the body of Hotspur he is carrying. But beyond this obvious meaning, who can doubt that Falstaff, in the phrase "double man," is also having a thrust at the dual role of the man he is addressing, or that Shakespeare, in letting Falstaff deny his own doubleness, is thereby calling our attention to it? At the very least the expression proves that the world did not have to wait for Dostoevsky before it heard of the double man.

Truth has made it necessary to say some harsh things about Prince Henry; so it is a pleasure to recognize the character of his conduct on the field of Shrewsbury: his valor in his encounter with Hotspur, his courage and loyalty in rescuing his father from Douglas, and his generosity in letting Falstaff take credit for Hotspur's death. Dover Wilson makes much of this last point—too much, I think, for the good of his own case—declaring that it proves the Prince thought nothing of renown, of "the outward show of honour in the eyes of men, so long as he has proved himself worthy of its inner substance in his own." But if he was as self-effacing as all that, why did he cry at the moment he met Hotspur?—

> all the budding honours on thy crest
> I'll crop, to make a garland for my head.

Those words flatly contradict the "grace" he does Falstaff in surrendering to him so easily the greatest honor of his life. The paradox arises, I think, from the presence of those conflicting personalities, Hal and the Prince. Touched momentarily at the sight of what he believes to be his old companion dead at his feet, the fast-disappearing Hal returns and survives long enough after the surprise and joy of finding him still alive to accept Falstaff's lie for truth. But we wonder how much longer. Wilson's assumption that the Prince would or could have kept up the fiction permanently is refuted by the fact that Morton had observed the death of Hotspur at Henry's hands and reports the event correctly:

> these mine eyes saw him in bloody state,
> Rendering faint quittance, wearied and outbreath'd,
> To Harry Monmouth; whose swift wrath beat down
> The never-daunted Percy to the earth,
> From whence with life he never more sprung up.

Everything, from the famous first soliloquy on, proves that the Prince not only craved renown but craved it in its most theatrical form.

## IX

In the fourth scene of the fourth act of the second part of the play, King Henry, surrounded by his lords, returns to his earlier proposal of a crusade to Jerusalem. If God crowns our arms with success in our present quarrel, he promises,

We will our youth lead on to higher fields
And draw no swords but what are sanctified,

a way of phrasing it that suggests a buried doubt about the sanctity of the sword he has drawn against the Percys. The scene is the Jerusalem Chamber in Westminster. As the King's confession,

Only, we want a little personal strength,

reveals, the hand of death is already on him.

Meanwhile, things have been happening in Yorkshire. John of Lancaster, a younger brother of Hal, has been guilty of the most despicable piece of treachery recorded anywhere in these plays. Just after berating the Archbishop of York for misusing his office

As a false favourite doth his prince's name,
In deeds dishonourable,

he proceeds, in the King's name, to an act of dishonor of exactly the same kind. By a cold-blooded lie, a promise he makes and breaks in a breath, he tricks the leaders of the rebellion into laying down their arms, condemns them to the block as traitors, and gives credit for the fraud to God:

God, and not we, hath safely fought today.

Safely, indeed! One more example of "honour."

News of this "victory" is brought to the King in the ironical line,

Peace puts forth her olive everywhere.

But the good tidings are too much for Henry. He is stricken with sudden illness and we next see him in another room to which he has been borne, lying in bed listening to music. He calls for his crown. It is placed beside him on his pillow. Music, a dying king, and a crown: it is a symbolic picture.

Prince Henry enters. And then comes one of those little scenes, that seem at a first reading utterly superfluous, wherein Shakespeare was so fond of dropping the clue to what is coming. Whoever would understand the critical crown scene that is to follow must attend to its preface in these eleven apparently casual lines.

"Who saw the Duke of Clarence?" the Prince demands as he comes in. The Duke, his brother, is in the room at the moment, but overcome with grief at his father's illness has apparently withdrawn into a corner. He is weeping.

How now! rain within doors and none abroad!

exclaims the Prince, catching sight of him. The jest in the circumstances is poor enough and is not much improved even if the King is too weak to hear it. Henry inquires for his father and, being told that he is "exceeding ill," declares that he will recover without medicine if he is sick with joy over the good news. Warwick reprimands him for speaking too loudly:

> Sweet prince, speak low;
> The king your father is dispos'd to sleep.

Clarence suggests that they all retire into another room. The Prince says he will remain and watch by the King. Such is Shakespeare's introduction to one of the most critical scenes of the play.

Left alone with the sick man, the Prince immediately spies the crown upon the pillow and breaks into an apostrophe to it. In the midst of it he notices that a feather near his father's lips does not stir and concludes that the King has suddenly expired.

> My gracious lord! my father!
> This sleep is sound indeed; this is a sleep
> That from this golden rigol hath divorc'd
> So many English kings. Thy due from me
> Is tears and heavy sorrows of the blood,
> Which nature, love, and filial tenderness
> Shall, O dear father, pay thee plenteously:
> My due from thee is this imperial crown,
> Which, as immediate from thy place and blood,
> Derives itself to me. Lo, here it sits,
> > (*Putting it on his head*)
> Which God shall guard: and put the world's whole strength
> Into one giant arm, it shall not force
> This lineal honour from me. This from thee
> Will I to mine leave, as 'tis left to me.

We wonder why Henry, on the discovery of his father's death, did not instantly recall his brother and the nobles who have just gone out. Yet even after his address to the dead man is done, the Prince, now self-crowned king, does not do so, but passes into an adjoining chamber with the symbol of his new power still on his head.

But his assumption of the crown turns out to have been premature. His father is not dead, and waking at the moment and missing the crown, calls out in dismay, "Warwick! Gloucester! Clarence!" They come, and when they tell him that they left the Prince watching by him, he realizes that it is he who has taken the crown and breaks into lamentations over what he is convinced is the Prince's craving for his death:

> Is he so hasty that he doth suppose
> My sleep my death?

Warwick, who has gone in search of the missing heir, returns to report that he found him weeping in the next room,

> Washing with kindly tears his gentle cheeks.

(Whether he was, or not, we shall never know.) But the King, unsatisfied, asks again:

> But wherefore did he take away the crown?

> I never thought to hear you speak again,

protests the Prince. He has entered at the moment and overheard.

> Thy wish was father, Harry, to that thought.
>             . . . O foolish youth!
> Thou seek'st the greatness that will overwhelm thee,

cries the disillusioned servant of Commodity.

> Thou hast stol'n that which after some few hours
> Were thine without offence. . . .
> What! canst thou not forbear me half an hour?
> Then get thee gone and dig my grave thyself,

and he goes on to forecast the undoing of the realm under his son's coming reign when "apes of idleness," ruffians and the scum of the earth will

> commit
> The oldest sins the newest kind of ways,

until England is finally reduced to a wilderness, peopled with wolves, its old inhabitants. The self-pity of the speech has the exact accent of Richard II. The wheel has come full circle. Henry has become the image of the man he injured.

Under his father's indictment the Prince has stood speechless. What can he say? His conduct in putting on the crown at such a moment is indefensible. And so he does what anyone is likely to do in such a predicament: he swears, he promises, he exaggerates, he lies, he calls God to witness, and, in general, "doth protest too much." Now we see why Shakespeare was at pains to contrast the conduct of the Prince's younger brother with the Prince's. Clarence melts into tears and near silence at the sight of his father's illness. Henry, at the sight of what he supposes his death, is dry-eyed (we cannot but infer) and able to make a perfectly self-controlled speech (I almost said oration) in which he declares that his father's due from him is tears which he "shall" weep, while his due from his father is the crown that "sits" by his own immediate act on his head. Why the careful discrimination in tenses? Why the postponement of the emotion? Why the question in our minds whether Warwick *did* find Hal in tears in the next room—whether his report that he did may not be an exaggeration, or even a lie, to comfort the dying man? That there are tears in Henry's eyes when he comes back and finds his father still alive we need not go so far as to question. There must have been mixed emotions back of them, however, vexation at himself being one of them. But the culminating proof of the Prince's duplicity is the account he gives his father of his apostrophe to the crown while he was watching by the bedside. His father did not hear his words. But we did. It is revealing to put what he said beside what he says he said.

Here is what he said:

> Why doth the crown lie there upon his pillow,
> Being so troublesome a bedfellow?
> O polish'd perturbation! golden care!
> That keep'st the ports of slumber open wide
> To many a watchful night! Sleep with it now!
> Yet not so sound and half so deeply sweet
> As he whose brow with homely biggen bound
> Snores out the watch of night. O majesty!
> When thou dost pinch thy bearer, thou dost sit
> Like a rich armour worn in heat of day,
> That scalds with safety. By his gates of breath
> There lies a downy feather which stirs not:
> Did he suspire, that light and weightless down
> Perforce must move. My gracious lord! my father!
> *Etc.*

And here is what he says he said:

> I spake unto the crown as having sense,
> And thus upbraided it: "The care on thee depending
> Hath fed upon the body of my father;
> Therefore, thou best of gold art worst of gold:
> Other, less fine in carat, is more precious,
> Preserving life in medicine potable;
> But thou, most fine, most honour'd, most renown'd,
> Hast eat thy bearer up." Thus, my most royal liege,
> Accusing it, I put it on my head,
> To try with it, as with an enemy
> That had before my face murder'd my father,
> The quarrel of a true inheritor.

The changes Henry quietly slips into his account of his own humiliating blunder are quite human and understandable. But if we want to understand

Henry we cannot overlook them. Actually the address to the crown is half over before he discovers the supposed death of his father. But he tells the King he realized he was dead as soon as he came into the chamber and *for that reason* denounced the crown:

> God witness with me, when I here came in,
> And found no course of breath within your majesty,
> How cold it struck my heart!

Bringing God into the matter is in itself suspicious, and when a moment later he repeats what he has just said, we know that a bad conscience is back of the double protestation:

> Coming to look on you, thinking you dead,
> And dead almost, my liege, to think you were,
> I spake unto the crown. . . .

The theme of the actual apostrophe is the crown as a disturber of slumber—of royalty in general it might almost seem. Its theme, as Henry recounts it, is the crown as murderer—specifically of "my father." The tone of the real speech is meditative and reflective—not unlike that of Henry IV's own address to sleep. The tone of the supposed one is that of an upbraiding or accusation (the Prince's own words), and the act of putting the crown on his head a trial with an enemy

> That had before my face murder'd my father.

He even inserts new details. Where, for instance, in the original is the reference to potable gold that he says he made? No, the revised version is doubtless what Henry now wishes he had said. What he did say was something quite different. And the vehemence with which he denies at the end— for we interrupted him—that he had any selfish motive in what he said or did is enough in itself to convict him. If he were innocent, words like these would be superfluous:

> But if it did infect my blood with joy,
> Or swell my thoughts to any strain of pride;
> If any rebel or vain spirit of mine
> Did with the least affection of a welcome
> Give entertainment to the might of it,
> Let God forever keep it from my head
> And make me as the poorest vassal is
> That doth with awe and terror kneel to it!

"I didn't take any cake," the guilty child protests even before he is accused, putting the hand that holds the cake behind him. Quite as boldly, if not quite so naïvely, the Prince puts behind him the words he spoke but a moment before. What he expressly declares he did not say or feel fits what he did say and obviously did feel with a damning neatness. In substance, he protests: "I, Prince Harry, feel any pride or offer the least welcome to the might of the crown! God keep it from me if I did." Yet this is what he said:

> put the world's whole strength
> Into one giant arm, it shall not force
> This lineal honour from me. This from thee
> Will I to mine leave, as 'tis left to me.

If that is not dynastic pride and the poison of power, what is it? *Infection:* we have the Prince himself to thank for the one word that describes it best. And there comes to mind by way of contrast, as Shakespeare must have specifically intended that it should, the vow of Faulconbridge with which *King John* concludes:

> Come the three corners of the world in arms,
> And we shall shock them. Naught shall make us rue,
> If England to itself do rest but true.

So similar, yet so antipodal! Such is the difference, Shakespeare seems to say, between love of country and family pride, between an uncrowned and a self-crowned king.... Years afterward the poet passed judgment on Prince Henry's conduct in this scene in a singular and possibly unconscious way. The feather! Every lover of Shakespeare will instantly think of another feather that did not stir, the one King Lear held to the lips of Cordelia. The depth and genuineness of the emotion there become a measure of its absence here.

But the Prince's explanation and apology (to come back to the scene) assuage the dying King. Begging his son to sit by him on the bed, he tells him of the "indirect crook'd ways" by which he came by the crown, of the disillusionment of power and the futility of his reign. He even admits that the long-planned crusade to the Holy Land was a political blind designed to distract the attention of the overinquisitive:

> Lest rest and lying still might make them look
> Too near unto my state.

So the long and pious address on peace with which the first of these two dramas opens turns out to have been a piece of political-religious duplicity. If ever the end of a work of art altered its beginning, it is this one. (Yet there are those who tell us that Shakespeare was concerned only with what the ordinary Elizabethan playgoer could take in at a first performance!)

But whatever his former words were, the King's present ones sound like a deathbed repentance, with entreaties from the father to the son to make *his* reign as different from his own as possible. But no! men generally die as they have lived, and just as we are ready for a miracle Henry reverts to his normal selfish self and concludes:

> Therefore, my Harry,
> Be it thy course to busy giddy minds
> With foreign quarrels; that action, hence borne out,
> May waste the memory of the former days.
> More would I, but my lungs are wasted so
> That strength of speech is utterly denied me.
> How I came by the crown, O God, forgive!
> And grant it may with thee in true peace live.

Was there ever such a "therefore"? "My reign was a futile one: therefore, go thou and do likewise. Use the trick I planned to use." Or to put it even more cynically: "Make war, dear boy, and God grant your reign may be a peaceful one." It sounds so incredible, so like a parody, that it is necessary to requote the text to substantiate its meticulous accuracy:

> Therefore, my Harry,
> Be it thy course to busy giddy minds
> With foreign quarrels. . . .
> How I came by the crown, O God, forgive!
> And grant it may with thee in true peace live.

The end forgets the beginning. Such is the level to which a fine brain may be reduced by a life of lies. Such is a king's idea of peace. And the new king, standing where his father formerly did, gives no sign that he so much as notices this typical piece of monarchical hypocrisy, but calmly replies:

> My gracious liege,
> You won it, wore it, kept it, gave it me;
> Then plain and right must my possession be:
> Which I with more than with a common pain
> 'Gainst all the world will rightfully maintain.

The son's "then" is like an antiphony to his father's "therefore." And immediately the stage direction reads: *"Enter John of Lancaster."* *"Enter the Prince of Liars,"* it might as well have been, *"fresh from the blackest act of treachery on record."* It is one of those symbolic entrances that are better than pages of criticism.

> Thou bring'st me happiness and peace, son John,

whispers the dying King. This entire family seems to have a curious conception of peace.

Turning to Warwick, the King asks the name of the chamber in which he was stricken.

> 'Tis call'd Jerusalem, my noble lord,

and the fast-failing monarch at his own request is carried into it that the prophecy may be fulfilled that he should die in Jerusalem. His crusade has at last begun—and ended—in a bitterly ironical sense. We are reminded of Tolstoy's story of *The Two Old Men* who set out for Jerusalem. They both arrived, one literally but not spiritually, the other spiritually but not literally. Henry IV arrived neither literally nor spiritually.

## X

The two scenes that follow the King's death were made to go together. In them we see justice, first under its mundane, then under something more nearly resembling its eternal aspect.

We are taken to Gloucestershire and see Master Robert Shallow, rural justice of the peace, planning to keep Sir John Falstaff, "the man of war" as Shallow's servant Davy calls him, overnight at his home. The scene might be called *Peace and War Preparing to Swallow Each Other*, and the result is a foregone conclusion, for Shallow is as thin and spare a man as Falstaff is fat, and his wits and spirit as starved as Falstaff's are well fed. The news of the old king's death has not yet come, but Master Robert knows that Sir John is close to the man who will soon rule England. He lends him a thousand pounds on that security a little later. "A friend i' the court is better than a penny in purse," he declares, and accordingly nothing is too good for the man of war. Davy perceives that this is the moment to put in a plea for a friend of his, one William Visor. "Visor is an arrant knave, on my knowledge," says Shallow. "I grant your worship," Davy admits, "but yet, God forbid, sir, but a knave should have some countenance at his friend's request. . . . I have served your worship truly, sir, this eight years; and if I cannot once or twice in a quarter bear out a knave against an honest man, I have but a very little credit with your worship." "He shall have no wrong," declares the Justice.

The scene shifts to Westminster and we see the Lord Chief Justice of England awaiting the entrance of the new king. He awaits it with no illusions, for this new king is no other than the Prince Hal whom in his father's time he sent to prison for striking him in his "very seat of judgment." The power is now Henry's and the Chief Justice expects him to take revenge. And sure enough the new monarch has little more than entered than he reminds the Justice of the great indignities he once heaped upon him:

> What! rate, rebuke, and roughly send to prison
> The immediate heir of England!

But the Chief Justice, whose character proves that honor in its true sense is not obsolete, defends himself with such cogency and dignity that the King, quite won, replies:

> You are right, justice; and you weigh this well.

He reappoints him to his office and begs him to go on administering the laws of his kingdom in this "bold, just, and impartial spirit." Offering him his hand, Henry declares (in lines that call for the very closest scrutiny):

> You shall be as a father to my youth;
> My voice shall sound as you do prompt mine ear,
> And I will stoop and humble my intents
> To your well-practis'd wise directions.
> And, princes all, believe me, I beseech you:
> My father is gone wild into his grave,
> For in his tomb lie my affections;
> And with his spirit sadly I survive,
> To mock the expectation of the world,
> To frustrate prophecies and to raze out
> Rotten opinion, who hath writ me down
> After my seeming. The tide of blood in me
> Hath proudly flow'd in vanity till now:
> Now doth it turn and ebb back to the sea,
> Where it shall mingle with the state of floods
> And flow henceforth in formal majesty.
> Now call we our high court of parliament:
> And let us choose such limbs of noble counsel,
> That the great body of our state may go
> In equal rank with the best govern'd nation;
> That war, or peace, or both at once, may be
> As things acquainted and familiar to us;
> In which you, father, shall have foremost hand.
> Our coronation done, we will accite,
> As I before remember'd, all our state:
> And, God consigning to my good intents,
> No prince nor peer shall have just cause to say,
> God shorten Harry's happy life one day!

Here is Henry at his finest, it will be said. Here is the first fruit of the great reversal he has been keeping in reserve ever since that first soliloquy. Here is the sun about to emerge from the clouds. Here is the Prodigal Son putting off Vanity and adopting Justice as his father and guide. It is just as Dover Wilson said. His theory of the morality play is vindicated in this scene.

It would be churlish indeed to suggest that Henry did not mean, or at least think he meant, what he said to the Chief Justice. But that does not excuse our overlooking the fact that both his words and his attitude also happen to be the most expedient ones he could conceivably have uttered and adopted at a moment when a decorous impression was so imperative to his success, when the unexpected was the indispensable. (Even Richard III stood up to be seen of all men between two bishops.) It was Henry's luck on this occasion that the most generous action was also the most politic. In such cases the judging of motives becomes ticklish.

Whether Henry did at this moment turn from Vanity to Justice depends not at all on what he promised his future "father" at the moment, but on what he did during the days and months to come. It depends, that is, on what he did in the little that is left of this play and on what he did throughout the succeeding one. Except in the matter of the rejection of Falstaff, then, it would seem as if judgment must be suspended until we have taken the next play into account.

But, as we have seen over and over, Shakespeare is in the habit of revealing the embryo of the future in the present, and Henry's preview of his own reign in the last half of his apology to the Chief Justice will bear examination from this point of view. What a man thinks he is saying is often at odds with what he is really saying. Shakespeare is a master at giving us both at once, the one in the thought, the other in the imagery and accent. Prosaic men like Henry use metaphors at their peril.

The sense of Henry's speech seems plain enough. "Here is my promise," he says in effect to the Chief Justice, "to subject my inexperience to your experience, to bow my will to yours. My father is dead, but I survive to surprise the world by defeating its ominous expectations concerning my reign. Hitherto I have given my life to vanity; henceforth I will give it to good counsel to the end that England may be as well governed as any nation on earth. You, My Lord Chief Justice, shall be my foremost adviser in both war and peace. With God's help, no one will wish my reign abbreviated by a single day."

Here, apparently, is a complete subjection of himself on Henry's part to the wisdom of the Chief Justice. But examine it more closely and it bears every mark of being, actually, an abject surrender to the spirit of his father. Henry himself supplies the metaphor that proves it. Just as his own word "infect" gave the clue to the effect upon him of putting on the crown, so his own word "ebb" shows what is happening here. Hitherto I have flowed, he says, now I will ebb. An ominous figure! And one that utterly reverses all he has previously vowed. His carousing with Falstaff, he told us (if under a different metaphor) was to be just a temporary ebbing—a little eddy—in the main stream of his life, which thereafter would flow steadily forward. Now it is the other way around. He has been flowing with Falstaff; now he will "turn and ebb back to the sea." What he means, of course, is that his vanity has increased and now will decrease. But it is not superficial things like vanity that ebb and flow. It is elemental things like the tide and the blood of man. *The tide of my blood now turns and ebbs back to the sea*, he declares. He thinks that thereby he is saying that from now on he will control his passions. But what are those passions but that very sea? The word "sea" is older and Henry's imagination is wiser than he is, and what it describes, in spite of him, is precisely the process that psychologists today call a regression into The Father, the sacrifice to ancestral forces and the past of freedom to control the present and to be a unique individual. The formal and dignified accent and movement of the verse confirm the reactionary state of mind of the speaker. And so does his vocabulary with its insistence on such words as "state," "rank," "formal," "majesty," "governed." This is not the language of moral emancipation. It is just the opposite. What practically clinches the matter is an obviously intentional ambiguity on Shakespeare's part in the line,

> In which you, father, shall have foremost hand.

Ostensibly this is addressed to the Chief Justice whom Henry has chosen as his father and counselor in war and peace. But, in its context, it fits far better that dead father with whose spirit he expressly says he survives:

> My father is gone wild into his grave,
> For in his tomb lie my affections;
> And with his spirit sadly I survive. . . .

These Delphic lines permit at least three interpretations. At a casual reading they mean no more than: my father is no longer living, but my love is still with him in the grave. But that leaves the word "wild" out of account. My father and I have executed an exchange, is what Henry says: my wild youth lies buried forever in his tomb, while his spirit has transmigrated into me (or, if that seems too strong, attends me as a guardian). And the lines will bear still another construction: my father is in his tomb and buried with him lie my powers to feel (the usual Elizabethan use of the word "affections"), while I survive with his spirit (which, the reader of these plays knows, was one lacking in human warmth). Henry, naturally, did not intend this. Shakespeare, I am convinced, did. In fact, the rejection of Falstaff, I should say, is specifically inserted to confirm it. But it is confirmed by something less debatable than that famous scene.

The final test of Henry's sincerity in his words to the Chief Justice depends neither on them nor on anything we may find under their surface, but, as I said, on what Henry does in the time to come. If we find that he did make the Chief Justice his political guide and counselor in war and peace, and if justice was the dominating note of his reign, then the promise was kept and the moral is unexceptionable. If not, not. We see Henry and the Chief Justice together just once more in *II Henry IV*, and on that occasion, instead of asking the Justice's advice, the King issues him an order. Then, except for three or four brief sentences not in Henry's presence, the Chief Justice passes out of the story forever, and at the beginning of the next play we find the King seeking counsel of an Archbishop and a Bishop who are morally at the opposite pole from the man who is supposed to be the symbol of his own regeneration. The characters who are absent from Shakespeare's plays are often as significant as those who are present. What became of the Chief Justice in *Henry V?*

The unconscious hypocrisy of Henry's ostentatious promises to him confirms the King's regression into the spirit of his father (the archhypocrite) just as the buried fears of that father confirm in turn *his* regression into the spirit of Richard II (the archvictim of fear). The Prince's insincerity to his father in the crown scene is the promise of the King's insincerity to the Chief Justice in the "father" scene. The one interpretation supports the other. But we must await the next play for the crowning evidence (in all senses) on this point.

Both the older and the younger Henry illustrate in extreme degree the law of moral compensation which anyone with any power of introspection may observe in himself. Whenever they say or do anything unwontedly frank or generous it becomes necessary to ask what they may just have done or are just about to do that is disingenuous or ungenerous. If Falstaff had overheard Henry's words to the Chief Justice, he might have guessed what was in store for him.

## XI

Pistol brings word of the King's death to Falstaff in Shallow's garden. The fat man's hour has come—or so he believes:

Away, Bardolph! saddle my horse. Master Robert Shallow, choose what office thou wilt in the land, 'tis thine.... We'll ride all night.... I know the young king is sick for me. Let us take any man's horses; the laws of England are at my commandment. Blessed are they that have been my friends; and woe to my Lord Chief Justice!

When we next greet Falstaff, he is standing in the street near Westminster Abbey waiting for the King to ride by. He comes and Falstaff hails him. "God save thy grace, King Hal! my royal Hal! . . . God save thee, my sweet boy!"

"I know thee not, old man," the King replies—and amplifies those half-dozen words into twenty-five lines.* It is the Rejection of Falstaff, one of the three or four most debated scenes in Shakespeare. To have them before us, the familiar lines must be quoted once more:

> I know thee not, old man: fall to thy prayers;
> How ill white hairs become a fool and jester!
> I have long dream'd of such a kind of man,
> So surfeit-swell'd, so old, and so profane;
> But, being awak'd, I do despise my dream.
> Make less thy body hence, and more thy grace;
> Leave gormandizing; know the grave doth gape
> For thee thrice wider than for other men.
> Reply not to me with a fool-born jest:
> Presume not that I am the thing I was;
> For God doth know, so shall the world perceive,
> That I have turn'd away my former self;
> So will I those that kept me company.
> When thou dost hear I am as I have been,
> Approach me, and thou shalt be as thou wast,
> The tutor and the feeder of my riots.
> Till then, I banish thee, on pain of death,
> As I have done the rest of my misleaders,
> Not to come near our person by ten mile.
> For competence of life I will allow you,
> That lack of means enforce you not to evil;
> And, as we hear you do reform yourselves,
> We will, according to your strengths and qualities,
> Give you advancement. Be it your charge, my lord,
> To see perform'd the tenour of our word.
> Set on.

The sun has come out from behind the clouds.

But what a strange sun! It is the function of a sun to illuminate. But who-ever heard of a sun that sermonized, or that refused to shine on the just and the unjust alike, particularly on one of its satellites, however ancient? Who, we ask, is this new king, to adopt this top-lofty manner toward an old man whom he could so easily have passed by in silence and rebuked, if he must, in private? "As we hear you do reform yourselves"! How long, in de-cency's name, has he been reformed himself? It is not Henry's rejection of tavern life with which we quarrel. That, naturally, had to go. It is not with his new sense of responsibility. That we welcome. What we inevita-bly remember is the beam and the mote (not to imply that "mote" does justice to Falstaff's vices).

---

* Here is perhaps the place to recall that in Dostoevsky's *The Devils* "Prince Harry" had a liaison with a certain lady whom he afterward publicly insulted.

The best we can say for Henry is that it is an outburst of that temper of which his father told us he was a victim ("being incens'd, he's flint"), sudden anger at Falstaff's highly untactful appearance at such a time and place. The worst we can say is that the King had deliberately planned to rebuke Falstaff publicly at the first opportunity for the sake of the moral contrast with his own past and in fulfilment of the promise of his first soliloquy. Unfortunately for Henry, however much anger he may have felt at the moment, Falstaff's explanation of the calamity to Shallow: "He must seem thus to the world," seems the most psychologically plausible account of what happened. But in what a different sense from that intended for Shallow! And we remember how Henry's father publicly pardoned Carlisle with his right hand, so to speak, while he was secretly murdering Richard with his left. Henry's vow to let his father "have foremost hand" in all his doings was being fulfilled, whomever he thought he was choosing as his guide. If it is a wise child that knows his own father, Henry was acquiring wisdom.

What did Shakespeare think?

Anyone is free to conjecture. And, however we take it, there is plenty of evidence.

This much at any rate is certain: we cannot imagine Shakespeare, no matter how high he might have risen in worldly place or esteem, rejecting a former friend by preaching him a sermon in public, no matter how low his friend might have fallen. So unthinkable is it that it seems almost silly to reduce the idea to words.

"A new commandment," said the smiling Muse,
"I give my darling son, Thou shalt not preach";—
Luther, Fox, Behmen, Swedenborg, grew pale,
And, on the instant, rosier clouds upbore
Hafiz and Shakspeare with their shining choirs.

Surely in those lines "Shakespeare's younger brother"—as John Jay Chapman called Emerson—gave utterance to the innermost spirit of Shakespeare. It has become a commonplace that the poet rated ingratitude among the deadliest of the sins. What would he have thought of ingratitude supplemented by preaching?

Nor can we imagine Falstaff himself doing what Henry did, if, in some inconceivable way, their roles had been reversed. And we love him for that incapacity. I wonder if Shakespeare has not been at pains to point this out. In the very first scene in which we see Hal and Falstaff together the latter tells of a casual incident that takes on an entirely fresh meaning in the light of this very last scene in which we see them together, "together" now in what a different sense.

> FALSTAFF: An old lord of the council rated me the other day in the street about you, sir, but I marked him not; and yet he talked very wisely, but I regarded him not; and yet he talked wisely, and in the street too.
>
> PRINCE: Thou didst well; for wisdom cries out in the streets, and no man regards it.

Wisdom does indeed cry out in the streets, but generally without opening her mouth, and certainly not in the form of moral diatribe. It is Morality that indulges in moral indignation. Wisdom, like Shakespeare, speaks in more oblique fashion, as she does, if I am not mistaken, in this very scene.

When Falstaff has been rebuffed, and he and his followers have been carried off to the Fleet, the play is a dozen lines from its end. Those lines (except for six significantly terse and reticent words from the Chief Justice) are all spoken by John of Lancaster. Why does Shakespeare, who is so fond of remarking that "the end crowns the whole," give the crowning speeches of this play to a person whose sole distinction lies in the fact that he is the most dastardly character in it? Why does he permit him, and him alone, to pass judgment on his brother's act in rejecting Falstaff?

> I like this fair proceeding of the king's.

If you know the devil's opinion, you can infer the angels'. The safest way to vote is to find out how the most "intelligently" selfish man in the community is voting and then vote the other way. It was in recognition of this principle, I believe, that Shakespeare reserved the most emphatic place in his play for the judgment on the King's rejection of Falstaff by the man whom Falstaff, in just six words, caused *us* to cast forth into everlasting darkness: "a man cannot make him laugh." Dostoevsky declares that a man's character can be read by the way he laughs. By that token John of Lancaster had no character. He "doth not love me," said laughing John of sober John. And so when sober John welcomes the humiliation and degradation of laughing John by saying,

> I like this fair proceeding of the king's,

it sounds like a statement straight from Shakespeare that the proceeding was not fair and that he did not like it.*

* This chapter was written, except for stylistic changes and interpolations in answer to Dover Wilson's book on Falstaff, before the publication of Charlton's *Shakesperian Comedy*. I was interested to find that the author makes the same point about John of Lancaster.

## XII

But there is more evidence than this (not counting that in the next play). In Shakespeare, as in life, things do not happen unprepared for. If we look back, we find a little scene in which the rejection of Falstaff was specifically forecast. More than forecast, rehearsed.

The place is the Boar's Head Tavern in Eastcheap, and the time just after the "discomfiture" of Falstaff in the matter of the robbery. Mistress Quickly, the hostess, enters to announce that a nobleman of the court has a message for the Prince from his father. Falstaff goes to the door to send the interloper packing, but comes back with news that the Percys are in revolt and civil war is on in the North. The Prince must be at court in the morning.

FALSTAFF: Tell me, Hal, art thou not horribly afeard? thou being heir apparent, could the world pick thee out three such enemies again as that fiend Douglas, that spirit Percy, and that devil Glendower? Art thou not horribly afraid? doth not thy blood thrill at it?

PRINCE: Not a whit, i' faith; I lack some of thy instinct.

FALSTAFF: Well, thou wilt be horribly chid to-morrow when thou comest to thy father: if thou love me, practise an answer.

PRINCE: Do thou stand for my father, and examine me upon the particulars of my life.

FALSTAFF: Shall I? content.

And Sir John instantly arranges the properties in a manner that reveals equally deep insight into the affairs of the state and of the stage, anticipating Goethe's principle that nothing is right in the theater that is not a symbol to the eye. "This chair shall be my state," he says, "this dagger my sceptre, and this cushion my crown"—a treatise on political science in a sentence—and he proceeds to impersonate King Henry with a perfection that wrings tears of ecstasy from Mrs. Quickly:

O Jesu, this is excellent sport, i' faith! . . . O, the father, how he holds his countenance! . . . he doth it as like one of these harlotry players as ever I see!

This "harlotry" King Henry chides his son for defiling himself with pitch by consorting with such loose companions—always excepting one "goodly portly man, i' faith, and a corpulent," in whose looks he perceives virtue. "Him keep with, the rest banish."

Whereupon the roles are reversed. "Do thou stand for me," says Hal, "and I'll play my father."

"Depose me?" cries Falstaff.

And then, if ever, we behold the future in the instant. It is as if something in the air and accent of the Prince, merely playing as he is, enables Falstaff to catch as in a magic mirror the bearing and voice of King Henry V as he was to pause near the Abbey on that fateful day and call out for all to hear, "I know thee not, old man." "If thou dost it half so gravely, so majestically, both in word and matter," Falstaff goes on, laying aside his role for a moment, "hang me up by the heels for a rabbit-sucker or a poulter's hare." But Henry *was* to do it gravely and majestically, and Falstaff *was*, figuratively, to be hung up by the heels. That one sentence should be enough to show that what Shakespeare is giving us here is a rehearsal of the rejection of Falstaff. But the little scene it introduces is such a masterpiece in its own right that it throws us off the track of its connection with what has come before, and what is to follow, in the main play. Poetry, like the sun, can blind as well as illuminate.

When in a gay moment we are off guard, we give utterance under the shield of wit to convictions and intentions from the bottom of our hearts that in any other mood we wouldn't for the world reveal. This principle is the key to this little scene. *Playing the part of his father*, Henry proceeds to castigate "that villanous abominable misleader of youth, Falstaff, that old white-bearded Satan," to which Falstaff, *playing the part of Hal*, retorts with a defense of himself that ends in a revelation of deep acquaintance with his own soul and with Henry's: "but for sweet Jack Falstaff, kind Jack Falstaff, true Jack Falstaff, valiant Jack Falstaff, and therefore more valiant, being, as he is, old Jack Falstaff, banish not him thy Harry's company, banish not him thy Harry's company: banish plump Jack, and banish all the world." To which the Prince in turn, *playing the King*, replies with unconscious divination of the future: "I do, I will." He will indeed. Now he pretends to be his father and *does* banish Falstaff. A little later he will become like his father and *will* banish him. Now he plays king. Then he will be king. Beware of what you play—it will come true. "Rehearsal" is not too strong a term for this scene.

Instantly following the Player-King's "I do, I will," the stage direction reads: "*A knocking is heard.*" It is one of Shakespeare's earliest uses of the device he employs so subtly in *Julius Caesar*, and, as everyone knows, so tremendously in *Macbeth*, to betoken at a fateful moment the knocking of the inner mentor. . . . But no, it is only the sheriff at the door, just as it was only Macduff; and Hal, though he stands on the inside, does not heed, or even hear, the warning from within. Yet there it is, saying plainly, if he could only hear it: "Banish sweet Jack Falstaff and banish all the world."

(The sweet Jack Falstaff, be it most particularly noted, not the malodorous one.) The difference in tone between this scene and the one in *Macbeth* should not mislead us. Even in a tavern, life may be lived well.

This little play within a play, two plays within a play, each with its player-king, may well warn us that *Hamlet* itself is barely around the corner. Indeed, this mousetrap catches not only the conscience of a king but the conscience of a king-to-be. The play scene in Shakespeare's tragic masterpiece to come scarcely surpasses this one in the subtlety of its psychology or the intricacy of its interwoven meanings. Here, if anywhere, here, if ever, the truth is brought home that we are not single personalities, nor even double ones, but bundles rather of actual and potential, emerging and expiring selves, as many as there are people who love or hate us, or whom we love or hate. Each one out there evokes a different one in here. The relation between two individuals is itself an individual relation, and, when it is set up, something that never was before on sea or land is created. Within the confines of this brief scene, to the success of which Mrs. Quickly, as audience, makes a memorable if mainly silent contribution, half-a-dozen Falstaffs and Henrys jostle and elbow, come in and go out, split, disintegrate, and recombine, a veritable phantasmagoria of spiritual entities. Who would undertake even to enumerate, let alone characterize them? When Falstaff plays Hal's father, for instance, he is partly King Henry rebuking the Prince for his wildness and partly the Falstaff who loves Hal as if he were his own son, and who longs to have Hal love him as if he were his father and consequently pictures himself as the sort of ideal father he would actually like to be to him. When, the parts exchanged, Falstaff plays Hal, he is first the subdued and respectful Prince in the presence of authority, and then the Hal whom Falstaff loved, and who, as Falstaff acts him, loved him as the real Falstaff longed to have the real Hal love him, and as, alas, he never did. When Hal acts himself, he is modest and reticent, not to say a bit scared, speaking scarcely a dozen words, but when he becomes his father he grows dominating and forbidding, and evokes in his description of his son's dissolute misleader the drunken debauched Falstaff who, it is especially worth noting, is otherwise totally and conspicuously absent from the scene. The Prince, *as his father*, says exactly what Sir John's bitterest enemies among critics and readers have been saying of him ever since:

That bolting-hutch of beastliness. . . . Wherein is he good, but to taste sack and drink it? wherein neat and cleanly, but to carve a capon and eat it? wherein cunning, but in craft? wherein crafty, but in villainy? Wherein villanous, but in all things? wherein worthy, but in nothing?

—while Hal, *impersonated by Falstaff*, describes the sweet, kind, true, valiant Jack that all the world loves, except the above-mentioned dissenters. It is all wonderful fun and we laugh. Yet underneath the mirth, how beautiful and tragic the implications, how beyond comprehension the miracle by which so much is compressed into so little! And hovering over it all, over all these subordinate personalities that glide in and glide out like ghosts, is the evoker and master of them all (for it is only in his presence that Hal ever rises to such imaginative height), the Immortal Falstaff, the sweet Jack Falstaff whom Henry should never have rejected to the end of his days.

## XIII

If anyone asks how Henry could have rejected one Falstaff and kept the other, there is both a general and a specific answer.

The first may be put in the form of another question: In what do love and friendship consist if not in a perpetual acceptance of the angels and rejection of the devils that we discover in everyone with whom we are brought into intimate contact? Here is merely an extreme instance of this truth.

Falstaff had been both Henry's tempter and his tutor. Tempter may seem the wrong word when we remember that Henry entered on his dissipations with both eyes open; but, like some of the critics of these plays, perhaps he was more seduced by Falstaff than he was willing to admit. At any rate he abandoned himself along with him to dissolute courses and moral irresponsibility. But this does not alter the fact that Falstaff gave him unconscious instruction in wit, humor, good-fellowship, understanding of human nature, and above all in imaginative love of life for its own sake. Even Mr. Stoll, remember, admits that Falstaff is "supremely poetic."

Practically all teachers have their good points, and even teachers of genius have their weaknesses. It is the art of the pupil to profit by the good points, to let himself be taken captive by the genius, and to overlook or reject the weaknesses.

> There is some soul of goodness in things evil,
> Would men observingly distil it out.

It was Henry himself who said that (in a moment of unusual insight), and it fits the case of himself and Falstaff so perfectly that one could think Shakespeare had him say it for that reason. Falstaff was a teacher of genius with lamentable weaknesses. Henry should have rejected those weaknesses and turned the genius to account in his position as king. Instead of distilling out the soul of goodness and throwing away what was left, he carefully kept what was left and threw away the soul of goodness. It is a strong statement, but the text of the next play, if not of this one, amply justifies it.

Consider what Henry might have done. The true pupil perpetuates the genius of his teacher not by adopting his ideas or imitating his conduct but by carrying on and living out his spirit under the peculiar conditions of his own life.

There is something like critical agreement that Shakespeare's three great-est achievements in character portrayal are Falstaff, Hamlet, and Cleopatra, to whom Iago is sometimes added as a diabolic fourth. Now Falstaff, Ham-let, and Cleopatra, different as they are in a hundred ways, have this in common: they are all endowed with imagination, and especially with dra-matic and histrionic power, to something like the highest degree. Each is a genius of play. (Even Iago is in his perverted way.) In a word, they all are in this respect like their creator, a kind of proof that even Shakespeare could draw people better who resembled himself than he could others. Who would not like to have had Shakespeare as a teacher? Prince Henry did. A huge slice of him at least. And then he went and threw away his education.

Having glanced at Henry's teacher, consider next his opportunity. War is not the supreme tragedy of men and nations. The supreme tragedy of men and nations is that the moment war ceases they give themselves over to the pursuit of pleasure or power: either to idleness, amusement, diver-sion, dissipation, or sport; or to money, business, intrigue, politics, domi-nation in some one of its diverse aspects—either, that is, to "peace" in that soft sense which indirectly makes more war inevitable, or to the hard self-ishness that is nothing but war in its slumbering form. A third way that is neither pleasure nor power is humanity's supreme desideratum. What that third way is is no secret. How to get humanity to take it is the prob-lem. The way itself is that of the imagination: of the love of life for its own sake, of human friendship or the good family on a social scale, of play in its adult estate. Shakespeare himself is an example of one who took that way. He taught us all to play. Think of the thousands who have "played" him in a dozen senses and perpetuated his spirit among tens of thousands of others who never or scarcely ever heard his name. Plato held that human-ity will be saved only when philosophers become kings or kings philoso-phers. Falstaff-Hamlet-Cleopatra-Shakespeare go Plato one better. They cast their vote for the poet–and–player-king.

Now Henry had a marvelous chance to begin being such an ideal ruler. He was obviously endowed by nature with a spirit of good-fellowship. He had an imaginative genius for a teacher. He had the opportunity of a king. He ought to have taught all England to play. But what did he do? Instead of leading his kingdom first to justice under the spirit of the Chief Justice and then to good-fellowship under the spirit of Falstaff, he led it to war under the ghost of his father. He accepted his father's advice to "busy giddy minds with foreign quarrels" and *in precise imitation of his father* went out, as the next play shows, to appropriate a throne that did not belong to him. Shakespeare did not invent this colossal irony. He merely perceived it.

But it was not only the ghost of his father that Henry was obeying; he was following in the footsteps of the very Immoral Falstaff whom he thought he had rejected. From snatching travelers' purses in pure fun, Henry goes on to annexing crowns that do not belong to him in dead earnest. He goes Falstaff many times better. An amateur retail robber becomes a professional wholesale one. "Leave gormandizing," he says to Falstaff, and turns to his attempt to swallow France. As usual, moral indignation against others indicates more often than not that the man who feels it is guilty in some subtler or symbolic form of the very sin he is castigating. Remember Antonio and Shylock.

And so the pattern of this supposed morality play of the reformed prodigal grows more and more demoralized. As we get the four plays that begin with *Richard II* in perspective, we see that from the moment when Henry Bolingbroke usurped a throne, stealing has been a main theme of the tetralogy. So taken, the two parts of *Henry IV* are not an alternation of historical scenes and comic relief. The history and the comedy are concerned with the same thing. It is no longer necessary to say that Falstaff runs away with the author or "steals the show." (Even if he does, what could be more appropriate?) The poet was beginning to perceive that history has no significance until it is seen as comedy—and tragedy. Imagination was beginning to assert its mastery of fact.

Prince Hal's first soliloquy now becomes clear. It was spoken by two persons. "Someday I shall be king. And then good-by to fun. Let me have some while I can," was the nonchalant Hal's innocent version of it. "I'll sow some wild oats for a year or two, and then I'll reap a harvest of wheat —and market it at the highest price," was the cold calculating heir-apparent's version. "I'll eat my cake and have it." It is a fascinating theory. But it never works. We do *not* have what we have eaten. And we reap what we sow, except that we reap rather more than we sow, and if we sow the wind we sometimes reap the whirlwind. "I won't count this year" is not a whit sounder than "I won't count this drink." Life counts every minute. How she does so is most minutely and convincingly set down in this dramatic biography of Henry, Prince of Wales, later King Henry V, by William Shakespeare. So much profounder is the truth than a moral.

To recognize that here is the truth we need make no dusty study of history. The story of Prince Hal is the usual one. It is as contemporary as this morning's sun. It can be duplicated in its essential features in any American university, college, or private school:

The charming and talented son of an able and ambitious father (the basis of whose business success had better not be scrutinized too closely), foreseeing the career the paternal fortune has cut out for him, decides to enjoy himself while he can. Though he is at college, he will see a bit of life (which after all is a better teacher than books), have a taste of gaiety before the responsibilities of his inheritance compel him to settle down. He does. He has a "royal" time, and he is not guilty of anything particularly bad, though some of his companions, on the strength of his allowance, go a bit further than he does. Relying on his native wit, he neglects his college work rather scandalously and his stock falls pretty low in official quarters. Everyone knows, however, the high quality of the work he could do if he only wanted to, and with the help of those who are willing to count this as an asset, he manages to scrape through. When he is graduated he has lost his boyish bloom and something seems to have tarnished his charm, yet he is still a delightful youth and everyone expects great things of him—all but a few keen observers who have seen the same thing too often. He travels for a year or so and then goes into the business in which his father has been too deeply buried to notice much about his son one way or the other, except to half-smile and half-frown at certain rumors about wild oats, and to observe with regret that his interest in his father's business (and incidentally his scholastic record) is not to be compared with that of the promising son of one of his associates.

And then the young man goes back to his tenth class reunion and his friends are gratified—and the few discerning ones are shocked. Our Prince Charming has settled down—no more fast living for him—in fact he is well on the road to becoming a Successful Man. His delightful modesty has given way to an air of command. His eyes have lost their roguish twinkle. He has put on more flesh. People begin to remark his resemblance to his father, who, by the way, is now dead. (Whether the son took a look into the paternal ledgers just before he died under the impression that he had already expired is not recorded.) Those with insight have a pretty accurate picture of him in mind as he will be at his twenty-fifth reunion, and, if he is still alive, at his fortieth.

Put your American college youth back five centuries, make him heir to the throne, and give him as boon companion one of the greatest wits and humorists that ever lived, and you have the case of Hal–Prince Henry– King Henry V in its main outlines.

Why, then, is it not all perfectly obvious? For the same reason that most of his friends and classmates go on taking our American hero for a Successful Man. He is, in their sense. And maybe in that sense Henry is destined to be an ideal king. Moreover, we loved him in his youth, and love is notoriously unconscious of changes for the worse in its object—like the mother who goes on treating the cynical worldling of thirty-five as if he were still the innocent boy of ten. So we do not notice the gradations by which Henry ceases to be Hal.

> Crumbling is not an instant's act,
> A fundamental pause;
> Dilapidation's processes
> Are organized decays.
>
> 'Tis first a cobweb on the soul,
> A cuticle of dust,
> A borer in the axis,
> An elemental rust.
>
> Ruin is formal, devil's work,
> Consecutive and slow—
> Fail in an instant no man did,
> Slipping is crash's law.

Those lines of Emily Dickinson put in succinct form the truth that these dramas about Henry document in such detail. Hal had said that the sun would rise clouded and then suddenly burst forth in all his glory. It was just the other way around. The sun rose clear and was gradually obscured. Is it any wonder Shakespeare stresses that metaphor?

If the evidence so far presented for this view of Henry seems insufficient, more, in abundance, is found in the next play.

## XIV

Undoubtedly the profoundest study of the father-son relationship since Shakespeare—possibly the profoundest in all literature—is Dostoevsky's in *The Brothers Karamazov*. That book, from one angle, is just an exhaustive contrast between natural and spiritual fatherhood. In it we see the sons of Fyodor Karamazov standing between him, their natural, and Zossima, their spiritual, father. This pure and saintlike man seems at the opposite pole from the debauched Falstaff. (To mention them in the same sentence will be an offense to some.) And so he is—from the *debauched* Falstaff, who indeed resembles in not a few respects the debauched Fyodor Karamazov. Yet Zossima's role in the story is in a way like the role of the finer Falstaff. Opposite as are their terminologies—that of religion and that of play—their creeds, in spirit, are startlingly alike. Zossima's is life for the joy of it as against Fyodor's pursuit of sensual pleasure. Falstaff's is life for the fun of it as against Henry IV's belief in power. The differences are, admittedly, abysmal, but the affinity is clear. And so when we see the sons (one son in particular) in the one case and the son in the other, standing between the racial father and the imaginative father, we recognize the same situation. And the conclusion reached by the two supreme geniuses who brought them into being is an identical one: namely, that in proportion as the child fails to be himself he falls back into the likeness of the racial father, while in proportion as he finds an imaginative father he rises, not into that father's image, but into his own soul's image, into himself. The negative side of this truth is clearly demonstrated in these History Plays; its positive aspect had to await the Tragedies for complete clarification.

*Chapter XVII*

# Henry V

Sweet, sweet, sweet poison for the age's tooth.

A good and virtuous nature may recoil
In an imperial charge.

---

## I

There is near-unanimity among critics that *Henry V* is not a marked success as a play. For once, it is said, his material was too much even for Shakespeare. A great military victory is epic, or even lyric, rather than dramatic matter, and though the piece contains much that is splendid and picturesque, these merits cannot atone for its intellectual and dramatic poverty. "A thing of shreds and patches, held together by the Choruses," one of the best of recent critics pronounces it. "A spirited and stirring piece of drum-beating and flag-waving," says another, "full of national pride and of rhetoric suitable for recitation." And Dr. Johnson's remark, aimed especially at the last act, that "not even Shakespeare can write well without a proper subject," is quoted over and over. The play remains history, it seems to be agreed, instead of being history transmuted into drama. To make up for this lack of the dramatic, Shakespeare, it is intimated, was not above truckling to the patriotic emotions of his audience. To say right out what many have insinuated: the poet in this play proves himself something of a jingo.

Before accepting these judgments as final, it is worth noting the presumptive unlikelihood that Shakespeare would have produced a poor play, or even a second-rate one, at this time or on this occasion. Here was to be the climax of the eight History Plays which, so far as Shakespeare was concerned, began with *Henry VI* and, so far as history was concerned, with *Richard II*. Here was King Henry himself, a figure whom the author had carefully portrayed throughout what were perhaps the two greatest plays he had written (with a glimpse of him in a third). No titular hero of a Shakespearean play ever had or ever was to have such meticulous preparation. Here is a play produced on the heels of *Henry IV*, practically contemporary with *As You Like It* and *Julius Caesar*, and just preceding *Twelfth Night*, *Troilus and Cressida*, and *Hamlet*. Judged by these titles, Shakespeare was incapable of producing anything but masterpieces at this time. (Even *The Merry Wives of Windsor* is one in its inferior kind.) And yet we are to believe that in the culminating play of his great historical series Shakespeare more or less goes to pieces as a playwright and substitutes pageantry and patriotism for his proper business, drama. It may be true, for these a priori arguments prove nothing. But it certainly is not what might have been expected. That Shakespeare loved England, all his plays prove, and these historical ones in particular. But there is nothing, unless it be this play, to show that he was a flag-waver. To think of him as a jingo is as difficult as to think of him as a Jew-baiter. Our examination of *The Merchant of Venice* demonstrated, I hope, that he was not the latter. The charge that he was the former is equally worthy of examination.

But there are the Choruses of *Henry V*, it will be said, which all in themselves, without going any further, prove the point.

The Choruses of *Henry V* are indeed full of a windy chauvinism. But who said they are Shakespeare? Who said, I mean, that they represent the author's ideas or attitude? A good many have said so, it is true, in the face of the fact that they are like nothing else in the poet's works that has ever been convincingly identified with his spirit.

The Chorus differentiates himself specifically from the author on his first appearance by asking the audience to

> Admit me Chorus to this history,
> Who prologue-like your humble patience pray....

"Me Chorus" is plainly not the author; and that the speaker of a prologue may be anything but the representative of the poet or the playwright is proved in most specific fashion by the Chorus-prologue of *Troilus and Cressida*, who says:

> hither am I come
> A prologue arm'd, *but not in confidence*
> *Of author's pen or actor's voice*, but suited
> In like conditions as our argument,
> To tell you, fair beholders, that our play
> Leaps o'er the vaunt and firstlings of those broils,
> Beginning in the middle.

And the words of the Chorus in the epilogue of *Henry V* confirm the distinction:

> Thus far, with rough and all-unable pen,
> Our bending author hath pursu'd the story.

The poet would not refer to himself as "*our* bending author." It is somebody else who is speaking.

Who, then, is the Chorus? He appears to be a mixture of several things. He is in part History filling in the gaps of the story by making abridgments of what is necessarily left out in the theater. He is in part the stage manager apologizing for that necessity and for the general inadequacy of the stage to the poet's theme. (The stage is incapable of doing justice to the storm in *King Lear*, but Shakespeare creates no Chorus to point it out.) And, in accordance with one of the traditional functions of the Chorus, he is in part an abstract of average public opinion.

This last point is the crucial one. A military hero at the top of his success is always elevated by the populace into something like a god. And that is just the note that is struck with regard to the warlike Harry throughout these Choruses. But can anyone believe that Shakespeare in his own person would have called Henry "the mirror of all Christian kings" and then let him threaten to allow his soldiers to impale French babies on their pikes and dash the heads of old men against the walls; or called him "this grace of kings" and then let him declare of the prisoners,

> we'll cut the throats of those we have,
> And not a man of them that we shall take
> Shall taste our mercy;

that he would have pronounced Henry "free from vainness and self-glorious pride," after dedicating a good part of two plays to showing how he wanted to imitate the sun and astound the world by emerging suddenly from behind clouds—and not only wanted to, but did?

Soldiers before battle are exposed to martial music and often given even stronger intoxicants, that when they begin to fight they may not be coldly aware of the exact nature of what is before them. Shakespeare offers the martial music of a Chorus before each act of this play, possibly with a similar motive with regard to his auditors and readers. As word music and rhetoric, they are indeed intoxicating. But poetry in any high sense, except perhaps for a few touches, they are not. We have ourselves to blame if we let them put us in a condition in which we cannot see what is going on before us in the play. Shakespeare's procedure was quite justified. As playwright, he must get a hearing for his play. As poet, he must tell the truth. But to tell the truth about a great national hero at a time when patriotism is running high calls for courage. To tell it and to keep the piece in which you tell it popular calls for more than courage. Shakespeare did as life does. Life places both its facts and its intoxicants before us and bids us make out of the resulting clash what we can and will. So does the author of *Henry V*. Through the Choruses, the playwright gives us the popular idea of his hero. In the play, the poet tells the truth about him. We are free to accept whichever of the two we prefer. God does not indicate what we shall think of his world or of the men and women he has created. He puts them before us. But he does not compel us to see them as they are. Neither does Shakespeare.

*Henry V* opens with war on France as good as decided on. Henry would have resented it if someone had told him that. Who doesn't resent being told that his mind is made up when he thinks it is still open? The resentment is a confession that it is closed.

The previous play ended with these words from John of Lancaster:

> I will lay odds, that, ere this year expire,
> We bear our civil swords and native fire
> As far as France. I heard a bird so sing,
> Whose music, to my thinking, pleas'd the king.
> Come, will you hence?

The present play, after a Chorus that forecasts the coming conflict, opens with a conversation between the Archbishop of Canterbury and the Bishop of Ely that takes war for granted, though Canterbury does not refer to it in so blunt a term but, more tactfully, as "causes now in hand . . . as touching France." What the King's brother, a little bird, a Chorus, and two Bishops agree in foreseeing is certainly coming. Henry has obviously made up his mind to follow his father's advice to busy giddy minds with foreign quarrels.

War being deemed desirable, the next thing is to find a reason for it. The opening of the play is dedicated to a search for sound moral ground for the attack on France. Fortunately for Henry, the Archbishop of Canterbury not only has such a sanction at hand but has a motive for bringing it forward. By a happy chance, he has discovered that what is good for the church coincides with what the King has decided is good for his kingdom. In Henry IV's reign a bill had been introduced to confiscate the better half of the church's wealth. Because of the troubled times it had never come to passage. But now it has been revived:

CANT.:                     Thus runs the bill.
ELY:    This would drink deep.
CANT.:             'Twould drink the cup and all.

ELY: But what prevention?
CANT.: The king is full of grace and fair regard.
ELY: And a true lover of the holy church.
CANT.: The courses of his youth promis'd it not . . .

and the two men digress from the subject in hand to comment on the miraculous change that has come over Henry. "But, my good lord," says Ely, returning to the main point,

> How now for mitigation of this bill
> Urg'd by the commons? Doth his majesty
> Incline to it, or no?

CANT.:                  He seems indifferent,
> Or rather swaying more upon our part
> Than cherishing the exhibiters against us;
> For I have made an offer to his majesty. . . .

This offer, he goes on to explain, is that the clergy shall make the greatest contribution ever recorded to the war chest of the sovereign. It will obviously be better for the church to make a large gift and so forestall confiscation than to give little or nothing and have its wealth expropriated.

ELY: How did this offer seem receiv'd, my lord?

(There is another word, also of five letters, that would define the nature of the proposed transaction more precisely than "offer." But it would be too much to expect either of these churchmen to employ it.)

> With good acceptance of his majesty,

says Canterbury, answering Ely's question,

> Save that there was not time enough to hear,—
> As I perceiv'd his Grace would fain have done. . . .

and the Archbishop proceeds to tell of another trump card he had up his sleeve which an interruption prevented him from putting on the table before the King:

> The severals and unhidden passages
> Of his true titles to some certain dukedoms,
> And generally to the crown and seat of France
> Deriv'd from Edward, his great-grandfather.

In a word, the Church will supply not only treasure for the war chest but a justification for making the war. What more could Henry ask? This is far more than his spiritual and political "father," the Lord Chief Justice of the previous play, would have had to offer in the circumstances. That may seem a cynical way of putting it, and Henry's words, when he resumes the interrupted conversation in the next scene, seem to make it utterly unwarranted. The King begins by warning the Archbishop not to incite him to war on specious grounds. Think of the blood that will be spilt, he reminds him, every drop of which will be a just complaint against whoever begins an unrighteous conflict.

> We charge you in the name of God, take heed. . . .
> Under this conjuration speak, my lord,
> And we will hear, note, and believe in heart,
> That what you speak is in your conscience wash'd
> As pure as sin with baptism.

Nothing could sound more moral and humane (though a suspicious mind might find a Chaucerian ambiguity in that last phrase). But we must judge Henry by his acts, not by his words.

The King must have an irreproachable reason for making war. The one thing that his claim to the French throne must be is *clear*. But when the Archbishop goes on to expound that claim, clear is the one thing it does not seem to be. The sixty-odd lines Canterbury devotes to it make one of the most complicated passages of pure exposition in Shakespeare and one of the most difficult to assimilate without an opportunity to study it minutely. No one could possibly take it in in the theater. Any stage director would be certain to cut it drastically. Yet attention to it in detail is indispensable to an understanding of the scene.

The gist of Henry's claim rests on the fact that his great-great-grandmother was the daughter of Philip IV of France, the only bar to its legitimacy being the Salic law under which succession through the female line is illegal. Even if the title had been a technically good one, time had had the same effect on it as a statute of limitations. But its very age seems to recommend it all the more to the learned Archbishop. His speech consists of an elaborate discrediting of the Salic law. Under analysis it turns out to be (as it is even in Holinshed whom Shakespeare follows closely here) a colossal piece of ecclesiastical casuistry with a highly ironical application to the situation in which Henry finds himself.

That situation itself, without any historical assistance, is ironical enough. Henry's father had seized the English throne—with disillusioning consequences. His son now proposes to seize the French throne in the hope—shall we say, of wiping out his father's sin? The Archbishop's speech rubs in the irony, for all the genealogical details he cites fit with damning neatness the situation in which Henry finds himself, and tend to undermine the very claim they are brought forward to substantiate. How far the learned Archbishop is intentionally obscuring the issue, and how far it is obscuring him, is difficult at times to make out. But if the style is the man we are entitled to believe the worst.

To prove that Henry will not be a usurper if he seizes the crown of France in defiance of the Salic law he cites the cases of three French kings who themselves inherited through the female. The first one deposed another king (*as Henry IV did Richard II*). The second "usurped the crown" by pressing his title

> with some shows of truth,
> Though in pure truth it was corrupt and naught,

(*just as the Archbishop is urging Henry to press a similar title at the moment*). The third, who was sole heir to this usurper (*as Henry V was to Henry IV*), was so uneasy in his mind about his title (*as the first Henry was*) that he could not keep quiet in his conscience (*as the second Henry is now, by his present enterprise, proving that he cannot*). The allusiveness of all this to the pending question makes cynical in the extreme the citation of titles "corrupt and naught" as precedents in support of a claim supposed to be pure and substantial. It is like pointing to a dog's mongrel ancestors to prove it a thoroughbred. But the effrontery of the Archbishop's reasoning exceeds even this. The kings of France unto this day, he says to Henry in conclusion, want to bar your title to their throne because you inherit it through the female line, when, all the while, their own titles are crooked and were usurped from you and your progenitors because they were inherited in precisely the same way. The very thing that proves the title of a French king crooked—namely, inheritance through the female—serves, by some twist of ecclesiastical logic, to prove the title of an English king good. Heads you lose, tails I win.

Canterbury's long argument and its conclusion, which he pronounces "as clear as is the summer's sun," bewilder Henry as much as they do the reader. Or perhaps he prefers not to understand, that the responsibility may rest on the Archbishop. At any rate, quite as if he had not taken in a word of Canterbury's magnificent effort, he merely reiterates his original question:

> May I with right and conscience make this claim?

To which the Archbishop replies:

> The sin upon my head, dread sovereign!
> For in the book of Numbers is it writ,
> When the son dies, let the inheritance
> Descend unto the daughter.

The Book of Numbers! The Archbishop has been holding back his ace. All those tedious genealogical details, then, were only a foil against which the crowning precedent should shine forth. (Quite in Henry's own style.) It was a considerable step back to the King's great-great-grandmother. But Moses, or whoever wrote the Pentateuch, is an even more venerable authority. When, in the next act, Exeter, in Henry's name, demands that the French King resign the crown and adds, as he presents his sovereign's pedigree:

> That you may know
> 'Tis no sinister nor no awkward claim,
> Pick'd from the worm-holes of long-vanish'd days,
> Nor from the dust of old oblivion rak'd,
> He sends you this most memorable line,
> In every branch truly demonstrative,

we remember the learned Archbishop's researches and the Book of Numbers, and perceive that Exeter's vehement denial that there is anything shady or far-fetched in Henry's claim is the poet's oblique way of telling us that shady and far-fetched is exactly what it is.

And there is irony in this scene at a still deeper level. Henry bases his title on inheritance through the female line. But by this very rule under which he claims the French, he must surrender the English throne, for, allow inheritance through the female, and Edmund Mortimer, who is descended from the third son of Edward III through his grandmother, has a prior claim over Henry, who is descended from the fourth son. Shakespeare leaves it to anyone who will to remember this little fact. With it, the play is one thing; without it, quite another.

> Cheerly to sea! the signs of war advance,

cries Henry when the decision to cross the Channel is announced,

> No king of England, if not king of France.

"I am not worthy to be your king," he means, "if we cannot beat these Frenchmen." But attending to truth rather than to meter, the line ought to read:

> No king of England, if king of France.

Between war and law, Henry is bound to lose. If he wins the war, he confirms inheritance through the female and is "no king of England." If he loses it, he is no king of France.

We interrupted the Archbishop at the Book of Numbers. Let us return to his speech. "Gracious lord," he exclaims, passing from learning to exhortation,

> Gracious lord,
> Stand for your own! Unwind your bloody flag!
> Look back into your mighty ancestors!
> Go, my dread lord, to your great-grandsire's tomb,
> From whom you claim.

It is indeed a tombstone claim.

> For in his tomb lie my affections,

Henry, we may recall, said of his father. Now they go still deeper into the family burial chambers. Could anything make clearer the atavistic character of the change that is coming over Henry than these references to blood and ancestry and graves? His nobler self is regressing not merely into his father but into "the fathers."

In what follows one might imagine that that nobler self makes a final attempt to assert itself, for Henry says nothing for forty lines, while Canterbury, Ely, Exeter, and Westmoreland vie with one another in urging him to rouse himself like "the former lions" of his blood to "forage in the blood of French nobility" as did that "lion's whelp," the Black Prince, in his great-grandfather's day. Their verbal violence suggests both a suppressed thirst for blood on their own parts and a fear that Henry is hesitating to give the final word. Your subjects' hearts have already left their bodies and lie pavilioned on the fields of France, says Westmoreland.

> O, let their bodies follow, my dear liege,

cries the Archbishop,

> With blood and sword and fire to win your right;
> In aid whereof we of the spiritualty
> Will raise your highness such a mighty sum
> As never did the clergy at one time
> Bring in to any of your ancestors.

Fire, blood, lucre, and spiritualty! The witches' brew in *Macbeth* scarcely exceeds that.

It is evidently at just this moment that Henry overcomes any lingering scruples. With the tension removed, all these men, including the King, let themselves go a bit and their metaphors grow correspondingly revealing. The Scots, who are likely to attack England when her back is turned, are called petty thieves, snatchers, and weasels who suck princely eggs. England is an eagle in prey—and a cat. But the Archbishop's comparison is a worse giveaway than any of these. He likens human polity in a well-ordered state to that of the bees. The bees, it turns out, have nearly everything in their community that men have except archbishops and armies.

No high churchmen of the hive are mentioned. And as for fighters, this
is the way the Archbishop tries to squeeze them in:

> Others, like soldiers, armed in their stings,
> Make boot upon the summer's velvet buds,
> Which pillage they with merry march bring home
> To the tent-royal of their emperor.

As if bees hovering above flowers, or the fruitful communion of the two,
could be compared to the clash of enemies on the battlefield, or honey
to the spoils of war! The Archbishop is as deficient in his science as in his
symbolism. His childhood was plainly not spent in the meadows of Stratford. And his logic, that theological and ecclesiastical specialty, is no better.
The bees are united and harmonious in a perfect division of labor, he says;
"therefore" Henry should "divide" his forces into four parts, attack France
with one, and leave the other three for home defense. What these two
kinds of division have to do with each other only a mind more concerned
with words than realities could figure out. What fun Shakespeare must
have had making such a fool of his Archbishop, knowing all the while that
his audience would swallow his utterances as grave political wisdom.

The King evidently accepts them as such, for as the Archbishop concludes, he gives the order:

> Call in the messengers sent from the Dauphin.
> Now are we well resolv'd.

The French ambassadors enter and ask whether they shall speak their sovereign's intent plainly or veil it in diplomatic language.

Henry tells them to speak out:

> We are no tyrant, but a Christian king;
> Unto whose grace our passion is as subject
> As are our wretches fetter'd in our prisons:
> Therefore with frank and with uncurbed plainness
> Tell us the Dauphin's mind.

The metaphor is worth noting, for it is presently going to escape, as prisoners sometimes do, and stab its user in the back. "Whatever praises itself but
in the deed," Shakespeare was to write a year or two later, "devours the
deed in the praise." He knew it already.

Accepting Henry's invitation not to mince their words, the ambassadors
declare that the Dauphin thinks Henry's claims (to certain lands in France
—they have not yet heard his claim to the throne) "savour too much of
your youth," a plain allusion to the part Hal had taken in *robberies;* that
he cannot *dance* and *revel* himself into French dukedoms. Therefore he

sends Henry, in satisfaction of his claims and as more appropriate to his spirit, a tun of treasure. The treasure turns out to be—tennis balls!

This allusion to his gay youth touches Henry where he is sorest. On the instant his passions, which a moment before he had boasted were his subjects and prisoners, break their chains in such a threat of violence that it sounds more like the barbarous license of some Goth or Norseman in the days of Beowulf than the utterance of a supposedly responsible monarch. Go tell the Dauphin that

> many a thousand widows
> Shall this his mock mock out of their dear husbands;
> Mock mothers from their sons, mock castles down;
> And some are yet ungotten and unborn
> That shall have cause to curse the Dauphin's scorn.

Diplomatic insults have often precipitated wars, and it isn't easy even for the Mirror of all Christian Kings to be twitted in the presence of his court on the subject of his misspent youth. Yet somehow all those widows and mothers and unborn babes seem more than an equivalent for a few tennis balls.

Intoxicated by his own strong speech, the King becomes so consumed with this idea of dominating France that England begins to seem like a mere side issue, a vacation spot where he has given himself up to gaiety while absent from his "home," the throne of France:

> We never valu'd this poor seat of England;
> And therefore, living hence, did give ourself
> To barbarous license; as 'tis ever common
> That men are merriest when they are from home.

(What would Faulconbridge and John of Gaunt have said to that?) But when I come back to that home, Henry declares,

> I will rise there with so full a glory
> That I will dazzle all the eyes of France,
> Yea, strike the Dauphin blind to look on us.

That same old metaphor of the sun is still troubling him! Possessing him rather, we should say, for the sun is now turning from a glorious thing into a deadly one.

Evidently the "barbarous license" that the rejection of Falstaff supposedly ended forever did not include the barbarous license of speech in which Henry indulges in this interview with the ambassadors. But something within his unconsciousness (where the rejected Hal, it should be remembered, now resides) is evidently uneasy and attempts to strike a balance by making Henry introduce references to God, three in a score of lines, immediately following his bragging outbreak. This is one of the King's most interesting psychological symptoms. Those tennis balls shall turn to cannon balls, he boasts in one breath, and the Dauphin's soul at the Judgment Day shall be charged for the vengeance they bring.

But this lies all within the will of God,

he adds in the next breath, as if catching himself up, "in whose name . . . I am coming on," he concludes in a third breath, "to venge me." He cannot leave himself out after all. *Vengeance is mine, saith the Lord*—and Henry V of England is my instrument. So reads Henry's revised version.

And thus the first act ends. One wonders whether any who find it lacking in drama may possibly have missed some of its irony.

## II

If Act I ends with a quarrel made, Act II opens with a quarrel composed. If there is to be war in France, there is peace for the moment at any rate in the tavern. The title that figures here is one not to a portion of the earth but to a woman. Pistol has married the Hostess of the Boar's Head, Mistress Quickly, to whom Corporal Nym was troth-plighted. But his legal claim has not allayed fears of a rival:

O hound of Crete, think'st thou my spouse to get?

And his trepidation is deepened by a gambling debt that he owes Nym of no less than eight shillings. Bardolph, the red-nosed, seeks to prevent bloodshed and to bring the two angry men together: "I will bestow a breakfast to make you friends; and we'll be all three sworn brothers."

It is all very vulgar, if you will, food for the groundlings. But putting its vernacular simplicity of utterance (except of course for Pistol) and the good sense of its outcome over against the hypocrisy, the moralizing, and the rhetoric of the previous act, and their outcome, one is tempted to feel that wisdom has fled to the underworld.

"I dare not fight," Corporal Nym confesses, "but I will wink and hold out mine iron." His sword, he says, "will toast cheese." A cheese-toaster is not a bad tavern-equivalent for the biblical pruning hook.

"Good Corporal Nym," cries Nell Quickly when she sees him about to go to it with her husband, "show thy valour and put up your sword." It might be a motto for nations! Indeed it awakens echoes of that profound but ill-starred phrase: "Too proud to fight."

"Why the devil should we keep knives to cut one another's throats?"

asks Bardolph, unconsciously condensing into a sentence the question of the centuries, as he seeks to compel the loud-mouthed and cowardly Pistol to keep the peace and pay his debt. "Base is the slave that pays," retorts Pistol, unaware that about twenty seconds later he will pay. "An thou wilt be friends, be friends," says Bardolph, "an thou wilt not, why then, be enemies with me too." And a touch on his sword is enough to remind the two that Bardolph means business and that his use for his weapon is to prevent a quarrel, not to prick one on. Whereat, Pistol meekly pays.

How far Shakespeare has juxtaposed intentionally the boastings of Pistol in this scene and those of Henry in the previous one, each reader must decide for himself. The fact is that he has juxtaposed them.

> O braggart vile and damned furious wight!

Shocking as it may sound to say it, that line is a vulgar, but nonetheless a psychologically accurate description of Henry, when, beside himself with anger, he resents the insults of the Dauphin. Not Henry, note, but Henry-beside-himself. ("Thou art essentially mad without seeming so.") Shakespeare can never be trusted not to comment on his main plot in his underplot.

This seemingly casual little scene is also the one that brings the news of Falstaff's mortal illness, and in it we get the reaction of this group of his friends to Henry's rejection of him. "The king has killed his heart," laments Mistress Quickly. "The king hath run bad humours on the knight; that's the even of it," says Nym.

> Nym, thou hast spoke the right;
> His heart is fracted and corroborate,

echoes Pistol—and it is as if the invisible Falstaff were almost causing the two men who were about to fight each other to embrace. Dying, he makes peace, while Henry, living, makes war. "The king is a good king," Nym concludes fatalistically, "but it must be as it may; he passes some humours and careers."

It will be impossible to analyze in detail all the scenes that make up the underplot of this play. The little one we have just glanced at is typical of the way the author relates them to his main theme and so makes them immensely more than comic relief. There are those who hold that the sins of men in high places should be less stressed than the sins of those in private life. There is no evidence that to Shakespeare right and wrong are one thing for kings and another for commoners or even for the underworld. There is plenty of evidence to the contrary.

### III

The Chorus of Act II has informed us that three Englishmen, Richard, Earl of Cambridge, Henry, Lord Scroop of Masham, and Sir Thomas Grey, knight, of Northumberland, have conspired to murder Henry before he embarks with his army at Southampton. In the second scene of Act II, the three men, unaware that evidence of their conspiracy has been intercepted, are brought under another pretext into the presence of the King. The situation is dramatic: the intended victim talking with his would-be murderers, he knowing their thoughts, they not knowing his. The opportunity is too good to be missed, and Henry, with his usual instinct for the theatrical, proceeds to stage a play within a play wherein to catch the consciences of the traitors. But the situation is even more dramatic than Henry realizes, for all the while Unseen Powers are reading his heart, even as he is reading the hearts of the traitors, and have decided that this very play's the thing wherein to catch the conscience of the King.

In the presence of the three conspirators Henry orders a man released who had been committed to prison the day previous for railing against the royal person. It was excess of wine, the King says, rather than treason that set him on. His pardon is an act quite in the family tradition of what might be called "clemency in the limelight," but it is a test, too, of course, of the traitors, and they walk unsuspectingly into the trap (an early model of a more famous mousetrap). They all protest that Henry shows an excess of mercy. "But if I do not wink at little faults what penalty will be left for capital crimes?" Henry asks in effect and thrusts papers into their hands that make them turn pale. Perceiving that their secret has been uncovered, they confess and beg for mercy. To which Henry can naturally retort:

> The mercy that was quick in us but late,
> By your own counsel is suppress'd and kill'd:
> You must not dare, for shame, to talk of mercy;
> For your own reasons turn into your bosoms,
> As dogs upon their masters, worrying you.

And after a scathing denunciation of the inward rottenness of men whose outside seemed so fair, he dismisses these "English monsters" to execution. He does it for the good of the kingdom, disavowing all desire for personal vengeance and thanking God for the timely revelation of the plot.

Now, for anything that appears in the Chorus to this act or on the surface of the story, there is no reason for not taking this scene at its face value: the lucky exposure of three vile traitors who have sold their honor to the enemy "for a few light crowns." But view it against its remoter background, or recall scene 5 of the second act of *Henry VI, Part I*, and a little fact comes to mind that radically alters its character. That fact is that these three men, one of them in particular, are bent in their conspiracy on exactly the same end on which Henry is ostensibly bent at the very moment, only with better historical and legal justification: the restoration, namely, to his proper throne of a man dispossessed because his claim to succession is derived from the female side. That man, of course, is Edmund Mortimer, brother-in-law of the Earl of Cambridge, one of the present conspirators, the Edmund Mortimer whom Richard II (for whose murder Henry's father was responsible) had designated as his heir, and who has been held by Henry in "loathsome sequestration" in the Tower of London, as he himself says just before his death, "since Henry Monmouth first began to reign"—Henry Monmouth being the present King. And so it turns out that at the very least the Earl of Cambridge, instead of having sold his soul for French gold, is conspiring in behalf of what he conceives to be, and what, according to the very principle on which Henry is now making war, is his family right and honor. This, it will be granted, somewhat alters the case and puts a second edge that the King does not perceive on his

> You must not dare, for shame, to talk of mercy;
> For your own reasons turn into your bosoms.

Little is Henry thinking of his own family history as he utters words that fit it so fatally. Nor are we. The long shadow that the incarcerated Mortimer casts across this play is not visible from a seat in the theater. But it is from the higher vantage point of poetry read in solitude. And right in this scene itself, family history apart, enough is revealed to show that the Higher Powers are here submitting Henry to the same test to which he submitted the three traitors in the episode of the drunken man. "Forgive us our trespasses as we forgive those. . . ." It is a play within a play within a play.

The King finds the treachery of Lord Scroop toward him incredible:

> 'tis so strange
> That, though the truth of it stands off as gross
> As black from white, my eye will scarcely see it.

Formerly Henry was a specialist in the foil. Once he consciously contrived the black background for the white to shine upon. Now Fate turns his own method against him and one by one lets him point out his own sins, without knowing it, in the sins of the three traitors—until we are tempted to cry in his own further words to Scroop:

> And whatsoever cunning fiend it was
> That wrought upon thee so preposterously
> Hath got the voice in hell for excellence.

THE MEANING OF SHAKESPEARE

The first sin of which the King finds the traitors guilty is ingratitude: that men he has so loved (like Cambridge), so taken into his confidence (like Scroop), should turn on him so basely:

> What shall I say to thee, Lord Scroop? thou cruel,
> Ingrateful, savage, and inhuman creature!
> Thou that didst bear the key of all my counsels,
> That knew'st the very bottom of my soul,
> That almost mightst have coin'd me into gold,
> Wouldst thou have practis'd on me for thy use!

This comes with poor grace from the man who rejected Falstaff. "Practis'd on me for thy use" seems like a phrase expressly coined to describe that incident. And if it be objected that Hal at least never conspired against Falstaff's life, Mistress Quickly will not agree. "The king hath killed his heart," she said. And Nym and Pistol said essentially the same.

Treason and murder are the next count in the King's indictment:

> Treason and murder ever kept together.

They did when Henry IV had Richard II murdered. And Henry's son has retained and is at this very moment enjoying the fruits of that crime, as he himself admits, when in a different mood, the night before Agincourt.

For the rest, Henry lumps it all together in a general charge of hypocrisy: that the traitors have seemed to be one thing and have turned out just the other.

> Show men dutiful?
> Why, so didst thou: seem they grave and learned?
> Why, so didst thou: come they of noble family?
> Why, so didst thou: seem they religious?
> Why, so didst thou: or are they spare in diet,
> Free from gross passion or of mirth or anger,
> Constant in spirit, not swerving with the blood,
> Garnish'd and deck'd in modest complement,
> Not working with the eye without the ear,
> And but in purged judgement trusting neither?
> Such and so finely bolted didst thou seem.

This is the worst of all from a man who planned to deceive all of England about his youth, who embraced the virtuous Chief Justice in public only to turn to a worldly archbishop in private to put his blessing on a dubious title and an unholy war, who preached a sermon in the street in turning off an old friend, and who is indulging at the moment in a long moral discourse aimed at three men who have only planned the same kind of crime which his father actually committed and in which he has become in a sense an accomplice after the fact.

All other devils that suggest by treasons
Do botch and bungle up damnation
With patches, colours, and with forms being fetch'd
From glistering semblances of piety.

Henry's words depict himself.

"The wrath of Henry," says Dowden of this passage, "has in it some of that awfulness and terror suggested by the apocalyptic reference to 'the wrath of the Lamb.' It is the more terrible because it transcends all egoistic feeling." Henry does indeed appear in this scene to arrogate to himself certain of the prerogatives of God. But that his wrath transcends all egoistic feeling is not so certain. The picture Henry draws of the traitors as they seemed is an almost perfect picture of the ideal king so many have found in Henry himself. But the discrepancy between what the three men seemed to be and what they were is hardly greater than that between the ideal king of the critics (to pick a single one of his virtues),

Free from gross passion or of mirth or anger,
Constant in spirit, not swerving with the blood,

and the actual Henry we saw in the tennis-ball scene, giving way utterly to his anger and indulging in an orgy of boasting and threatened vengeance. And yet there was something like the possibility of the ideal king in the original Hal. And so when the King concludes his indictment of the traitors with the words

And thus thy fall hath left a kind of blot,
To mark the full-fraught man and best indu'd
With some suspicion. I will weep for thee;
For this revolt of thine, methinks, is like
Another fall of man,

it is as if Henry V were condensing his own story into four words. *Another fall of man.* It was not Falstaff that Hal rejected. It was himself.

That so many have been willing to accept the man Henry became, with all his defects, as Shakespeare's portrait of the ideal king, is a fact of the highest psychological interest. One could almost fancy that Shakespeare foresaw how many would be taken in by his "hero" and was speaking of them through Henry's own mouth:

If that same demon that hath gull'd thee thus
Should with his lion gait walk the whole world,
He might return to vasty Tartar back,
And tell the legions, "I can never win
A soul so easy as that Englishman's."

IV

The three conspirators are sentenced to death. Shakespeare quietly places beside the King's condemnation of them Mistress Quickly's account of Falstaff's death. The poet evidently expended every power at his command in this scene, and it is enough to say that the story does not suffer when put in comparison with the deaths of Hamlet and Othello, of King Lear and Cleopatra. The familiar lines must again be quoted. Their meaning can never be exhausted:

PISTOL: Bardolph, be blithe; Nym, rouse thy vaunting veins;
　　　　Boy, bristle thy courage up; for Falstaff he is dead,
　　　　And we must yearn therefore.
BARD.: Would I were with him, wheresome'er he is, either in heaven or in hell!
HOST.: Nay, sure, he's not in hell: he's in Arthur's bosom, if ever man went
　　　　to Arthur's bosom. A' made a finer end and went away an it had
　　　　been any christom child; a' parted even just between twelve and
　　　　one, even at the turning o' the tide: for after I saw him fumble
　　　　with the sheets and play with flowers and smile upon his fingers'
　　　　ends, I knew there was but one way; for his nose was as sharp as
　　　　a pen, and a' babbled of green fields. "How now, Sir John!" quoth I;
　　　　"what, man! be o' good cheer." So a' cried out "God, God, God!"
　　　　three or four times. Now I, to comfort him, bid him a' should not
　　　　think of God; I hoped there was no need to trouble himself with
　　　　any such thoughts yet. So a' bade me lay more clothes on his feet:
　　　　I put my hand into the bed and felt them, and they were as cold
　　　　as any stone; then I felt to his knees, and they were as cold as any
　　　　stone, and so upward and upward, and all was as cold as any stone.
NYM: They say he cried out of sack.
HOST.: Ay, that a' did.

Four times in his speech at the end of the previous scene, three times within a dozen lines, Henry has referred to God: (1) praying that God may have mercy on the men to whom he is showing no mercy; (2) begging that God may give them true repentance and strength to endure their execution; (3) thanking God for bringing the conspiracy to light; and (4) delivering into God's hand his present military enterprise. "God," "God," "God," "God."

"So a' cried out 'God, God, God!' three or four times. Now I, to comfort him, bid him a' should not think of God; I hoped there was no need to trouble himself with any such thoughts yet." The man who invokes God's aid in an unholy war of conquest: the woman who does her best to comfort a conscience-stricken and dying sinner (who has wronged her cruelly) by bidding him not to trouble himself with thoughts that she knows can bring him only terror! Here it seems as if for once we are close to the heart of Shakespeare's own religion, and we remember the words of Jack Cade about the noble and innocent Lord Say in *II Henry VI*: "He speaks not o' God's name. Go, take him away, I say, and strike off his head presently." Eckhart, the German mystic, declares that the purpose of true religion is "to get rid of God." Anyone who fails to understand that paradox may well meditate on the last words of Falstaff and Mistress Quickly's last words to him. How many other wise men have put more directly the truth that Shakespeare dramatizes in this scene. "The learned talk of God and His name is on their lips," says Langland, "but the poor have him in their hearts." "Cleave to God against the name of God," says Emerson. "You don't believe in Christ," says one character to another in Chekhov's *The Duel;* "why do you mention his name so often?" "Mention but the word divinity, and our sense of the divine is clouded," says Samuel Butler. God moves in a mysterious way. . . .

## V

With Falstaff's death Bardolph feels that the fuel is gone that maintained the fire of his life. But Pistol is less downcast, and his inferences are more in the spirit of Commodity:

> Come, let's away. My love, give me thy lips.
> Look to my chattels and my movables:
> Let senses rule; the word is "Pitch and Pay."
> Trust none;
> For oaths are straws, men's faiths are wafer-cakes,
> And hold-fast is the only dog, my duck:
> Therefore, *Caveto* be thy counsellor.
> Go, clear thy crystals. Yoke-fellows in arms,
> Let us to France; like horse-leeches, my boys,
> To suck, to suck, the very blood to suck!

"And that's but unwholesome food, they say," the Boy remarks, though nobody seems to notice. Falstaff's page is perhaps referring to "blood-pudding." Yet it is into just such casual utterances that Shakespeare is most likely to slip his own opinion.

"Now, lords, for France!" Henry had said at the end of the previous scene—a phrase to which Pistol's "Let us to France" is antiphonal. Stripped of its chivalric and religious nomenclature, what Henry goes on to say is: let us engulf France in our empire and if she refuses to be swallowed freely let us apply "bloody constraint"—and he sends his uncle ahead to threaten the enemy with fiery tempest, thunder, and earthquake. It is interesting that the French King, in contemplating the coming conflict, picks on

Pistol's very metaphor of sucking, though with less suggestion of the leech:

> For England his approaches makes as fierce
> As waters to the sucking of a gulf.

Hoping to avert the catastrophe, he offers Henry, the Chorus tells us,

> Katharine his daughter, and with her, to dowry,
> Some petty and unprofitable dukedoms.

But what are dukedoms and daughters (the alliteration reminds us of ducats and daughters) to a man whose blood is up? We are not told that Henry so much as sends a refusal, and we see him at the beginning of the next act addressing his soldiers before Harfleur:

> Once more unto the breach, dear friends, once more,
> Or close the wall up with our English dead!

Trite as it has become from schoolboy declamation, the passage is a crucial one and cannot be omitted:

> In peace there's nothing so becomes a man
> As modest stillness and humility:
> But when the blast of war blows in our ears,
> Then imitate the action of the tiger;
> Stiffen the sinews, summon up the blood,
> Disguise fair nature with hard-favour'd rage;
> Then lend the eye a terrible aspect;
> Let it pry through the portage of the head
> Like the brass cannon; let the brow o'erwhelm it
> As fearfully as doth a galled rock
> O'erhang and jutty his confounded base,
> Swill'd with the wild and wasteful ocean.
> Now set the teeth and stretch the nostril wide,
> Hold hard the breath, and bend up every spirit
> To his full height!

What this boils down to is the doctrine that in peace the manly virtues are all right but that in war man ought to become a beast. That men often do become beasts when they fight is notorious. But that it is the duty of the soldier deliberately to transform himself into a beast in advance is a totally different proposition, and Henry's unabashed advocacy of it shows how nearly dead, at such a moment at least, the chivalric conception of honor was in his mind.

What did Shakespeare think of this red-blooded doctrine?

The question, "What did Shakespeare think?" about this or that is frequently a futile one. But on this particular point his plays are so full of evidence, converging to one conclusion, that I believe we are entitled to say exactly what Shakespeare thought down to the very noun he would have used to characterize Henry. He thought Henry was talking like a savage. "Fie, savage, fie!" was the retort of Hector to his younger brother Troilus (in *Troilus and Cressida*) when the latter began ranting in precisely Henry's vein:

TRO.:     For the love of all the gods,
   Let's leave the hermit pity with our mothers,
   And when we have our armours buckled on,
   The venom'd vengeance ride upon our swords,
   Spur them to ruthful work, rein them from ruth.
HECT.: Fie, savage, fie!

Now Hector is a man we cannot imagine giving way to tigerish passion in any circumstances, a man immeasurably closer than Henry, I believe, to Shakespeare's ideal of the warrior-hero.

But we do not need to go beyond the present play. In the last act, in one of the wisest speeches on peace in Shakespeare, the Duke of Burgundy observes that a people long plunged in war

   grow like savages,—as soldiers will
  That nothing do but meditate on blood.

Ironically, Henry's own picture, in another mood, of the type he most admired was, as we have seen, that of a man

  Free from gross passion or of mirth or anger,
  Constant in spirit, not swerving with the blood.

This is Hamlet's ideal of the man who is not passion's slave but whose blood and judgment are well commingled. What Shakespeare himself thought of this ideal, passage after passage in the plays and poems of this period makes plain, none better than the 94th sonnet:

  They that have power to hurt and will do none,
  That do not do the thing they most do show,
  Who, moving others, are themselves as stone,
  Unmoved, cold, and to temptation slow;
  They rightly do inherit heaven's graces,
  And husband nature's riches from expense;
  They are the lords and owners of their faces,
  Others but stewards of their excellence.
  The summer's flower is to the summer sweet,
  Though to itself it only live and die,

> But if that flower with base infection meet,
> The basest weed outbraves his dignity:
>> For sweetest things turn sourest by their deeds;
>> Lilies that fester smell far worse than weeds.

If anyone thinks Shakespeare considered this self-control possible in peace only, and not in war, all his greatest warriors give that idea the lie: Faulconbridge, Hector, Othello, even Coriolanus.

Henry's idea of war and the warrior is as antithetical to the classical as to the chivalric conception. "The Greek battle-pieces are calm," says Emerson, "the heroes, in whatever violent action engaged, retain a serene aspect; as we say of Niagara that it falls without speed." Here the virtues of war are the virtues of peace carried to their highest pitch. But in Henry's doctrine the virtues of war are the vices of peace carried to their highest pitch. Followed through, this is the totalitarian conception. Its logical upshot is one nation leaping suddenly on another out of the air in undeclared war, like a beast from ambush.

The Battle of Agincourt has long been considered a turning point in military history because it was the first victory of massed yeomen over armored knights. In so far as his "tiger" speech is representative of its victor, Shakespeare makes that battle an even more significant turning point in military morality. There is everything to indicate that the poet admired the hero who kept his head on the battlefield. (Even Falstaff does that.) He has a special term for the opposite condition.

> To be furious,
> Is to be frighted out of fear; and in that mood
> The dove will peck the estridge; and I see still,
> A diminution in our captain's brain
> Restores his heart. When valour preys on reason,
> It eats the sword it fights with.

So Enobarbus describes the defeated and desperate Antony. And Caithness says much the same of Macbeth after he had begun to run amuck:

> Some say he's mad; others that lesser hate him
> Do call it valiant fury.

Whoever holds that Shakespeare indorses Henry's advice about imitating the action of the tiger should trace, with the aid of a concordance, the poet's use of the word "fury."

It would be superfluous to quote the rest of the King's oration with its equation of force and "the fathers," its allusion to Alexander the Great, its animal metaphors and similes. "The game's afoot," he exclaims in conclusion:

Follow your spirit, and upon this charge
Cry "God for Harry! England and Saint George!"

Whereupon Nym, Bardolph, Pistol, and the Boy enter, and Bardolph cries: "On, on, on, on, on! to the breach, to the breach!" Evidently Shakespeare's game's afoot as well as Henry's. "The humour of it is too hot," says Nym of Bardolph's battle cry. It might have been said of the King's. And the rest of the scene, with Fluellen's "Up to the breach, you dogs!" etc., contains what look like a number of other oblique glances at the main action, especially in certain lines of the Boy. His companions have been trying to teach him filching. But he says it is against his manhood "if I should take from another's pocket to put into mine; for it is plain pocketing up of wrongs. I must leave them and seek some better service: their villainy goes against my weak stomach, and therefore I must cast it up." Boy as he is, his sense of *mine* and *thine* is more highly developed than Henry's. It is Captain Macmorris, the Irishman, who comes closer to the King. His words indeed sound at times like a parody of Henry's extraordinary collocations of God and war: "There is throats to be cut . . . so Chrish sa' me, la! . . . so Chrish save me, I will cut off your head."

## VI

We next see the King with his forces before the gates of Harfleur attempting to complete the reduction of the town by threats in place of cannon balls. It is economy to let words save munitions.

If I begin the battery once again,
I will not leave the half-achiev'd Harfleur
Till in her ashes she lie buried.
The gates of mercy shall be all shut up,

and then follows a picture of violence and licentiousness let loose such as would be hard to duplicate in Shakespeare: bloody soldiers seizing by the hair shrill-shrieking virgins, old men with their brains dashed out against the walls, naked infants spitted upon pikes, mothers run mad as in the days of Herod. (The reference to Herod is fitting, for it out-herods Herod.) Even the threats of that Marlowesque "fiend of hell," Talbot, in a like situation before Bordeaux in *I Henry VI*, read like a weak dilution of Henry V's outburst. But the inevitable contrast is that between Henry before Harfleur and Faulconbridge before Angiers. Faulconbridge was not squeamish. But instead of threatening the city with all the details of destruction he ingeniously put it in a dilemma. The wit, humor, and even reticence he displayed on this occasion put Henry's verbal orgy of blood lust in the sorriest light. What would the Bastard have said to it? Presumably just what he said to the First Citizen of Angiers:

> Here's a stay
> That shakes the rotten carcass of old Death
> Out of his rags! Here's a large mouth, indeed,
> That spits forth death and mountains, rocks and seas . . .
> What cannoneer begot this lusty blood?
> He speaks plain cannon fire, and smoke, and bounce;
> He gives the bastinado with his tongue:
> Our ears are cudgell'd: . . .
> Zounds! I was never so bethump'd with words
> Since I first call'd my brother's father dad.

The most ominous parallel of all is Shakespeare's description of Tarquin's emotional state just before the rape of Lucrece.* Those in our day who wrote into international law the doctrine that offensive war is a crime were hailed as pioneers. They were anticipated by Shakespeare.

If Henry had not proved his physical courage at Shrewsbury, there would be every Shakespearean precedent for doubting it on the basis of this speech before Harfleur.

> We'll have a swashing and a martial outside,

says Rosalind to Celia when they are about to disguise themselves,

> As many other mannish cowards have.

And Brutus declares that

> hollow men, like horses hot at hand,
> Make gallant show and promise of their mettle;
> But when they should endure the bloody spur,
> They fall their crests, and, like deceitful jades,
> Sink in the trial.

Let no one imagine that I quote such passages as characterizations of Henry. But they may well set us questioning whether the hero of Shrews-

---

* "His rage of lust by gazing qualified;
  Slack'd, not suppress'd; for standing by her side,
    His eye, which late this mutiny restrains,
    Unto a greater uproar tempts his veins:

"And they, like straggling slaves for pillage fighting,
  Obdurate vassals fell exploits effecting,
  In bloody death and ravishment delighting,
  Nor children's tears nor mothers' groans respecting,
  Swell in their pride, the onset still expecting:
    Anon his beating heart, alarum striking,
    Gives the hot charge and bids them do their liking."

bury and King Henry V are quite the same man. "Men who wish to inspire terror," says Emerson, "seem thereby to confess themselves cowards."

Oh, but Henry was just trying to frighten Harfleur out of fighting, it will be said. (And, incidentally, he succeeded.) When it came to actual warfare he was the soul of mercy. Here, for example, is the real Henry:

and we give express charge, that in our marches through the country, there be nothing compelled from the villages, nothing taken but paid for, none of the French upbraided or abused in disdainful language; for when lenity and cruelty play for a kingdom, the gentler gamester is the soonest winner.

What could be more exemplary, more impeccable? His soldiers are not to indulge even in abusive words, let alone deeds. It sounds incredible—coming from the same man. But these Lancasters as a family have taught us to ask what they have just been doing or are just about to do when their words become especially generous or merciful. What are the circumstances in this case?

The circumstances are that Fluellen, the Welsh captain, has announced that Bardolph is to be executed for robbing a church. Bardolph, we recall, was one of Hal's cronies of the wild-oats days, and time was when he and Hal went stealing together. Does Hal remember this at a moment so critical for his old friend? It is hard to see how he could have failed to. But he does not mention it. "We would have all such offenders so cut off," is his laconic comment, whereupon he plunges in his next breath into his order against plundering. Much ink has been spilled over the rejection of Falstaff. This much briefer rejection of Bardolph has scarcely been noticed. But it is psychologically hardly less interesting. The King spares Bardolph (who indeed is not present) the sermon he preached on the other occasion. In place of it, he gives orders for lenity and mercy on his soldiers' part. Henry covers his unmerciful deed by his merciful words. "I give orders for the death of a friend, but let my soldiers beware of stealing a spoon from the enemy or even speaking impolitely to them."* That is the compensatory logic of it. But as usual with Shakespeare, the most interesting thing is behind. Robbing a church! Had Henry, even in his wildest days, ever broken into a church edifice and stolen a pyx? There is no record of anything of the sort. But he had accepted the bribe of a large slice of ecclesiastical property for the purpose of launching his proposed conquest of France. It makes a difference whether you steal retail or wholesale, and whether you do it openly or slyly, legally or illegally. The plot and underplot of this play grow more and more mutually illuminating.

* "We would have all such offenders so cut off; *and* we give express charge," etc. "And" is a little word but it can have a big significance. The psychological truth clearly called for a "but."

## VII

The fourth act of *Henry V* is dedicated to the Battle of Agincourt and what preceded it. The last scene of the previous act supplies the foil. In it we catch a glimpse of the French camp the night before the battle, with its mingled frivolity, light conversation about horses, mistresses, and sonnets, and wishes for the dawn of the morning that will summon them to the easy extinction of the English. It is all like some hopelessly overconfident university football squad contemptuous of the team of a backwoods college that by some freak of fortune they have been compelled to condescend to play.

And then, with the new act, the scene shifts to the English camp on the same night and we have one of the most dramatic and symbolic scenes that Shakespeare, up to that time, had conceived.

The King wraps himself in a borrowed cloak, and, Haroun-al-Raschid-like, mingles incognito with the common soldiers. And forthwith, a miracle! His royal habiliments hidden, Henry is at first almost the old Hal with whom we were formerly acquainted. The man had had to disguise himself to become a king; now the king must disguise himself to become a man. Wrapped in the double obscurity of his cloak and of night, he engages in conversation three of his soldiers, John Bates, Alexander Court, and Michael Williams. Their Christian names, in each case, I think, are intended to have significance, and in the case of Court the surname certainly does, for his first speech in the play turns out to be his last, possibly, in proportion to its length, as remarkable a role as is to be found in Shakespeare.

"Brother John Bates," he says, "is not that the morning which breaks yonder?" Just eleven words—and the rest is silence. But those words let us into the secret thoughts of a man who never expects to see another dawn, and in his silence we hear his heartbeats. We hear them to the end of the scene—of the act—of the play. Did he fall in the battle? We never know. Even Shakespeare seldom packed so much into so little. Put the one word "brother" over against its plural "brothers" as used by Henry. Put all eleven words—with the silence that follows them—over against the speech of the Constable of France that opens the previous scene: "Tut! I have the best armour of the world. Would it were day!" with the loquacity that follows *it*, and it is scarcely too much to say that in the two we have the reason why, in this play at any rate, the English won the Battle of Agincourt. "When matched armies encounter," says Laotse, "the one instinct with sadness conquers." Bates and Williams too are filled with dark forebodings, but they are at least able to speak. All three of them are plainly men of sincerity and worth. Somehow Shakespeare convinces us that it is of this stuff that England is made. The three men evoke a responsive sincerity from Henry. "I think the king is but a man," he says—in words that are a clear echo of Shylock's memorable words on a similar theme—and we can feel the relief with which in the darkness he puts aside not merely the trappings but the very accent of state. "A little touch of Harry in the night." Like the others, significantly, he speaks in prose.

This is the scene widely relied on by Henry's admirers to prove his simplicity, his modesty, his democracy. If only this *were* Henry! Those who think it is forget that it is night. This is the suppressed Henry. Which is real? the old man who lies in bed and remembers his youth or the youth the old man lies in bed and remembers? If only we were what we lie awake in the night and wish we were! It is what a man makes of himself in the daylight that he *is*. One might as well go to the soliloquy on sleep to find Henry IV as to this scene to find Henry V. The father poured forth the unrealized poetry and hidden regrets of his life in that magnificent apostrophe. Nocturnal history is repeating itself—with certain differences. Our daytime personality, though in the background, is always there along with our three-o'clock-in-the-morning one. The King lay in bed with the man who uttered the address to sleep. And the King is present in this scene as well as the ghost of Hal. In coming to the defense of the King, Hal begins to pass back into him.

> BATES: He may show what outward courage he will, but I believe, as cold a night as 'tis, he could wish himself in Thames up to the neck, and so I would he were, and I by him, at all adventures, so we were quit here.[*]
>
> K. HEN.: By my troth, I will speak my conscience of the king: I think he would not wish himself any where but where he is.
>
> BATES: Then I would he were here alone; so should he be sure to be ransomed, and a many poor men's lives saved.
>
> K. HEN.: I dare say you love him not so ill to wish him here alone, howsoever you speak this to feel other men's minds. Methinks I could not die any where so contented as in the king's company,

and then, as if Bates' words had revived some old doubt, the ghost of Hal adds, "his cause being just and his quarrel honourable."

"That's more than we know," says Williams.

Bates assuages his conscience with the thought that, even if the King's cause is bad, the soldier's obedience wipes out the crime of it for him.

---

[*] "I would it were bed-time, Hal, and all well," said Falstaff the night before Shrewsbury.

But the more assertive Williams turns it the other way around and points out how heavy in that case is the responsibility of the king.

> WILL.: But if the cause be not good, the king himself hath a heavy reckoning to make, when all those legs and arms and heads, chopped off in a battle, shall join together at the latter day and cry all "We died at such a place"; some swearing, some crying for a surgeon, some upon their wives left poor behind them, some upon the debts they owe, some upon their children rawly left. I am afeard there are few die well that die in a battle; for how can they charitably dispose of any thing, when blood is their argument? Now, if these men do not die well, it will be a black matter for the king that led them to it; whom to disobey were against all proportion of subjection.

It is an unanswerable argument. And does it not have a familiar ring? It should have. For it is the precise argument that Henry himself used when he told the Archbishop of Canterbury that it would be a black matter for him, the Archbishop, if he incited him, the King, to a bad war:

> We charge you in the name of God, take heed;
> For never two such kingdoms did contend
> Without much fall of blood, whose guiltless drops
> Are every one a woe, a sore complaint
> 'Gainst him whose wrongs give edge unto the swords
> That make such waste in brief mortality.

The King was willing to put the responsibility on an archbishop but he is unwilling to let his soldiers put the responsibility on a king. As in the case of the three traitors, Henry is caught in his own trap. The King gives no sign that he remembers his former words, but if any proof were needed that he knows in his heart of hearts that this is a bad war we have it in the squirming sophistry—almost worthy of a Pandulph—with which he vainly attempts to refute the simple and straightforward statement of Williams.

"So, if a son that is by his father sent about merchandise do sinfully miscarry upon the sea," reasons Henry, "the imputation of his wickedness, by your rule, should be imposed upon his father that sent him." Was ever logic more topsy-turvy? Henry has it exactly upside down. What he should have said, to parallel Williams' argument, is: "If a merchant send his son forth with orders to cheat, the father, by your rule, should bear the blame if his son is dishonest." And that would have been true! "Besides," Henry goes on, still further side-stepping the issue and forgetting that the question is the justice of the war, not the morals of the soldiers, "there is no king, be his cause never so spotless, if it come to the arbitrement of swords, can try it out with all unspotted soldiers. Some peradventure have on them the guilt of premeditated and contrived murder; some, of beguiling virgins with the broken seals of perjury; some, making the wars their bulwark, that have before gored the gentle bosom of peace with pillage and robbery. Now, if these men have defeated the law and outrun native punishment, though they can outstrip men, they have no wings to fly from God. War is his beadle, war is his vengeance."

It would be both cruel and repetitious to examine these sentences in the light of Henry's unlicensed youth and his parentally instigated, deliberately contrived, casuistically and ecclesiastically supported motives for the war in which he is engaged.

"I myself heard the king say he would not be ransomed," says Henry, confessing thereby that his argument needs backing up with something more solid.

"Ay, he said so, to make us fight cheerfully," says the penetrating Williams, "but when our throats are cut, he may be ransomed, and we ne'er the wiser." (Falstaff in his speech on honor said something close to this, if in a different key.) "If I live to see it," says Henry, shifting to wit—the defeated man's only alternative to anger—"I will never trust his word after."

"You'll never trust his word after! come, 'tis a foolish saying."

It was, as Henry as good as admits in his reply.

"Your reproof is something too round. I should be angry with you, if the time were convenient." He is shifting to the other alternative.

Whereat Williams takes him up. They exchange gloves and their words of honor to settle their quarrel after the battle. Henry declares that he will challenge him "though I take thee in the king's company," a wording of his promise to be especially noted in view of what happens later. Meanwhile Bates exclaims, precisely as Bardolph had exclaimed to the pugnacious Nym and Pistol: "Be friends, you English fools, be friends; we have French quarrels enow, if you could tell how to reckon." And a moment later the three soldiers go out.

Though he has been compelled to revert to his assumed self in his argument in defense of the King, the genuineness of these common men has affected Henry profoundly, and, left alone, he breaks forth, as man, not king, into the soliloquy on Ceremony—the counterpart of his father's on Sleep and of his son's on the Simple Life—which shows how his soul loathes the burden of monarchical make-believe under which the man is all but interred:

> O ceremony, ...
> Art thou aught else but place, degree, and form,
> Creating awe and fear in other men?

> Wherein thou art less happy being fear'd
> Than they in fearing.
> What drink'st thou oft, instead of homage sweet,
> But poison'd flattery? O, be sick, great greatness,
> And bid thy ceremony give thee cure!
> Think'st thou the fiery fever will go out
> With titles blown from adulation?

The contempt with which he turns on "the farced title running 'fore the king," indicates how far he is at this moment of soul-revelation from the ambitious boy who put the crown on his head when his father was dying, or the leader who urged his soldiers to imitate the action of the tiger. He is closer, indeed, as the rest of his speech with its envious references to those of low degree shows, to the spirit of his son-to-be, Henry VI. And every word of it is as straightforward and true as his argument with Williams was twisted and false. Is it any wonder that those who want to make out that Henry was the ideal king always appeal to this passage? If only good thoughts could be credited as good deeds!

Word comes that the lords and nobles are searching for the missing King. He asks for only a moment more of solitude, and, granted it, falls on his knees (or so we suppose) and pours forth his anguish, and sense of guilt, in a prayer:

> O God of battles! steel my soldiers' hearts;
> Possess them not with fear; take from them now
> The sense of reckoning, if the opposed numbers
> Pluck their hearts from them. Not to-day, O Lord,
> O, not to-day, think not upon the fault
> My father made in compassing the crown!
> I Richard's body have interr'd anew,
> And on it have bestow'd more contrite tears
> Than from it issu'd forced drops of blood.
> Five hundred poor I have in yearly pay,
> Who twice a day their wither'd hands hold up
> Toward heaven, to pardon blood; and I have built
> Two chantries, where the sad and solemn priests
> Sing still for Richard's soul. More will I do;
> Though all that I can do is nothing worth,
> Since that my penitence comes after all,
> Imploring pardon.

"The sins of the fathers"! So false have Henry IV's dying words been proved when he said that all the "soil" of Richard's murder would go with him into the grave, leaving his son with an unspotted title. Those two chantries and those five hundred poor are convincing testimony to the contrary. Indeed as we read those last lines our memories are haunted with a sense of familiarity.

> all that I can do is nothing worth,
> Since that my penitence comes after all,
> Imploring pardon.

Where have we heard something like that before?

> That cannot be; since I am still possess'd
> Of those effects for which I did the murder,
> My crown, mine own ambition, and my queen
> May one be pardon'd and retain the offence?

Shakespeare, to be sure, had not yet written those words, but it is precisely poetry's function to put us above time.

Yes, another guilty king, kneeling in prayer—and the same inevitable question: was he sincere? and the same inevitable answer: yes, and no. Claudius, Hamlet's uncle.

What! the ideal king and the murderer-adulterer in the same attitude, uttering the same thoughts? There are important differences, certainly. It was the father, not the son, who was personally guilty of the crime in the present case. But the central fact of a throne founded on murder is the same. The parallelism is so startling that the familiar passage takes on a fresh meaning in its new context:

> In the corrupted currents of this world
> Offence's gilded hand may shove by justice,
> And oft 'tis seen the wicked prize itself
> Buys out the law. But 'tis not so above:
> There is no shuffling, there the action lies
> In his true nature; and we ourselves compell'd,
> Even to the teeth and forehead of our faults,
> To give in evidence. What then? What rests?
> Try what repentance can. What can it not?
> Yet what can it when one can not repent?

Shakespeare finds the right word. *Shuffling!*

## VIII

And then we get another glimpse of the two camps. The French knights are boasting that a puff of their breath would be enough to put the English to rout or that they themselves might stand idly by, watching, and let the camp lackeys and peasants beat their base foe. Meanwhile they observe the "knavish crows" flying over the field "impatient for their hour." The

English are contemplating the fearful odds against them, five to one, sixty thousand against ten or twelve, and Westmoreland expresses the wish that just "one ten thousand of those men in England That do no work today" (it was Sunday) were with them.

"Not one man," says the King, entering just in time to overhear the remark, and crying

> if it be a sin to covet honour
> I am the most offending soul alive,

he goes on to expound the doctrine of "the fewer men, the greater share of honour," quite in the manner of Hotspur before the Battle of Shrewsbury. It grows increasingly evident that the outmoded notion of "glory" of the man Prince Henry killed on that occasion transmigrated from the soul of the slain into the soul of the slayer. Let any man depart, Henry orders it proclaimed, "which hath no stomach to this fight,"

> We would not die in that man's company . . .
> We few, we happy few, we band of brothers;
> For he to-day that sheds his blood with me
> Shall be my brother; be he ne'er so vile,
> This day shall gentle his condition;
> And gentlemen in England now a-bed
> Shall think themselves accurs'd they were not here,
> And hold their manhoods cheap whiles any speaks
> That fought with us upon Saint Crispin's day.

Westmoreland, who, a moment ago, was longing for reinforcements, is so carried away by the King's eloquence that he cries to him,

> would you and I alone,
> Without more help, could fight this royal battle!

—which ought to have satisfied even Henry's mathematical method of reckoning honor. These words to his little "band of brothers" have perhaps been quoted oftener than anything else in Henry's entire role to prove his democratic spirit. They are indeed fair words. But we have heard fair words from this man often enough before to make us prefer to wait and see how well he will live up to them. Shakespeare has further evidence to offer on this point. Indeed, apart from both Henry and Shakespeare, the experience of two world wars has made our own generation a bit suspicious of extreme protestations of democracy from those in high position if uttered at a moment when national safety depends on the loyalty of those of lower situation.

A French herald enters, begging the English to have the sense to compound before they are slaughtered. Henry, reminding him of the man who sold the lion's skin in advance and then was killed while hunting the lion, proceeds, with a "let me speak proudly," to do a little modest boasting of his own, his references to the "robes" and "gay new coats," in which his soldiers, if God please, shall be arrayed ere night, coming ominously near the idea of the lion's skin. In terms of a day, Henry killed his lion; in terms of the years the lion killed him. But one prophecy that he makes is especially worth noting. Our very dead, he predicts, though buried in your dung hills, shall have fame,

> for there the sun shall greet them,
> And draw their honours reeking up to heaven;
> Leaving their earthly parts to choke your clime,
> The smell whereof shall breed a plague in France.
> Mark then abounding valour in our English,
> That being dead, like to the bullet's grazing,
> Break out into a second course of mischief,
> Killing in relapse of mortality.

It is a singularly unpleasant metaphor, but a singularly prophetic one—though the "second course of mischief" turned out to be something quite different from what Henry had in mind, as the three parts of *Henry VI* and *Richard III* testify. "The name of Henry the Fifth hales them to a hundred mischiefs"—the very word!—cries Jack Cade of his rebels. That glancing bullet ricocheted across the Channel. And as for the plague that the corpses of Henry's soldiers engendered, the English suffered from it in a figurative if not in a literal sense quite as much as the French. The fact that the Henry of history died in France at the age of thirty-five (probably of a fever complicated with stomach trouble, and, according to one account, after infernal visitations and acute pangs of conscience) tempts one to fancy that the King's prophecy here of the aftereffects of his conquest was a preparation on Shakespeare's part, now he had completed the cycle, for a reference to Henry's death which he intended to, but for some reason never did, insert in *I Henry VI*. That of course is the sheerest conjecture and can have no part in the story. But the truth remains that the omission of all details with regard to Henry's end is the one great hiatus and artistic flaw in these eight Chronicle Plays as they stand. This much at any rate is clear: seen in long perspective, the King's speech before the battle, in spite of his triumph, was selling the lion's skin in advance. The battle itself bred a century of plagues for England. It is never safe to overlook the metaphors in Shakespeare.

IX

Agincourt! "It was a famous victory." Five scenes are dedicated to the battle.

In the first one we see Pistol capturing a French soldier ("a gentleman of a good house") and agreeing to spare his life for a ransom of two hundred crowns. The frequency with which, after Henry has indulged in boasting, Shakespeare introduces Pistol in the next scene grows increasingly suspicious. This one is obviously food for the groundlings. But is it only that? If Pistol, that brief extract and chronicle of all the cowards who ever cringed before nothing, can capture a French gentleman (in a scene that, by the way, reads like a parody of Falstaff's capture of Colville), pass himself off as "the most brave, valorous, and thrice-worthy signieur of England," and extort from him two hundred crowns, what, one wonders, will soldiers like Court and Williams and officers like Fluellen not be able to do? We have noted that the French were frivolous and overconfident. But Pistol! His exploit helps explain the inexplicable victory.

The second battle scene is but a few lines long and gives us a glimpse of the shame of the French at being worsted by the weaklings and slaves they had just been playing dice for:

Shame, and eternal shame, nothing but shame!

The third scene shows Henry receiving word of the deaths of the Duke of York, who led the van, and the Earl of Suffolk. Exeter, who brings the report, draws a pathetic picture of their final moments, and declares that on the field he wept at the sight. "I blame you not," says Henry,

For, hearing this, I must perforce compound
With mistful eyes, or they will issue too.

Why should Shakespeare give nearly a whole scene to the deaths of two men who have played practically no part in the story? For the sake of the battle atmosphere, it will be said. But Shakespeare generally subordinates his picturesque effects to drama. And so he does here. The last four lines of the scene reveal why the first thirty-four were written. An alarum sounds, and the King cries:

But hark! what new alarum is this same?
The French have reinforc'd their scatter'd men:
Then every soldier kill his prisoners!
Give the word through.

From tears to orders for the death of the prisoners—all in a second. The complete presence of mind of a great field commander! So it might seem.

But we recall the King's directions to his troops, just after he sent Bardolph to his death, which ended: "when lenity and cruelty play for a kingdom, the gentler gamester is the soonest winner." Then he followed a cruel act by gentle words. Now he follows tearful words by a cruel act. These sudden polar reversals are too characteristic of Henry to be attributed at bottom to anything but his own nature. But perhaps in this case the killing of the prisoners was "necessary," it may be suggested. Shakespeare does not make us wait long for more evidence on that point.

The fourth battle scene seems to digress even further. Yet it is one of the best illustrations in all the author's works of the rule that the more casual and incidental one of his scenes appears to be, the more significant and central it often is. What this one appears to be is just a bit of conversation between Fluellen and Gower, two of the King's officers, precipitated by the killing of the prisoners. What it is, if I am not mistaken, is nothing less than Shakespeare's last judgment on the rejection of Falstaff.

Gower and Fluellen, the Welsh officer who is forever quoting the military precedents of the Greeks and Romans, imply that the killing of the prisoners is an act of retaliation because French stragglers killed the English boys guarding the luggage. But the previous scene proves that this is not the case. Gower suggests the additional motive of personal revenge: "besides, they have burned and carried away all that was in the king's tent; wherefore the king, most worthily, hath caused every soldier to cut his prisoner's throat. O, 'tis a gallant king!" Do not suppose for a moment that Gower is ironical, however sarcastic those last words sound.

"Ay," says Fluellen, taking up the reference to the King's gallantry, "he was porn at Monmouth, Captain Gower. What call you the town's name where Alexander the Pig was born?"

"Alexander the Great," Gower returns, not relishing Fluellen's Welsh English. But Fluellen will not accept the correction:

"Why, I pray you, is not pig great? The pig, or the great, or the mighty, or the huge, or the magnanimous, are all one reckonings, save the phrase is a little variations."

"I think Alexander the Great was born in Macedon," says Gower, coming back to Fluellen's inquiry.

Whereupon Fluellen, taking up the alliteration of Monmouth and Macedon, proceeds to draw a parallel—how deadly, not Fluellen but only the attentive reader realizes—between Harry of Monmouth and Alexander the Pig of Macedon. That "Pig," of course, must have delighted the groundlings. But there is more in it than that. For consider: Alexander the Great has become the symbol for all time of insatiable lust for blood and conquest. "No more lands to conquer." The allusion in itself, in a play whose theme is imperialism, would be suspicious. Henry is bent on the subjection of France by force. Once upon a time he had admonished Falstaff to "leave gormandizing." But that was long ago. The parallel between Henry and Alexander, Shakespeare more than hints (and now we see the reason for Court's first name), goes considerably beyond the fact that the places where they were born both begin with the same letter. Even Fluellen sees that much, innocent as he is of the deeper import of what he is saying:

There is a river in Macedon; and there is also moreover a river at Monmouth. It is called Wye at Monmouth; but it is out of my prains what is the name of the other river; but 'tis all one, 'tis alike as my fingers is to my fingers, and there is salmons in both. If you mark Alexander's life well, Harry of Monmouth's life is come after it indifferent well; for there is figures in all things,

and he goes on to draw a parallel between Alexander's killing, when drunk, of his best friend Cleitus, and Henry's rejection of Falstaff. (Like the soul of Banquo, Falstaff will not down.)

FLU.: Alexander, God knows, and you know, in his rages, and his furies, and his wraths, and his cholers, and his moods, and his displeasures, and his indignations, and also being a little intoxicates in his prains, did, in his ales and his angers, look you, kill his pest friend, Cleitus.

Gow.: Our king is not like him in that: he never killed any of his friends.

FLU.: It is not well done, mark you now, to take the tales out of my mouth, ere it is made and finished. I speak but in the figures and comparisons of it: as Alexander killed his friend Cleitus, being in his ales and his cups; so also Harry Monmouth, being in his right wits and his good judgments, turned away the fat knight with the great belly-doublet: he was full of jests, and gipes, and knaveries, and mocks; I have forgot his name.

Gow.: Sir John Falstaff.

FLU.: That is he: I'll tell you there is goot men porn at Monmouth.

Gow.: Here comes his majesty.

And King Henry enters.

" 'There's no art to find the mind's construction in the face.' *Enter Macbeth*." Henry's entrance is like that, casting back a reversed significance over the scene that has gone before.

Fluellen, in comparing Henry and Alexander, has pointed out one incidental contrast: that whereas Alexander "in his ales and his angers" murdered Cleitus, Harry "in his right wits and his good judgments" turned away Falstaff. But *was* the King, whether angry or not, in his right wits and good judgments at that fatal moment? That is the debated point. And now, as if in living answer to the question, Henry enters with the words:

I was not angry since I came to France
Until this instant.

And he commands a herald to ride up to certain horsemen on the hill that "offend" his sight and order them either to come down and fight, or to quit the battle, under the threat of being hurled to death. And he adds:

Besides, we'll cut the throats of those we have,
And not a man of them that we shall take
Shall taste our mercy. Go and tell them so.

Fluellen's parallel is more pitiless than he realized. Alexander the Pig himself could hardly have been more magnificently angry than Henry is at this moment. It is one thing to kill prisoners in an emergency, or through "necessity." It is another to kill them on principle—and to promise to kill those not yet taken. Henry is drunk with wrath. How venial Falstaff's addiction to sack compared with this intoxication! Henry's father had warned us of this weakness of his son:

give him line and scope,
Till that his passions, like a whale on ground,
Confound themselves with working,

and we remember Henry's reproach against the three traitors who seemed, but were not,

Free from gross passion or of mirth or anger.

Thus, unobtrusively, near the end of another play, does Shakespeare slip quietly in his own comment on the rejection of Falstaff. For what else can it be? What other purpose has the scene? And how it confirms what went before!—the rehearsal of the rejection in the tavern; the rejection itself on the street; and now this reversion to it on the battlefield, when we see it in true perspective. Shakespeare "manifests no disapproval," says George Brandes, "where the King sinks far below the ideal, as when he orders the frightful massacre of all the French prisoners taken at Agincourt. Shakespeare tries to pass the deed off as a measure of necessity." Brandes has just remarked in the previous paragraph: "Shakespeare was evidently unconscious of the naïveté of the lecture on the Salic law." But possibly the poet is less guilty of casuistry in the one case, and naïveté in the other, than Brandes thinks.

A French herald who, the last time he left the English camp, had said,

Thou never shalt hear herald any more,

enters, granting the French defeat and begging an opportunity to bury their dead and separate the corpses of the nobles from those of peasants and mercenaries to which they lie disgracefully close. Henry grants the request, gives the battle its name from the neighboring castle of Agincourt, and around memories of Crécy and the Black Prince, of St. Crispin and St. "Tavy," he and Fluellen felicitate each other over their Welsh blood: "By Jeshu, I am your majesty's countryman, I care not who know it; I will confess it to all the 'orld: I need not to be ashamed of your majesty, praised be God, so long as your majesty is an honest man."

> God keep me so!

says Henry.

It takes less time than that between Peter's profession and the crowing of the cock to prove that Henry, judged by the chivalric code that he professes, is not an honest man, or, if you will, that God does not keep him so.

Henry espies his own glove in the cap of Williams. "Soldier, why wearest thou that glove in thy cap?" And Williams explains the mutual challenge exchanged between him and the "swaggering rascal" of the night before and his promise to strike his own glove from the other's cap when he finds it.

"What think you," says Henry, turning to Fluellen, "is it fit this soldier keep his oath?"

"He is a craven and a villain else."

But maybe his unknown opponent is of higher degree than he, Henry suggests.

That makes no difference, says Fluellen, though he be as good a gentleman as the devil himself, as Lucifer, or Belzebub, he must keep his oath. Evidently, to Fluellen fidelity or infidelity to an oath is not a mere matter of rank.

In that case, how about the King's oath?

He swore, when in disguise, to challenge his glove in his opponent's cap and to meet him in personal combat to defend his idea of where the guilt lies as between a sovereign and his soldiers in war. "If ever I live to see it I will challenge it," were his words. "I will do it," he added, "though I take thee in the king's company." Indeed Henry now admits quite casually to Warwick that he made this promise. He has given Fluellen Williams' glove—he tells Warwick after Fluellen has gone out—inventing a false account of where he got it and bidding Fluellen wear it in his cap.

> It is the soldier's; I by bargain should
> Wear it myself.

*Bargain!* It is a bourgeois word. Henry has pawned his *honor*—supposedly a noble word. But what is the word of honor of a king when given to a

commoner? Thus does Shakespeare demonstrate how long it takes after
the battle—half an hour?—for Henry's protestations of democracy and
equality before the battle to evaporate:

> We few, we happy few, we band of brothers;
> For he to-day that sheds his blood with me
> Shall be my brother; be he ne'er so vile,
> This day shall gentle his condition.

The victory is won; it is daylight now, not night; and the King is no longer
disguised—or should we say he is again disguised? All these things make a
difference. Williams is neither brother nor gentleman, but just a commoner. "Such is the breath of kings." It all has a subtle allusiveness on another
plane to John of Lancaster's broken oath.*

In the last of what I have loosely called the battle scenes, Warwick and
Gloucester, who are in the secret, and then Henry himself, intervene just
in time to prevent a combat between Fluellen and Williams, who, true to
his word, has struck the Welshman on perceiving his glove in his cap. The
King reveals the identity of the "swaggering rascal":

> It was ourself thou didst abuse.

The anouncement does not abash or embarrass Williams. He stands his
ground like a man. If the King is unwilling, or, if anyone insists, unable, to
meet Williams in bodily encounter, nemesis contrives to bring them together in spiritual combat. And again by day, as in their argument before
by night, it is the king rather than the man who comes off second best.

The brief scene between the two gives us Shakespeare near the top of
his ironic power. It is a little drama complete in itself. Its theme is: Which
is greater, a man or a king? And one need not go beyond it to find an
answer to that everlasting question: Was Shakespeare a democrat? Democrat in any dogmatic or narrowly political sense of course he was not. But
in the wider and deeper sense in which we speak of Lincoln as a supreme
democrat—well, let the scene itself decide:

K. HEN.: It was ourself thou didst abuse.
WILL.: Your majesty came not like yourself: you appeared to me but as
a common man; witness the night, your garments, your low-
liness; and what your highness suffered under that shape, I
beseech you take it for your own fault and not mine: for had

* The situation also brings to mind the famous "fourteen points" that Germany, at
the end of World War I, found to her undoing had one meaning before the Armistice
and quite another after it. Hitler made the most of this broken promise. It was Woodrow
Wilson who once declared: "There is more of a nation's politics to be got out of its
poetry than out of all its systematic writers upon public affairs and institutions."

> you been as I took you for, I made no offence; therefore, I
> beseech your highness, pardon me.
>
> K. HEN.: Here, uncle Exeter, fill this glove with crowns,
> And give it to this fellow. Keep it, fellow;
> And wear it for an honour in thy cap
> Till I do challenge it. Give him the crowns:
> And, captain, you must needs be friends with him.
>
> FLU.: By this day and this light, the fellow has mettle enough in his
> belly. Hold, there is twelve pence for you; and I pray you to
> serve God, and keep you out of prawls, and prabbles, and
> quarrels, and dissensions, and, I warrant you, it is the better
> for you.
>
> WILL.: I will none of your money.
>
> FLU.: It is with a good will; I can tell you, it will serve you to mend your
> shoes: come, wherefore should you be so pashful? your shoes
> is not so good: 'tis a good shilling, I warrant you, or I will
> change it.

The King compounds his honor for crowns—just as his father had for an English crown, and as he himself had even now been doing for a French one. The man whose shoes need mending will not touch so much as a penny. Here is what honor in another and higher sense means to a simple citizen. Here is one other man who, like the Chief Justice at the other end of the social scale, can spurn Faulconbridge's devil, Commodity. Here is a man who has no price. Falstaff himself would have failed, or rather never would have tried, to make fun of honor in this sense. And the best of it is that Williams (unlike Henry) does not so much as mention the word. He deals in the thing itself. "No longer consider what sort of man the good man ought to be," says Marcus Aurelius, "but be that man."

A herald enters and the King inquires: "Are the dead number'd?" "Here is the number of the slaughter'd French," the herald replies, and delivers papers showing that ten thousand French have been slain and twenty-nine English. No, not twenty-nine thousand, nor twenty-nine hundred. Twenty-nine! A battle? Call it rather, according to your point of view, a massacre or a miracle. And the disparity is even more startling in another respect. Henry takes particular satisfaction in the fact that most of the French dead are of high estate:

> in these ten thousand they have lost,
> There are but sixteen hundred mercenaries;
> The rest are princes, barons, lords, knights, squires,
> And gentlemen of blood and quality,

and he reads the names of the noblest of them. (Shakespeare can make even a list of proper nouns significant.) But for the English it turns out that they have lost one duke, one earl, one baronet, and one esquire. Among those of "blood and quality," then, the proportion is somewhat more than eighty-four hundred French to four English! The inference seems inescapable that it must have been the English commoners who accounted for a large number of the French knights and nobles. Henry should have been grateful surely to the rank and file. Was he? This is the way he announces it:

> Where is the number of our English dead?
> Edward the Duke of York, the Earl of Suffolk,
> Sir Richard Ketly, Davy Gam, esquire:
> None else of name; and of all other men
> But five and twenty.

"Be he ne'er so vile, this day shall gentle his condition." "None else of name." Again, it makes a difference whether it is before or after the battle. And instead of expressing gratitude to the Bateses and Courts and Williamses of his army of yeomen, Henry characteristically attributes his triumph wholly to God and within the space of a little more than a dozen lines declares:

> O God! thy arm was here.
>
> Take it, God,
> For it is none but thine!
>
> And be it death proclaimed through our host
> To boast of this or take the praise from God
> Which is his only.
>
> God fought for us.

And he orders that *Non nobis* and *Te Deum* be sung.

We have no quarrel with Henry's gratitude to heaven for a victory that must indeed have seemed to him like a miracle, but his reiteration of it becomes psychologically suspicious in the highest degree. It ends by looking less like giving thanks to God for the victory than like putting the responsibility on God. We recall those two chantries and those five hundred poor. Like his father with his crusade to Jerusalem, Henry is haunted by the specter of Richard II. For him, too, the wheel is coming full circle, and in license in bringing God into military matters he comes perilously close to talking like the Richard who placed his faith in celestial armies. "So Chrish save me, I will cut off your head." Anybody can get the irony of that. Henry's confusion of Mars with the Christian God is of the same order. Any one of his references to the God of Battles with which this play is filled is a trifle. In the aggregate they become an avalanche.

And so is brought to a close the story of Agincourt. Anyone fresh from a reading of it thinks the fourth act of this play gives the picture of a dashing hero leading his little army with indomitable courage, physical and moral, to victory over a foe overwhelmingly superior in numbers. But if asked for the evidence of Henry's part in the battle he searches the text in vain. He has carried over his impression from the Choruses, from Henry's "tiger" speech to his soldiers, from previous indirect knowledge of the hero-king from history or secondhand accounts of this very play, or, if he has seen it on the stage, from the unwarranted interpolations of some stage director. (That there were such interpolations in the poet's own day is entirely probable.) Shakespeare has portrayed many battles and shown many military leaders in combat, but not King Henry V in the Battle of Agincourt.

The magician makes us see things that are not there. Shakespeare does something similar to the imagination of the man who finds the heroism of Henry in the five scenes devoted to this battle, which, in the interest of the facts, may be summarized as follows:

1. Pistol captures a French gentleman.
2. The French lament their everlasting shame at being worsted by slaves.
3. Henry weeps at the deaths of York and Suffolk and orders every soldier to kill his prisoners.
4. Fluellen compares Henry with Alexander and his rejection of Falstaff to the murder of Cleitus. Henry, entering angry, swears that every French prisoner, present and future, shall have his throat cut. . . . The battle is over. The King prays God to keep him honest and breaks his word of honor to Williams.
5. Henry offers Williams money by way of satisfaction, which Williams rejects. Word is brought that 10,000 French are slain and 29 English. Henry gives the victory to God.

If Shakespeare had deliberately set out to deglorify the Battle of Agincourt in general and King Henry in particular it would seem as if he could hardly have done more.*

* This summary of the battle shows the liberties which the producers of the Olivier film version of *Henry V* took with the text. The picture of the battle with its colorful array of galloping horses and knights with streaming banners is magnificent and unsurpassed as photography and artistic design, but as far as Shakespeare goes it is sheer

But, it may be asked, how about this passage:

You may imagine him upon Blackheath,
Where that his lords desire him to have borne
His bruised helmet and his bended sword
Before him through the city. He forbids it,
Being free from vainness and self-glorious pride;
Giving full trophy, signal and ostent
Quite from himself to God.

That is from the Chorus of the fifth act. If what the Chorus says "you may imagine" is to be accepted as fact, Henry is once for all the Mirror of Humility of all Christian Kings, and that ends it. But if, when the Chorus and the play contradict each other, the text of the latter should be arbiter, the conclusion may be a different one. "You may imagine him," if you will, dealing and receiving blows from the beginning to the end of the battle, but you will be put to it to find in the text the scene in which he bruised his helmet and bent his sword. Indeed, the whole account comes closer to giving the impression that the King saw the battle from a vantage point than that he mixed in the fighting. The Duke of York led the van and perished with the Earl of Suffolk. "Thrice within this hour," says Henry when Exeter comes to announce York's death,

I saw him down; thrice up again, and fighting.
From helmet to the spur all blood he was.

Henry too may have been covered with blood (though he plainly had leisure enough to observe what was going on), yet in spite of his "he to-day that sheds his blood with me," he came through, for anything the text says to the contrary, without a scratch.

The evidence for all this, it is true, is negative. It lies in what is omitted. But is it not strange that the text should not be explicit on this point, that it should permit us for a moment to entertain such thoughts concerning this supreme hour of the hero-king? No one, of course, can question the valor of the man who killed Hotspur. What anyone can question—and, it seems to me, must question—is whether Henry at Agincourt is the man who killed Hotspur. There is much indeed to indicate that Shakespeare deliberately created a detailed contrast between Henry's conduct at Shrewsbury and his conduct at Agincourt.

At Shrewsbury we hear his father begging Henry to withdraw from the battle because of his loss of blood. He refuses:

---

invention. It throws the impression which the poet intended to create utterly out of focus, whereas these scenes to the modern moviegoer are probably the most vivid and memorable in the film.

> God forbid a shallow scratch should drive
> The Prince of Wales from such a field as this.

A little later the King is attacked by Douglas. His son comes to his rescue and Douglas flees. Scarcely has he had time to catch his breath when Hotspur enters. They fight and Hotspur falls. After the battle the Prince begs of his father the disposition of Douglas, who has been captured. It is granted and he gives Douglas his freedom. All this prowess and personal courage is conspicuous by its absence at Agincourt, except in so far as we choose to imagine it. Henry, for instance, makes no move to come to the rescue of York, though three times he sees him sorely beset, as he did to the rescue of his father. And if it be objected that Henry is now king and in command, there are too many Macbeths and Coriolanuses in Shakespeare to make that an acceptable explanation.

Does the poet offer any reason why Henry should have been less heroic at Agincourt than at Shrewsbury? He does.

More and more since his accession, we have seen Henry growing like his father. What was Henry IV's part in the Battle of Shrewsbury? No very glorious one, as those counterfeit kings made clear. Indeed, Henry would undoubtedly have been slain by Douglas, had not his son intervened at the critical moment. The elder Henry was no poltroon. Why was he not more valiant? Because his conscience was troubling him. So was his son's conscience on this later occasion, as his prayer before the battle shows. There is much to suggest that the son's inner state at Agincourt may have been closer to that of his father at Shrewsbury than we would ever have supposed, had we not seen him in disguise and heard him in soliloquy and prayer the evening before the battle. Henry V sent no counterfeit kings into the fray, but he confessed to God that he was little better than a counterfeit king himself:

> all that I can do is nothing worth,
> Since that my penitence comes after all.

His statement about himself on his accession has come true in a sense he did not anticipate:

> My father is gone wild into his grave....
> And *with his spirit* sadly I survive.

The contrast between Shrewsbury and Agincourt has interest beyond the character of Henry. Shrewsbury was still a feudal battle. Agincourt, as we have already noted, was the first victory of massed yeomen over knights and so registers the end of feudal war. We are dealing, however, not with the battle itself but with Shakespeare's account of it, and he puts no stress on the unarmored archers with their longbows to whom the victory has generally been attributed. The poet was plainly more interested in the moral than in the military aspects of the battle.

In the play, the English army before the encounter is described as a bedraggled brigade of pale and pining wretches about to confront the legions and flower of French chivalry and nobility. How could this "ruin'd band" have conquered at such odds? Partly, of course, because of the softness and vanity of "the confident and over-lusty French" and their contempt for their foe. But to leave it at that would do injustice to men like Court and Bates and Williams. Men who are modest and soft-spoken in peace, it has long been noted, often show the most courage on the battlefield. By a random choice, Shakespeare convinces us that Henry's army contained many such. They wished they were at home in bed, or even up to their necks in Thames, rather than where they were. In their very courage of hopelessness we have a better explanation of the miracle as the poet portrays it than in the personal heroism and leadership of Henry. In all this Shakespeare comes startlingly close to the same conclusion Tolstoy reaches in his analysis of the grounds of military victory in *War and Peace*.

The Chorus of the fifth act likens the celebration after Agincourt to an imperial triumph in ancient Rome and to an imaginary welcome in London of the Earl of Essex after a hypothetical suppression of the Irish rebellion. These dubious references to imperialism, Roman and Elizabethan, stress once more the distinction that must be drawn between the Chorus and the poet. In the light of the consistently disparaging allusions to Caesar throughout Shakespeare's works, the implied comparison of Essex to a "conquering Caesar" defines plainly enough what Shakespeare conceived to be the relation of his play to the events of his own day.

But, even without this, the cumulative testimony to what Shakespeare thought of Henry V's French conquest is utterly crushing. The irony of his rejecting Falstaff with his petty robberies only to embrace the shade of his father with his stolen crown and his advice to commit mightier thefts; the shaky character of his title to the throne of France, his unwillingness to understand that title, and his insistence that it be underwritten by the church; the passion into which he was sent by those innocent symbols of his youth, the tennis balls; his acceptance of church property to carry on his war, coupled with his swift dispatch of Bardolph to death for stealing from a church; his democratic protestations before the battle along with his quick consignment of them to oblivion after the victory; the continual juxtaposition of his boastfulness and Pistol's; his confession the night before Agincourt that even his own throne was not his own; the little loot of the underworld and the huge conquest of the King:

all these things, and others, confirm the fact that he had turned his back on the wildness of his youth only to confirm it on a grand scale in the anarchy of war. No one but a person very ignorant of the mathematics of chance could attribute to coincidence the agreement of so many details. "Who, I rob? I a thief? Not I, by my faith," cries Hal when the Gadshill escapade is first proposed. To which Falstaff replies that the Prince comes "not of blood royal" if he cannot steal. "Well, then," Hal relents, "once in my days I'll be a madcap." Did cap ever fit better than this madcap fitted the future? What wonder that the future put it on! What it all adds up to is that the Battle of Agincourt was the royal equivalent of the Gadshill robbery. If Shakespeare did not mean it, it means itself.

The analogy between imperialism and highway robbery is no invention of modern radicals. It is probably as old as the organization of men into predatory groups. "You know as well as we do," Thucydides makes the cynical Athenians say to the helpless Melians on the eve of the former's piratical conquest of their little isle, "you know as well as we do that right, as the world goes, is only in question between equals in power, while the strong do what they can and the weak suffer what they must."

> He looks upon the mightiest monarchs' wars
> But only as on stately robberies,

says Samuel Daniel, Shakespeare's contemporary. "Justice is as strictly due between neighbor nations as between neighbor citizens," says Benjamin Franklin; "a highwayman is as much a robber when he plunders in a gang as when single; and a nation that makes an unjust war is only a great gang." A comparison common to the ages could not have escaped a mind as acute as Shakespeare's. That it did not, Hamlet's one phrase, "a cutpurse of the empire," is enough to prove. And in plays like *Troilus and Cressida* and *Timon of Athens* the poet says right out what he says more or less under cover in *Henry V*. "Shall the son of England prove a thief and take purses? a question to be asked," says Falstaff impersonating Henry IV in the tavern. "Shall the King of England prove a thief and take kingdoms?" A question both asked and answered by Shakespeare in *Henry V*.

If this play, with its historical predecessors, is not enough to show what Shakespeare thought of imperialism, there are the four more on the reigns of Henry VI and Richard III in which he had already studied its fruits, for, as we have seen, it may well have been the disorder of the later fifteenth century that first sent Shakespeare in search of the causes of such chaos. And if all this is not enough, there is a later and greater masterpiece on the subject which is like all eight of these plays telescoped into one, and a still later one in which the theme is finally gathered up in the form of a parable. When Henry "embraced" the Chief Justice as his father, rejected Falstaff, and embarked on his conquest of France, it was not a new leaf, but the oldest of leaves, that he turned over.

## X

After the Battle of Agincourt, the fifth act of *Henry V* strikes one at first reading as the worst anticlimax in any of Shakespeare's greater plays. The poet, it is pretty generally agreed, ran out of matter, and the act has been put down as more of an epilogue than anything else—a sort of tailpiece. But we had better be on guard. Supreme poets, when approaching the crest of their power, are not in the habit of attaching tailpieces to masterpieces.

Following the Chorus, with its reference to Essex, we see Pistol in the first scene, after having sworn by Cadwallader and all his goats that he will not do it, compelled by Fluellen to eat a leek. Fluellen offers him a groat to square the injury, and, when Pistol hesitates, tells him he has another leek in his pocket, whereat Pistol complies:

I take thy groat in earnest of revenge,

but when his tormentor is gone he swears, "All hell shall stir for this." And our last glimpse of this unholy braggart-in-blank-verse reveals him setting out for England to embark on one of those criminal careers that it is one of the curses of war in all ages to leave in its wake. The Immoral Falstaff and Henry's "Gallia wars" have between them given Pistol the education and the opportunity for his future vocation as bawd and cutpurse.

We pass to the palace in Troyes and behold the two Kings, French and English, embracing like brothers just as if nothing had happened. In this last scene of *King Henry V,* if anywhere in Shakespeare, we are introduced to that Ceremony which was the subject of Henry's soliloquy the night before Agincourt. There we heard what he thought about it. Here we see what he does about it. Indeed this scene is so smothered in ceremony that only by disregarding the words and concentrating on the deeds can we get any notion of what is really happening. What does happen, to call a spade a spade, is this: one king compels another to eat a leek (or two leeks, if you will). The administration of the dose is so disguised by sentiment and diplomacy, so sugared over with protestations of "love" and exchanges of "brother France" and "brother England," that the leek to all appearances might have been a piece of wedding cake. But leek it is, nevertheless. And we remember Pistol's "All hell shall stir for this," and wonder if it shall.

In high contrast with all the palaver of the Kings and the Queen, one speech stands out: the Duke of Burgundy's on peace. It is sincere, profound, and imaginative, a touchstone by which to try everything that is said and done in the play. In *Richard II*, a well-weeded and well-tended garden was the metaphor for peace. Burgundy uses the same figure. He draws a picture of France, "this best garden of the world," from which Peace has been too long expelled: her unpruned vines, overgrown hedges, rusty plows, meadows that were formerly covered with sweet clover where now

> nothing teems
> But hateful docks, rough thistles, kecksies, burs,
> Losing both beauty and utility;
> And as our vineyards, fallows, meads, and hedges,
> Defective in their natures, grow to wildness,
> Even so our houses and ourselves and children
> Have lost, or do not learn for want of time,
> The sciences that should become our country,
> But grow like savages,—as soldiers will
> That nothing do but meditate on blood,—
> To swearing and stern looks, diffus'd attire,
> And everything that seems unnatural.

And he asks the two Kings what there is to prevent the restoration of peace with all her former blessings.

If you want all those blessings, Duke of Burgundy, Henry replies,

> you must buy that peace
> With full accord to all our just demands;
> Whose tenours and particular effects
> You have enschedul'd briefly in your hands.

Under the ceremony there is no nonsense about Henry. If peace is a garden to Burgundy, it is a commodity to be bought to the King. The language of horticulture—and the language of the market place. So, while his uncle Exeter, his brothers, and other lords go out to discuss with the French King and Queen the terms under which peace can be bought, Henry turns to the "wooing of Katharine"—if it may be called wooing when the lover has demanded the lady from her father as a condition of settlement:

> Yet leave our cousin Katharine here with us:
> She is our capital demand, compris'd
> Within the fore-rank of our articles.

It is a bit frank to refer to Kate in her own presence as a "capital demand." But the remark may have been intended only for her father's ear, and, when Kate and the King are left alone, under the influence of gentler feelings the original Hal, we hope, may come to the surface as he did once before under the cover of night.

The Court retires, only Alice, lady-in-waiting to Kate, who, as interpreter and chaperone, is a necessary party to the tête-à-tête, remaining, and the scene that follows, with its wit and its queer mixture of halting French and lame English, is indeed delightful. But love! Shade of Romeo, no! Not a spark of it, not a trace. And Romeo's ghost is the right one to invoke, for this is a case, like his, of an alliance that crosses the battle lines. "The quality least present in love," says Stendhal, "is gallantry." This interview between Henry and Kate might have been written to prove the truth of the maxim. It is right here that Shakespeare achieves unity between the two themes of the act, diplomacy and courtship, for just as gallantry is the ceremony of "love" so is ceremony the gallantry of politics.

All the zest of love-making rests in the uncertainty of the result, but in this case the result is a foregone conclusion. Yet Henry goes through the motions of pretending that his fate is in the lady's hands. He begins by calling her an angel. To which she replies, "*O bon Dieu! les langues des hommes sont pleines des tromperies,*" or, as rendered by Alice into English, "de tongues of de mans is be full of deceits."

Henry is glad her English is imperfect. Otherwise, he fears, "thou wouldst find me such a plain king that thou wouldst think I had sold my farm to buy my crown." But the swashbuckling way in which he goes at it does not sound at all like a farmer's mode of making love:

"If I could win a lady at leap-frog, or by vaulting into my saddle with my armour on my back, under the correction of bragging be it spoken, I should quickly leap into a wife. Or if I might buffet for my love, or bound my horse for her favours, I could lay on like a butcher and sit like a jack-an-apes, never off."

It does sound like a butchering of love.

"These fellows of infinite tongue, that can rhyme themselves into ladies' favours, they do always reason themselves out again." We remember Orlando's rhymes to Rosalind on the trees of the forest of Arden, and wonder.

Henry pretends to none of the qualities of a lover but plain-spokenness, constancy, and a good heart. "A good heart, Kate, is the sun and the moon." The moon is an ominous addition to the metaphor of his youth. Henry's figures of speech, as we have seen, are forever betraying him, but for once he perceives his slip in time to correct it: "or rather the sun and not the moon; for it shines bright and never changes, but keeps his course truly. If thou would have such a one, take me; and take me, take a soldier; take a soldier, take a king. And what sayest thou then to my love? speak, my fair, and fairly, I pray thee." (The awkward repetitions in those last two sentences remind us of nobody in the world so much as Shallow! Do his inadvertent allusion to the moon and his assertion that he, like the sun, has kept his course truly, cause Henry a moment of unconscious embarrassment?)

"Is it possible dat I should love de enemy of France?" Kate comes back at him very pertinently.

"No; it is not possible you should love the enemy of France, Kate; but, in loving me, you should love the friend of France; for I love France so well that I will not part with a village of it, I will have it all mine; and, Kate, when France is mine and I am yours, then yours is France and you are mine."

"I cannot tell vat is dat," Kate interjects. And neither can we, except that it is closer to a rapacity for land than it is to the love of woman.

Henry tries it over again in French, but with no better success, so he takes another tack: that of appealing to her maternal instinct. "I love thee cruelly," he protests, letting slip a Janus-faced adjective. "If ever thou beest mine, Kate, as I have a saving faith within me tells me thou shalt, I get thee with scambling,* and thou must therefore needs prove a good soldier-breeder. Shall not thou and I, between Saint Denis and Saint George, compound a boy, half French, half English, that shall go to Constantinople and take the Turk by the beard? Shall we not? What say'st thou, my fair flower-de-luce?" Imagine Shakespeare's genuine warrior-lover, Othello, speaking to Desdemona in that vein!

And who was this boy that, his prospective father hopes, is to make his grandfather's unfulfilled crusade to the East and take the Turk by the beard? The sainted Henry VI!

"I do not know dat," says Kate.

So Henry falls back on calling her goddess and divine—"*la plus belle Katharine du monde, mon très cher et devin déesse.*" To which she wittily retorts: "Your *Majesté ave fausse* French enough to deceive de most *sage demoiselle* dat is *en France.*"

"Now, beshrew my father's ambition!" cries Henry, disgusted at his lack of progress with the lady, "he was thinking of civil wars when he got me; therefore was I created with a stubborn outside, with an aspect of iron, that, when I come to woo ladies, I fright them." So throwing all

* *Scamble:* to struggle indecorously or rapaciously to obtain something.

England, Ireland, and France into the scale with himself, he asks directly: "Wilt thou have me?"

"Dat is as it sall please de *roi mon père*." The father shall decide.

"Nay, it will please him well, Kate," says Henry, and knowing that the father really has no choice in the matter, he cannot resist adding, "It shall please him, Kate." Henry may know little about love, but he understands the distinction between shall and will.

"Den it sall also content me."

The conquest is over.

This is Henry's second Agincourt and it throws as much light on the first one as anything in the play. They are both overwhelming victories won by force (actual and potential) in the face of odds not nearly as great as they appeared. They both turn, in different senses, on the will of the father. Their ultimate fruits are respectively (1) the loss of France by England, and (2) King Henry VI: both, judged by what Henry V stood for, calamities of the first order; both, for England, blessings in disguise. And the second helped, negatively, to bring about the first. If this scene is a "tailpiece," it is at least a prophetic one.

The French King returns and Henry asks for the sake of form: "Shall Kate be my wife?"

"So please you," says Kate's father, knowing where the compulsion lies.

"I am content," says Henry, not forgetting the bride's dowry, "so the maiden cities you talk of may wait on her."

This also is agreeable to King Charles. Nor does he deny Henry's new title of King of England and Inheritor of France. It is all in the family now, and Kate's father expresses his faith that "this dear conjunction" may plant

> Christian-like accord
> In their sweet bosoms, that never war advance
> His bleeding sword 'twixt England and fair France,

—a wish over which the figure of Joan of Arc, awaiting her cue, casts a certain shadow. And Queen Isabel outdoes her husband. She compares the union of the two kingdoms to a marriage of man and wife, which, she hopes, unlike human marriage, will never know divorce. This touch clinches the unity underlying the politics and the love-making of the fifth act of the play and proves again that it is far more than an epilogue.

Henry, however, is thinking of the immediate, not the distant, future, and in spite of all the flow of sentiment he sees that everything is done in binding legal shape:

> My Lord of Burgundy, we'll take your oath,
> And all the peers', for surety of our leagues.

Then shall I swear to Kate, and you to me;
And may our oaths well kept and prosperous be!

With which characteristic last line "this star of England," who has figured in four plays, disappears forever—except as a corpse at his own funeral and in the possible good and the certain evil that lived after him—from Shakespeare's dramatic firmament.

But not from Shakespeare's imagination.

## XI

If the events of this play be taken at face value, if Henry is accepted at his own estimate, or if we go even further and believe with the Chorus that he is the mirror of all Christian kings, or with the majority of critics that he is Shakespeare's portrait of the ideal king, then there is no contesting the view that the play is epic and lyrical rather than dramatic. There is in that case none of that disparity between inner and outer upon which all poetic drama depends for its effect. But grant that Henry is the golden casket of *The Merchant of Venice*, fairer to a superficial view than to a more searching perception, and instantly the play becomes pervaded with an irony that imparts intense dramatic value to practically every one of its main scenes: the interview with the Bishops, the tennis-ball incident, the entrapping of the traitors, the "tiger" speech and the one before Harfleur, the rejection of Bardolph, the Haroun-al-Raschid scene before the battle with the soliloquy and prayer that follow it, the "we few, we happy few" address to the King's little "band of brothers," the battle itself with its echo of the rejection of Falstaff and the killing of the prisoners, the second encounter with Williams, the giving of the victory to God, and, finally, the making of "peace" and the "wooing" of Kate. It is all woven into a web of high psychological, political, symbolical, and (if so much be granted) dramatic value. And this does not take into account the "comic relief" which is enough in itself, with its oblique comments on the main plot, to relieve the play of the charge of being undramatic. If this play is undramatic, *Hamlet* itself, one is tempted to say, is undramatic. The difference is that Hamlet is at least partly conscious of psychological events which in Henry, except on rare occasions, take place below the threshold of apprehension. Whether *Henry V* is theatrical as well as dramatic is another question the answer to which will depend on the acting and the audience at a particular performance. It has been said that no actor can fail as Hamlet. Any actor can fail as Henry.

"It is well to seem merciful, faithful, humane, sincere, religious, and also to be so," says Machiavelli, prescribing right conduct to the ideal ruler in *The Prince*, "but you must have the mind so disposed that when it is needful to be otherwise you may be able to change to the opposite qualities. . . . A prince must take great care that nothing goes out of his mouth which is not full of the above-named five qualities, and, to see and hear him, he should seem to be all mercy, faith, integrity, humanity, and religion. And nothing is more necessary than to seem to have this last quality, for men in general judge more by the eyes than by the hands, for every one can see, but very few have [power] to feel. Everybody sees what you appear to be, few feel what you are."

Not maliciously and in cold blood but against the grain of his own na-ture and by insensible degrees, the man who began as Hal and ended as Henry V made himself into something that comes too close for comfort to Machiavelli's ideal prince. "Then why did not Shakespeare make it plain?" those will exclaim who hold that at any sacrifice everything must be clear in the theater. (That everything must seem to be clear may be readily granted.) But how, will they tell us, could Shakespeare draw a character whose first requisite is that he shall appear to be the opposite of what he is except by drawing a character who appears to be the oppo-site of what he is? "If Machiavelli had had a prince for disciple," wrote Voltaire in his *Memoirs*, "the first thing he would have recommended him to do would have been to write a book against Machiavellism." Samuel Butler has demonstrated in convincing detail that no art or mental process is perfect until it becomes unconscious. The perfect thief is the klepto-maniac, who steals as it were automatically. In that sense Henry V was possibly the perfect Machiavellian prince. In that sense Richard III was a mere bungler: he was still conscious of his evil.

Seldom has a conquest begun to crumble more immediately than did Henry's. Hardly is his body cold in death (if we may glance again at *Henry VI*) when losses across the Channel are reported. Successive mes-sengers interrupt his funeral procession to tell of cities retaken by the enemy, the crowning of the Dauphin, the defeat of Talbot, the cowardice of Sir John Fastolfe. It is as if with the departure of the King's spirit from his body the extremities of his kingdom begin to grow cold and to shrink. And not just the extremities. Dissension at home between church and state, rivalries of the nobles, street fighting between retainers, show what a counterfeit is the "unity" that emerges in time of war, what a forgery the "order" imposed by a "strong" man. Much has been made, based mainly on a famous speech in *Troilus and Cressida*, of Shakespeare's love of unity and order. It was harmony and peace, not unity and order, that Shakespeare loved. The feudal system had said and done what it could for an organization of human life founded on an analogy with the solar system, with the king, like the sun, at the center and nobles around him, like the planets, revolving in fixed orbits. Richard II and Henry V, with their perpetual likening of themselves to the sun, are relics of this system. The anarchy of the fifteenth century is compensation for the order of Henry IV and Henry V, the inevitable ebb of the tide before the emergence of Richard III. Shakespeare evidently detected very early the resemblance between anarchy and order, realizing that the two are merely extremes that meet. Anarchy he abhorred, and order, he perceived, is only the counterfeit of peace. Henry VI gives us a tiny, if abortive, glimpse of a spirit that can exorcise them both and usher in that balance of opposites within which alone a genuine society can be brought into being. "Such harmony is in immortal souls."

*Richard III*, as we saw when we discussed that play, is a sort of biography of Force, a fitting close to the series of nine plays that begin chronologically with *King John*, a confirmation of the Bastard's belief that Truth in the long run gets the better of Commodity, a crowning demonstration of the diabolic rather than the divine right on which absolute power rests, of the nemesis that is bound in the end to overtake the "strong" man. How likely is it that Shakespeare would have composed this pitiless exposure of the hollowness and rottenness of power, only to turn a few years later to a glorification of it on an imperialistic scale? That is the paradox and the question with which the conventional interpretation of *Henry V* confronts us. And more than that: it involves the further contradiction of Shakespeare's almost immediate reconversion to his earlier view in plays that follow. Was Shakespeare, then, just a turncoat and "fool of time" himself? That he should take advantage of the winds of patriotic emotion of his day is just what we would expect of him. It was his duty as good playwright and sailor to do exactly that. But that he abandoned his ship to them is unthinkable—or so it seems to me. If he did, we might just as well give up first as last any attempt to discover continuity or integrity in his works.

*Chapter XVIII*

# Henry VIII

*The Tempest* makes such a fitting conclusion to Shakespeare's works, and *Henry VIII* is such an anticlimax after it and the other late plays, that in spite of its unchallenged inclusion in the First Folio one is tempted to assign to him just as little of it as the evidence will permit.

Doubt concerning Shakespeare's sole responsibility for *Henry VIII* had been expressed about the middle of the eighteenth century, and Johnson remarked that "the genius of Shakespeare comes in and goes out with Katherine." Emerson in 1850 sensed two rhythms in the play and attributed what he took to be the original underneath Shakespeare to someone "with a vicious ear." Tennyson suggested that many passages were "very much in the manner of Fletcher," and James Spedding, on the basis of a careful analysis of the versification and style, assigned to Shakespeare only five scenes and part of a sixth (I, i, ii; II, iii, iv; III, ii, 1–203; and V, i), giving the rest to Fletcher. Critics generally, though not unanimously, have acquiesced in this conclusion.

The fact that under Spedding's arrangement Shakespeare introduces most of the leading characters would suggest that he had something to do with the planning of the play rather than that he was a mere reviser, but if so he permitted himself a constructive looseness such as he had never previously revealed. The work is conspicuously lacking in unity.

The first act, along with a little of the second, makes up what is almost a separate story of the fall of Buckingham. It is effectively handled but it contributes little to the rest of the drama except for its forecast of the part Wolsey is to play in influencing the King.

And the last act is even more detached. Against all dramatic and artistic principles it initiates a fresh line of interest in the account of the threat against Cranmer by the nobles and his defense by the King, in the face of the fact that Cranmer has figured scarcely at all in what has preceded.

The other three acts, which partly interweave the fates of Katherine and Wolsey, are slightly more compact, though it is only in the account of his death that Wolsey comes into Act IV.

The sympathy of the reader or spectator is all with Katherine as against both Wolsey and Henry, and this fact makes a poor preparation for the glowing prophecies with regard to Anne Bullen's daughter with which the play concludes. Indeed, the portrait of the selfish, lustful, and unscrupulous Henry affords a somewhat inappropriate background for the extravagant glorification of his daughter. One wonders what Elizabeth would have thought of the play if she could have seen it.

This shift of sympathy is just what we might expect if the work were the product of more than one author. And its lack of coherence and harmony in other respects confirms the view that it was not conceived and executed by one imagination. It is compelled to depend for such unity as it has on the continuity provided by Henry himself and on the theme of "the fall of princes," Buckingham, Wolsey, and Katherine.

Buckingham and his friends; Wolsey, Henry, and Katherine, as first introduced; such a minor figure as Anne's Old Lady: these and others have the authentic Shakespearean ring. The Queen—whether or not Shakespeare is responsible for the rest of her role—makes a fit companion for Hermione in her modesty, bravery, and dignity under suffering. But these effects are not numerous or sustained enough to impart anything like a Shakespearean quality to the play as a whole. Indeed, *Henry VIII* is more pomp and pageantry than drama, however dramatic single moments in it may be, and its "fine" speeches along with the opportunities it provides for rich costuming, brilliant spectacle, and general pictorial appeal account better than any more universal qualities for the fact that it has frequently been revived. The critic of the London *Times*, writing in 1811 of a contemporary production, pronounced the play

the most laborious in its construction, and the most exhausting in its effect, of any that has ever been produced by diligent servility. Processions and banquets find their natural place in a work of this kind; and without the occasional display of well-spread tables, well-lighted chandeliers, and well-rouged maids of honour, the audience could not possibly sustain the accumulated *ennui* of *Henry the Eighth*.

That is an extreme estimate. But the modern reader who remembers *Hamlet* and *King Lear* will understand.

## Chapter XIX

# Much Ado about Nothing

### I

It has often been noted that the titles of the three comedies that Shakespeare wrote just on the threshold of his supreme tragic period, *Much Ado about Nothing*, *As You Like It*, and *What You Will* (alias *Twelfth Night*), indicate a rather nonchalant attitude on his part toward these productions, not to say an innocently condescending one toward his audience. Each is a masterpiece in its kind, and yet, when we think of *Othello* and *Macbeth*, they do give us the impression of having been tossed off, so to speak, by a genius that was ready for immensely greater things. It is as if the author wrote them with his little finger.

*Much Ado about Nothing* is in some ways Shakespeare's most enticing title. Superficially it seems to suggest that the content of the play itself is trifling or inconsequential. Someone who would have it taken less lightly has pointed out that "nothing," in Elizabethan times, was pronounced almost as "noting" is today and would have us note that noting, or eavesdropping, plays an important role in the play. It would be quite like Shakespeare to intend something of the sort. But those who seek a deeper meaning in the title should not stop at that level.

Of the four words in it, *Nothing* is the most interesting. Indeed, in all of Shakespeare's immense vocabulary there are few more interesting words. He uses it often of course in its usual signification. But he uses it also in a way of his own.

If I draw a circle on the sand or on a piece of paper, instantly the spatial universe is divided into two parts, the finite portion within the circle (or the sphere if we think of it in three dimensions) and the infinite remainder outside of it. Actuality and possibility have a similar relation. Actuality is what is within the circle. However immense it be conceived to be, beyond it extends not merely the infinite but the infinitely infinite realm of what might have been but was not, of what may be but is not. In this realm are all the deeds that were not done when the other choice was made, all the roads that were not traveled when the other fork was taken, all the life that did not come into existence when its seeds failed to germinate. And in it no less is all that still may be: all the possible combinations of chemical elements that have never been made, all the music that is still uncomposed, all the babies that have not yet been born. This is the realm of NOTHING. In one sense it has no existence. In another, existence is nothing without it. For out of it ghosts are perpetually being summoned by our hopes and fears—which are themselves made of nothing—to be incorporated into the world of FACT. The interflow and union between these two realms is the type and father of all the alchemies and chemistries. "He who has never hoped shall never receive what he has never hoped for." Thus Heraclitus packs it into a sentence. *Ex nihilo nihil fit* is but a half-truth. For out of something nothing new ever came without the aid of "nothing" in this high potential sense. Nothing is thus practically a synonym for creativity. It is that realm of pure possibility that alone makes freedom possible. It is one of the two constituents of the imagination, the other being fact.

Shakespeare delighted in using the word "nothing" in this high metaphysical sense. It is easy to see why any artist might.

Today a sheet of white paper on the table; tomorrow a poem on the same paper. Today a white canvas; tomorrow a painting. "And God said, Let there be light: and there was light." The poem or the picture is the same miracle on a smaller scale. How could Shakespeare have failed to feel the wonder of it when at last he held in his hands a completed *Hamlet* or *King Lear?* Where had it come from? Out of nothing. He says as much himself in *A Midsummer-Night's Dream:*

> as imagination bodies forth
> The forms of things unknown, the poet's pen
> Turns them to shapes, and gives to *airy nothing*
> A local habitation and a name.

Here is one of the first and one of the clearest instances in which he equates nothing and the idea of pure creativity.

Beyond doubt the most impressive use of the word "nothing" in this sense in all Shakespeare is Cordelia's in the opening scene of *King Lear,* though Cordelia was of course unconscious, at the time, that she was using the word in any but its ordinary sense. Having elicited their effusive and hypocritical protestations of love from his two older daughters, Lear turns to his youngest and asks her what she can say to outdo them. She says nothing. Her silence, which says everything, presently becomes unbearable. "Speak," her father commands.

Cor.: Nothing, my lord.
Lear: Nothing?
Cor.: Nothing.
Lear: Nothing will come of nothing.

But when we have finished the story we see that everything came of nothing. King Lear was right in prophesying that nothing in the way of material inheritance would come of Cordelia's "nothing." But her whole spiritual inheritance came from nothing else. Between the covers of Shakespeare's works it would be hard to find one word more instinct with creativity than that "nothing" of Cordelia's. "Nothing brings me all things," exclaims Timon of Athens, brought at last to that ultimate bound where everything turns to its opposite. That sentence sums it up, puts the final stamp of the positive on this most negative of words.

Now if our eyes are not so dazzled by Beatrice and Benedick and the glitter of their wit, or our risibilities so tickled by Dogberry and his companions, that we cannot attend to the play as a whole, we shall see that it is dedicated to this idea of Nothing. It is full of lies, deceptions (innocent and not so innocent), and imagination, and these things grade into one another as imperceptibly as darkness does into light. Yet, notwithstanding that fact, the extremes—namely, lies and imagination—are seen to be as opposite as night and noon.

Nature, unless we watch her long and closely, appears to be neutral and unmoral, equally hospitable to either of these opposites, able to digest the one or the other with the same facility. But like poison given to work a long time after, the lie in the long run (if not in the short) fails to get on with the facts of the world into which it has been introduced, and has the effect of a grain of sand in a watch or other fine mechanism. It sends nature back, however slightly, toward chaos. Whereas imagination has the opposite effect of enabling more facts to get on better with one another than would have been the case without it. It introduces harmony, as do reconciliation and atonement. False and blatant advertising and publicity may sell a shoddy novel for a time. But the works of Shakespeare go on gaining more readers indefinitely on their own momentum. Here are two kinds of success that it behooves us not to confuse. "The end justifies the means," we say. Does it? Yes, or no, according to the interpretation we put on those five Delphic words, for if ever a maxim embraced the extremes of virtue and knavery, it is this one.

The end justifies the means: the end crowns the whole; the harvest is the test of the garden, the apple of the apple tree; the arrival at the summit is proof that the climber took a right way up. "By their fruits ye shall know them." This is the pragmatism of Jesus, the bringing of truth to the test of life, life in his high sense of more abundant life, that fulness for which each new creature is by its nature fitted. Over against this authentic pragmatism is the shabby pragmatism of all the self-seekers, opportunists, and deluders of mankind from Machiavelli to Mussolini, or, to go further back and come further down, from Satan himself to the last American who says "Anything goes, so long as you can get away with it." It is the doctrine that a high purpose sanctifies and sanctions any means, however base, of attaining it. Raskolnikov reasoned that it was right to rob and kill so long as he intended to put the money to good use. Hitler made his vision of a New Order his excuse for plunging the world into war. Jesus and Hitler, Christ and Anti-Christ: such are the opposite philosophies hidden in the same five words. On a confusion between them both self-delusion and deliberate malice thrive. *Much Ado about Nothing* might have been written to make the distinction between them clear.

## II

The main plot of *Much Ado* is founded on two deceptions. Don John and his fellow-conspirators spread the lie that Hero is false to Claudio, when she is really true to him. Friar Francis gives it out that Hero is dead, when she is still alive. The first deception is false in fact and false in purpose and intention. It is a lie in the fullest sense. The second deception is false in fact, but is imaginatively and symbolically true. The Hero whom Claudio maligned *is* dead, never to revive. Out of the illusion of her death a new Hero emerges not only in herself but in Claudio's heart and imagination. And so the illusion turns into the fact, and looking retrospectively we see there was no deception. If I begin saying, "Now the eclipse is total!" a moment before it is total only to find it total before I have finished my sentence, I have spoken the truth more nearly than I would if I had tried to keep strictly to the evidence of the moment. The same principle holds when the interval is longer. Imagination simply anticipates the fact, with the difference that it not merely foresees (as in the case of the eclipse) but actually helps to bring the fact to birth, as we might conceive the sun saying to the seed: "You are not a seed; you are a flower," and then setting about to transform it into a flower. Literally the sun's statement would be false; but prospectively and creatively it would be true. This is the pivot on which turns the much-maligned doctrine of the will to believe of William James. "This world is good, we must say, since it is what we make it—and we shall make it good," says James.

*Much Ado about Nothing* is saturated with this idea of the power of Nothing (of the creative ingredient of the imagination, that is) to alter the nature of things for good or ill, for, as Shakespeare's History Plays so abundantly show, fear and hate, as well as faith and love, have the capacity to attract facts to them and so, temporarily at least, to confirm their own hypotheses. But the changes fear and hate effect are destructive and pointed in the direction of chaos, whereas imagination integrates, makes for synthesis and reconciliation of clashing interests. The play is full of phrases that imply this fluidity of facts, their willingness to flow for good or evil into any mold the human mind makes for their reception. Antonio brings news to Leonato. "Are they good?" asks the latter. "As the event stamps them," the former replies. "You have of late stood out against your brother," says Conrade to Don John, "and he hath ta'en you newly into his grace; where it is impossible you should take true root but by the fair weather that you make yourself: it is needful that you frame the season for your own harvest." The children of this world, as Jesus divined, are often wiser in these matters than the children of light. But not so in the case of Friar Francis. "Die to live," is his advice to Hero, which is only a more succinct summary of his prophecy of the effect on Claudio of the "nothing" of Hero's death:

> for it so falls out
> That what we have we prize not to the worth
> Whiles we enjoy it, but being lack'd and lost,
> Why, then we rack the value, then we find
> The virtue that possession would not show us
> Whiles it was ours. So will it fare with Claudio:
> When he shall hear she died upon his words,
> The idea of her life shall sweetly creep
> Into his study of imagination,
> And every lovely organ of her life
> Shall come apparell'd in more precious habit,
> More moving-delicate, and full of life
> Into the eye and prospect of his soul,
> Than when she liv'd indeed.

### III

Between Don John's lying plot and the Friar's imaginative experiment, the black and white respectively of the play's pragmatic theme, are incidents of various shades of gray, tamperings with the facts of different degrees of justification or its opposite. Of these the masked wooing of Hero by Don Pedro in behalf of Claudio, with the distorted reports of it that come through eavesdropping to Leonato and Don John—leading to the loss of faith in Don Pedro by Claudio himself—is the most complicated example.

But it is the underplot, or, as we might call it, the second main plot, that confirms the theme and proves that we are not reading things into Shakespeare's play in making it center about Nothing.

Beatrice and Benedick are in love with each other without knowing it. Their friends contrive to have them overhear conversations in which Benedick listens in one scene to reports of Beatrice's hopeless passion for him and she listens in the next to similar accounts of his for her and, in addition, to condemnations of her pride and scorn. The effect in both cases is instantaneous. "When I said I would die a bachelor," cries Benedick, "I did not think I should live till I were married." "Can this be true?" asks Beatrice,

> Stand I condemn'd for pride and scorn so much?
> Contempt, farewell!

Where faith in the fact can help create the fact, says William James, it would be an insane logic that would deny our right to put our trust in it. If the friends of Beatrice and Benedick had concocted their whole plot out of nothing, as Don John did his against Hero, their means of bringing the two together would not have been "justified." But sensing the existence of the seed they brought just enough "nothing" to bear on it in the form of imaginative sunshine to bring it to the flower of actuality, to give to that "airy nothing" a local habitation and a name. They merely gave nature a nudge, as it were. The love thus elicited justified the faith. But if this was enough to make the two lovers confess their love to themselves, it took the wrong done to Hero to get them to confess it to each other. "Kill Claudio," cries Beatrice, shaken into sincerity. She doesn't mean it. Yet it is the truest thing she had ever said up to that moment. So far can truth be from the merely literal meaning of the words that try to convey it.

Emerson, in his essay on *Self-Reliance,* has a famous paragraph on consistency beginning: "A foolish consistency is the hobgoblin of little minds." Looking at it later in life, he remarked that he might better have substituted for the whole passage simply: "Damn Consistency." It would be hard to find two words that come closer to summing up a Shakespearean character than those two do Benedick when he bids good-by to wit-cracking and opens his arms to Beatrice. If this Emersonian distillation of Benedick be joined to Beatrice's own "Contempt, farewell!" we have four words that not only characterize the transformations which take place in these two for whom the play has come to stand in most minds but that show also what the drama stands for in Shakespeare's development. It is his own as well as Benedick's repudiation of "wit," his own as well as Beatrice's farewell to contempt, his own as well as their declaration of independence of the past. He still had to write two more comedies, to be sure, in a not wholly different vein (*As You Like It* and *Twelfth Night*), in which to develop and consolidate that declaration of independence and step further in the direction in which his genius was leading him. More than that. He had to write three dark and in some respects perplexing plays (*All's Well That Ends Well*, *Troilus and Cressida*, and *Measure for Measure*) and one tragedy centered around a figure of measureless contempt (*Hamlet*), before the dragon of satire was slain and he could emerge on the mountain peaks of pure tragedy. That Shakespeare's supreme accomplishment took place on those heights the world has come pretty nearly to agree. The story of Benedick and Beatrice, who loved each other from the first but came to recognize it only after a long "comic" detour, is a kind of partial allegory of the progress of Shakespeare's own soul. At the risk of being far-fetched we might even detect a vague repetition of the same theme in Claudio's vicarious wooing of Hero and his repudiation of her, followed at the end by their reunion. Even apart from possible unconscious spiritual autobiography, the more we stress this parabolic aspect of their love the less unacceptable the otherwise somewhat unpalatable denouement of the Claudio-Hero story becomes.

## IV

*Much Ado about Nothing* is a study in the egotism of youth, its sentimental and romantic egotism in Claudio, its antiromantic and intellectual egotism in Beatrice and Benedick. The two tendencies reduce to pretty much the same thing and are as natural to youth as mumps and measles, phases through which it normally passes, largely harmless if that passage is not arrested. If it is, love may grow soft or even rotten (Claudio's "rotten orange" at the altar is more nearly a description of himself at the moment than it is of Hero), or, at the other extreme, it may harden into a shell of pride. These are the respective dangers that Claudio (if we can believe in his conversion) and Beatrice and Benedick are represented as escaping. The suspense and interest of the play lie in the danger—its point in the escape. And so, oddly, whoever likes this play too unreservedly comes under its own condemnation. It has always been a favorite with actors and theatergoers. But with many twentieth-century readers it leaves the impression that its author regarded it lightly, saw it more nearly as we do than as his contemporaries did. Everything conspires to show that though he seldom used words more brilliantly than in this very play his attitude toward them was growing more and more like Hamlet's: "Words, words, words." Words can say only a little. But they can reveal a great deal by what they conceal. This is the difference between wit and poetry. In this sense Shakespeare was getting less and less interested in wit and more and more interested in poetry.

Fencing, which Shakespeare likens to wit, may be developed for its own sake into an art, but it reveals its true nature only as we consider it a prelude to dueling or deadly combat in battle, and when that comes there are other things more important than the polish on the rapiers and the glitter they make in the sun. The same is true of words. They can be made to scintillate, but they have a more serious and fatal function, as no one can better understand than he who has mastered them in this lower sense. We grow a bit contemptuous of what we can do easily or perfectly. We crave a full challenge to our capacities, something that will make us stretch ourselves to the limit, as a tennis player does not care for a match against an unworthy opponent. He had rather lose to a superior player than win against an inferior one. "For absolute power of composition, for faultless balance and blameless rectitude of design," says Swinburne, "there is unquestionably no creation of [Shakespeare's] hand that will bear comparison with *Much Ado about Nothing*." It is one of Swinburne's absurd superlatives, but there is just enough truth in it to make it illuminating. It is as if Shakespeare said to himself: "I'll do it once more, give them what they want as utterly as I can, and then be done with that sort of stuff forever." And he was done with it. There is plenty of wit in later plays but never again does it occupy the central position that it does here. "But how about Rosalind?" it will be asked. An objection that only serves to drive the point home. For by way of Rosalind, in whom wit begins to transcend itself, Shakespeare takes a long stride in the direction of those great tragic heroines whose central endowment is love rather than wit. Beatrice can talk, but the play is nearing its end before we have full evidence that she can act and love as well as talk. But Rosalind can act and love from the beginning and her wit is exercised mainly in the service of love and not for its own sake. Just where between Beatrice and Desdemona Rosalind comes in it would be hard to say. But the point is that she does come between them.

And so, paradoxically, *Much Ado* is in the end a sort of repudiation of itself and of the very thing that has given it its immense theatrical reputation. And that, in turn, is our excuse in discussing it for stressing a single word in its title at the price of saying little about the pair who always packed the theater in Shakespeare's own day, whom actors and actresses will long love to impersonate, and about whom so many critics have had so many witty things to say. "There is only one thing worse than the Elizabethan 'merry gentleman,' and that is the Elizabethan 'merry lady.'" says Bernard Shaw just after having declared that Benedick is "not a wit, but a blackguard." And he expresses the hope that the very thought of Benedick covered Shakespeare with shame in later years. But so far from having to be contrite, my guess would be that, quite without benefit of Bernard Shaw and without going to the extreme of his dissenting opinion, the creator of this incomparable pair was perfectly aware, at the time he made them, of the superficiality of their wit and the shallowness of most of their talk, however brilliant the style in which it is dressed.

## V

Finally, it remains for Dogberry and his fellows, who to some readers are the top of the play, to put the last seal of approval on this way of interpreting it. Dogberry likes to hear himself talk as well as Beatrice and Benedick do, and he, too, is interested in words for their own sake. The parody is apparent. Verbality for verbality, loquacity for loquacity, it sets us wondering how much there is to choose between the repartee of the wits and the mental meanderings of the constable, between the polishing of the King's English by Beatrice and Benedick and the murdering of it by Dogberry. The latter has at any rate contributed more than the former to posterity's stock of familiar quotations.

And the realistic clowning of this part of the story ties in with the theme as well as with the plot of the rest. What culture could not compass, the dumb luck or instinct of the unlettered brings to light. Here sheer witlessness becomes the highest wit, the ridiculous almost sublime; here dulness is sublimated into philosophy. It is all a perfect commentary on the antithesis drawn by Dostoevsky between intelligence and stupidity. "The stupider one is," says Ivan Karamazov whose prime gift was intelligence, "the closer one is to reality. The stupider one is, the clearer one is. Stupidity is brief and artless, while intelligence wriggles and hides itself. Intelligence is a knave, but stupidity is honest and straightforward." How in keeping with this Shakespeare is in having these plain watchmen in the routine performance of their duty uncover the truth that has evaded the clever and sophisticated. Dogberry himself is loquacious and inane, anything but "straightforward" it would seem. Yet he is straightforward in Dostoevsky's sense, right on the fundamentals, that is, and when it comes to these he can hit the nail on the head. "Write God first," he commands. And to Borachio he says, "I do not like thy look," which, while it may not constitute legal evidence, does credit to his perception. His instant distrust of the man is the counterpart of Beatrice's instant faith in her cousin. Shakespeare even imparts to some of his most muddleheaded blunders overmeanings that seem like nature uttering unconscious wisdom through his mouth. "Master constable," says the Sexton at the end of the preliminary examination, "let these men be bound." "Let them be opinioned," says Dogberry, rejecting as not dignified enough for his office the Sexton's simpler word. "Opinioned": is it a slanting glance at the main theme of the play? It might well be. To be a sophisticated man is to be opinioned, and to be opinioned is to be bound. It is the stupid and the imaginative, at the extremes, who are unopinioned and therefore free, free like the Creator and like the creator of the characters in this play, to make something out of NOTHING.

## Chapter XX

# As You Like It

### I

*As You Like It* is far from being one of Shakespeare's greatest plays, but it is one of his best-loved ones. "I know nothing better than to be in the forest," says a character in Dostoevsky, "though all things are good." We are in a forest, the Forest of Arden, during four-fifths of *As You Like It*, but it is a forest that by some magic lets in perpetual sunshine. And not only do we have a sense of constant natural beauty around us; we are in the presence, too, almost continuously, of a number of the other supremely good things of life, song and laughter, simplicity and love; while to guard against surfeit and keep romance within bounds, there is a seasoning of caustic and even cynical wit, plenty of foolishness as a foil for the wisdom, and, for variety, an intermingling of social worlds from courtiers and courtly exiles to shepherds and country bumpkins. In this last respect *As You Like It* repeats the miracle of *A Midsummer-Night's Dream*.

As might be expected of a work that is a dramatized version of a pastoral romance (Lodge's *Rosalynde*), the play is the most "natural" and at the same time one of the most artificial of the author's. Yet we so surrender ourselves after a little to its special tone and atmosphere that there is no other work of Shakespeare's in which coincidences, gods from the machine, and what we can only call operatic duets, trios, and quartettes trouble us less or seem less out of place. The snake and lioness that figure in Oliver's sudden conversion might be thought to be enough for one play, but when on top of that in the twinkling of an eye an old religious man turns the cruel usurping Duke, who is on the march with an army against his enemies, into a humble and forgiving hermit, instead of questioning the psychology we accept it meekly and merely observe inwardly that the magic of the Forest of Arden is evidently even more potent than we had supposed.

It is customary to find the main theme of *As You Like It* in the contrast between court and country. "If we present a pastoral," said Thomas Heywood, "we show the harmless love of shepherds, diversely moralized, distinguishing between the craft of the city and the innocency of the sheepcote." The play does indeed involve the question of the relative merits of these types of life, and the conclusion implied seems on the surface to be similar to George Meredith's in "Earth's Secret," namely, that wisdom is to be found in residents neither of the country nor of the city but in those rather who "hither thither fare" between the two,

> Close interthreading nature with our kind.

But whoever goes no deeper than this does not get very near the heart of *As You Like It*. Shakespeare was the last person to believe that geography makes the man.

There is generally an Emersonian sentence that comes as close to summing up a Shakespearean play as anything so brief as a sentence can. "A mind might ponder its thought for ages and not gain so much self-knowledge as the passion of love shall teach it in a day." There, compressed, is the essence of *As You Like It,* and, positively or negatively, almost every scene in it is contrived to emphasize that truth. As *Love's Labour's Lost*, to which Emerson's sentence is almost equally pertinent, has to do with the relation of love and learning, *As You Like It* has to do with the relation of love and wisdom. Rosalind is the author's instrument for making clear what that relation is.

## II

In no other comedy of Shakespeare's is the heroine so all-important as Rosalind is in this one; she makes the play almost as completely as Hamlet does *Hamlet*. She seems ready to transcend the rather light piece in which she finds herself and, if only the plot would let her, to step straight into tragedy. When Celia, in the second scene of the play, begs her cousin to be more merry, Rosalind, in the first words she utters, replies:

> Dear Celia, I show more mirth than I am mistress of; and would you yet I were merrier?

> I am not merry; but I do beguile
> The thing I am by seeming otherwise,

says Desdemona on the quay at Cyprus and on the edge of her tragedy. The similarity is startling. It clinches, as it were, the impression Rosalind makes on those who admire her most: that she had it in her, in Cordelia's words, to outfrown a falser fortune's frown than any she is called on to face in this comedy. In so far as she has, she is a transitional figure.

*As You Like It* has no lack of interesting characters, but most of them grow pretty thin in Rosalind's presence, like match flames in the sun. However less brilliant, Celia suffers less than she otherwise would because of her loyalty and devotion to her cousin and freedom from jealousy of her. Adam, Corin, and Rosalind's father are characters in their own right, but minor ones. Orlando at his best is thoroughly worthy of the woman he loves, but by and large she sets him in the shade. For the rest, Rosalind exposes, without trying to, their one-sidedness or inferiority, whether by actual contact or in the mind of the reader.

> Heaven Nature charg'd
> That one body should be fill'd
> With all graces. . . .

It is this wholeness of hers by which the others are tried, and in the comparison Touchstone himself (so named possibly for that very reason) fades into a mere manipulator of words, while that other favorite of the commentators, Jaques, is totally eclipsed.

## III

One way of taking Jaques is to think of him as a picture, duly attenuated, of what Shakespeare himself might have become if he had let experience sour or embitter him, let his critical powers get the better of his imagination, "philosophy" of poetry. As traveler-libertine Jaques has had his day. Now he would turn spectator-cynic and revenge himself on a world that can no longer afford him pleasure, by proving it foul and infected. The more his vision is darkened the blacker, naturally, what he sees becomes in his eyes. He would withdraw from society entirely if he were not so dependent on it for audience. That is his dilemma. So he alternately retreats and darts forth from his retreat to buttonhole anyone who will listen to his railing. But when he tries to rationalize his misanthropy and pass it off as medicine for a sick world, the Duke Senior administers a deserved rebuke. Your very chiding of sin, he tells him, is "mischievous foul sin" itself.

Jaques prides himself on his wit and wisdom. But he succeeds only in proving how little wit and even "wisdom" amount to when indulged in for their own sakes and at the expense of life. His jests and "philosophy" give the effect of having been long pondered in solitude. But the moment he crosses swords with Orlando and Rosalind, the professional is hopelessly outclassed by the amateurs. Extemporaneously they beat him at his own carefully rehearsed game. Being out of love with life, Jaques thinks of nothing but himself. Being in love with Rosalind, Orlando thinks of himself last and has both the humility and the insight that love bequeaths. When the two men encounter, Jaques' questions and answers sound studied and affected, Orlando's spontaneous and sincere.

> JAQ.: Rosalind is your love's name?
> ORL.: Yes, just.
> JAQ.: I do not like her name.
> ORL.: There was no thought of pleasing you when she was christened.
> JAQ.: What stature is she of?
> ORL.: Just as high as my heart.
> JAQ.: You are full of pretty answers. Have you not been acquainted with goldsmiths' wives, and conn'd them out of rings?
> ORL.: Not so; but I answer you right painted cloth, from whence you have studied your questions.
> JAQ.: You have a nimble wit: I think 'twas made of Atalanta's heels. Will you sit down with me? and we two will rail against our mistress the world, and all our misery.
> ORL.: I will chide no breather in the world but myself, against whom I know most faults.

There is not a trace of any false note in that answer. It has the ring of the true modesty and true wisdom that only true love imparts. Jaques, of course, misses the point diametrically:

> JAQ.: The worst fault you have is to be in love.
> ORL.: 'Tis a fault I will not change for your best virtue. I am weary of you.

(To tell the truth we are a bit weary of him too.)

And Rosalind outphilosophizes Jaques as utterly as Orlando has outjested him.

> JAQ.: I prithee, pretty youth, let me be better acquainted with thee.
> ROS.: They say you are a melancholy fellow.
> JAQ.: I am so; I do love it better than laughing.
> ROS.: Those that are in extremity of either are abominable fellows, and betray themselves to every modern censure worse than drunkards.
> JAQ.: Why, 'tis good to be sad and say nothing.
> ROS.: Why, then, 'tis good to be a post.
> JAQ.: I have neither the scholar's melancholy, which is emulation; nor the musician's . . .

and after enumerating seven different types of melancholy, he concludes,

... but it is a melancholy of mine own, compounded of many simples, extracted from many objects; and indeed the sundry contemplation of my travels, in which my often rumination wraps me in a most humorous sadness—

Ros.: A traveller! By my faith, you have great reason to be sad. I fear you have sold your own lands to see other men's; then, to have seen much, and to have nothing, is to have rich eyes and poor hands.

Jaq.: Yes, I have gained my experience.

Ros.: And your experience makes you sad. I had rather have a fool to make me merry than experience to make me sad; and to travel for it too!

Love bestows on those who embrace it the experience and wisdom of the race, compared with which the knowledge schools and foreign lands can offer is at the worst a mere counterfeit and at the best a mere beginning. What wonder that Jaques, after being so thoroughly trounced by the pretty youth whose acquaintance he was seeking a moment before, is glad to sneak away as Orlando enters (what would they have done to him together?), or that Rosalind, after a "Farewell, Monsieur Traveller," turns with relief to her lover.

Even Jaques' most famous speech, his "Seven Ages of Man" as it has come to be called, which he must have rehearsed more times than the modern schoolboy who declaims it, does not deserve its reputation for wisdom. It sometimes seems as if Shakespeare had invented Adam (that grand reconciliation of servant and man) as Jaques' perfect opposite and let him enter this scene, pat, at the exact moment when Jaques is done describing the "last scene of all," as a living refutation of his picture of old age. How Shakespeare loved to let life obliterate language in this way! And he does it here prospectively as well as retrospectively, for the Senior Duke a second later, by his hospitable welcome of Adam and Orlando, obliterates or at least mitigates Amiens' song of man's ingratitude ("Blow, blow, thou winter wind") that immediately follows.

## IV

When I read the commentators on Touchstone, I rub my eyes. You would think to hear most of them that he is a genuinely wise and witty man and that Shakespeare so considered him. That Shakespeare knew he could pass him off for that in a theater may be agreed. What he is is another matter. A "dull fool" Rosalind calls him on one occasion. "O noble fool! a worthy fool!" says Jaques on another. It is easy to guess with which of the two Shakespeare came nearer to agreeing. The Elizabethan groundlings had to have their clown. At his best, Touchstone is merely one more and one of the most inveterate of the author's word-jugglers, and at his worst (as a wit) precisely what Rosalind called him. What he is at his worst as a man justifies still harsher characterization.

In her first speech after he enters the play in the first act, Rosalind describes him as "the cutter-off of Nature's wit," and his role abundantly justifies her judgment. "Thou speakest wiser than thou art ware of," she says to him on another occasion, and as if expressly to prove the truth of what she says, Touchstone obligingly replies, "Nay, I shall ne'er be ware of mine own wit till I break my shins against it." Which is plainly Shakespeare's conscious and Touchstone's unconscious way of stating that his wit is low. And his manners are even lower, as he shows when he first accosts Corin and Rosalind rebukes him for his rude tone:

| | |
|---|---|
| Touch.: | Holla, you clown! |
| Ros.: | Peace, fool; he's not thy kinsman. |
| Cor.: | Who calls? |
| Touch.: | Your betters, sir. |
| Cor.: | Else are they very wretched. |
| Ros.: | Peace, I say. Good even to you, friend. |

Nothing could show more succinctly Rosalind's "democracy" in contrast to Touchstone's snobbery. (No wonder the people thought highly of her, as they did of Hamlet.) The superiority in wisdom of this "clown" to the man who condescends to him comes out, as we might predict it would, a little later.

| | |
|---|---|
| Touch.: | Wast ever in court, shepherd? |
| Cor.: | No, truly. |
| Touch.: | Then thou art damned. |
| Cor.: | Nay, I hope. |
| Touch.: | Truly, thou art damned, like an ill-roasted egg all on one side. |

It is an almost invariable rule in Shakespeare, as it is in life, that when one man damns another, even in jest, he unconsciously utters judgment on himself, and the rest of the scene, like Touchstone's whole role, is dedicated to showing that he himself is his own ill-roasted egg, all "wit" and word-play and nothing else.

| | |
|---|---|
| Cor.: | For not being at court? Your reason. |
| Touch.: | Why, if thou never wast at court, thou never sawest good manners [*We have just had, and are now having, a sample of the manners of this "courtier" who greeted Corin as a "clown."*]; if thou never sawest good manners, then thy manners must be wicked; and wickedness is sin, and sin is damnation. Thou art in a parlous state, shepherd. |

Corin may be a "silly" shepherd but he is not taken in by this silly verbal legerdemain. He stands up to his "better" stoutly:

COR.: Not a whit, Touchstone: those that are good manners at the court, are as ridiculous in the country as the behaviour of the country is most mockable at the court,

and he illustrates by pointing out that the habit of kissing hands at court would be uncleanly among shepherds. Whereupon, as we might expect, Touchstone, forgetting his own rule that he who calls himself wise is a fool, cries "Learn of the wise," and descends to an even lower level of sophistry than before. Corin, sensing that it is futile to argue with such a man, refuses to continue, but refuses with a courtesy at the opposite pole from Touchstone's rudeness, and we suddenly realize that Shakespeare has contrived the whole episode as a refutation on the plane of life of the conclusion for which Touchstone is contending: that good manners are impossible for a countryman.

COR.: You have too courtly a wit for me; I'll rest.

In reply to which we have an example of courtly wit and manners:

TOUCH.: Wilt thou rest damned? God help thee, shallow man!

Shallow man! the best possible characterization of Touchstone himself at the moment. And as if to show by way of contrast what a deep man is, Shakespeare lets Corin condense his life into a sentence which, if a sentence ever was, is a perfect blend of modesty and pride:

COR.: Sir, I am a true labourer: I earn that I eat, get that I wear, owe no man hate, envy no man's happiness, glad of other men's good, content with my harm; and the greatest of my pride is to see my ewes graze and my lambs suck.

It is one of the tersest and one of the finest "creeds" to be found anywhere in Shakespeare, at the farthest possible remove from Touchstone's own which Jaques overheard and quoted. And with all his "wit" the only thing Touchstone can think up by way of retort is the taunt that Corin by his own confession is a "bawd" because, forsooth, he makes his living by the multiplication of his stock. A Hottentot would be ashamed of such reasoning, and as for the jocosity of it, it is close to Touchstone's "low," which is saying a good deal. To the crass animality and ribaldry of this courtier Shakespeare, with another of his sudden switches, instantly opposes the "sanctity" of the man whose very kisses are like "the touch of holy bread": Rosalind, as Ganymede, enters reading snatches of the verses her lover has been hanging or carving on the trees.

> Her worth, being mounted on the wind,
> Through all the world bears Rosalind,

verses which Touchstone, as we would expect, proceeds to parody in such choice lines as:

> If the cat will after kind,
> So be sure will Rosalind.

What wonder that Rosalind rebukes the man as a "dull fool" and tells him that, like a medlar, he will be rotten ere he is ripe. The simile is a manifest double allusion on Shakespeare's part, first, to Touchstone's own "ill-roasted egg" (the same idea under another image), and, second, to Touchstone's summary of human life:

> And so, from hour to hour we ripe and ripe,
> And then from hour to hour we rot and rot.

If we know anything about the man who through the mouth of Edgar in *King Lear* declared that "Ripeness is all," we know what he must have thought of this philosophy of Touchstone's. He must have thought it rotten—rotten not in any modern colloquial sense of the term but rotten in the full implication of the horticultural metaphor.

But even with all this mauling, Shakespeare is not done with Touchstone. Having demonstrated to the hilt that his wit instead of sharpening has dulled his wits, he proceeds to show that his wit has also withered his heart. It is in his interlude with Audrey that we see Touchstone at his moral nadir. It will be said, of course, that this episode is pure farce and that to take it seriously is to show lack of humor. The objection need disturb nobody but the man who makes it. For of all the strange things about this man William Shakespeare one of the most remarkable is the fact that he could contrive no scene so theatrical, no stage effect so comic or dialogue so nonsensical, as to protect himself from the insertion right in the midst of it of touches of nature scientific in their veracity. Such was the grip that truth seems to have had on him.

Audrey is generally dismissed as a country wench expressly set up as a butt for Touchstone. And a theater audience can be duly counted on to roar with laughter at her. She is indeed just a goatherd, plain in appearance (though doubtless not as plain as Touchstone would make out) and so unlettered that most words of more than one syllable bewilder her simple wits. Touchstone's literary and mythological puns and allusions are naturally lost on her. But the attentions of this stranger from the court have awakened unwonted emotions and aspirations in her breast, and nothing could be clearer than her desire to be modest and true and pure. Love is the great leveler as well as the great lifter, and Audrey, perhaps for the first time in her life, feels that even she may have a place in God's world. And this is the way Touchstone deals with the emotion he has awakened:

TOUCH.: Truly, I would the gods had made thee poetical.

AUD.: I do not know what "poetical" is. Is it honest in deed and word? Is it a true thing?

TOUCH.: No, truly, for the truest poetry is the most feigning; and lovers are given to poetry, and what they swear in poetry may be said as lovers they do feign.

AUD.: Do you wish then that the gods had made me poetical?

TOUCH.: I do, truly; for thou swearest to me thou art honest; now, if thou wert a poet, I might have some hope thou didst feign.

AUD.: Would you not have me honest?

TOUCH.: No, truly, unless thou wert hard-favour'd; for honesty coupled to beauty is to have honey a sauce to sugar.

JAQ.: (*Aside*): A material fool.

AUD.: Well, I am not fair, and therefore I pray the gods make me honest.

TOUCH.: Truly, and to cast away honesty upon a foul slut were to put good meat into an unclean dish.

AUD.: I am not a slut, though I thank the gods I am foul.

TOUCH.: Well, praised be the gods for thy foulness! sluttishness may come hereafter.

As "theater" this is doubtless what a modern director might call "sure-fire stuff." As life it comes close to being the sin against the Holy Ghost. Touchstone of course is planning to marry Audrey ("to take that that no man else will") and abandon her as soon as he is sick of his bargain, and when Sir Oliver Martext, a marrying parson, enters, he is ready to go ahead with the ceremony then and there. Jaques, who has been eavesdropping, coming forward offers at first to "give the woman." But on second thought the scandalous procedure is too much for even him to stomach and he rebukes Touchstone roundly for his conduct, about the best thing Jaques does in the play:

> And will you, being a man of your breeding, be married under a bush like a beggar? Get you to church, and have a good priest that can tell you what marriage is.

But a good priest and a binding marriage are precisely what Touchstone does not want.

Later, Shakespeare treats us to a little encounter between Touchstone and William, the forest youth who "lays claim" to Audrey. Setting out to make a fool of him, Touchstone asks him if he is wise.

Will.: Ay, sir, I have a pretty wit.

Touch.: Why, thou sayest well. I do now remember a saying, "The fool doth think he is wise, but the wise man knows himself to be a fool."

But in that case Touchstone stands condemned as a fool by his own rule, for about twenty lines back in this same scene he had said, "By my troth, we that have good wits have much to answer for." And about ten lines farther on he again convicts himself by his own rule even more convincingly:

Touch.: You do love this maid?

Will.: I do, sir.

Touch.: Give me your hand. Art thou learned?

Will.: No, sir.

Touch.: Then learn this of me....

Whereupon, addressing William as "you clown," he announces that he, Touchstone, is the man who is to marry Audrey, and orders his rival on pain of death to abandon her company, meanwhile drowning him under such a flood of unfamiliar words that the bewildered youth is only too glad to decamp. "Oh, but Touchstone's threats to kill are just jest," it will be said, "and his superiority and condescension just mock-heroics and mock-pedantics. Again you are guilty of taking seriously what is mere fooling, making a mountain out of a molehill of the text, and treating William as if he were a real human being instead of the theatrical puppet that he is." (As if Shakespeare did not make even his most minor characters human beings!) Granted that to Touchstone the whole thing is a huge joke; that does not make his torrent of talk any less perplexing or menacing to William, nor the theft of Audrey any less mean or immoral. It is merely a consummation of what this man in motley has revealed throughout: his snobbery and bad manners, and ultimately his hard heart. Touchstone, if you insist, is making a fool of this rustic simpleton, William. It is another William who is making a fool of Touchstone.

So even the tormented comes off better than the tormentor. Indeed nearly everybody in the play does who comes in contact with Touchstone. "A touchstone," says the dictionary, is "a black siliceous stone used to test the purity of gold and silver by the streak left on the stone when rubbed by the metal." Not precious itself, it reveals preciousness in what touches it. That seems to be precisely the function assigned to Touchstone in this play, so perhaps its author knew what he was doing when he named him. Near the end two of the banished Duke's pages enter and Touchstone asks them for a song. They comply with his request by singing

It was a lover and his lass,

and when they are done Touchstone rewards them by remarking, "Truly, young gentlemen, though there was no great matter in the ditty, yet the note was very untuneable." "You are deceived, sir," the First Page protests, "we kept time; we lost not our time." "By my troth, yes," Touchstone persists, "I count it but time lost to hear such a foolish song." Here again Shakespeare lets Touchstone judge himself in judging others, for though as manikin he will doubtless long continue to entertain the crowd in the theater, as man he is even more empty of both matter and music than the foolish song he counts it time lost to listen to. Touchstone is "wit" without love.

## V

And Rosalind is wit with love, which is humor, humor being what wit turns into when it falls in love. But humor is almost a synonym for many-sidedness and reconciliation of opposites, and in her versatility, her balance of body, mind, and spirit, Rosalind reminds us of no less a figure than Hamlet himself, the uncontaminated Hamlet. As there is a woman within the Prince of Denmark, so there is a man within this Duke's daughter, but never at the sacrifice of her dominant feminine nature. "Do you not know I am a woman? when I think, I must speak," she says to Celia. She changes color when she first suspects that the verses on the trees are Orlando's, and cries "Alas the day! what shall I do with my doublet and hose?" when the fact that he is in the Forest is confirmed. And she swoons when she hears he is wounded. Yes, Rosalind is a woman in spite of the strength and courage of the man within her. All of which makes her disguise as a boy immeasurably more than a merely theatrical matter.

> That you are fair or wise is vain,
> Or strong, or rich, or generous;
> You must add the untaught strain
> That sheds beauty on the rose.

So says Emerson (in lines enough in themselves to acquit him of being what he is so often called, a "puritan"). Rosalind is all of these things: fair and wise and strong and rich (except in a worldly sense) and generous. But not in vain. For she has also, as her name betokens, the untaught strain that sheds beauty on a rose. The Forest of Arden, for all its trees, is, as we remarked, forever flooded with sunshine. There is no mystery about it. Rosalind is in the Forest and she supplies it with an internal light. "Be like the sun," says Dostoevsky. Rosalind is. She attracts everything that comes within her sphere and sheds a radiance over it. She is the pure gold that needs no touchstone.

Rosalind has the world at her feet not just for what she is but because, being what she is, she so conducts her love with Orlando as to make it a pattern for all true love-making. Unimaginative love, whether sentimental or overpassionate, overreaches and defeats itself because it cannot keep its secret. Intentionally or otherwise, it spills over—confesses or gives itself away. (Juliet is no exception: she admitted her love so soon only because Romeo had overheard her in soliloquy by accident.) The love of Silvius for Phebe and of Phebe for Ganymede in this play are examples. Imaginative love is wiser. Taking its cue from the arts, of which it is one and perhaps the highest, it creates a hypothetical case in its own image, a kind of celestial trap under cover of which (only the maddest mixture of metaphors can do it justice) it extorts an unconscious confession from the loved one, all the while keeping a line of retreat fully open in case the confession should be unfavorable, in order that no humiliation may ensue.

In this play Rosalind undertakes to cure Orlando of his love by having him come every day to woo her under the illusion that she is just the boy Ganymede impersonating Rosalind. Thus the love between the two is rehearsed in the kingdom of the imagination, where all true love begins, before any attempt is made to bring it down to the level of everyday life, a situation that permits both lovers to speak now as boldly, now as innocently, as though they were angels or children. (The only conceivable situation that could surpass it as a model of right love-making would be one where each of the lovers was simultaneously luring the other into a confession without that other being aware of what was happening.)

Again we are reminded of the Prince of Denmark. In *Hamlet* a literal play within the play becomes a device (inspired or infernal according to your interpretation of the play) whereby to catch the guilty conscience of a murderer. Here a metaphorical "play" within the play becomes a celestial trap in which to expose the tender heart of a lover. Heaven and hell are at opposite poles, but the one is a model of the other. "Upward, downward," says Heraclitus, "the way is the same." It is not chance that *As You Like It* and *Hamlet* were written not far apart in time.

Love between man and woman having the importance that it does in life, what wonder that a drama that depicts it in perfect action under its happiest aspect should be popular, even though not one in a hundred understands the ground of its fascination. How many a woman who sees or reads *As You Like It* either believes in secret that she does resemble Rosalind or wishes that she did! And how many a man projects on its heroine the image of the woman he loves best, or, if not, the memory of some lost first love who still embodies the purest instincts of his youth, and hears her voice instead of the words printed on the page! Which is why the imaginative man will always prefer to read the play rather than to have some obliterating actress come between the text and his heart. And so Rosalind is a sort of universal image of Woman as Sweetheart, just as Cressida is an image of Woman as Seductress, and Cleopatra of Woman, both good and evil, in a still more universal sense.

In her own way, and on a lower level, Rosalind contributes her mite to our understanding of why Dante chose the Rose as a symbol of the ultimate paradise.

*Chapter XXI*

# Twelfth Night

## I

*Twelfth Night,* as its stage history proves, is one of the most effective theater pieces Shakespeare ever wrote. It is an almost unbroken succession of telling scenes. As has often been pointed out, the play is a sort of recapitulation. It is as if Shakespeare, for his last unadulterated comedy, summoned the ghosts of a dozen characters and situations with which he had triumphed in the past and bade them weave themselves into a fresh pattern. *The Comedy of Errors, The Two Gentlemen of Verona, The Merchant of Venice, Henry IV,* and even such recent successes as *Much Ado about Nothing* and *As You Like It* were laid under contribution. He pilfered from himself in this play as shamelessly as he ever had from others but, as usual, turned all his thefts to original account. And he named what came out of it all *Twelfth Night; or, What You Will*—as if he had selected the first title that came into his head and were quite willing that any auditor should rechristen the play to his own liking. All this seems to stamp *Twelfth Night* as a potboiler. But we had better beware, for whenever Shakespeare tried a potboiler some of his genius had a habit of boiling over into the pot.

In general, we go to the theater to be entertained. As we enter we are either in a gay mood already or in search of gaiety—of something at any rate that will carry us out of ourselves. And everything before the play begins collaborates. The bright costumes, the chatter, the laughter—in the modern theater the lights and the music—to say nothing of the mere fact of becoming part of a crowd, all tend to one end. They prepare us for emotion, make us ready to laugh and weep, to be amused or absorbed. Of anything that will achieve these results we are not too critical. So with *Twelfth Night*. In spite of Fabian's remark at one point, "If this were played upon a stage now, I could condemn it as an improbable fiction," we do not submit it in the theater to the tests or judge it by the standards we would use in real life, nor even to those we may apply to it afterward when we recollect it in solitude and tranquility. With the crowd around us to suggest what our own reaction should be, Sir Toby's drunkenness, even to his belchings, is without reservation funny; Maria's practical joking, even to Malvolio's confinement as a madman, without qualification clever and side-splitting; the steward's combined vanity and virtue fair game to any limit, and his discomfiture, even in the dark house, nothing but deserved. And when at the end we reach for coat and hat we are too theatrically intoxicated to pay much attention to the Clown's closing song, which, if we listened to it, might have a sobering effect.

It is only afterward, if at all, that we realize we might have probed a little deeper, might even have seen a little deeper in the theater with the aid of actors of genius, especially such a one in the part of Malvolio, as Charles Lamb's superlative criticism of this play in "On Some of the Old Actors" makes clear. *Twelfth Night!* So far from being a casual title, it is one of the most revealing ones Shakespeare ever used, however aware or unaware he may have been of all it implied. For Twelfth Night, January 6—though it is something else too—marks the end of the Christmas festivities. In half-a-dozen senses Shakespeare's *Twelfth Night* brings festivity to an end. To begin with, it is the third and last of the poet's own farewells to "wit" (*Much Ado* and *As You Like It* of course being the other two). In a wider sense it is his farewell to comedy. It is his transition from prince to king, his rejection of "Falstaff," not for the purpose of ascending the throne and conquering France, but of becoming "king" in the sense of mastering the domain of tragedy and tragicomedy. It marks an end too in more than a personal and professional way. It marks the end of Merry England, of the great day of the great Tudor houses where hospitality and entertainment were so long dispensed, one of the ends even (if I may use that expression) of feudalism itself whose long-drawn-out death never permits the historian to put a finger on any particular hour or event and say, Here it finally died. With its own reference to the pendulum swing of things, the whirligig of time that brings in his revenges, it seems like an intimation of the Puritan revolution with its rebuke to revelry—down even to the closing of the theaters. Merry England after the Armada certainly has its points of difference from the America of the twenties after World War I. (In the amount of genius produced that difference is abysmal.) But it has its points of likeness too. There was a descent and, if in a different sense, a Great Depression in store in both cases.

Did Shakespeare know what he was doing when he wrote and named this play? Did he appreciate its irony? Not entirely, of course. We have to wait for history to read its ironies into literature as it does into its own facts. But if Shakespeare's own development means anything, *Twelfth Night* is merely the culmination and consummation of something he had been saying almost from the beginning. If in *The Two Gentlemen of Verona* he gives us two revealing specimens of the species gentleman; if in *Romeo and Juliet* he shows us to what tragedy the code of the gentleman may lead; if in *The Merchant of Venice* he exposes the hollowness, and even cruelty, lurking under the silken surface of a leisured society; if in all these plays and in *Much Ado about Nothing* and *As You Like It* he tears the mask off wit and word-play, he does all these things at once in *Twelfth Night* (except that the tragedy that emerges fully in *Romeo and Juliet* is here only hinted at), but does them so genially that his very victims were probably loudest in their applause. We can imagine the Elizabethan gentlemen swarming to see *Twelfth Night* and paying for the privilege! It is almost as if the dead man were expected to pay an entrance fee to his own funeral and enjoy the proceedings. The poet just holds the mirror up to nature and gets a more devastating effect than the fiercest satire could achieve. It is the Chaucerian method. Indeed *Twelfth Night* makes one wonder whether justice has been done to the indebtedness of Shakespeare to the spirit of his great predecessor as distinguished from his indebtedness to him as source in the narrower sense (as in *Troilus and Cressida*). In *Twelfth Night* at any rate Shakespeare does something similar to what Chaucer does in *The Legend of Good Women*: so sweetens the medicine he is administering to his victims (in Chaucer's case the women) that they swallow it as if it were the most refreshing draught.

And yet there have been critics so incapable of shaking off their theater mood as to suggest that in this play Shakespeare is unreservedly on the side of revelry, of cakes and ale as against "virtue," of drunkenness and riot and quarreling as against sobriety and decency and some semblance of order. (Not that he is on the side of those things either!) In their dislike of Malvolio they forget that he is merely carrying out Olivia's orders, in however annoying a manner. She objects quite as much as he to having her house turned into a bedlam at any and all hours; she calls her drunken parasite of an uncle a wretch and a ruffian and declares that he is

> Fit for the mountains and the barbarous caves,
> Where manners ne'er were preach'd,

which, according to any considered judgment, he is. The unconscious logic of these critics seems to run something like this: (1) Shakespeare believed in laughter; (2) Sir Toby and his cronies make us laugh; therefore (3) Shakespeare approved of Sir Toby and his cronies. Imagine thinking that of the man who at this very time may have been creating the drunken court at Elsinore and its princely critic! Imagine thinking it of the author of the 146th sonnet:

> Why so large cost, having so short a lease,
> Dost thou upon thy fading mansion spend?
> Shall worms, inheritors of this excess,
> Eat up thy charge? Is this thy body's end?
> Then, soul, live thou. . . .

## II

If ever there were mansions fading from excess, they were those of Olivia and the Duke in this play, and that that is what Shakespeare set out to show is strongly indicated by the opening and the close of the piece (of its end we will speak at the end). Taken together they practically prove as much. The familiar speech of the Duke with which *Twelfth Night* opens is like a musical overture in which Shakespeare, as so often, announces his main theme:

> If music be the food of love, play on;
> Give me excess of it, that, surfeiting,
> The appetite may sicken, and so die.
> That strain again! It had a dying fall.
> . . . Enough, no more!
> 'Tis not so sweet now as it was before.

Excess! Surfeit! Sicken! Dying fall! Enough, no more! 'Tis not so sweet now as it was before! Even at a second reading this play is not so sweet as it was before—but it is more tartly significant. Pretty nearly everybody in it but Viola and Sebastian—and those two outskirt characters the sea captains—is at the extreme point where from excess of something or other he is about to be converted into something else. Sir Toby, who is the feudal retainer at his vanishing point, is in the "third degree of drink," drowned in it, namely. (Those who liken him to Falstaff are in some still higher degree of obfuscation.) Feste the jester is in the third degree of "wit." (There is another wiser Feste, emerging from the "dry" one like a butterfly from a chrysalis, of whom we will speak later.) Sir Andrew is in the third, nay, the $n$th, degree of fatuity—the complete gentleman so attenuated that he is indistinguishable from the complete fool. He is class transmigrated into ass, with not "so much blood in his liver as will clog the foot of a flea." He is a great consumer of beef and thinks that life consists of eating and drinking—and pretending to fight. He is Sir Toby's gull, as Roderigo is Iago's.

Maria's third degree is of another sort. She is a lively, alert, resourceful, mocking person. Her vitality and intelligence (to call it that) have, in her servile position, made her ambitious and envious, especially so of the steward whose merits her mistress prizes so highly. It is important to realize that it is not just because he is Malvolio that she hates him. She would have resented anyone in his place. "I can hardly forbear hurling things at him." The remark is a giveaway. There is a vague premonition of the Iago-Cassio theme here on the comic level as her simile, "I have dogged him like his murderer," is enough to show. Her "humor" is of that low order that must always have a physical outlet. She has her jests, she says, at her fingers' ends (not at her tongue's). She will make her fellow-conspirators laugh themselves into stitches. Her sport must always bear immediate fruit that others can see and feel. In this case to show off her talents before Sir Toby is as strong a motive as to humiliate Malvolio. She tickles and catches her trout. And Toby rewards her by asking, "Wilt thou set thy foot o' my neck?" (which she doubtless did with a vengeance after they were married) and calling her "thou most excellent devil of wit!" What wonder that in her the spirit of fun passes from the cathartic prank of the cross garters and yellow stockings to the cruel and perilous practical joke of the dark room. Fabian and finally Sir Toby himself see that they have gone too far. But Maria plainly means it when she says that if Malvolio really does go mad, it will be well worth it: the house will be the quieter! There is a cruel streak in her as there generally is in practical jokers. She is in that third degree of fun where what might originally have been a sense of humor becomes perverted and commits suicide. But her excesses will trouble few people in the theater. They have made them laugh too heartily.

Malvolio and his function in the play seem plain enough during its performance or at a first reading. He is simply the antitype of the revelers, their excess drawn out equally in the opposite direction. If they are levity, he is gravity—dignity, decency, decorum, servility and severity in the cause of "good order," carried to the third degree and beyond—and as such fair game for his tormentors. No more than this is necessary to make Malvolio a success on the stage. But that more is possible even there, and much more in the imagination of a reader who reads deeper, is shown in Charles Lamb's famous reminiscences of Bensley and his own comments on the part. Lamb's main point, it will be remembered, is that Malvolio is not essentially ludicrous, that his pride is neither mock nor affected—and

TWELFTH NIGHT

so not a fit object, as such, to excite laughter. He thinks the man had it in him to be brave, honorable, accomplished. Maria calls him a kind of puritan, but quickly takes it back and calls him a time-pleaser instead. She could not have been more mistaken. Malvolio is a man of principle rather, and being, like all "men of principle," lacking in imagination in its creative sense, is all the more prone to become a victim of it in its primitive form. In Malvolio's love of Olivia, Shakespeare has stolen from his own account of Bottom's love of Titania. Like that, this love is calculated in the theater to excite nothing but laughter. Bottom's love, however, eventuating as it did in Bottom's dream, was, we saw, "at bottom" beautiful, a sort of allegory of the birth of imagination in matter. But if inexpressible things can be born in the head of a weaver, why not in the head of a steward? If that seem fanciful, again we have Charles Lamb for authority, Lamb and the man who inspired him here, the actor Bensley, who showed that a different and subtler reading of Malvolio is possible even on the stage: "You would have thought that the hero of La Mancha in person stood before you.... You rather admired than pitied the lunacy while it lasted; you felt that an hour of such mistake was worth an age with the eyes open.... The man seemed to tread upon air, to taste manna, to walk with his head in the clouds, to mate Hyperion." If anything can prove that a part can be one thing to the average man and something quite different to the actor or reader of genius, Lamb's interpretation of Malvolio does. It is an infallible rule after reading a play of Shakespeare's: read it once more and read deeper.

That Malvolio keeps his head during his confinement in darkness and does not lose his dignity when he charges his mistress with having done him notorious wrong is further proof of a kind of moral solidity in the man. "I confess I never saw the catastrophe of this character, while Bensley played it," Lamb concludes, "without a kind of tragic interest." Surely Lamb is right: the shadow of Shakespeare's coming tragic period casts its shadow back over Malvolio as it does over Shylock.

The Dark House in which Malvolio is incarcerated is in some respects the central symbol of the play, for the houses of Olivia and the Duke, for all their apparent brightness, are dark houses in a deeper sense.

I am as mad as he,

says Olivia (meaning as mad as Malvolio),

If sad and merry madness equal be.

It is one of the key lines of the play and opens our eyes to the fact that with an exception or two it is little more than an anthology of madnesses, sad and merry ("Are all the people mad?" asks Sebastian); for what after all is madness but a slightly stronger term for that excess of which we have been speaking?

## III

Orsino and Olivia are both victims of their emotions. The Duke is the *ne plus ultra* of the melancholy characters we have met in Shakespeare. His love is the sentimentalism that idleness is sure to breed in potentially fine natures if it does not turn to something worse. He is in the third degree of "love," as much drowned in it as Toby is in drink, a fact that makes his fondness for the sea as metaphor significant. But he does not keep it consistent. (He keeps nothing consistent; his mind, as the Clown perceives, is "a very opal.") He says in one place that his love is "as hungry as the sea, and can digest as much." But unfortunately he has admitted in his opening speech that whatever enters this sea-like love begins within a minute to lose its value. Olivia, with her inordinate grief for her brother, looks at first like Orsino's twin. But when we get a glimpse behind her veil we see that her emotionalism is of another brand. Her carefully announced, absurdly long period of mourning, with its withdrawal from society, is evidently a pretext, however unconscious, for singling herself out, making herself interesting, as black does its wearer in a crowd of bright costumes. There is much of the grand lady about Olivia. She is the efficient head of a great house, managing its affairs and commanding her followers with smoothness and discretion. But like Portia, whom she resembles at more than one point, she cannot take her own advice: "O, you are sick of self-love, Malvolio, and taste with a distempered appetite. To be generous, guiltless, and of free disposition, is to take those things for birdbolts that you deem cannon bullets." If in proper degree she could have applied this principle to her grief for her brother, she might have assuaged its supposed violence and abbreviated its seven-year term by at least a little. But it is precisely her strict adherence to outer form that accounts for her highly unconventional falling in love with the Duke's "man," Cesario. We like her for that capacity, but we cannot help noticing that she inquires about his parentage and makes certain he is a gentleman before letting her emotions have their way. Also, we wish she had not taken occasion to compliment her own countenance so early in their acquaintance. If she could not hide her feelings from him, she might at least not have blurted them out so precipitately. (And she might have concealed them from her household.) There is a finer Olivia within her that senses all this and rebukes her for her headstrong love-making:

There's something in me that reproves my fault.

But that doesn't prevent her from fairly dragging the supposed Cesario to the altar, when, in the person of the wonder-struck Sebastian, the resistance of the man at whom she has fairly flung herself apparently breaks down. On the whole, criticism has been overkind to Olivia as it has to Portia.

## IV

And so the "upstairs" and the "downstairs" parts of Shakespeare's plot are not so much interwoven as identified. Excessive revelry and excessive sentimental love, the poet seems to be saying, are just opposite forms of the same infection. Barbarism and "civilization" are extremes that meet.

But in the midst of all the madness of these two dark houses two figures, Viola and Feste, stand out for their essential sanity—not Feste the jester but that wiser being into whom we can see him being transformed under our eyes.

In Feste the Shakespearean clown (with intimations of it in Launce) comes, as it were, to self-consciousness. Touchstone seems perpetually delighted with himself and his vocation. But the first thing we hear about Feste is that he has been playing truant. Why he has absented himself from his duties as jester in Olivia's household we are never told. But the rest of the play makes it a fair inference that, whatever the immediate occasion, he was sick of his fool's costume, as his protestation that he does not wear motley in his brain is almost enough in itself to show. (No wonder: Olivia's is the second generation during which he has been jesting!) The main function of a clown is to juggle with words until everything, often including the truth, is upside down and inside out. All Shakespeare's clowns do it, but Feste not only does it but perceives and proclaims that he does it. "A sentence is but a cheveril glove to a good wit. How quickly the wrong side may be turned outward! . . . Words are grown so false I am loath to prove reason with them." He is not Olivia's fool, he says, but her corrupter of words. Even Viola at first mistakes him for the conventional merry fellow who cares for nothing. "I do care for something," Feste protests, and the fact that he is frequently apologetic, even a bit sad, about his joking goes far to prove it. His disillusionment about himself and his profession betokens a sense of humor that is lacking almost by definition in the mere wit. His is a gentle and attractive melancholy that avoids sentimentalism. He loves to sing, and his songs are all plaintive and in a minor key. Wise observations about life spring up like flowers amid the weeds of his professional jesting, as, for instance, his contention that his foes are his best friends because they tell him the truth about himself. They tell him plainly that he is an ass. He seems truly concerned, too, with the moral welfare of those around him. He sees through the artifice of Olivia's grief for her brother and would gladly cure her of it. He tells the Duke to his face what a hopelessly self-contradictory mind he has, and understands the nature of his "passion" for Olivia. He enters with no particular zest into the plot against Malvolio and, when he assumes his disguise as Sir Topas, remarks that "to be said an honest man and a good housekeeper goes as fairly as to say a careful man and a great scholar," an opinion which it is safe to guess his creator shared and which betokens a simplicity of mind at the opposite pole from the snobbery of Touchstone. Rosalind even called the latter a dull fool, while Viola comes to find a philosopher in Feste. And he can be friend as well as philosopher. Near the end he promises to fetch Malvolio not only ink and paper but light also and to transmit his appeal to Olivia. All of which he obviously does. With folly bringing light to darkness and "madness" we can almost feel the fool in *King Lear* being conceived.

But it is Viola far more than Feste who offers the telling contrast with the revelers and sentimentalists. She appears out of her element among them, and Shakespeare seems to be saying as much in the second line she speaks in the play:

> Vio.:  What country, friends, is this?
> Capt.:  This is Illyria, lady.
> Vio.:  And what should I do in Illyria?

And, sure enough, what should she?

> My brother he is in Elysium,

Viola goes on,

> Perchance he is not drown'd.

Illyria—Elysium. What light that echo throws! (Yes, in poetry echoes can throw light.) Having read the play, we are in a position to see, on reading, that Illyria is a counterfeit Elysium, a fool's paradise, where nearly everybody *is* drowned, drowned in pleasure. Illyria is a sort of counter-symbol of the Forest of Arden. There there was freedom and happiness (at least a good bit of it). Here there is pleasure and slavery to self. And this bondage is the more sad and tragic just because the inhabitants are socially and economically free. It is the seventeenth-century version of *Heartbreak House* with the difference that whereas Bernard Shaw depicts his heartbreaking society with blasts of satire and on top of that writes a blistering preface that nobody may miss his point, Shakespeare just holds up what is essentially the same world and allows it to amuse or break our hearts as we choose. *What You Will.*

But that does not mean that Shakespeare does not slip in at odd moments, when we are not looking, perfectly plain statements of his main conception.

> . . . nature with a beauteous wall
> Doth oft close in pollution,

says Viola on the threshold of entering a world of just that character. "Virtue is beauty," says Antonio, as if echoing her (Antonio, that grand old sea captain from whom Shaw might have taken a hint for his Captain Shotover):

> Virtue is beauty; but the beauteous evil
> Are empty trunks, o'erflourish'd by the devil.

Ironically it is Viola herself, mistaken for Sebastian, whom Antonio is charging with ingratitude in the matter of the money he has lent her brother.

> I hate ingratitude more in a man,

she retorts,

> Than lying, vainness, babbling, drunkenness,
> Or any taint of vice whose strong corruption
> Inhabits our frail blood.

Viola is speaking to the particular situation. But when we attend to the list of sins she has picked out, we feel that through her her creator (who agreed with her as to which the worst of them was) was indicting one by one and all together the inhabitants of this parasitical world of which they are typical. Lying, vainness, babbling, drunkenness are pretty sure to be characteristics of any leisured society, as they were of this one. But ingratitude is certain to be, if for no other reason than that such a society rests on the unrecognized labor of others. If anyone thinks such an idea out of Shakespeare's ken, he should remember *King Lear*.

In one sense Viola herself descends to the deceptions of this world when she enters it in disguise.

> Disguise, I see, thou art a wickedness,

she cries later, when she realizes in what entanglements it has involved herself and others. (And for my part, as I have said elsewhere, I hear Shakespeare the playwright, who had condescended to the conventions of Elizabethan comedy, echoing his heroine and resolving perhaps to renounce the cheap and easy ways of holding an audience that the cruder forms of disguise and mistaken identity afford.) Yet, after all, as mythology shows, how can a being of a higher order enter a lower world except in disguise?

And Viola is such a being. She is a Lady from the Sea. Sincere, modest, sweet, gentle, generous, tender, true, she is absolutely loyal and devoted to Orsino. And she is quick-witted, practical, and resourceful as well, utterly free of the sins and sentimentalisms of the world she has been washed up on from shipwreck. What an opportunity she had, if she had been willing to adopt its code, of complicating for emotional purposes the misunderstanding Olivia is under with regard to her sex! She never toys with that possibility for a moment. Though she wears masculine attire, Viola is no boy-girl as Rosalind was. She is purely feminine. Psychically it is as if Viola-Sebastian were Rosalind split in two. It takes two of them to be what she was alone, and the play here becomes one more variation on the theme of hermaphroditic man.

> Prove true, imagination, O, prove true,

Viola cries when she first realizes that she may be about to be reunited with her "drowned" brother. It is one of the supremely integrating lines in all Shakespeare, and it shows in a flash that the play deals not only with madness in its lower sense but with that divine madness of the imagination that comes into being when things long or far separated are united, or when dreams too wonderful to be true nevertheless submit themselves successfully to the tests of sight and touch:

> SEB.: This is the air; that is the glorious sun;
> This pearl she gave me, I do feel't and see't;
> And though 'tis wonder that enwraps me thus,
> Yet 'tis not madness.

Probably the most disappointing thing about *Twelfth Night* to most readers is the fact that such a rare girl as Viola should have fallen in love with such a spineless creature as the Duke. And Sebastian seems too good for Olivia. There is the whole point! The play leaves us with the question whether these two beings from outside Illyria, these two who were thought drowned, this spirit, Sebastian-Viola, from beyond ("A spirit I am indeed," says Sebastian, and we know that Viola is) will be sucked down into the pleasure-seeking parasitical world of Orsino-Olivia or will redeem that world by lifting it at least a little toward a more spiritual level. These marriages are parabolic as well as realistic unions. Are all aristocracies destined by their very nature to decay, life doomed to die off at the top? It is the question of the ages.

## V

The theme of the main plot as well as that of the enveloping action, we suddenly see, is rescue from drowning: drowning in the sea, drowning in the sea of drunkenness and sentimentalism. (There is a reason why with the exception of *The Tempest* the word "drowned" occurs oftener in this play than in any other of Shakespeare's.) Is it possible that Orsino's renunciation, repudiation rather, of the "marble-breasted tyrant" Olivia is not just his opaline fickleness but the indication of a genuine change under Viola's influence? His

> Come, boy, with me. My thoughts are ripe in mischief,

might make us think so. They sound a new note in his role. However that may be, Olivia's ringing rebuke of Cesario when she thinks he is denying their marriage (which was really hers with Sebastian) gives us ground for hope in her case. We never heard anything so fine from her lips before, though she is doubtless unaware at the moment of the universality of the truth she is uttering:

> Alas, it is the baseness of thy fear
> That makes thee strangle thy propriety.
> Fear not, Cesario; take thy fortunes up;
> Be that thou know'st thou art, and then thou art
> As great as that thou fear'st.

All we can say with certainty is that Viola will make a man of Orsino if any woman can and that Sebastian seems fitted to make a woman, as distinct from a lady, of Olivia. Her defense of Malvolio at the end and the Duke's line when the steward goes out swearing revenge,

> Pursue him and entreat him to a peace,

array the two squarely against those whom Charles Lamb calls the "sottish revellers."

Feste's song at the end, as we hinted, puts the keystone in place and sums it all up. The thing that this society of pleasure-seekers has forgotten is the wind and the rain. It's all right to play with toys while we are children, and later we may thrive for a little time by swaggering or crime. But knaves and thieves are soon barred out. There is such a thing as coming to man's estate, such a hard reality, for instance, as marriage, which all the cakes and ale will not turn into what it is not. The world, with its weather, is an ancient fact. There is even a kind of rain that raineth not just occasionally but every day. "Our play is done."

When that I was and a little tiny boy,
    With hey, ho, the wind and the rain,
A foolish thing was but a toy,
    For the rain it raineth every day.

But when I came to man's estate,
    With hey, ho, the wind and the rain,
'Gainst knaves and thieves men shut their gate,
    For the rain it raineth every day.

But when I came, alas! to wive,
    With hey, ho, the wind and the rain,
By swaggering could I never thrive,
    For the rain it raineth every day.

But when I came unto my beds,
    With hey, ho, the wind and the rain,
With toss-pots still had drunken heads,
    For the rain it raineth every day.

A great while ago the world begun,
    With hey, ho, the wind and the rain,
But that's all one, our play is done,
    And we'll strive to please you every day.

Was there ever a song at the end that made plainer the meaning of what has gone before? It seems almost inconceivable that the poet did not expressly intend it as his own comment on the play it brings to an end, a piece that for all its gaiety is somehow touched with an ominous shadow. But even if the author did not mean it so, time did. So it makes little difference.

When Shakespeare wrote *Twelfth Night* he could only surmise what the future had in store for him. But we know. To us this play, with the song that brings it to a conclusion, looks both ways. It is a bridge between the poet's Comedies and his Tragedies as *Julius Caesar* more obviously is between his Histories and his Tragedies. Compared with most other men, Shakespeare was a man from the beginning. Compared with himself, he is now for the first time about to confront the full force of the wind and the rain, to come to man's estate. *King Lear* is not far under the horizon. His "play" is done.

*Twelfth Night.* The work, like the festival, is a recapitulation and looks back over what it brings to an end. But Twelfth Night is also Epiphany, a commemoration of the coming of the Magi to Bethlehem, the first manifestation of Christ to the Gentiles! Did Shakespeare somehow sense that he was on the verge of a visitation of new wisdom from the East? It is not necessary to think so. But he was.

## Chapter XXII

# Julius Caesar

## I

*Julius Caesar* is a bridge. That it is a bridge between Shakespeare's Histories and his Tragedies has often been pointed out. It is neither quite the
one, it is said, nor quite the other. Undoubtedly this is a suggestive way of
taking the play. But held too rigidly, this view of it rests on the assumption that *Hamlet* is Shakespeare's first real tragedy, *Romeo and Juliet*
being ruled out because of the part that accident plays in its plot, and
*Julius Caesar* because its protagonist is not its titular hero. I have given
what I hope are sound reasons for questioning this attitude toward *Romeo
and Juliet*. To exclude *Julius Caesar* on account of its title is quite as unjustifiable. It is to subordinate its spirit and total effect to the demands of
mere classification and definition. If the story of Brutus is not tragedy, it
is hard to know what it is.

Nevertheless, *Julius Caesar* is a bridge—in a far deeper sense. By way of
it Shakespeare finally passes from one world to another. Or, rather, he
shifts the center of his universe. *Julius Caesar* is his Copernican revolution. There are plenty of premonitions in his earlier works of the coming
change: in the last act of *Richard III*, in *A Midsummer-Night's Dream*,
throughout *Romeo and Juliet* especially, and in scattered scenes and passages of other plays. But it is in *Julius Caesar* that the poet finally crosses
the Rubicon.

> For he is superstitious grown of late,

says Cassius of Caesar.

> Caesar, I never stood on ceremonies,
> Yet now they fright me,

says Calphurnia.

> You know that I held Epicurus strong,
> And his opinion; now I change my mind,
> And partly credit things that do presage,

says Cassius near the end. These are not coincidences. It is not that Shakespeare was growing superstitious, or beginning to be frightened by "ceremonies." Nor on the other hand had he ever held Epicurus strong. But he too at this time was tending in a profounder sense than Cassius to give more and more credit to things that do presage.

> He is a dreamer; let us leave him: pass,

says Caesar, dismissing the Soothsayer who called out to him "Beware the ides of March." The event showed that he dismissed him at his peril. Shakespeare was growing more convinced that we neglect dreams and dreamers at our peril. He was a humanist, to be sure, and remained one to the end of his days. But from *Julius Caesar* on, his greater characters and greater plays are touched with the dream-light and dream-darkness of something that as certainly transcends the merely human as do the prophets and sibyls of Michelangelo. There were presentiments and visions in *Romeo and Juliet*. But this play is fairly saturated with omens and ironies, portents and wonders. There were fairies in *A Midsummer-Night's Dream*, and ghosts in *Richard III*. But the ghost of Julius Caesar is a being of another order. Brief as are his three utterances, just sixteen words in all, he speaks with a new accent. And it is not the accent of tradition, nor of folklore however well assimilated. Nor of the theater. It is the accent, we instantly know, of something that has happened in Shakespeare's own soul. The secret of human life, it seems to say, lies beyond that life as well as within it. The ghost of Julius Caesar was as truly a part of Brutus as it was of Caesar. "The soul knows no persons." That is why a play whose protagonist is one of the two is appropriately named for the other.

In spite of this new note, *Julius Caesar* is tied to the plays that precede it—and to those that follow—as intimately as anything Shakespeare ever wrote. Which makes it a bridge in a still further sense.

Brutus is one more study of a man who undertakes a role for which nature never intended him. In this respect he is a direct descendant of Richard II, Antonio, Romeo, and, in a somewhat different sense, of Hal. Often the best summary of a play of Shakespeare's is some line or couplet in the next or a closely succeeding play that seems hidden there by the poet as if on purpose.

> He would be crown'd,

says Brutus in soliloquy, of Caesar;

> How that might change his nature, there's the question.

That was the crucial question about Prince Henry, which *Henry IV* was written to ask and *Henry V* to answer—the question Falstaff failed to ask himself in time. The young Henry V "killed" his old friend when he rejected him, putting what he held to be the public good above personal feeling. Brutus did precisely the same thing when he assassinated Caesar. The analogy is startling. Sir John and the mighty Julius make strange bedfellows, but their situations are so similar that it is easy to imagine Falstaff saying to himself at the moment he was rejected, in whatever would have been its Falstaffian equivalent: "*Et tu*, Henry!" Indeed, that is just what his silence does say.

But if Henry V at the end of *Henry IV* has an affinity with Brutus, he has a deeper one with Caesar himself in *Henry V*. (His affinity with Alexander the Great, Shakespeare himself more than hints at, as we have seen, through the mouth of Fluellen.) Far apart as the two men seem, the common theme of the two plays to which their names give the titles is imperialism. The point is that we see the imperialist at different stages of his career. A conqueror at the outset is different from a conqueror at the end.

The unflattering character of the portrait Shakespeare draws of Julius Caesar is notorious. The name and spirit of Caesar ring as imperially through the play as they do through history. But the trembling epileptic the poet depicts seems like a parody of the figure that shook the ancient world. Historical critics will say that Shakespeare is following Plutarch. He is, but what of it? He had no need of Plutarch to teach him what a "strong" man becomes in his last days or at death. He had already drawn unforgettably the final hours or moments of Cardinal Beaufort, of Warwick, of Richard III and others, to demonstrate that the nemesis of worldly strength is spiritual weakness (a truth that need not be labored in a generation that has witnessed the downfall of so many men of this type). And he was to go on doing it. "To be called into a huge sphere, and not to be seen to move in't, are the holes where eyes should be, which pitifully disaster the cheeks." That description of a weakling (Lepidus) in his prime is a good characterization of this strong man (Caesar) on the edge of death.

> Now does he feel his title
> Hang loose about him, like a giant's robe
> Upon a dwarfish thief.

Those words concerning Macbeth in his decline fit Shakespeare's Caesar in his. If the poet had given us a picture of Caesar's youth, it might have been as fascinating as that of Hal, or, of his prime, as masterful as that achieved by Bernard Shaw. But his purpose here is different, and it bears an interesting relation to the story that was cut short by the death of Henry V. If Henry had lived and held France, it is obvious in what direction he would have developed. But he died, and the chief defect of Shakespeare's story is its failure to give any account of the circumstances of his death. At his funeral, however, the poet has Bedford call upon Henry's ghost and link it specifically with Julius Caesar:

> Henry the Fifth! thy ghost I invocate:
> Prosper this realm, keep it from civil broils!
> Combat with adverse planets in the heavens!
> A far more glorious star thy soul will make,
> Than Julius Caesar, or bright—

At which moment, a messenger enters to announce the beginning of the end of Henry's conquests. It is easy to see what happened in Shakespeare's imagination. In a dream, a character will sometimes grow blurry and begin to undergo a change just as another character enters. What has happened is that the original character has split in two. So here. It is as if after the "death" in the poet's mind of Henry V the split indicated by the hyphenated name Hal-Henry widened still further, and what was originally one man with a dual nature became two men, Brutus and Caesar. So regarded, the play in which the two men figure is a sort of metempsychosis of Henry V.

## II

As in life, there are characters in Shakespeare about whom men hold antipodal opinions. Brutus is among them. There are those who consider him one of the most noble and lovable figures the poet ever created. Others cannot conceal their scorn for him. He was a fool, they say, an egotist, an unconscionable prig. If this be true, it is a bit odd that almost everyone in the play seems to think highly of him. "This was the noblest Roman of them all," Antony declares. And Antony was Brutus' enemy. "His life was gentle," he goes on to say, and we get the impression that, until the idea of assassinating Caesar infected it, that life was a pattern of domestic and civic virtue. Integrity was its keynote, a balanced mixture of the elements. And Antony, as if bent on surpassing what he has already said, shifts at the end from a Roman to a human standard. He imagines Nature standing up, proud of her masterpiece, declaring to all the world, "This was a man!"

JULIUS CAESAR

And yet the detractors of Brutus have a case. They are merely talking about another person. They have turned their attention from the man Nature made to the man Brutus marred. There is little evidence that Brutus was particularly conscious of his own virtue until he began to consider Caesar's assassination. Then he had to exaggerate his own goodness to compensate for the evil that he contemplated. After which, Nature's formula no longer fully characterizes him. We are compelled to add four other words to her original four: "This was a man"—*and Brutus knew it.* And there lies the tragedy, for a man should have no more acquaintance with his virtue than a woman with her beauty.

The shadow on the wall, or the reflection in a distorting mirror, of the most nearly perfect human figure ever created can be grotesque. Those who disparage Brutus are talking of his shadow.

> Tell me, good Brutus, can you see your face?

asks Cassius on the occasion when he first hints at the assassination.

> BRU.: No, Cassius; for the eye sees not itself
> But by reflection, by some other things.
> CASS.: 'Tis just;
> And it is very much lamented, Brutus,
> That you have no such mirrors as will turn
> Your hidden worthiness into your eye,
> That you might see your shadow.

It is a case where the speaker uses a word in one sense and Shakespeare in another. Shadow! it evokes ominous memories of Richard, the Shadow King; and certainly the envious Cassius was not the one to offer a reflecting surface serene enough for the "good Brutus" to catch his image in, whatever may be true of "that poor Brutus, with himself at war" whom Brutus himself has just mentioned. It was not for nothing that Shakespeare put "good Brutus" and "poor Brutus" side by side. And so the story is at once the story of a man, and, like that of Hal, of "another fall of man."

Hence, whether we attend to the contrast between Caesar and the noblest Roman of them all, or to the conflict within that Roman between his nobility and his pride, the theme is the same. It is *King John* over again with its antithesis between the real and the titular hero. *King John* remains history because John was only a king and not a "man," while Faulconbridge, who was both man and "king," did not fall. *Julius Caesar* becomes tragedy because Brutus both was a "man" and did fall. *Emperor and Galilean* is the title of the play Ibsen considered his masterpiece. *Emperor and Man* might have been the name of *Julius Caesar*, had Shakespeare been given to comment in his titles. He was given to it, but in a more subtle way than Ibsen. The pride of Brutus *is* the ghost of Caesar within him as certainly as if at the moment Caesar expired it had literally transmigrated from the dead man to the living one. And so this Tragedy of Brutus is the story of Julius Caesar's spirit after death. The title of the play is precisely the right one.

As the political theme of *Henry V* is imperialism and war, so the political theme of *Julius Caesar* is imperialism and revolution. To say that Shakespeare in this play is asserting that assassination as a political instrument is always, everywhere, for any man, under any circumstances, morally unjustifiable would be asserting too much. Shakespeare is not given to defending or attacking universal propositions. Even when Camillo, asked by Leontes to kill Polixenes in *The Winter's Tale*, declares:

> If I could find example
> Of thousands that had struck anointed kings,
> And flourish'd after, I'd not do't; but since
> Nor brass nor stone nor parchment bears not one,
> Let villany itself forswear't,

it is Camillo's opinion and not necessarily Shakespeare's, though the absoluteness of the statement is indeed interesting, coming from the author of *Julius Caesar*. "Shakespeare is no partisan in this tragedy," says Professor Kittredge. "He sides neither with Caesar and his avengers nor with the party of Brutus and Cassius. The verdict, if there must be a verdict, he leaves to history." It is a safe statement, if for no other reason than that Shakespeare is never a political partisan. But if ever Shakespeare left anything beyond doubt it is that this particular man Brutus should never have had anything to do with this particular deed. Practically every scene of the play contributes something toward this conclusion. So true is it indeed that *Julius Caesar*, if you care to take it so, becomes a sort of manual on the art of knowing what your soul is telling you to do, or not to do, of finding out what you think in contrast with what you think you think.

Brutus is an exceptional man. Yet Brutus is Everyman in the sense that every man is Brutus at some hour of his life. Whoever is aware of the disparity between what he would be and what the world seems bent on making him is a Brutus in a general sense. More specifically, Brutus is the man of sensitive nature who, outraged by the cruelty and tyranny around him, sadly and reluctantly concludes that there is no way to oppose the world but with the world's weapons, that fire must drive out fire and force force.

The lofty character of the end intended, the preservation of the liberties of Rome, blinds Brutus to the low character of the means proposed.

He represses, but he cannot eradicate, that abhorrence of force which, by definition, must be inherent in every lover of liberty. The result is war in that psychological realm where all war begins.

> Since Cassius first did whet me against Caesar,
> I have not slept.
> Between the acting of a dreadful thing
> And the first motion, all the interim is
> Like a phantasma or a hideous dream.
> The genius and the mortal instruments
> Are then in council; and the state of man,
> Like to a little kingdom, suffers then
> The nature of an insurrection.

Dreadful, hideous, mortal! His own words ought to have been warning enough. But reason does not understand the language of the imagination. In the conflict of instincts let loose within Brutus, Lucius and Portia are his good angels, Caesar and Cassius his evil ones. With or without knowing it, they strive for the possession of his soul.

## III

Portia is one of the first of a number of Shakespearean heroines who have brief roles of supreme importance. Speaking to Brutus, she refers to herself as "your self, your half." The phrase "better half" as applied to a wife has been so prostituted to jocosity that it is scarcely possible to use it seriously. Yet it describes precisely Portia's relation to Brutus. She is all that is fine in his unconscious nature, and their conjugal partnership is as lovely as any Shakespeare ever pictured, even including that between Coriolanus and Virgilia. The point is underlined by the fact that Calphurnia bears somewhat the same relation to Caesar. These women through their dreams and intuitions draw from deeper springs of wisdom than any to which their husbands have access. And Caesar because of his vanity and ambition, Brutus because of a strain of cold rationalism that runs through his nature, are in peculiar need of the insight of their wives.

If Portia is Brutus' wisdom, the boy Lucius is his original innocence. "Become what thou art," says Pindar. Brutus was well on his way toward obeying that injunction when this business of Caesar's assassination intervened. Lucius is Brutus before he was contaminated, and in him his master can see himself as he came from the hand of God. Innocence does not mean unsophistication. It means the state of being unpoisoned.

Lucius, naturally, does not know the role he is playing in Brutus' life. Portia is only partly conscious of her participation in his fate. Nor can Caesar suspect the evil he has unloosed within him. But it is quite otherwise with Cassius. He is cynically aware of every step he takes. He is the Seducer. He proceeds to lay siege to Brutus' integrity exactly as a seducer in a commoner sense does to a woman's chastity. Cassius looks up to Brutus, even loves him. Why, then, does he not let him alone and find someone more fit for the business he has in hand? Because the conspiracy needs the moral prestige that only Brutus can lend it.

> Into what dangers would you lead me, Cassius,
> That you would have me seek into myself
> For that which is not in me?

Like the woman who thinks it is not in her, he thinks it is not in him, but proves that it is by remaining to hear more—just as Ivan Karamazov once remained to hear more from Smerdyakov.

Cassius knows his brother will entertain no proposal save for the general good. So he attacks him where virtue and its opposite are forever getting confused, in his pride, pride in his ancestors' dedication to republicanism:

> O, you and I have heard our fathers say,
> There was a Brutus once that would have brook'd
> Th' eternal devil to keep his state in Rome
> As easily as a king.

The fathers once more! It is the clinching argument. Like Romeo and Hal, Brutus capitulates to the past, or rather to Cassius' subtle perversion of it (the earlier Brutus did not kill the tyrant). "I sense what you are driving at," Brutus confesses in effect. "Indeed, I have been meditating on these very things myself, and will confer about them—later."

> What you have said
> I will consider; what you have to say
> I will with patience hear, and find a time
> Both meet to hear and answer such high things.

The lines have a familiar ring.

> Yet when we can entreat an hour to serve,
> We would spend it in some words upon that business,
> If you would grant the time.

Macbeth to Banquo! a sinister parallel.

Caesar with his train enters, and when he has retired, Casca tells how he was three times offered the crown and three times refused it. As Casca goes out, Brutus changes his appointment with Cassius from some indefinite time in the future to a definite one on the morrow at his home. Cassius has won. He soliloquizes:

Well, Brutus, thou art noble; yet, I see,
Thy honourable metal may be wrought
From that it is dispos'd. Therefore it is meet
That noble minds keep ever with their likes:
For who so firm that cannot be seduc'd?

Seduced: he is honest enough to use the very word. With cynical frank-
ness he admits that he has corrupted his friend, that his own conduct has
been ignoble, that, if the roles had been reversed, Brutus would never have
done to him what he has done to Brutus. And yet, in the face of all this
from the arch-conspirator, men have argued whether Brutus did right or
wrong to enter the conspiracy!

## IV

His evil angels have had their way with Brutus in the first act. As the
second act opens, we find him invoking his good angel. But he does not
know it: he thinks he is just a sleepless man arousing a sleeping child.

What, Lucius, ho!
I cannot, by the progress of the stars,
Give guess how near to day. Lucius, I say!
I would it were my fault to sleep so soundly.
When, Lucius, when! Awake, I say! What, Lucius!

Here the metaphor of daybreak that figures so significantly through the
play is beautifully introduced. The daybreak of the fatal day of Caesar's
death is but an hour or so away. Following close upon it will be the daybreak of new liberty for Rome, or so Brutus believes. Finally, there is the
daybreak of life itself incarnated in the child. Brutus cannot estimate by
the stars how near day is. But he looks in the wrong place. The dawn that
might save him is as near as the next room, as near as the child, as near as
himself, and when he cries "Awake!" he is beseeching the child within to
awaken before it is too late. The boy enters, and his master sends him
to light a taper in another room, not realizing that the child himself is the
best light. From end to end the role of Lucius is permeated with this symbolism. Caesar, just before his fall, announces that he is the Northern Star
that alone holds a fixed place in the moving firmament. Lucius is that star.
It is not by chance that the moment the boy is gone Brutus begins to lose
his way, to strike the note of darkness: "It must be by his death."

Presently Lucius comes back with a paper that was thrown in at the
window of Brutus' study:

"Brutus, thou sleep'st; awake, and see thyself!"

How different that "Awake" from the one that opened the scene, and
what ironical words to address to a victim of insomnia who has been

awake all night! Lucius, whom Brutus has sent out for a calendar, re-
enters, and the Janus-like stage direction is *"Knocking within."* The boy
goes to the gate and reports that Cassius has come with others he cannot
identify because their hats are plucked about their ears and half their
faces buried in their cloaks. "O conspiracy!" cries Brutus, and the speech
that follows shows how his soul abhors the enterprise he is nevertheless
bent on undertaking. Dangerous, dark, monstrous; night, cavern, evil;
shame, mask, hide: adjectives, nouns, and verbs conspire fairly to shout
the truth in his ears. But he is deaf. And this lover of truth stoops to the
abjectest hypocrisy when he bids the conspiracy hide itself in smiles and
affability.

> To beguile the time,
> Look like the time; bear welcome in your eye,
> Your hand, your tongue: look like the innocent flower,
> But be the serpent under't.

These lines are Lady Macbeth's. Except perhaps for the touch about the
serpent, where she goes a bit beyond him, they might pass unchallenged
if assigned to Brutus at this point.

As Brutus and Cassius whisper together, several of the other conspirators take up, as if the scene were music, the theme of daybreak with
which it opened:

DECIUS: Here lies the east. Doth not the day break here?
CASCA: No.
CINNA: O, pardon, sir, it doth; and yon grey lines
        That fret the clouds are messengers of day.
CASCA: You shall confess that you are both deceiv'd.
        Here, as I point my sword, the sun arises,
        Which is a great way growing on the south,
        Weighing the youthful season of the year.
        Some two months hence, up higher toward the north
        He first presents his fire; and the high east
        Stands as the Capitol, directly here.

"While Brutus and Cassius confer," says Kittredge, "the others courte-
ously occupy themselves with casual talk about indifferent matters." It
may have seemed casual and indifferent to the speakers. But it was not
to their imaginations, nor to Shakespeare's. If there is a passage in the play
that lets us into the secret of what the author thought of the conspiracy
it is this. (This, and possibly two others yet to be mentioned.) As we have
seen, Shakespeare is forever using such apparent parentheses for uttering
his own convictions under the protection of a metaphor. These men think

they are about to bring a new day to Rome when they cannot even agree as to where the geographical east lies. They promise a new spiritual morning before they have even learned where the material sun comes up! And when Casca cries:

> Here, as I point my sword, the sun arises,

we feel the presumption of expecting a new day to break at the command of a sword. Casca has surpassed Chaunticleer in egotism. Thus is the political message of the play condensed into a metaphor, its whole point suspended, as it were, on the point of a sword.

Cassius suggests in succession that the conspirators bind themselves to one another by an oath, sound out Cicero, and mark Antony to fall with Caesar. Brutus negatives each of these proposals, revealing in each instance how unfitted he is for the business he is undertaking. In the case of Cicero, the reason he gives,

> For he will never follow anything
> That other men begin,

strongly implies that he does not want to share his prestige as moral head of the conspiracy. In the other two cases he is unconsciously attempting to compensate for an ignoble major decision by minor nobler ones.

If there were no other evidence whatever, the speech in which Brutus seeks to justify the sparing of Antony would be enough in itself to show how completely the true Brutus recognizes in advance the futility of the course on which the false Brutus is embarking. Without knowing it, he puts his finger on the precise reason why the conspiracy was bound to fail. As in Richard II's tribute to Peace, or Henry V's argument with Williams about the king's responsibility for the consciences of his soldiers, the imagination of the man tells the truth over his head. He thinks he is saying one thing when actually he is saying just the opposite.

> Our course will seem too bloody, Caius Cassius,
> To cut the head off and then hack the limbs,
> Like wrath in death and envy afterwards;
> For Antony is but a limb of Caesar.
> Let us be sacrificers, but not butchers, Caius.
> We all stand up against the spirit of Caesar,
> And in the spirit of men there is no blood;
> O, that we then could come by Caesar's spirit,
> And not dismember Caesar! But, alas,
> Caesar must bleed for it! And, gentle friends,
> Let's kill him boldly, but not wrathfully;
> Let's carve him as a dish fit for the gods,

> Not hew him as a carcass fit for hounds;
> And let our hearts, as subtle masters do,
> Stir up their servants to an act of rage,
> And after seem to chide 'em. This shall make
> Our purpose necessary and not envious;
> Which so appearing to the common eyes,
> We shall be call'd purgers, not murderers.
> And for Mark Antony, think not of him;
> For he can do no more than Caesar's arm
> When Caesar's head is off.

Disentangle the syllogism underlying the verbiage in the first part of this speech and this is what we have: (1) The spirit of men contains no blood. (2) We wish to destroy the spirit of Caesar. Therefore (3) we must spill Caesar's blood. No one will question that major premise. All lovers of liberty will second the minor one. The tragedy is dedicated to demonstrating the absurdity of the conclusion. The true inference from the premises is obviously: Therefore it is useless to spill Caesar's blood. Moral pride prevents Brutus from seeing it.

The logic is false, but the metaphors, as usual, slip in the truth.

> Let us be sacrificers, but not butchers, Caius . . .
> Let's carve him as a dish fit for the gods.

Dropping out the six lines that intervene between those two reveals the tricks his mind is playing upon Brutus—for who ever carved what had not previously been butchered? And the figure of the master and servants betrays him even more ignominiously. The conspirators seek the end of the man who would make himself master of Rome. Brutus tells them they must imitate the subtle master who stirs up his servants to a violent act and then appears to chide them for committing it. Thus the assassination will be received as a deed of necessity rather than envy:

> We shall be call'd purgers, not murderers.

Purgers! the very word that in our day has been used so often to camouflage murder. The example establishes the point it is supposed to refute and stamps the act it is used to justify as murder.

Brutus' opinion prevails, Antony is spared, and to an ominous striking of the clock, anticipating the ringing of the bell that summoned Macbeth "to heaven or to hell," the conspirators disperse as Cassius cries, "The morning comes upon's," and Brutus warns,

> Let not our looks put on our purposes,
> But bear it as our Roman actors do.

He is indeed, himself, playing a part. And when he turns to the child, it is as if he were bidding a final farewell to his true but discarded self:

> Boy! Lucius! Fast asleep? It is no matter.

No matter that his innocence slumbers? He did not think so when the scene opened.

But if one of Brutus' good angels is asleep, the other is not. Portia enters to inquire why her lord has left her bed at this unwonted hour. And with a skill that would do credit to a twentieth-century psychiatrist she lists the symptoms she has noted of his mental perturbation, signs of a nervous irritability that has altered him almost past recognition. He protests that he is merely physically unwell. She will have nothing of that explanation, and piercing directly to the truth, she cries:

> No, my Brutus,
> You have some sick offence within your mind.

She kneels to him, begging him to reveal his secret.

> There is a tide in the affairs of men . . .

It was at this moment, not when, too late, he uttered those famous lines to Cassius, that Brutus should have recognized that his last chance to save himself from becoming an assassin had come.

> O ye gods!
> Render me worthy of this noble wife!

If ever a prayer was sincere, it is this. If ever a man had a chance to help answer his own prayer, this is he. Again, the stage direction registers the spiritual crisis with a *"Knocking within."* It is as ominous a knocking as the more famous one in *Macbeth*.

And what does Brutus say and do?

> Hark, hark! one knocks. *Portia, go in awhile,*
> And *by and by* thy bosom shall partake
> The secrets of my heart.
> All my engagements I will construe to thee,
> All the charactery of my sad brows.
> *Leave me with haste. (Exit Portia)*
>                     Lucius, who's that knocks?
> *(Re-enter Lucius with Ligarius)*
> Luc.: Here is a sick man that would speak with you.
> Bru.: Caius Ligarius, that Metellus spake of.
> *Boy, stand aside.* Caius Ligarius! how?

If the poet had had Brutus say, "My Wisdom, go in awhile! My Innocence, stand aside! Sickness, let me embrace you!" he could hardly have made his point clearer. There are few stage directions in his plays more pathetic than those two words: *Exit Portia*. It might have been: *Exit the Soul of Brutus*.

Brutus tells Ligarius that great things are afoot, and, summoning his failing forces, the latter inquires, "What's to do?"

> A piece of work that will make sick men whole,

replies Brutus.

> But are not some whole that we must make sick?

asks Ligarius, suspecting the truth. He does not know that his words fit the man to whom he is speaking better than they do the intended victim, who in an hour or two will be beyond both sickness and wholeness. "That must we also," replies Brutus, equally ignorant of the application of the words to himself. "Set on your foot," says Ligarius,

> And with a heart new-fir'd I follow you,
> To do I know not what: but it sufficeth
> That Brutus leads me on.

> Follow me then,

says Brutus, and he too might well have added, "to do I know not what." It is tragic when a nobility that might have led only follows, when it consents to be used by envious men for their base purposes. It adds to the tragedy when weak men, trusting that nobility, follow it blindly into that baseness.

## V

Brutus is not the only one whose sleep is interrupted the night before the assassination and who will not let his wife save him. The same is true of Caesar. Three times Calphurnia dreams that her husband is murdered, that his statue runs blood in which many Romans bathe their hands. And the augurers confirm her fear. Caesar decides not to go to the Capitol. But Decius Brutus, by a strained reinterpretation of the dream and by dangling the hope of a crown before him, gets him to change his mind. Brutus leads him to Brutus. The crown he is to receive is death.

Even at the last moment he might have been saved if he had regarded the Soothsayer or had received the petition of Artemidorus, the philosopher, who in some unexplained way—possibly because the conspirators had not bound themselves to secrecy by an oath—had got a hint of the conspiracy.

> What touches us ourself shall be last serv'd,

he cries, brushing Artemidorus aside. What looks like magnanimity is inverted pride.

Metellus Cimber kneels before Caesar begging the repeal of his brother's banishment. If Caesar's decision had been made a genuine test of his fitness to live, the spectator might feel more sympathy with the conspirators. But his death is ordained regardless of how he decides. Brutus, with a kiss that reminds us more of Judas than of the Brutus who expelled Tarquin from Rome, seconds the petition of Metellus Cimber. Caesar, refusing, justifies his unwillingness to change his mind by comparing himself to the Northern Star and to Olympus. It is assumption of divinity. The man is infatuated. The moment has come. Casca stabs him from behind, the others follow, Brutus, significantly, striking last. "*Et tu, Brute?* Then fall, Caesar!" How much deeper into Brutus' heart those words must have sunk than did the dagger that made "the most unkindest cut of all" into Caesar's flesh. It was Caesar who stabbed Brutus.

## VI

Liberty! Freedom! Tyranny is dead!

cries Cinna.

Liberty, freedom, and enfranchisement!

cries Casca.

Peace, freedom, and liberty!

cries Brutus, and unconsciously fulfilling Calphurnia's dream, he bids his fellows bathe their hands to the elbows in Caesar's blood. (Is this the man we saw bending over a sleeping child but a few hours before?)

How many ages hence
Shall this our lofty scene be acted over
In states unborn and accents yet unknown!

cries Cassius as he complies with Brutus' bloody suggestion.

How many times shall Caesar bleed in sport,
That now on Pompey's basis lies along
No worthier than the dust!

cries Brutus, echoing Cassius. It is significant that while the first prophecy is political, the second is theatrical. How many times since then both have been fulfilled. "So oft as that shall be," Cassius concludes,

So often shall the knot of us be call'd
The men that gave their country liberty.

What they did give it is best seen by turning over a few pages of the text to the opening of Act IV, where Antony, Octavius, and Lepidus, the new rulers of Rome, sit around a table pricking off the names of those who must die that their own regime may base itself in safety. So soon can tyranny succeed violent revolution. And if the immediate fruits of the assassination as depicted in this play are insufficient, the reader may turn to *Antony and Cleopatra* to behold its remoter harvest.

But this is anticipating.

Antony, whom Brutus spared, begs leave to speak over Caesar's body at his funeral, and, in the face of Cassius' protest, Brutus consents. In a speech that will precede Antony's he will placate the people. The two orations, or rather Brutus' oration and Antony's speech, have been declaimed and dissected in innumerable classrooms. Yet the contrast between them remains a better treatise on the relation of sincerity to style than a shelf of textbooks.

Though everybody sees that the wily Antony puts his speech over, as we say, while Brutus does not, just as a speech Brutus' effort has usually been declared a good one by academic authority. It was merely too good for the mob, it is said. On the contrary it is one of the worst speeches ever made by an able and intelligent man. Its symmetrical structure, its balanced sentences, its ordered procedure, its rhetorical questions, its painfully conscious and ornamental style, its hopelessly abstract subject matter, all stamp it as the utterance of a man whose heart is not in his words. It is a dishonest speech.

The cry of the Third Citizen, "Let him be Caesar," measures its practical effectiveness. Those four words have often been pointed out as one of the most crushing ironies in the play. They are, and with the other comments of the populace show how hopeless the cause of the conspirators was. These people did not deserve liberty. They were ready for slavery.

Antony's speech, on the other hand, for all its playing on the passions of the people, and for all its lies, is at bottom an honest speech, because Antony loved Caesar. Because to that extent he has the truth on his side, he is as concrete as Brutus was abstract. A sincere harangue by a demagogue is better than the most "classic" oration from a man who speaks only with his lips. It is like Henry IV and Falstaff. The good form is on one side, the veracity on the other.

> Now let it work,

cries Antony in an accent with which our own day has made us well acquainted,

> Mischief, thou art afoot,
> Take thou what course thou wilt!

And Shakespeare devotes a little scene to Cinna, the poet, whom the mob mistakes for Cinna the conspirator. What if they do have hold of the wrong man! They go ahead anyway—on sound lynching principles. It is the Jack Cade motif over again. Mythology is wrong. It is not love, it is passion that is blind.

Meanwhile, before this, word has come to Antony that Brutus and Cassius

> Are rid like madmen through the gates of Rome.

Instead of liberating Rome, Rome has "liberated" them. But a few hours before they were crying "Tyranny is dead!" and so soon it all seems like a dream.

## VII

After the proscription, at which we took a glance in advance, the scene shifts to Sardis. Assassination and revolution have eventuated in war, and already the two brother-generals are blaming each other for their predicament.

> Thou hast describ'd
> A hot friend cooling. Ever note, Lucilius,

says Brutus to his servant who has just come from Cassius,

> When love begins to sicken and decay,
> It useth an enforced ceremony.
> There are no tricks in plain and simple faith.

If only Brutus had remembered that truth when, at its inception, he bade the conspiracy hide itself in smiles and affability!

Cassius enters with the salutation,

> Most noble brother, you have done me wrong,

and, the two beginning to wrangle, Brutus draws his friend into his own tent that their dissension may not be overheard.

A guilty conscience invariably finds in others the evil it will not admit to itself. The quarrel scene is Brutus' specific confession that the conspiracy and assassination were terrible errors.

As usual, he takes a high idealistic line. He charges Cassius with protecting bribery. "In such a time," Cassius answers, one cannot be meticulous. Brutus implies that Cassius has "an itching palm" and has sold offices for gold. Cassius declares that if he were not Brutus that speech would be his last.

Remember March, the ides of March remember,

cries Brutus in a tone that reminds us of the very dog he mentions:

> Did not great Julius bleed for justice' sake?
> What villain touch'd his body, that did stab
> And not for justice? What, shall one of us,
> That struck the foremost man of all this world
> But for supporting robbers, shall we now
> Contaminate our fingers with base bribes,
> And sell the mighty space of our large honours
> For so much trash as may be grasped thus?
> I had rather be a dog, and bay the moon,
> Than such a Roman.

Shall we who made away with the great Injustice, the great Robber, stoop to little injustices and petty thefts? But in that case, we feel like asking, how about imitating the great Apostle of Force by practicing a little assassination? Brutus is not pushing analogy that far.

> Brutus, bait not me;
> I'll not endure it,

Cassius exclaims, and the quarrel descends to common scolding with Brutus immeasurably the worse offender.

> There is no terror, Cassius, in your threats,

he declares, when Cassius warns him not to go too far,

> For I am arm'd so strong in honesty
> That they pass by me as the idle wind,
> Which I respect not.

It is the perfect echo of an earlier speech in the play. The arrogation of moral infallibility is but a step below the affectation of divinity. Brutus has become like Caesar! His victim has infected him with his own disease. It is the special nemesis of the revolutionist. He comes to resemble what he once abhorred.

And the irony goes even further. "I did send to you," Brutus goes on,

> For certain sums of gold, which you denied me;
> For I can raise no money by vile means.
> By heaven, I had rather coin my heart
> And drop my blood for drachmas than to wring
> From the hard hands of peasants their vile trash
> By any indirection. I did send
> To you for gold to pay my legions,
> Which you denied me. Was that done like Cassius?

He will not wring gold from the peasants by any indirection. But he will take it, even demand it, of Cassius, who, of course, has no other ultimate source from which to obtain it than just those peasants. Brutus is doing what in the same breath he declares that he would rather die than do. "I won't rob myself, but I will rob by way of you, for I can do nothing indirectly." That is what his astounding argument reduces to. "Indirection": Pandulph's word, Polonius' word. Brutus thinks he is angry with Cassius for his countenance of petty thefts and bribes. Actually he is angry with himself for robbing Rome, for robbing Portia, for robbing himself.

Cassius, stung to the quick, does just what Caesar once did to the mob: presents his bosom to Brutus' dagger—and instantly Brutus relents. But when so huge a fire is suddenly quenched some sparks are bound to escape. A Poet, overhearing and sensing something wrong between the generals, breaks boldly in in an attempt to reconcile them. In ejecting him, Brutus vents what is left of his anger. But in doing so he speaks and behaves more like Hotspur than like Brutus.

Alone again with Cassius, Brutus chooses the moment to reveal the hidden tension he has been under during their quarrel. Portia is dead— by her own hand.

In keeping this secret from his audience as well as from Cassius, Shakespeare violates a fundamental rule of stagecraft. It is one of the clearest of many indications in his plays that he cared for something more than the first impressions of a theater audience. Reread, or seen a second time on the stage, the quarrel scene sounds harmonics that the ear misses completely the first time the scene is encountered.

Brutus attributes Portia's suicide to his absence and to the successes of Octavius and Antony. We can guess, only too easily, the deeper reason why

> she fell distract
> And, her attendants absent, swallow'd fire.

As fact, Portia's death by swallowing fire is perhaps incredible. As truth, it rises to an order beyond the invention possibly even of a Plutarch or a Shakespeare, to the level of myth itself. But the poet has at least made the most of what he inherited. As he uses it, this incident becomes the second of his three main comments on his own play (the first being the passage on the location of the East). He has made plain in the one scene where we see them together that Portia is Brutus' other "half." As the mirror of his soul, she is bound to reflect so tremendous an event as his spiritual death in accepting the code of violence. And that is exactly what her death does.

On entering the conspiracy Brutus metaphorically swallowed fire. Portia swallows it literally as an allegory of his act. It is both a picture of his dereliction and a measure of the agony she underwent because of it. The whole meaning of the drama seems somehow concentrated in this symbol.

## VIII

The boy brings wine and Brutus and Cassius pledge each other and "bury all unkindness" in the cup. But Brutus will never by swallowing the fire of wine bury the memory of how Portia died. At the very moment indeed he is to be reminded of her end. Messala enters bringing news from Rome. Not knowing whether Brutus has heard of his wife's suicide, he sounds him out, and, on Brutus' insistence that he reveal what he is hinting at, tells the truth. Brutus pretends he has not heard and receives the word with stoic calm. The double report of Portia's death has often been held an error in the text, a sign of unfinished revision. But surely it is just one more bit of evidence that Brutus is acting a part. The unnatural restraint he puts himself under in this personal matter may have more than a little to do too with the rash plan of battle we find him advocating a few minutes later. He turns to it with an abruptness that would have been cruel, had the situation been what Messala supposed.

Shall Brutus and Cassius march down to the enemy and give battle at Philippi or await him where they are on the heights? Brutus is for the former course, Cassius for the latter. The decision is motivated by unseen forces. The quarrel and reconciliation, with the news of Portia's death, have left Cassius melancholy and in no mood to cross Brutus again. The unnatural restraint that Brutus has imposed upon himself with regard to Portia's death helps perhaps to make him impulsive. At any rate he argues —in words the world knows by heart—that they are now at their high tide and should strike immediately. But whatever may be true of the military situation, Brutus' moral tide is at its ebb, and the strategy he favors is ultimately dictated by that fact. Whatever the immediate reasons for it, it conforms finally to nothing less than the pattern of his whole life. His is the story of a man who instead of keeping to "the hills and upper regions" has by the assassination come down to "the enemy." Had he still had hope in his heart, his unconscious might have tried to compensate for his moral decline by insisting that his forces keep to the heights. But with the death of Portia a dark fatalism begins to possess him. He is the victim of a desperation he does not yet realize. And so the plan of battle becomes a symbolic picture of his life. He has gone down before and led other men down. He will do it for the last time. As when he entered the conspiracy, his willingness to descend to their level suits "the enemy" exactly. Reluctantly Cassius consents. He who had once led Brutus lower now follows him. "Time is come round." The nemesis is inevitable. Thus, Shakespeare seems to be saying, our particular decisions, which appear to be made freely and on the merits of the occasion, are overruled by the total pattern of our lives. Cause and effect may reign in the physical world, but likeness and unlikeness are sovereign in the realm of the imagination. In our day the man who has plunged too heavily in the stock market leaps from the twentieth story of a skyscraper to his death. The type of suicide he chooses is not chance. It was not chance that Caesar had the "falling" sickness. Nor that the man who killed him becomes a victim of that sickness in another form.

Brutus is left alone with the boy Lucius, and, as usual in his presence, his true self comes to the surface. He is all tenderness. This man who could kill Caesar cannot ask a tired child to watch one hour more. He calls in Claudius and Varro, but bids them lie on cushions rather than stay awake, so sensitive is he to their feelings. It is compensation, of course. He finds the book for which he has searched—revealing touch—in the pocket of his gown, but before beginning to read—another revealing touch—he begs for a strain or two of music from Lucius. The drowsy boy complies, but after a note or two falls asleep over his instrument, and we have Henry IV's soliloquy on sleep dramatized before us. The scholar-assassin finds the leaf turned down where he left reading and composes himself to go on. But noting something strange about the taper, he looks up, and beholds a "monstrous apparition" coming toward him. It is the Ghost of Julius Caesar!

Is the specter a creature of his own fantasy, nothing at all, or, if something, angel or devil? "Speak to me what thou art."

> Thy evil spirit, Brutus.

The Delphic answer leaves open the question whether it is from within or from without. But it leaves no doubt, in either case, of its infernal origin. With a promise to meet Brutus again at Philippi, it vanishes.

> O, that we then could come by Caesar's spirit,
> And not dismember Caesar!

Too late Brutus discovers that when his dagger entered Caesar's body it released a power as towering and uncontrollable as the genie freed by the fisherman in the Arabian tale. Julius Caesar is dead. But his spirit has volatilized into something as invulnerable as the air. "In the spirit of men there is no blood."

"Some angel, or some devil?" Brutus had asked. And promptly on the disappearance of the devil, the angel appears—as if the one had exorcised the other. Coming suddenly to himself on the exit of the Ghost, Brutus cries out:

> Boy, Lucius! Varro! Claudius! Sirs! Awake!
> Claudius!

> The strings, my lord, are false,

murmurs Lucius. The child is dreaming, and out of some divine confusion in his mind between his instrument and the trouble he has read on his master's brow his unconsciousness frames this inspired answer. (It is Shakespeare's third supreme comment on his own play.) If up to this point anyone has doubted what Lucius symbolizes, this should convince him. Brutus' slumbering innocence, awakening, gives him a last warning. On the lips of a child, from out of that borderland between sleeping and waking where it so often resides, the truth speaks. "The strings, my lord, are false." Brutus is out of tune. But a musical instrument that is out of tune is not a musical instrument. Brutus is not Brutus.

And because he is not himself, he cannot read the oracle. Victim of an auditory hallucination, he mistakes the cry of his own soul for the nightmare of one of his companions. He projects his inner conflict into the outer world and sends to Cassius to "set on his powers."

## IX

Things draw to a close and the tragedy is finished at the Battle of Philippi fought on Cassius' birthday, a coincidence he turns to fatal effect:

> This day I breathed first; time is come round,
> And where I did begin, there shall I end.

The pathos of the parting predicts the outcome:

> For ever, and for ever, farewell, Cassius!

> For ever, and for ever, farewell, Brutus!

The battle has been fought and decided in the bottom of their hearts before it is even begun. It is more the conviction of certain defeat than the forces arrayed against them that determines the issue.

> ... men may construe things after their fashion,
> Clean from the purpose of the things themselves.

So Cassius does in mistaking the shouts of joy of friends at the arrival of his messenger for the exultation of enemies at his capture. Not even wait-

ing to confirm his conjecture, he covers his face and bids a servant run
him through with the very sword with which he had assassinated Caesar—

> Caesar, thou art reveng'd,
> Even with the sword that kill'd thee.

The advantage the impulsive Brutus had gained over Octavius on the
other wing of the battle is thrown away.

> O Julius Caesar, thou art mighty yet!

cries Brutus when he gazes down at his dead friend,

> Thy spirit walks abroad, and turns our swords
> In our own proper entrails.

The Ghost promised to meet Brutus again at Philippi. He has kept his
word. What Brutus did not reckon on was what the Other World would
say to his deed. He realizes at last that he has brought down on Rome in
hundred-fold measure the very spirit to exorcise which he sold his soul
to the conspiracy. Alive, Julius Caesar was a feeble epileptic. Dead, he has
become an annihilating tide.

> O hateful error, melancholy's child,
> Why dost thou show to the apt thoughts of men
> The things that are not? O error, soon conceiv'd,
> Thou never com'st unto a happy birth,
> But kill'st the mother that engender'd thee!

The whole plot against Caesar had been such an error. Brutus returns to
the field, but he is soon convinced that there is nothing left him but to
follow Cassius. "Caesar, now be still," he cries as he runs on his sword
held by a servant (after three others have refused that office):

> I kill'd not thee with half so good a will.

Those ten words are the Last Judgment of Brutus on a conspiracy the
morality of which other men, strangely, have long debated.

From the level of practical affairs, of politics, of drama, imperialism and
a violent hatred of imperialism look like opposites. But from the level of
poetry, of those high pastures of the soul where, as Thoreau once remarked on a famous occasion, the state is nowhere to be seen, the two can
have a curious resemblance. If anything was needed after *Henry V* to
make plain what Shakespeare thought of imperialism, this play supplies it.
Readers of William Blake will remember his habit of using names like
Locke, Newton, and Voltaire as symbols for ideas and attitudes of mind
that he disapproved of, quite without reference to the men themselves or

the details of their thinking. Caesar and Alexander apparently came to stand for Imperialism in Shakespeare's mind in a somewhat similar fashion. Falstaff speaks of Caesar as "the hook-nosed fellow of Rome." Rosalind refers to his "thrasonical brag." Hamlet has him turned to clay and stopping a hole in the wall along with Alexander who performs the same office for a beer barrel. And we remember Alexander the Pig. Fluellen, Falstaff, Rosalind, and Hamlet. Can anyone imagine Shakespeare having sympathy for what those four scorned?

After the indictment of imperialism in *Henry V, Julius Caesar* is just the combined confirmation of that indictment and compensation for it that might have been expected. It makes plain that those who oppose imperialism with force run the risk of being no better than the imperialists themselves. Bernard Shaw once remarked that *Julius Caesar* glorifies a murder which Goethe described as "the most senseless of deeds." A queer way of glorifying it: to demonstrate that it brought on its perpetrators precisely what they committed it to avert. No, Shakespeare agreed with Goethe. The path of violence and the path of the violent opposition to violence can easily be the same.

> And 'mid this tumult Kubla heard from far
> Ancestral voices prophesying war!

The real opposition, Shakespeare seems to say, is not between the state and the enemies of the state. It is between those ancestral voices and the voice of the soul.

*Chapter XXIII*

# Hamlet

When such a spacious mirror's set before him,
He needs must see himself.

---

I

There is no mystery in a looking glass until someone looks into it. Then, though it remains the same glass, it presents a different face to each man who holds it in front of him. The same is true of a work of art. It has no proper existence as art until someone is reflected in it—and no two will ever be reflected in the same way. However much we all see in common in such a work, at the center we behold a fragment of our own soul, and the greater the art the greater the fragment. *Hamlet* is possibly the most convincing example in existence of this truth. In a less "spacious mirror" it is often concealed or obscured. But "Hamlet wavered for all of us," as Emily Dickinson said, and everyone admits finding something of himself in the Prince of Denmark. *Hamlet* criticism seems destined, then, to go on being what it has always been: a sustained difference of opinion. It is quite as if *Hamlet* were itself a play within a play. *The Murder of Gonzago* was one thing to the Prince, another to the King, and others still to the Queen, Polonius, Ophelia, and the rest. So *Hamlet* is to us. The heart of its hero's mystery will never be plucked out. No theory of his character will ever satisfy all men, and even if one should convince one age, it would not the next. But that does not mean that a deep man will not come closer to that mystery than a shallow man, or a poetic age than a prosaic one— just as Hamlet saw more in "The Mouse-trap" than Rosencrantz or Guilden- stern could conceivably have seen. No one but a dead man can escape pro- jecting himself on the Prince of Denmark. But some will project themselves on many, others on only a few, of the innumerable facets of his personality. The former, compared with the latter, will obtain a relatively objective view of the man. And this process will continue to create what might be called the world's slowly growing portrait of Hamlet. Over the years the cairn of *Hamlet* criticism is more than any stone that has been thrown upon it.

## II

To nearly everyone both Hamlet himself and the play give the impression of having some peculiarly intimate relation to their creator. What that relation may originally have been we shall probably never know. But it is hard to refrain from speculating. When we learn that Dostoevsky had a son, Alyosha (Alexey), whom he loved dearly and who died before he was three, and that the father began writing *The Brothers Karamazov* that same year, the temptation is irresistible to believe that its hero, Alexey Karamazov, is an imaginative reincarnation of the child, a portrayal of what the author would have liked the boy to become. In this instance the father bestowed an immortality that there is only a negligible chance the son would have achieved if he had lived. Shakespeare's son Hamnet died at the age of eleven, possibly not long before his father began to be attracted by the Hamlet story. Was there any connection? We do not know. But the name, in its interchangeable forms, must have had strong emotional associations for Shakespeare. Hamnet and Judith Sadler, neighbors and friends of the Shakespeares, were godparents to their twins, to whom they gave their names. When Shakespeare was sixteen, a girl, Katherine Hamlett, was drowned near Stratford under circumstances the poet may have remembered when he told of Ophelia's death. Resemblances between Hamlet and the Earl of Essex, who, in turn, figured significantly in Shakespeare's life, have frequently been pointed out.

However all this may be, there is no doubt that Shakespeare endowed Hamlet with the best he had acquired up to the time he conceived him. He inherits the virtues of a score of his predecessors—and some of their weaknesses. Yet he is no mere recapitulation of them. In him, rather, they recombine to make a man as individual as he is universal. He has the passion of Romeo ("Romeo is Hamlet in love," says Hazlitt), the dash and audacity of Hotspur, the tenderness and genius for friendship of Antonio, the wit, wisdom, resourcefulness, and histrionic gift of Falstaff, the bravery of Faulconbridge, the boyish charm of the earlier Hal at his best, the poetic fancy of Richard II, the analogic power and meditative melancholy of Jaques, the idealism of Brutus, the simplicity and human sympathy of Henry VI, and, after the assumption of his antic disposition, the wiliness and talent for disguise of Henry IV and the cynicism and irony of Richard III —not to mention gifts and graces that stem more from certain of Shakespeare's heroines than from his heroes—for, like Rosalind, that inimitable boy-girl, Hamlet is an early draft of a new creature on the Platonic order, conceived in the *Upanishads*, who begins to synthesize the sexes. "He who understands the masculine and keeps to the feminine shall become the whole world's channel. Eternal virtue shall not depart from him and he shall return to the state of an infant." If Hamlet does not attain the consummation that Laotse thus describes, he at least gives promise of it. What wonder that actresses have played his role, or that among the theories about him one of the most inevitable, if most insane, is that he is a woman in disguise! Mad literally, the idea embodies a symbolic truth and helps explain why Hamlet has been pronounced both a hero and a dreamer, hard and soft, cruel and gentle, brutal and angelic, like a lion and like a dove. One by one these judgments are all wrong. Together they are all right—

> These contraries such unity do hold,

a line which those who object to such paradoxes as "modernizing" should note is Shakespeare's, as is also the phrase "mighty opposites."

For what was such a man made? Plainly for the ultimate things: for wonder, for curiosity and the pursuit of truth, for love, for creation—but first of all for freedom, the condition of the other four. He was made, that is, for religion and philosophy,* for love and art, for liberty to "grow unto himself"—five forces that are the elemental enemies of Force.

And this man is called upon to kill. It is almost as if Jesus had been asked to play the role of Napoleon (as the temptation in the wilderness suggests that in some sense he was). If Jesus had been, ought he to have accepted it? The absurdity of the question prompts the recording of the strangest of all the strange facts in the history of *Hamlet:* the fact, namely, that nearly all readers, commentators, and critics are agreed in thinking that it was Hamlet's duty to kill, that he ought indeed to have killed much sooner than he did. His delay, they say, was a weakness and disaster, entailing, as it did, many unintended deaths, including his own. He should have obeyed much earlier the Ghost's injunction to avenge his father's murder. "Surely it is clear," says Bradley, giving expression to this idea for a multitude of others, "that, whatever we in the twentieth century may think about Ham-

---

* Hamlet himself condemns this word as inadequate to the idea of the pursuit of truth in his

> "There are more things in heaven and earth, Horatio,
> Than are dreamt of in your philosophy,"

"your philosophy" meaning, of course, not Horatio's, but philosophy in general.

let's duty, we are meant in the play to assume that he *ought* to have obeyed the Ghost." "As for the morality of personal vengeance," says Hazelton Spencer, "however abhorrent the concept we must accept it in the play as Hamlet's sacred duty, just as we must accept the Ghost who urges it." "John-a-dreams tarried long," says Dover Wilson at the end of *What Happens in Hamlet*, "but this Hercules 'sweeps' to his revenge." And with plain approval he pronounces Hamlet's "task accomplished," his "duty now performed."

Now whatever we are "meant" to assume, there is no doubt that nearly every spectator and reader the first time he encounters the play does assume that Hamlet ought to kill the King—and nearly all continue in that opinion on further acquaintance in the face of the paradox just stated.

How can that be?

It can be for the same reason that we exult when Gratiano cries, "Now, infidel, I have thee on the hip," and we see Shylock get what he was about to give, for the same reason that we applaud when Romeo sends Tybalt to death, and are enthralled by Henry V's rant before Harfleur or his injunction to his soldiers to imitate the action of the tiger. It can be because we all have stored up within ourselves so many unrequited wrongs and injuries, forgotten and unforgotten, and beneath these such an inheritance of racial revenge, that we like nothing better than to rid ourselves of a little of the accumulation by projecting it, in a crowd of persons similarly disposed, on the defenseless puppets of the dramatic imagination. There is no mystery about it. Anyone can follow the effect along his own backbone.

But if we are all repositories of racial revenge, we are also repositories of the rarer tendencies that over the centuries have resisted revenge. Against the contagion of a theater audience these ethereal forces have practically no chance, for in the crowd we are bound to take the play as drama rather than as poetry. But in solitude and in silence these forces are sure to lead a certain number of sensitive readers to shudder at the thought of Hamlet shedding blood. Let them express their revulsion, however, and instantly there will be someone to remind them that, whatever may be true now, "in those days" blood revenge was an accepted part of the moral code. As if Shakespeare were a historian and not a poet!

"Those days" never existed. They never existed poetically, I mean. No doubt the code of the vendetta has prevailed in many ages in many lands and revenge has been a favorite theme of the poets from Homer down. History itself, as William James remarked, has been a bath of blood. Yet there is a sense in which the dictum "Thou shalt not kill" has remained just as absolute in the kingdom of the imagination as in the

Mosaic law. Moralize bloodshed by custom, legalize it by the state, camouflage it by romance, and still to the finer side of human nature it is just bloodshed; and always where poetry has become purest and risen highest there has been some parting of Hector and Andromache, some lament of the Trojan women, to show that those very deeds of vengeance and martial glory that the poet himself is ostensibly glorifying have some-how failed to utter the last word. To utter that last word—or try to—is poetry's ultimate function, to defend man against his own brutality, against

> That monster, custom, who all sense doth eat,
> Of habits devil,

a much emended line-and-a-half of Hamlet that makes excellent sense exactly as it stands.

If Shakespeare was bent in this play on presenting the morality of a primitive time, why did he make the mistake of centering it around a man who in endowment is as far ahead of either the Elizabethan age or our own as the code of blood revenge is behind both? "The ultimate fact is," says J. M. Robertson, "that Shakespeare *could not* make a psychologically or otherwise consistent play out of a plot which retained a strictly bar-baric action while the hero was transformed into a supersubtle Eliza-bethan." *Hamlet*, the conclusion is, is a failure because the materials Shake-speare inherited were too tough and intractable. Too tough and intractable for what? That they were too tough and intractable for a credible histori-cal picture may be readily granted. But what of it? And since when was poetry supposed to defer to history? Two world wars in three decades ought to have taught us that our history has not gone deep enough. But poetry has. The greatest poetry has always depicted the world as a little citadel of nobility threatened by an immense barbarism, a flickering candle surrounded by infinite night. The "historical" impossibility of *Hamlet* is its poetical truth, and the paradox of its central figure is the universal psy-chology of man.

Yet, in the face of the correspondingly universal fascination that both the play and its hero have exercised, T. S. Eliot can write: "*Hamlet*, like the sonnets, is full of some stuff that the writer could not drag to light, contemplate, or manipulate into art. We must simply admit that here Shakespeare tackled a problem which proved too much for him. Why he attempted it at all is an insoluble enigma." In which case, why all this fuss over a play that failed? To reason as Eliot does is to indict the taste and intelligence of three centuries. If Hamlet is just a puzzle, why has the world not long since transferred its adulation to Fortinbras and Laertes?

They, at any rate, are clear. If action and revenge were what was wanted, they understood them. The trouble is that by no stretch of the imagination can we think of Shakespeare preferring their morality to that of his hero. They are living answers to the contention that Hamlet ought to have done what either of them, in his situation, would have done instantly. For what other purpose indeed did Shakespeare put them in than to make that plain?

But Hamlet himself, it will be said, accepts the code of blood revenge. Why should we question what one we so admire embraces with such unquestioning eagerness? With such *suspicious* eagerness might be closer to the mark. But waiving that for the moment, let us see what is involved in the assumption that Shakespeare thought it was Hamlet's duty to kill the King.

It involves nothing less than the retraction of all the Histories, of *Romeo and Juliet* and *Julius Caesar*. Private injury, domestic feud, civil revolution, imperialistic conquest: one by one in these plays Shakespeare had demonstrated how bloodshed invoked in their name brings on the very thing it was intended to avert, how, like seeds that propagate their own kind, force begets force and vengeance vengeance. And now in *Hamlet* Shakespeare is supposed to say: "I was wrong. I take it all back. Blood should be shed to avenge blood." And more incredible yet, we must picture him a year or two later taking his new opinion back and being reconverted in turn to his original conviction in *Othello, Macbeth, King Lear*, and the rest. If you find a term in a mathematical series fitting perfectly between what has gone before and what follows, you naturally assume it is in its right place, as you do a piece that fits into the surrounding pieces in a jigsaw puzzle. Only on the assumption that Hamlet ought not to have killed the King can the play be fitted into what then becomes the unbroken progression of Shakespeare's spiritual development. The only other way out of the difficulty for those who do not themselves believe in blood revenge is to hold that Shakespeare in *Hamlet* is an archeologist or anthropologist interested in the customs of primitive society rather than a poet concerned with the eternal problems of man.

### III

"But in that case why didn't Shakespeare make his intention clear?" A question that implies a profound misapprehension of the nature of poetic, if not of dramatic, art.

Of course Shakespeare expected his audience to assume that Hamlet should kill the King, exactly as he expected them to assume that Katharine was a shrew, and that Henry V was a glorious hero for attempting to steal the kingdom of France. He was not so ignorant of human nature as not to know how it reacts under the stimulus of primitive emotion. He understood too that what ought to be can be seen only against a background of what is. Carlyle spoke of the Paolo and Francesca incident in *The Inferno* as a thing woven of rainbows on a background of eternal black. And Hamlet himself declared:

> I'll be your foil, Laertes; in mine ignorance
> Your skill shall, like a star i' the darkest night,
> Stick fiery off indeed.

The contrast need not always be so extreme. The setting is more ordinarily terrestrial and diurnal than infernal, or even nocturnal. If, enthralled by its familiarity, we do not alter the focus of our eyes to see what may be unfamiliar and perhaps nearly invisible in the foreground, how is that the poet's fault? That is not his lookout. His business is to create a work of art. How it is taken is not his responsibility. "Here it is," he seems to say, as perhaps God did when he made the world, "take it, and see what you can make of it." And different men make very different things. To all of us in life appearances are deceitful. To all save the wisest characters in a work of dramatic art, if it be true to life, they should be even more so. The spectator or reader of that work takes delight in their delusions. But meanwhile from a higher level the poet may be deluding him. Living would lose all its challenge if everything were made so plain that anybody could understand it all the first time. And so would reading. You plunge into a poem as you plunge into battle—at your peril. "That which can be made explicit to the idiot," said Blake, "is not worth my care."

This procedure is not trickery. Even the alertest reader must be partly taken in the first time or he will miss more than he gains. A book that can be comprehended at a first reading is not imaginative literature. Dostoevsky's novels, for instance, contain many dreams and hallucinations which the reader is intended to mistake for occurrences in the objective world until, later, he realizes that the person having the experience was asleep or in a trance. That is as it should be. For dreams are true while they last, and Dostoevsky's technique leads us to identify ourselves with the dreamer. A too critical reader who sees through the device deprives himself of the very experience he would understand. Intellectuals cannot read. A child lost in a story is the model of right first reading. The more ingenuous we are the first time the better. But not the second and third times. Then the critical intellect should begin to check the imagination—or check on it rather. Shakespeare, I am convinced, wanted us at first to believe that Hamlet ought to kill the King in order that we might undergo his agony with him. But he did not want us, I am equally convinced, to persist in that belief. We must view Hamlet first under the aspect of time so that later we may view him under the aspect of eternity. We must be him before we can understand him.

And here, oddly, we have an advantage over Shakespeare. The author of *Hamlet*, when he wrote it, had not had the privilege of reading *King Lear* and other post-Hamletian masterpieces. But we have had it, and can read *Hamlet* in their light. This does not mean that we import into *Hamlet* from later plays anything that is not already there. A work of art must stand or fall by itself. It merely means that, with vision sharpened by later plays, we are enabled to see in *Hamlet* what was already there but hidden from us—as a later dream does not alter an earlier one but may render it intelligible because of a mutual relation. In some sense or other, as we have seen, Hamlet's problem must have been Shakespeare's. He doubtless wrote the play in part to make that problem clear, just as Tolstoy, to make his problem clear, wrote *Anna Karenina*. *Hamlet* being only a step in its solution, its author could not conceivably have caught its full import at once. But we can see, as later he could see, whither it was tending, as a prophecy is remembered and illuminated when it is fulfilled. However much above us Shakespeare may be in genius, at any particular moment in his development we are beyond him in time. To that extent we are on the mountain while he is on the road.

And even if we do not look beyond *Hamlet*, our vantage point enables us to see from the past the direction that road was taking. Roads, to be sure, may make unexpected turns, and even a long-maintained general course is no guarantee against its interruption. But highways of Shakespearean breadth seldom go off abruptly at right angles. And so it is permissible to ask as we come to *Hamlet*: What, judging from what he had been doing, might Shakespeare be expected to do next?

The answer is plain. Having given us in Hal-Henry (not to mention Romeo and Richard II) a divided man easily won by circumstances to the side of violence, and in Brutus a man so won only after a brief but terrible inner struggle, what then? Why, naturally, the next step in the progression: a divided man won to the side of violence only after a protracted struggle. And this is precisely what we have in Hamlet. Moreover, there is a passage in the play that confirms just this development. Indeed, as the word "development" suggests, a better metaphor than the road is the figure of an unfolding organism.

## IV

In the notes Dostoevsky made when composing *The Brothers Kara-mazov* there is one especially remarkable revelation: the fact that in its earliest stages the hero, who was to become Alyosha, is identified with the hero of a previous novel, *The Idiot*, being even called the Idiot by name. It shows how akin to the dream the creative faculty is—one character split-ting off from another. What was at first a vague differentiation ends as a distinct individual, but an individual always bearing traces of his origin, as traces of the parent can be found in the child and in the man.

Shakespeare is not Dostoevsky, and it is not likely that an early draft of *Hamlet* will ever be found in which the Prince's name is first set down as Brutus. Yet there is a bit of dialogue in the play as we have it that links the two almost as intimately as Alyosha is linked with Prince Myshkin. The passage is brief and apparently parenthetical. Shortly before the perform-ance of *The Murder of Gonzago*, Hamlet suddenly addresses Polonius:

HAM.: My lord, you played once i' the university, you say?
POL.: That did I, my lord, and was accounted a good actor.
HAM.: What did you enact?
POL.: I did enact Julius Caesar: I was killed i' the Capitol; Brutus killed me.
HAM.: It was a brute part of him to kill so capital a calf there.

It is interesting, to begin with, that Polonius was accounted a good actor in his youth. He has been playing a part ever since, until his mask has become a part of his face. The roles that men cast themselves for often reveal what they are and may prophesy what they will become. That Polonius acted Julius Caesar characterizes both men: Caesar, the synonym of imperialism, Polonius, the petty domestic despot—the very disparity of their kingdoms makes the comparison all the more illuminating.

But it is not just Caesar and Polonius. Brutus is mentioned too. And Brutus killed Caesar. In an hour or so Hamlet is to kill Polonius. If Polo-nius is Caesar, Hamlet is Brutus. This is the rehearsal of the deed. For to hate or scorn is to kill a little. "It was a brute part ... to kill so capital a calf there." The unconscious is an inveterate punster and in that "brute part" Hamlet passes judgment in advance on his own deed in his mother's cham-ber. Prophecy, rehearsal, judgment: was ever more packed into fewer words?* *Et tu*, Hamlet?

And it is not Brutus only who stands behind Hamlet. There is another behind him. And another behind *him*.

---

* A person interested in psychological symbols might find in "calf" an unconscious allusion to Ophelia, at whose feet Hamlet is to lie down a moment later and whom he

> A third is like the former. . . .
> . . . A fourth! start, eyes!
> What! will the line stretch out to the crack of doom?
> Another yet!

We need not follow it as far as did Macbeth to perceive that, as Hamlet listens to the spirit of his father, behind him are the ghosts of Brutus, Hal, and Romeo. "Beware, Hamlet," says Romeo, "my soul told me to embrace Juliet and with her all the Capulets. But my 'father' bade me kill Tybalt and carry on the hereditary quarrel. And I obeyed him." "Beware, Hamlet," says Hal, "my soul told me to hold fast to Falstaff's love of life. But, instead, I did what is expected of a king, rejected Falstaff, and following my dying father's advice, made war on France." "Beware, Hamlet," says Brutus, "Portia and my soul gave ample warning. But Cassius reminded me that there was once a Brutus who expelled a tyrant from Rome, and, in the name of 'our fathers,' tempted me to exceed him in virtue by killing one. And I did. Beware, Hamlet." Each of these men wanted to dedicate himself to life. Romeo wanted to love. Hal wanted to play. Brutus wanted to read philosophy. But in each case a commanding hand was placed on the man's shoulder that disputed the claim of life in the name of death. Romeo defied that command for a few hours, and then circumstances proved too strong for him. Hal evaded it for a while, and then capitulated utterly. Brutus tried to face the issue, with the result of civil war within himself. But death won. Brutus' suppressed compunctions, however, ejected themselves in the form of a ghost that, Delphically, was both Caesar and Brutus' own evil spirit, his reliance on force.

Hamlet is the next step. He is a man as much more spiritually gifted than Brutus as Brutus is than Hal. The story of Hamlet is the story of Hal over again, subtilized, amplified, with a different ending. The men themselves seem so unlike that the similarities of their situations and acts are obscured. Like Hal, Hamlet is a prince of charming quality who cares nothing at the outset for his royal prospects but is absorbed in playing and savoring life. Only with him it is playing in a higher sense: dramatic art, acting, and playwriting rather than roistering in taverns and perpetrating practical jokes. And, like all men genuinely devoted to art, he is deeply interested in philosophy and religion, drawing no sharp lines indeed be-

---

really kills in killing Polonius—just as Raskolnikov in *Crime and Punishment* kills the childlike Lizaveta in killing the Old Money Lender. Unlikely as this will sound to those who have never paid attention to the associative and prophetic ways of the unconscious mind, Shakespeare proves again and again that he is capable, exactly as dreams are, of just such psychological supersubtleties. Ophelia's life is sacrificed before it has reached maturity.

tween or among the three. Because he is himself an imaginative genius, he needs no Falstaff to spur him on. Hamlet is his own Falstaff.

Hamlet's father, like Hal's, was primarily concerned with war, and after death calls his son to a deed of violence, not to imperial conquest, as the elder Henry did, but to revenge. Like Hal, Hamlet accepts the injunction. But instead of initiating a change that gradually alters him into his father's likeness, the decision immediately shakes his being to its foundations. The "antic disposition" under which he hides his real design is an exaggerated counterpart of the "wildness" under which Hal had previously concealed his own political ambition—however much less selfish and better grounded Hamlet's deception was.

The far more shattering effect on Hamlet than on Hal or even on Brutus of the task he assumes shows how much more nearly balanced are the opposing forces in his case. Loyalty to his father and the desire to grow unto himself—thirst for revenge and thirst for creation—are in Hamlet almost in equilibrium, though of course he does not know it. Henry V was vaguely troubled by nocturnal stirrings of the spirit. He saw no ghost. Brutus became the victim of insomnia. He stifled his conscience by action and saw no ghost until after the deed. Hamlet saw his before the deed—as Brutus would have if his soul had been stronger—and it made night hideous for him. No spirit but one from below would have produced that effect, and the fact that "this fellow in the cellarage" speaks from under the platform when he echoes Hamlet's "swear" is in keeping with Shakespeare's frequent use of the symbolism that associates what is physically low with what is morally wrong. Hamlet's delay, then, instead of giving ground for condemnation, does him credit. It shows his soul is still alive and will not submit to the demands of the father without a struggle. If two forces pulling a body in opposite directions are unequal, the body will move in response to the preponderant force. If the two are nearly equal, but alternately gain slight ascendancy, it will remain unmoved except for corresponding vibrations. In a tug of war between evenly matched teams the rope at first is almost motionless, but ultimately the strength of one side ebbs and then the rope moves suddenly and violently. So mysterious, and no more, is Hamlet's hesitation, followed, as it finally was, by lightning-like action. "Shakespeare, as everyone knows," says Dover Wilson, "never furnishes an explanation for Hamlet's inaction." "No one knows," says Professor Alden, "why Hamlet delays." And many others have said the same. Yet Shakespeare puts in the mouth of Claudius words that seem expressly inserted to explain the riddle. The King, caught in the same way between opposing forces—desire to keep the fruits of his sin and desire to pray—declares:

> And, like a man to double business bound,
> I stand in pause where I shall first begin,
> And both neglect.

That seems plain enough. But what is true of Claudius in this one scene is true of Hamlet during all the earlier part of the play. It is as if his soul were a body in space so delicately poised between the gravitation of the earth and the gravitation, or we might say the levitation, of the sun that it "hesitates" whether to drop into the one or fly up to the other. It sometimes seems as if *Homo sapiens* were in just that situation.

People who think Shakespeare was just a playwright say Hamlet delayed that there might be a five-act play! Others, who calmly neglect much of the text, say he delayed because of external obstacles. Coleridge thinks it was because he thought too much. Bradley, because he was so melancholy.\* It would be nearer the truth to say he thought too much and was melancholy because he delayed. The more powerful an unconscious urge, the stronger and the more numerous the compensations and rationalizations with which consciousness attempts to fight it. Hence the excess of thought and feeling. Goethe, I would say, is far closer to the mark than Coleridge and Bradley in attributing Hamlet's hesitation to a feminine element in the man. But then he proceeds to spoil it all by implying that Hamlet is weak and effeminate: "a lovely, pure and most moral nature, without the strength of nerve that makes a hero, sinks beneath a burden which it cannot bear and must not cast away." The implication is that Hamlet ought to have killed the King at once; also that loveliness, purity, and moral insight are not sources of strength and heroism!

On the contrary, they are the very higher heroism that challenges a more primitive one in this play. Hamlet is the battlefield where the two meet. It is war in that psychological realm where all war begins. Hamlet is like Thermopylae, the battle that stands first among all battles in the human imagination because of its symbolic quality—a contest between the Persian hordes of the lower appetites and the little Greek band of heroic instincts.

---

\* I yield to no one in admiration of Bradley's *Shakespearean Tragedy* and indebtedness to it, but how little Bradley believes in his own theory of Hamlet is shown by the net of illogicality in which he entangles himself, a net that reminds one of the similar toils in which Henry V and Brutus get caught. On page 122 he says: "The action required of Hamlet is very exceptional. It is violent, dangerous, difficult to accomplish perfectly, on one side repulsive to a-man of honour and sensitive feeling. . . . These obstacles would not suffice to prevent Hamlet from acting, if his state were normal; and against them there operate, even in his morbid state, healthy and positive feelings, love of his father, loathing of his uncle, desire of revenge, desire to do his duty." Revenge, then, and loathing, are healthy and positive feelings; also, they are on one side repulsive to a man of honor and sensitive feeling! Nothing can be made of such an argument (A. C. Bradley, *Shakespearean Tragedy* [2d ed.; Macmillan, 1929]).

They have the numbers, we, the heights.

At Thermopylae the Persians won. Yet we think of it as a Greek victory because it was the promise of Salamis and Plataea. So with Hamlet. Hamlet lost. But *Hamlet* is the promise of *Othello* and *King Lear*.

## V

Is it the death of Hamlet's father or the marriage of his mother that has plunged their son into the depressed state in which we find him at the opening of the play? Obviously the two are too closely associated in his mind to permit their separation. One is the seed, the other is the soil, of all that follows.

Freud made the suggestion that the killing of the Elder Hamlet and the marriage of the murderer with Hamlet's mother were realizations of Hamlet's own repressed childish wishes. His condition when the action begins would be accounted for, then, by the workings of incestuous fantasy. And later, when he learns of the murder from the Ghost, the nephew cannot kill the uncle because he recognizes in him the image of his own desire. Dr. Ernest Jones has written an extended interpretation of the play founded on these ideas.*

"*The main theme of this story,*" says Dr. Jones, summing up his thesis in italics, "*is a highly elaborated and disguised account of a boy's love for his mother and consequent jealousy of and hatred towards his father.*" Whatever truth there may be in this view, it is certainly superfluous to posit any such pathological love to account for Hamlet's state of mind when the play opens. His father has died under mysterious circumstances, so mysterious that when the Ghost reveals the murder Hamlet cries, "O my prophetic soul!" as if he had already suspected the guilt of his uncle, an exclamation that immediately reminds us of his earlier:

> I doubt some foul play: would the night were come!
> Till then sit still, my soul: foul deeds will rise,
> Though all the earth o'erwhelm them, to men's eyes.

Before Hamlet has had time to recover from the shock of his father's death, his mother, with unseemly haste, marries his uncle. Even without the stigma of incest which such a union then carried, the impact of this disaster on top of the other is enough to explain the disillusionment and near-suicidal mood of a youth as sensitive as Hamlet, a son as devoted to

---

* I had not read Dr. Jones's essay when I wrote the present chapter. Apart from its intrinsic interest, the fact that the Rank-Olivier cinema production of the play has spread this conception far and wide justifies inserting a section on the subject at this point. The discussion will then be resumed as originally written.

his mother. Stunned by the double blow, he is halted dead in his tracks. Blocked by the double obstruction, his life energy flows backward and floods his mind with images of disintegration and death. If it is not sustained too long, there is nothing morbid in such a reaction. Who would have had as rare a man as Hamlet take these things casually or callously, or even stoically—not to mention taking them pugnaciously as Laertes and Fortinbras took the deaths of their fathers? All we know of what Hamlet was before his father's murder suggests that any abnormality in the man was on the side of genius and the future rather than on that of degeneracy and the past. That prolongation of "infancy" which is the special mark and glory of human nature (as Shakespeare himself shows in *Venus and Adonis*) is at the opposite pole from that pathological reversion to infancy that is a sign of the Oedipus complex. How many a genius has owed to a love of his mother preservation from too early initiation into sexual experience. This may well have been the case with Hamlet. But that his attachment to his mother was neither too strong nor too prolonged is indicated, first, by his friendship with Horatio, and second, by his falling in love with Ophelia—a girl of very different temperament from his mother—apparently at just the right time. If Hamlet had been a victim of the Oedipus complex, and the play a highly elaborated and disguised account of a boy's love for his mother, such a transference of his affections would have been unthinkable.

But the trouble with the psychoanalytic interpretation of *Hamlet* lies not so much in what it includes as in what it omits. What would we think of a study of *Romeo and Juliet* that traced everything in the play to the hereditary quarrel between the two houses? Every statement in such an analysis might be correct *as far as it went*, yet it would be destined in advance to miss the secret of the play because it would leave out the love of Romeo and Juliet as an autonomous and creative flame. The same is true of an analysis of *Hamlet* that makes an even more extreme sacrifice of the present and future to the past, that traces everything to the hero's infantile fantasies and has nothing to say of his imagination. The players and the play within the play figure scarcely at all in Jones's interpretation of the drama. But they are the heart of the whole matter. As well write a biography of Shakespeare and leave out his interest in dramatic art! It is like trying to explain the earth without taking the sun into account.

Here is the greatest character in all literature—or so at least many have called him. Here is the Shakespearean character who most resembles Shakespeare, the only one, as Bradley has observed, whom we can conceive of as the author of Shakespeare's plays. But to Freudian analysis all that is apparently nothing. And when it has done its probing work what is revealed? Not a genius who made an effort to transcend the morality of his time with thoughts beyond the reaches of his soul, but a mind reduced to its most infantile impulses, a body pushed about by the most primitive biological drives.

That these drives are present deep down in Hamlet as they are in all of us need not be denied. That Hamlet was ultimately overthrown by his instincts may not only be granted but should be insisted on. But the fact of interest is that he was conquered only after a protracted struggle. About this the Freudians have practically nothing to say. Jones does indeed speak of Hamlet's "desperate struggle" against Fate. But when we search his essay for an account of that struggle it turns out to be nothing but the struggle of a trapped animal. Hamlet's dramatic battle, which is a symbolic embodiment of the perennial attempt of life, in the face of the forces that would drag it backward, to ascend to a higher level, the Freudian interpretation reduces to nothing but the picture of a man foredoomed to destruction. If this be so, *Hamlet* may indeed be a supreme treatise on pathology. But it is no longer drama, let alone poetry.

Lucifer is the archetype of all tragic heroes. He fell. The fascination of his fate lies not in the fact that he fell, but in the fact that he who fell was the light-bearer—that his light, before he fell, was transformed into pride. What he did in hell is significant only because he was once an inhabitant of heaven. So with all tragic heroes. So with Hamlet. He too was a light-bearer ("in action how like an angel! in apprehension how like a god!"). His mind was focused on philosophy, on religion, and on art—regions into which something that stands above and is wiser than physical life has long been trying to channel the blind urgencies of selfish will and sex. Is it not immeasurably more in keeping with the character of such a man to attribute his aversion to sensuality and blood to these loftier aspirations of his soul than to primordial and atavistic instincts—to believe that he drew back from the killing of his uncle because he did not want to degrade himself to his level by becoming a murderer than to think he hesitated because he saw in him an image of his own incestuous fantasies?

It has been argued that if repugnance to the act of killing had been the ground of Hamlet's hesitation he would have been conscious of the reason for his delay.* But this is to forget the atmospheric pressure to which his mind was subjected. New moralities do not spring into existence in the face of intrenched custom in full-fledged conscious and conceptual form. They begin in dumb feelings around the heart ("thou wouldst not think how ill all's here about my heart") and in momentary gleams of the imagination.

* Ivan Karamazov is an example of a man of high intellectual power who thought he believed in just what he really didn't believe in.

What person of any sensitiveness looking back on his childhood cannot remember some occasion when he conformed to the morality of the crowd against the un-understood protests of what only long after he recognized was his own higher nature—or when possibly he did *not* conform, but instead of taking pride in what was an act of courage lashed himself inwardly for what he supposed was abject cowardice? Hamlet was like that. If he was indeed trying to repudiate the morals of his herd, it is absurd to suppose that he opposed to them a clear-cut moral theory of his own. What he opposed to them was a combined imaginative courage and unconscious compassion that embrace the strongest and the tenderest elements of his nature.

To the Freudians, Hamlet's hesitation comes from a literal jealousy of his father and a literal love of his mother. He wants to kill his uncle because he recognizes him as a rival for the possession of his mother. But he also does not want to kill him, because he recognizes in him an image of his own desire. Hence he hesitates. But one can argue just as cogently that Hamlet wants to kill his uncle because he has murdered the father whom Hamlet as a youth has idealized and loved. But also he does not want to kill him, because he would thereby be converting himself into an image of the father whose life was dedicated to violence and whom he therefore unconsciously hates—and at the same time into an image of his murderer-uncle. Hence he hesitates. Logically the one argument is as good as the other. But poetically and pragmatically there is simply no comparison between them, so much more creative and enlightening is the second. When the facts of a dream make it susceptible of either of two interpretations, how foolish the dreamer would be not to believe the one that makes for the richer unfolding of his own life. Our choice between two interpretations of a work of art, provided they are equally faithful to the text, should be similarly determined.

How much more illuminating to translate all this about Hamlet's "love" and "hatred," about his "father" and "mother," from crudely sexual into symbolic terms, thus giving the future as well as the past a share in their meaning. Hamlet's "mother" is then on one side his creativeness (for whoever gives birth to new life, as the artist does, is a mother) and on the other side his sensuality. The one he loves; the other he loathes. We see him in the play fluctuating between the two. And he responds in a similarly ambivalent way to his two "fathers." One, his sun and the source of his inspiration, is the product of that idealization of the older generation by the younger which ensures the continuity and, in so far as it is justified, the uplifting of life. This father Hamlet worships. The other is a type of that authority and violence that the racial father always represents and that his own father as renowned warrior (pirate in the original version) specifically incarnates. This father, however unconsciously, Hamlet abhors.

A full half of this picture the Freudian interpretation calmly omits. To it the dice are perpetually loaded on the side of the past. To it the flower is nothing but a differentiated root, and the tragic mysteries of Hamlet nothing but his infantile fantasies in disguise. What a "nothing but"! Echoing it, we may well say that a psychology that is contented with it is "nothing but" the last variation of that ancient and mildewed view that would make the universe itself "nothing but" a vortex of atoms. "Look you, this brave o'erhanging firmament, this majestical roof fretted with golden fire, why, it appears no other thing to me but a foul and pestilent congregation of vapours." There is Hamlet himself in a "nothing but" mood! But it is nothing but a fragment of Hamlet! It is Hamlet at his most abject, the Hamlet who went on down into Macbeth with his ultimate belief that life is nothing but a tale told by an idiot, full of sound and fury, signifying nothing. So is the Freudian interpretation of *Hamlet Hamlet* at its most abject. It is a reduction of the tremendous battle between spirit and the instincts, wherein the drama of life consists, to the spectacle of the mere writhings of a predestined victim.

If there is any truth in all this, it is as if Hamlet, of all characters in literature, were specifically created *not* to be understood by the Freudian psychology. For the things closest to Hamlet's heart are precisely the ones that Freud dismisses as mere by-products of the evolutionary process. Art, Freud declares, "does not seek to be anything else but an illusion." Philosophy is an interest of only a small number of "the thin upper stratum of intellectuals." Religion is nothing but an attempt to replace reality by a wish-world: "the truth of religion may be altogether disregarded." So are Laotse and Jesus, Plato and Aristotle, Homer and Dante, Michelangelo and Rembrandt, Bach and Beethoven wiped off the slate, as it were, in a single stroke. Talk about substituting a wish-world for reality! If Hamlet could have heard, would he not have exclaimed

> There are more things in heaven and earth, dear Sigmund,
> Than are dreamt of in your psychology.

"Shakespeare is a great psychologist," said Goethe, "and whatever can be known of the heart of man may be found in his plays." Yet the Freudians would have it that this great psychologist was unaware of the main meaning of what not a few consider his greatest play, that he projected that meaning on his material because of some hidden analogy in it to a situation in his own life. If this be so, we shall be compelled to ask whether Shakespeare himself was not mad. If this be so, we shall be put to it to explain *Coriolanus*—one of the most searching and obviously conscious accounts in all literature of a son under the unduly prolonged influence of his mother. And *Coriolanus* is not the only play that makes us wonder whether Shakespeare, though he had never heard of the super-ego and the id, may not have known as much in his own way about the deeper strata of the human mind as Freud himself. It is the familiar confusion of terminology with knowledge—a confusion that makes each age think it has discovered the truth for the first time because it has a new nomenclature in which to dress it. The unconsciousness of ignorance must be discriminated from the unconsciousness of genius, the unconsciousness of deficient mind, of which there is not a trace in Shakespeare, from the unconsciousness of superabundant imagination in which he abounds. It was in that latter unconsciousness indeed that Thoreau found the heart of the "Shakespeare miracle." If Shakespeare did not know what he was doing in *Hamlet*, we would at least like to know what he thought he was doing, and, even more, what his imagination *was* doing.

## VI

Commentators have in general been at one with the naïve reader in taking the picture Hamlet draws of his father for fact. But if it be fact, then the Elder Hamlet was a paragon of virtue indeed, embracing both in outward form and inward temper all noble qualities, human and divine:

> Where every god did seem to set his seal,

Hyperion, Jove, Mars, Mercury—glorious as the sun in appearance, dreadful as a thunderbolt in battle, gentle as a dove in love. If the portrait is faithful, it is more than ever inexplicable how Gertrude could so easily discard such a miracle of manhood and take up, in the latter's phrase, such a mess of garbage as his brother. She must have been as much an incarnation of folly as he was of valor.

Yet the Elder Hamlet, as ghost at any rate, in spite of his egotism, has no such notion of his own perfection:

> I am thy father's spirit,
> Doom'd for a certain term to walk the night,
> And for the day confin'd to fast in fires,
> *Till the foul crimes done in my days of nature*
> Are burnt and purg'd away.

We wonder what those foul crimes of this man-god were. "Foul," in fact, seems to have been a favorite word of the Ghost's, as it was of Hamlet's (a tiny link of perhaps deep significance):

> List, list, O list!
> If thou didst ever thy dear father love— . . .
> Revenge his foul and most unnatural murder. . . .
> Murder most foul, as in the best it is;
> But this most foul, strange, and unnatural.

Foul, foul, foul! The reiteration is curious, to say the least. The Ghost pronounces his own murder foul. He begs his son to kill his murderer, an act which, since it is revenge, is presumably killing at its least reprehensible level. But killing is killing, if it be wilful, no matter on what level, and whether or not it is denominated "murder." And so, without intending it, the Ghost pronounces "most foul" even the act he is urging on his son: "most foul, *as in the best it is!*" That "as in the best it is" looks like a logical slip on the Ghost's part. Slip it unquestionably is, and it reveals in a flash the state of Hamlet's mind. For, whatever else or more the Ghost may be, the facet of himself he here presents to his son matches exactly the projection of a like facet of Hamlet's unconscious mind, and that "as in the best it is" lets escape the fatal doubt he harbors about the whole business.

> Haste me to know't, that I, *with wings as swift*
> *As meditation or the thoughts of love,*
> May sweep to my revenge.

Wings, meditation, love: what inappropriate equipment for a deed of blood! As so often in Shakespeare, the metaphors undo the logic and tell the truth over its head.

This scene is permeated from end to end with this Janus-like quality, these symptoms of the divided mind. The Ghost one moment calls himself (by inference) "a radiant angel" and his brother "garbage" and the next moment he is complaining that his murderer cut him off "even in the blossoms of my sin," with no chance for confession, "with all my imperfections on my head." We remember, too, Horatio's "And then it started like a guilty thing," and Hamlet's astonishing admission—or slip—in the prayer scene:

> He took my father grossly, full of bread,
> With all his crimes broad blown, as flush as May.

Foul crimes, all his crimes, blossoms of sin, a host of imperfections: how out of keeping with a radiant angel! "Hyperion"—"satyr," says Hamlet comparing the two brothers before he has even seen the Ghost. "Radiant angel"—"garbage," says the Ghost, as if he were echoing him. "A form indeed Where every god did seem to set his seal"—"a mildew'd ear," says Hamlet, later, as if he were echoing the echo. The very accent is the same.

Plainly the contradictions of the Ghost are the doubts in Hamlet's own mind, and the fanatically ideal portrait he draws of his father, based though it may be on his boyish ideal, is his attempt to push the weight far out on the conscious side to counterbalance the deep distrust on the unconscious side. The principle of the lever enables us to estimate almost mathematically the heaviness of the doubts by the intensity, and even more the tone, of the superlatives. Indeed, when we come to think of it, what reason had this young lover of philosophy and art (courtier and soldier though he was as Prince) for falling into such rhapsodies of admiration over this warrior-father, who, so far as the record goes, except for a little love-making, over-eating, and sleeping, never did anything but fight?

And so, the moment we forget Hamlet's picture of his father, we frame a very different one. There are few things more significant in the saga from which *Hamlet* ultimately derives than the fact that the father of Hamlet was "a most notorious pirate."* Every reference to him in the opening scenes suggests a man whose life is dedicated to warfare: he is "our valiant Hamlet" to the whole Danish world; we have glimpses of his "fair and war-like form," his "solemn march," his "martial stalk," his armor, "the very armour he had on When he the ambitious Norway combated," his frown like that he wore "When, in an angry parle, He smote the sledded Polacks"—or poleaxe—"on the ice." And he comes in this same garb after death. "Armed at points exactly, cap-a-pe," says Horatio, describing the visitant he has seen:

| | |
|---|---|
| HAM.: | Arm'd, say you? |
| MAR. AND BER.: | Arm'd, my lord. |
| HAM.: | From top to toe? |
| MAR. AND BER.: | My lord, from head to foot. |

When the others retire, Hamlet exclaims:

> My father's spirit in arms! all is not well,

and later, when that spirit appears to him:

> What may this mean,
> That thou, dead corse, *again in complete steel*
> Revisit'st thus the glimpses of the moon,

and so on. Medieval armor was uncomfortable enough for a man dressed in his own flesh and bones. But for a ghost! Nothing could make clearer the fact that this is the spirit of War itself.

---

* Perhaps the hereditary wheel comes full circle when this "pirate's" son returns to Denmark for the last time on a pirate ship after agreeing to do the pirates a good turn. It would be like Shakespeare to intend symbolism here.

## VII

Critics and readers of *Hamlet* who lean toward what they call a psychological, but what is really a subjective, interpretation of the Ghost are puzzled by the fact that he appears to Horatio, Marcellus, and Bernardo in the opening scene and not just to Hamlet, as he does later.

But there is a reason for this. The kingdom is feverishly preparing for war. The Elder Hamlet had once upon a time conquered and slain Fortinbras of Norway, who, according to previous agreement, forfeited all his lands to Hamlet with his life. And now his son, young Fortinbras, threatens to retake what he considers his stolen inheritance. (The parallelism with the younger Hamlet's story is obvious.) But the new Danish King is more interested in feasting and sensuality than in war. War from abroad, sensuality at home: the realm stands between these dangers as certainly as the Earth moves between Venus and Mars. What wonder if at such an hour the threatened kingdom thinks of the Old King and longs for him as the English nobles under Henry VI longed for his dead father when France threatened retaliation; or that the spirit of the Old King, if it is still extant, thinks of his menaced country and longs to help it. His spirit alone can save it. In time of war men's imaginations revert to the martial history of their race and nation. They see what they need—as the English saw the Angel of Mons and reported a Russian army on British soil in August 1914, or as the Finns saw a cross in the clouds during their war with Russia. It was the most natural thing in the world that these men on the platform at Elsinore should have had a common nocturnal visitation. All men are likely to see ghosts at the threat of an invasion.

But it is not the public trouble that troubles Hamlet, though, in another sense, he stands under the same shadows of sensuality and violence. His is, relatively, a personal concern. So he must have a private conference with the Ghost. If to the state the Elder Hamlet comes as the spirit that will inspire his countrymen to resist the invader with war, to his son he comes as the spirit that will instigate him to kill the King who has stolen his inheritance. It is a nice point of nemesis that the dead King has himself "taken" the inheritance of Fortinbras. According to the code of the day it had been in fair fight. And fair fight certainly has its points of difference from surreptitious murder. Nevertheless, Shakespeare is plainly up to his old game of comparisons. He has an inveterate habit of detecting analogies between war and murder.

And just as Hamlet's father is the symbol of physical force, so his mother has now become in his mind the symbol of sensuality. Hamlet is the child of violence and lust. Racially, we all are. And Claudius, murderer-lover, is the link between the two. Could Shakespeare say more plainly that war and murder are brothers and that murder and lust are wedded to each other? Such is the parabolic scheme on which the action is based. Here we are close to the imaginative heart of *Hamlet*.

But to return to the Ghost.

Dawn approaches, and with a warning to his son to leave his mother to heaven and the stings of her own conscience, he vanishes with an "Adieu, adieu! Hamlet, remember me."

> O all you host of heaven! O earth! what else?
> And shall I couple hell?

cries the Prince, and vows by all those powers to remember nothing else.

Why, then (to revert to a postponed question), if Hamlet is doubtful about the deed to which the Ghost calls him, does he embrace his mission with such furious joy? For the same reason, of course, that he exaggerates the virtues of his father under the pressure of unadmitted doubts. In the depths of his nature, or rather on its heights, there are forces making against revenge. Hence the conscious forces of revenge must exert themselves instantly and to their limit lest they be defeated before they are mobilized.*

> Remember thee!
> Ay, thou poor ghost, while memory holds a seat
> In this distracted globe.

Distracted. Exactly! Thus in a single adjective or stray phrase the truth escapes. The Avenging Hamlet says he will make his mind a blank sheet of paper for everything but revenge:

> Yea, from the table of my memory
> I'll wipe away all trivial fond records,
> All saws of books, all forms, all pressures past,
> That youth and observation copied there,

but a moment later the Philosophic Hamlet is whipping out his notebook to write down one of those very saws, those very observations:

> That one may smile, and smile, and be a villain.

---

* On page 100 (*op. cit.*) Bradley says of the prayer scene: "The reason Hamlet gives himself for sparing the King is that, if he kills him now, he will send him to heaven, whereas he desires to send him to hell. Now, this reason may be an unconscious excuse, but is it believable that, if the real reason had been the stirrings of his deeper conscience, *that* could have masked itself in the form of a desire to send his enemy's soul to hell? Is not the idea quite ludicrous?" The idea is neither ludicrous nor unbelievable. Quite the contrary. Bradley forgets that this is a case where it is consciousness, not unconsciousness, that does the masking. Hamlet *thinks* he wants to kill the King, but he *feels* an impulse to spare him. His consciousness must explain the delay. Hence the rationalization.

"Now to my word," he cries as he puts up his tables. Why "word"? Why not, "now to my deed"? Because two Hamlets speak in one in an unconscious pun. By "now to my word" Hamlet thinks he means "now to my promise." But the Other Hamlet means "now to the world of words, the world of thought in contrast to the world of blood." Puns have been called the lowest form of wit. They do come, not infrequently, from the profoundest region of the mind.

Horatio and Marcellus enter, and Hamlet is torn between a desire to tell and the necessity not to tell. "There's ne'er a villain dwelling in all Denmark—," he begins boldly. "But he's an arrant knave," he ends ignominiously.

> There needs no ghost, my lord, come from the grave,
> To tell us this,

Horatio retorts, and Hamlet extricates himself in a speech that has the very accent of Polonius in one of his inaner moments.

> These are but wild and whirling words, my Lord,

says Horatio. It must have been at that instant that the idea of assuming an antic disposition flashed over Hamlet. How often there would be moments in the future when, as now, he would be forced to cover his real feelings with whatever happened to come to his lips! What a resource if he could pretend to be mad! A safety valve, it has been called. Yet some critics with more learning than psychology accuse Shakespeare of taking over this feature of his story from his source without properly motivating it. "It is just like one of us," I heard a young reader of the play remark, "when we say we 'want to scream'—only we don't. Hamlet assumed his antic disposition and under cover of it could scream all he wanted—and thus get rid of some of his nervous hysteria." That is well put. And the laughter the wild words would evoke would be as useful as the wildness itself. Whoever has put on hilarity to hide a sad heart will understand. But the device was as dangerous as it was inspired. For the mockery of insanity differs by a hairline only from the thing it mocks. It is perilous to release the brakes when going downhill, even in fun. It is generally easy to distinguish the passages where Hamlet deliberately puts on his antic disposition, as when he is teasing Polonius, from those where some demonic power quite beyond his control boils over from inside him, as in Ophelia's grave. But the one blends imperceptibly into the other.

Hamlet proposes an oath of secrecy to his friends, and we remember Brutus' words,

> unto bad causes swear
> Such creatures as men doubt.

And every time Hamlet says, "Swear by my sword," the Ghost, below, echoes, "Swear." Why, if it is a good ghost, should Hamlet not like to have him "underwrite" the proceedings, as it were? But the Other Hamlet knows it is a bad ghost, and, trying to get away from him, cries the first time, "then we'll shift our ground," and the second, "once more remove," but the third time he gives it up and lets the Ghost collaborate. This little scene is a prophecy and microcosm of the rest of the action. Hamlet's delay is a perpetual shifting of ground in an attempt to get away from the Ghost. But in the end the Ghost has his way.

## VIII

From the moment when Hamlet cries:

> The time is out of joint; O cursed spite,
> That ever I was born to set it right!

he becomes an example, unequalled in modern literature until Dostoevsky, of the Divided Man. "God and the Devil are fighting there, and the battle-field is the heart of man." That sentence of Dmitri Karamazov's expresses it, and because the infernal and celestial powers that are contending for the possession of Hamlet are so nearly in balance, the torture is prolonged and exquisite. He alternates between phases of anguished thought and feverish activity. Hence, as the one mood or the other is stressed, the opposing theories of his character. Hamlet is like a drunken man and you cannot determine where he is going from his direction at any one moment. He lurches now to the right, now to the left. He staggers from passion to apathy, from daring to despair. To select his melancholy as the key to his conduct, as Bradley does, is to offer the drunkard's fall as an explanation of his drunkenness. It is taking the effect for the cause, or fooling one's self, as Polonius did, with a word:

> Your noble son is mad:
> Mad call I it; for, to define true madness,
> What is't but to be nothing else but mad?
> But let that go.

Shakespeare is content with no such solution. To him melancholy is a symptom. He insists on getting under it to the cause that makes his melancholy characters melancholy.

Shakespeare dissects the cases of two such men, Richard II and Antonio, at length, two others, Jaques and Orsino, more briefly, and gives us a glimpse into the melancholy stage of still another, Brutus. Melancholy, he concludes in all these instances, is a sign that a man is living or trying to live a miscast, partial, or obstructed life—is functioning far under his capacity or against the grain of his nature. Richard II was a poetic soul attempting to enact a royal role. Antonio was a man made for better things who dedicated his life to trade. In *As You Like It* and *Twelfth Night* the record is not so complete, but it is sufficient. Jaques was a philosophic nature that had wasted itself in sensuality, Orsino an artistically gifted person who led an idle life. Brutus stifled his melancholy in action. He was a rare man who reverted to what any common ruffian can do—stab with a knife. There is no resisting so many instances.

Does the same diagnosis fit Hamlet? Obviously it does.

If these others were exceptional, Hamlet was as much one man among millions as Shakespeare was. He had precisely Shakespeare's interest in acting, playmaking, and drama. What if Shakespeare had turned from writing *Hamlets* and *King Lears* to go to war like Essex, or, like Hamlet, to run his rapier through an old man behind a curtain! What if Beethoven had fought with Napoleon instead of composing the *Eroica!* That, *mutatis mutandis*, is what Hamlet did. He did not know it. But his soul supplied plenty of evidence to that effect, if only he had had the power to read it.

We all hate in others the faults of which we are unaware in ourselves. And men of high endowment who are not doing what nature made them for exhibit this tendency in conspicuous degree.

> He that is giddy thinks the world turns round.

In that line Shakespeare caught in a striking image this propensity of the mind to project its unconscious contents. As early as *The Rape of Lucrece* he had written:

> Men's faults do seldom to themselves appear;
> Their own transgressions partially they smother:
> This guilt would seem death-worthy in thy brother,

and in the 121st sonnet:

> No, I am that I am, and they that level
> At my abuses reckon up their own:
> I may be straight, though they themselves be bevel;
> By their rank thoughts my deeds must not be shown.

Plainly Shakespeare had not merely observed this psychological effect in isolated instances. He understood it as a principle.

Now the moment we put Hamlet to this test we perceive that those around him become looking glasses in which, unknown to himself, his secret is reflected. (And this is particularly fitting in a work through which the symbol of the looking glass runs like a leitmotiv and whose central scene consists in the holding-up of a dramatic mirror in the form of a play within the play.)

To begin with, because Hamlet is trying to force himself to obey orders from his father to do something that his soul abhors, he hates with equal detestation those who issue orders and those who obey them, particularly fathers and children. This is plainly a main reason why Shakespeare allots to Polonius and his family so important a part in the play. Each of them seems expressly created to act as a mirror of some aspect of Hamlet. Polonius is a domestic tyrant wreaking on his son and his daughter revenge for his own spoiled life. His wife is dead, and except for one unrevealing allusion by her son, we are told nothing about her. Yet there she is! How she lived and what she died of we can readily imagine. As for Laertes, governments that want pugnacity in the younger generation should study his upbringing and act accordingly. But Ophelia is different. She is one more inexplicable daughter of her father (there are so many in Shakespeare). She is a mere child, just awakening into womanhood, and she unquestionably gives a true account of Hamlet's honorable "tenders of affection" to her. But Polonius fancies that Hamlet must be what he himself was at the same age ("I do know") and in the scene in which we are first introduced to Ophelia we see first Laertes, aping his father, and then Polonius himself, pouring poison in her ear. Both brother and father fasten on her like insects on an opening rosebud.

> Who plucks the bud before one leaf put forth?

It is like an echo of *Venus and Adonis* with the sexes reversed, the first step on the journey of which Ophelia's madness and death are the last. "Do not believe his vows." "I shall obey, my lord."

Who can doubt—what juxtapositions Shakespeare achieves!—that this scene was written to be placed just before the one between Hamlet and the Ghost? There another father pours poison of another kind into the ear of a son as innocent in his way as Polonius' daughter was in hers. The temptation this time is not to sensuality under the name of purity but to violence under the name of honor. It is Romeo's temptation as contrasted with Juliet's. The parallel is startling.

We tend to hate anyone we obey against the grain of our nature. "I'll shoot you!" says the small boy to his father, giving vent to his instincts. But after childhood, when anyone we love exacts obedience, unless we can forgive we suppress the hatred and to that extent become divided within. ("Who does not desire to kill his father?" says Ivan Karamazov.) Hamlet knows that he loved his father when he was alive. He does not know how he abhors that father when, dead, he orders him to kill. But any despotism is a kind of killing, and so he projects his abhorrence on another father who exacts obedience. How otherwise can we account for Hamlet's treatment of Polonius? After all, he was the father of the girl Hamlet loved. Stupidity and morality, it may be said, are always fair game for intelligence and virtue. And when Hamlet begins to suspect the father's part in the daughter's infidelity, it is easy to see how he could come to hate him. But even this does not explain the rattlesnake-like venom with which he strikes the old man at every opportunity. As in the case of Antonio's loathing of Shylock, only buried forces that Hamlet does not comprehend can account for it. Hamlet thinks he is pillorying Polonius, when, really, his insults are directed at the Ghost and himself, just as, later, he kills Polonius with the sword he thinks he is thrusting at the King. Scorn is a diluted form of murder.

Take one example. Hamlet has urged Guildenstern to play upon a pipe. Guildenstern has begged off: "I have not the skill." Whereupon Hamlet rebukes him for trying to make *him* a pipe to be played on. Polonius enters, and Hamlet proceeds to show how easily this yes-man can be played on by getting him to admit, in quick succession, that the same cloud resembles now a camel, now a weasel, and now a whale. Since the cloud doubtless resembled none of the three in any marked degree, what Hamlet pretended to see in it was the result of free association on his part. But free association is a basic method of modern analytical psychology for bringing to the surface the contents of the unconscious mind. A camel, a weasel, and a whale! A camel—the beast that bears burdens. A weasel—an animal noted for its combined wiliness and ferocity and for the fact that it can capture and kill snakes (remember the royal serpent!). A whale—a mammal that *returned to a lower element* and so still has to come to the surface of it occasionally for air, not a land creature, to be sure, nor yet quite a sea creature. What an astonishing essay on Hamlet in three words! (It is things like these that tempt one at moments to think that Shakespeare *was* omniscient.) This Prince piped on Polonius by his gibing experiment. What or who was piping upon him?

But Hamlet reads his own experience into Ophelia as well as into Polonius. Only in this case he knows what he is doing—up to a certain point. As unconsciously he sees the image of his father in the father, so consciously he sees the image of his mother in the daughter. That mother was false to his father. That daughter, he suspects, is false to him—if not in just the same sense. "Frailty, thy name is woman!" But Ophelia is not even a frail woman. She is still a child who obeys her father. She and Hamlet are two children who dare not trust the instinct to disobey. But this analogy he does not catch. And so, while he heaps conscious scorn on her for being like his mother, the unconscious scorn he heaps on her for being like himself is far more bitter. Read in this light, the nunnery scene is a revelation —not of Ophelia's but of Hamlet's soul. "I have heard of your paintings too, well enough; God hath given you one face, and you make yourselves another." There in a sentence is Hamlet's perfect indictment of himself for betraying the God within him (a reason why a main theme of this scene is prostitution). For who has made himself another face than the one God gave him if not this man who has put on an antic disposition to hide his revenge? His fierce onslaught on woman in general in this scene is motivated by his perfidy to the feminine element in his own nature. "Your everlasting attacks on female logic, lying, weakness and so on—doesn't it all look like a desire at all costs to force woman down into the mud that she may be on the same level as your attitude toward her?" The quotation is from Chekhov's *An Anonymous Story*, but it fits the nunnery scene as if it had been written about it.

Now all this only re-enforces what of course goes without saying: that Hamlet's treatment of Ophelia is profoundly affected by his attitude toward his mother. But for Gertrude's infidelity all might have been well— in spite of Polonius. Because of that infidelity, Hamlet's ideal of woman totters. And when Ophelia fails him, it falls. Deprived of its object, unless it can immediately find another, a love that believes itself deluded tends to revert to lust or violence, or both. Hamlet was no fickle lover to find another Ophelia overnight. And so he sinks into his instinctive nature. It is only in this generic sense that Hamlet loves his "mother" abnormally, a "loves" that might more accurately be written "loathes." His self-loathing is conspicuous not only in the nunnery scene, but in his conduct toward Ophelia at the play, and in the scene in his mother's closet. His "Get thee to a nunnery!" is a cry to his own polluted soul to purify itself, or, if "nunnery" be taken in its jocose Elizabethan sense, his notice to that soul that it is lost. His words to Ophelia at the play grate on the ear as do no others in his entire role. That Hamlet should descend to the level of Laertes is bad enough. But he goes below it. Here he actually pushes Ophelia toward the abyss of madness and the grave. It is from his coarsest utterance to her that Shakespeare has him pass instantaneously to his command to the murderer (Lucianus) to "begin." From sensuality to blood. And it is from Ophelia's side, when the play is broken up, that he goes to his mother's closet to brand her for an act that

> takes off the rose
> From the fair forehead of an innocent love
> And sets a blister there,

a perfect description of what he himself has just done, and enough in itself
to show that his excoriations of his mother in this scene are unconscious
denunciations of himself. (Of that more in its place.) What soil all this is
for the seed of violence! Shakespeare seems to have agreed with Dostoevsky that "a cruel sensuality" is close to the fountainhead of all human evil
whatsoever. It is "the expense of spirit in a waste of shame" of the 129th
sonnet, that scorching poem that packs into fourteen lines all the poet had
had to say on the subject in *Venus and Adonis* and *The Rape of Lucrece:*\*

> perjur'd, murderous, bloody, full of blame,
> Savage, extreme, rude, cruel, not to trust.

The adjectives fit war or murder. Actually they are applied to lust. The
union of cruelty and sensuality is one marriage to which the partners seem
to have remained faithful down the ages.

Even at the risk of supererogation, one further example of Hamlet's tendency to project himself must be added. Of all the glasses that catch his
image in the play none, oddly, is more revealing than that held up by Rosencrantz and Guildenstern. They are the Tweedledee and Tweedledee of the
genteel world and their very nonentity makes them perfect reflecting sur-
faces. It is their function to be nothing except what they give back from
the world around them. They are conformists. They follow the prevailing
mode. They contaminate their friendship for Hamlet by obeying the King
when he invites them to be spies. But what is Hamlet himself doing but
obeying another king and following another mode in accepting the code
of blood revenge? Moral customs may be quite as corrupting as worldly
fashions, and it may be as fatal to surrender one's will to a royal ghost as to
a flesh-and-blood sovereign. This unperceived analogy is unquestionably
the ground of Hamlet's devastating contempt for these harmless fashion
plates. He scorns Guildenstern for attempting to play on him as on a pipe
at the very moment when unseen forces are playing upon him. And he is
even more savage with Rosencrantz:

HAM.: Besides, to be demanded of a sponge! what replication should be made
 by the son of a king?
Ros.: Take you me for a sponge, my lord?
HAM.: Ay, sir, that soaks up the king's countenance, his rewards, his authorities. But such officers do the king best service in the end: he keeps
 them, like an ape, in the corner of his jaw; first mouthed, to be last
 swallowed: when he needs what you have gleaned, it is but squeezing
 you, and, sponge, you shall be dry again.

\* The detail that Tarquin was a king's son seems to have made an indelible impression
on the young Shakespeare's imagination.

Ros.: I understand you not, my lord.

HAM.: I am glad of it: a knavish speech sleeps in a foolish ear.

But Hamlet's own ear is asleep. Rosencrantz may indeed have soaked up orders to spy from a living king. But how is that worse than soaking up orders to kill from a dead one?

All this is repeated *forte* in another key and in another octave near the end of the play in the scene with Osric. That cockatoo of fashion and conformity carries the same theme to the edge, but never quite over the edge, of caricature.

## IX*

The first two acts of *Hamlet*, up to the coming of the players, make plain the character of the burden that has been placed on Hamlet's shoulders and what he ought *not* to do to discharge it. His soul cries out over and over: Do not obey your father. Do not kill the King.

What, then, ought he to do? With the entrance of the players, that, too, begins to be clear. Once more, Hamlet's soul speaks in unmistakable accents.

The highest duty of any man is to be true to the divinity within him, to remain faithful to his creative gift. But how can he tell when he is doing that? What is the mark? What are the signs? Perhaps no better brief answer to that question was ever framed than by the Elder in *The Brothers Karamazov*. Out of its context, it may sound disappointingly simple, to some ears even banal, but not in it. "Men are made for happiness," said Father Zossima, "and anyone who is completely happy has a right to say to himself, 'I am doing God's will on earth.'" It is as if Shakespeare had composed the scene in which the players come to Elsinore expressly to confirm that truth. Just prior to it, we have heard Hamlet, in his most melancholy vein, pronounce the earth a sterile promontory, the heavens a foul and pestilent congregation of vapors, and man the quintessence of dust; we have heard Rosencrantz predict that, with the Prince in this black mood, the players whose coming he announces will receive but "lenten entertainment." There are a few questions and answers about them, followed by a brief interlude

---

* Almost from my first careful study of *Hamlet* I have held, without realizing for a long time that it was not entirely orthodox, the view of Hamlet's conduct during the play scene set forth in the pages that follow. I had never heard of an article by W. W. Greg (*Modern Language Review*, October, 1917) until I found it referred to in Mr. Wilson's book (*What Happens in Hamlet*). I was excited to find someone who shared, so far as I could make out from what Mr. Wilson said, what I had come to consider *my* view of Hamlet's behavior during the play. I purposely refrained from reading Mr. Greg's article until my chapter on *Hamlet* was finished. I have now read it, and find, as I expected, with regard to the part Hamlet's conduct played in the interruption of *The Murder of Gonzago*, an opinion almost identical with the one I had been expounding to students for a number of years before the publication of Mr. Greg's article.

in which the Prince twits and insults Polonius—and then the players themselves enter. Instantly, we have another Hamlet—a man happy as a man can be only in the presence of the thing he was made for, as a woman is in the presence of the man she loves. The very tone of his voice alters. We hear the "sweet bells" as they sounded before they grew "out of tune and harsh." Here, we instinctively feel, is an echo of the young Shakespeare when the wonder of his destined vocation first dawned over him. Like his creator's, Hamlet's heart of heart is in dramatic and poetic art. This is his "enthusiasm," here is his "genius," in the original sense of those debased words. He is possessed. He cannot wait. Almost before the greetings are over he asks the First Player for a taste of his quality and hangs entranced on the recitation. Even when Polonius interrupts he says nothing, and at a second interruption though he can joke, he forgets to jeer, brushing the old man aside as casually as if he were a fly. At the end, he can even address to him in complete seriousness some of his deepest wisdom:

POL.: My lord, I will use them according to their desert.
HAM.: God's bodykins, man, better. Use every man after his desert, and who should scape whipping? Use them after your own honour and dignity. The less they deserve, the more merit is in your bounty.

That clinches it—proves how utterly the Prince's evil spirit is exorcised. For once, Hamlet can treat even Polonius as a man. This is God's Hamlet.

From the mountain peak on which they have dwelt for half an hour, Hamlet's thoughts descend abruptly to his father and the Ghost's injunction, and he finds himself poised between two universes: art and death. They are as far apart as heaven and hell. How can he inhabit both? Yet to do that is exactly what the opposite sides of his nature command. The fierce self-laceration of the soliloquy that follows ("O, what a rogue and peasant slave am I!"), in which he tears his passion to tatters in contrasting himself with the First Player, is a fresh measure of the dichotomy within him. Then suddenly as he says "About, my brain!" an idea, already adumbrated, formulates itself clearly, an idea for harmonizing, for the moment at least, the dual forces that are at war inside him. Why not make his art an instrument for finding out whether the King is guilty, an instrument, not of revenge, but of revelation?

> The spirit that I have seen
> May be the devil.

"The play's the thing" wherein to discover whether it was the devil or not. It is an inspiration if Hamlet ever had one—no injunction from a dead man but an intimation straight from his own innermost genius. His evil spirit had told him to kill the King. His good angel tells him to show the King to himself by holding up the mirror of art before him. The dagger or the play? That is the question. It is God's Hamlet who chooses the play.

But how hard it is going to be for this man to maintain that unique mixture of cold and warmth, of detachment and intimacy, which is the *sine qua non* of art, is shown in the first scene of the third act. In the "To be, or not to be" soliloquy he is in a mood of near-suicidal melancholy in reaction from the passion of the "Hecuba" speech. Thought is as predominant now as emotion was then. But on the entrance of Ophelia, with suspicion or certainty that Polonius is eavesdropping, he reverts in the nunnery scene to the note of self-laceration, only this time it is not a conscious laceration, as in the "peasant slave" lines, but, as we have seen, unconscious and projected. Little wonder that Ophelia exclaims, as he goes out:

O, what a noble mind is here o'erthrown!

Hamlet has proved himself capable in this scene of profound thought and of intense emotion, but not of that equilibrium of the two that is an indispensable condition of art.

## X

But with the opening of scene 2 of Act III (admittedly one of the half-dozen or so supreme scenes in all dramatic literature) Hamlet is once more himself. It is as if all that were needed to achieve this miracle was the presence of the players. Keats said he was "certain of nothing but of the holiness of the Heart's affections, and the truth of Imagination." Shakespeare might have written the advice to the players and Hamlet's ensuing confession of love to Horatio to confirm, in reverse order and in advance, that dictum of a poet who owed so much to his influence.

Hamlet's advice to the players, though universally admired, has often been accounted an organic excrescence—a splendid digression wherein a great dramatist, who was also an actor, does not resist the temptation to stop the action of his play for a few minutes to talk about his art. Criticism could not conceivably go more astray. A passage better integrated with the rest, or more essential, the play does not contain. Granted that we undoubtedly have here Shakespeare's ideas about the theater, about dramatic and histrionic art. That does not alter the fact that these ideas are also completely appropriate to the conscious Hamlet in the circumstances, and, what is immeasurably more important, that they are unconsciously the best imaginable advice to himself for the role he is about to enact. Though Hamlet has had a hand in the version of *The Murder of Gonzago* that is to be presented, he has naturally not cast himself for a part in the play. But he has a role in another play—along with the King one of the two leading roles—in the drama, namely, which he is even now shaping out of the unique conditions under which he has seen to it that *The Murder* is to be presented. So considered, that drama is not just a play within a play, but a play within a play within a play. The success or failure of this other play which Hamlet, unknown even to the players, is staging will depend on whether he himself, as playwright-spectator, can maintain precisely that temperance he has recommended to the players in his "advice" and whether he can avoid those excesses against which he has warned them. It is this above all that makes that advice integral and indispensable—and in the upshot tragically ironic. The affecting scene with Horatio, with its blessing upon those whose blood and judgment are so well commingled that they are not passion's slaves or a pipe for Fortune's finger, re-enforces the advice to the players in another more intimate and tender key. Here again is Hamlet himself. And that brings us to the play.

There are not a few respects in which a play within a play is the most dramatic of all conceivable theatrical situations. The reason is obvious.* A spectator at a play looks down on a piece of life much as God has long been supposed to look down on the world. To that extent the spectator becomes a god, though it is usually only emotionally that he apprehends that fact. But when he beholds actors in the scene he is watching looking down as spectators in their turn on a little world upon the stage, the truth with regard to himself comes closer to consciousness. He gets at least an inkling of the relation of art to life. And if he realizes that the play within the play is altering for the better any of the characters in the play itself, he may even perceive that art is a selective reflection of life meant to re-deem it.

The play within the play as arranged in *Hamlet* is typical of a situation that occurs time and again outside the theater. A mother tells a story to her children. They all listen, not knowing that her words are especially directed at just one. A teacher reads a poem to a class, but aims it in his heart at a particular member of it. A man relates an anecdote, or makes a seemingly casual remark, to a group, intending it, however, for a single individual. In each instance the desired effect will usually be produced in proportion as the speaker, if not full of love, is at least free of malice, and in proportion as the listener, if not free of all suspicion, is at least free of fear that he is being mocked or scorned—or preached at. Often, the more unconscious the reaction the better. Any suggestion that the analogy is a weapon, and the effect is spoiled or turned into resentment. Art that is directed in this sense against anyone has degenerated into moralizing or propaganda. It has become force on the mental plane. At its best, art ought to be left free to radiate, like the sun, in all directions, to scatter its pollen,

* See the chapter on *The Comedy of Errors.*

like a flower, wherever the wind wills. The least that should be *done* with it is to place it in a position where it will have a maximum opportunity to reflect or be disseminated. "To make a man better," says Chekhov, "you must first show him what he is"—hold a mirror up before him, that is, instead of threatening him with a dagger either literal or metaphorical.

This was the method of Shakespeare. There is nothing to show that he ever followed any other practice than that of leaving art free to produce its own effect, of letting a play speak for itself. Even his Choruses, as we have seen, are not *his* comment. The use of his *Richard II* by Essex's partisans on the eve of their rebellion shows how one of his works could be put to a perverted use. Shakespeare may have written *Henry V* or *Julius Caesar* partly as warnings to Essex, but if so he apparently left him to catch the analogy and draw the inference.

Hamlet has an opportunity to act like Shakespeare. It was plainly "the little Shakespeare" in his heart that sent him the inspiration to try out a work of dramatic art on his uncle. In so far as he regards *The Murder of Gonzago* as such a work and is willing to let it have its own way with the King, he is doing what his soul calls on him to do. But in so far as he regards it as a trap, an engine for torturing a victim, for catching not the King's conscience but the King himself, the play is nothing but a contrivance for murder on the mental plane. To be or not to be an artist. To be or not to be a murderer. Those were the questions.

The character of Claudius fits the situation as if explicitly created for it. It suggests what might have happened if Hamlet had had the power to follow his own advice and act like Shakespeare. The King, in spite of Hamlet's famous line about his smile, is no villain. It is plain that he becomes a criminal not through viciousness but through weakness, and that his nature contains the seeds of repentance. When Polonius remarks that we often sugar over the devil himself with devout countenance and pious action, Claudius, overhearing, exclaims:

> O! 'tis too true;
> How smart a lash that speech doth give my conscience!
> The harlot's cheek, beautied with plastering art,
> Is not more ugly to the thing that helps it
> Than is my deed to my most painted word.
> O heavy burden!

Here is no Cardinal Pandulph or Richard III, but a man conscious of his sin and longing to be rid of it—a fit subject for the redemptive power of art. Rarely have a man and an opportunity been more made for each other than Hamlet and the chance to save his uncle—and with him his mother and himself. It is enthralling but tragic to watch the Prince as he watches the play and its royal auditors, and to follow the crescendo of passion that ultimately masters him.

The dumb-show presents an outline of the action. Did Hamlet count on this, or was it introduced to his own surprise and consternation? His evident scorn for the players for "telling all" should settle that. Again, did the King and the Queen see the dumb-show, or were they in conversation at the moment and inattentive to the stage? The point has been much debated lately. It is possible to act the scene under either assumption. The question is obviously of concern to the stage director. But all that is really important is the fact that Claudius misses what is going on on the stage. Whether it is through failure to watch or failure to understand makes little difference. The whole point is that he is "asleep"—as the Elder Hamlet was, and as the Player King is. He is the third. That is enough to complete the analogy and to point the symbolism. Presently, Hamlet will pour the poison in his ear.

The Prologue enters and speaks three lines. "'Tis brief, my lord," says Ophelia. "As woman's love," Hamlet retorts. He is already fingering the mental dagger. The Player Queen spurns the suggestion of the Player King that on his death she will find another husband as kind as he has been.

> In second husband let me be accurst!
> None wed the second but who kill'd the first.

"Wormwood, wormwood," whispers Hamlet. The mental dagger is in his hand.

The Player King is unconvinced, and quite as if he had just been reading *Hamlet* and were propounding his own theory of the Prince's procrastination, he declares:

> What to ourselves in passion we propose,
> The passion ending, doth the purpose lose.
> The violence of either grief or joy
> Their own enactures with themselves destroy . . .
> Our wills and fates do so contrary run
> That our devices still are overthrown,
> Our thoughts are ours, their ends none of our own:
> So think thou wilt no second husband wed;
> But die thy thoughts when thy first lord is dead.

To which the Queen replies:

> Both here and hence pursue me lasting strife,
> If, once a widow, ever I be wife!

"If she should break it now!" cries Hamlet. He is beginning to lift the dagger. But he pauses.

HAM.:  Madam, how like you this play?
QUEEN:  The lady doth protest too much, methinks.
HAM.:  O, but she'll keep her word!

The flash of the dagger is caught in the way Hamlet pronounces that "she'll." He stresses it a shade too much and it attracts the attention of the King. Hamlet has given him his fatal opening:

Have you heard the argument? Is there no offence in't?

—a question which makes clear that the King has learned nothing from the dumb-show. There is fearful tension under the affected casualness of Hamlet's answer:

No, no, they do but jest, poison in jest; no offence i' the world.

However it may be in the dumb-show, it is not in jest but in dead earnest that Hamlet pours this poison in this King's ear. And it does not allay his aroused suspicion.

KING:  What do you call the play?

The dagger begins to descend.

HAM.:  The Mouse-trap. Marry, how? Trapically.

It is generally printed "tropically." The editor has to choose between the two. But Hamlet of course means both, and the actor must somehow achieve the two in one. The pun shows that Hamlet's unconscious is taking command. With a sarcasm that measures his mounting excitement he plunges recklessly ahead:

This play is the image of a murder done in Vienna: Gonzago is the duke's name; his wife, Baptista. You shall see anon; 'tis a knavish piece of work: but what of that? your majesty and we that have free souls, it touches us not: let the galled jade wince, our withers are unwrung.

How now about those "barren spectators" who laugh or interrupt "though in the mean time some necessary question of the play be then to be considered"? "That's villanous," he had pronounced such conduct a short while ago. What is it now? No, the "advice to the players" was not a digression. It is the perfect ironic "chorus" to this scene.

At this moment the Player Murderer enters and Hamlet makes haste to identify him:

This is one Lucianus, nephew to the king.

Nephew!* Who can doubt that that "nephew" was an improvisation of the Prince's rising passion or that he stresses the fatal word a full two shades too much? Had it been "brother," *The Murder of Gonzago* might have retained some semblance of a mirror. By a change of two syllables Hamlet lets the mental dagger become a literal one and finally converts what had begun as an imaginative experiment into a direct threat.

> You are as good as a chorus, my lord,

exclaims Ophelia innocently. What a thrust! It goes home. Hamlet accepts the role Ophelia assigns him, and throwing at her his most indecent utterance of all, turns back to the stage and cries:

> Begin, murderer; pox, leave thy damnable faces, and begin. Come; the croaking raven doth bellow for revenge.

We know who that raven is and can hear his ferocious tone. Half an hour ago Hamlet would have had a fellow whipped for this sort of thing. "It out-herods Herod: pray you, avoid it."

"Begin, murderer." And Lucianus does begin—in lines that anticipate the atmosphere of the witch-scenes in *Macbeth*—and pours the poison in the sleeping Gonzago's ear. How asleep, or how awake, is Claudius now?

It is the supreme moment.

There are many crises in *Hamlet*, but this is the crisis of crises—this, and not the sparing of the praying King or the killing of Polonius, which are but the inevitable outcome of what happens here. Now, for the last time, Hamlet is free. A second more and he will be bound by the fatality of his act. Fortune will have sounded on him what stop she pleased. The second passes, and Hamlet's blood finally overwhelms his judgment. Seeing Lucianus pour poison, he must pour poison too—all that is left in his vial. He breaks in to give a huddled summary of the rest of the plot:

> He poisons him i' the garden for's estate. His name's Gonzago; the story is extant, and writ in very choice Italian. You shall see anon how the murderer gets the love of Gonzago's wife.

The dagger has descended. Hamlet himself has o'erstepped the modesty of nature and betrayed the right of dramatic art to speak obliquely. He has produced an abortion. Forgetting that "the play's the thing," he has ruined his imaginative experiment by "telling all"—just what he damned the players for doing, far less blatantly and offensively, in their dumb-show. He is hoist with his own petar. He has sprung the mousetrap instead of letting it spring itself, and has caught two royal mice, himself as well as the King.

---

* To Dover Wilson belongs the credit of having made clear for the first time the full importance of this word. His sharp differentiation of three theories of Hamlet's madness—Polonius', Gertrude's, and Claudius'—is highly illuminating.

Exactly as Romeo thrust his fatal rapier between the fighting Mercutio and Tybalt, Hamlet has stepped between Claudius and his fighting soul. If there could be any doubt that this is the crisis, the King's conduct sets it at rest.

"The king rises," cries Ophelia.

But is it he who interrupts the play?

Of course it is—yet not a whit more than Hamlet. Hamlet and the King interrupt it *together*. The rising tides of emotion in nephew and uncle reach their flood at the same instant. The timing is perfect. It is as if the two had composed, and even rehearsed, the scene together.

"What! frighted with false fire?" cries Hamlet.

False fire! Could there be a better description of the counterfeit thing into which Hamlet has transformed what might have been true fire if it had been left to sear the King's conscience with its own Promethean heat? Instead of letting the fire burn, Hamlet has seized a brand from it and fairly thrust it in the King's face.

"Give o'er the play," Polonius commands, bringing Hamlet's imaginative venture to an official end.

"Give me some light! Away!" cries the King as he rushes out.

"Lights, lights, lights!" everyone echoes. To miss the symbolism here is to miss all. Light, not fire, is what Claudius craves. And light is what *The Murder of Gonzago* might have been to his soul. But Hamlet has debased it to fire, to false fire at that.

> Put out the light, and then put out the light.

And what did the court make of that fragment of the play which Hamlet permitted it to hear? How is it that in what follows there is no sign that anybody but Horatio had understood what had happened? Sycophancy is the usual explanation: they just kept mum. But we forget that the court at Elsinore had not had our privilege of witnessing a production of *Hamlet* up to the play scene. We know that a guilty king rises because he cannot endure the sight of his own crime, or a threat against his life, or both. The court merely sees a madman giving vent to his aberration. Reason enough for giving over the play. The court may realize that this crazed youth is menacing the King and sense some deeper mystery, may even think, as Dover Wilson holds, that here is a dispossessed heir threatening assassination to recover his crown. But even so, compared with us, they can only conjecture what it all means. We have been watching the King. They have been watching the madman. They think the King interrupts the performance because he cannot stand his nephew's insane conduct. It is we who see that he also cannot endure the play. *Hamlet* as a whole is thrown out of focus if this distinction is not made plain on the stage.

## XI

As the cry "Lights, lights, lights!" fades away, Hamlet, left alone with Horatio, dances about in a delirium of joy. The Ghost is justified! He sings snatches of song and calls for music. "Has this fellow no feeling of his business, that he sings at grave-making?" That later remark of his to Horatio in the churchyard is the tersest comment on his own conduct here, for it is many graves, including Ophelia's and his own, that he has just been digging. The state Hamlet is in is pictured a moment later when Rosencrantz and Guildenstern come to summon him to his mother's chamber. "Good my lord," exclaims Guildenstern, "put your discourse into some frame, and start not so wildly from my affair." That "start not so wildly" conveys vividly the delirious character of Hamlet's joy. There is nothing voluntary about this antic disposition. " 'Sblood, do you think I am easier to be played on than a pipe?" *That*, at just the moment his own blood is mastering him completely! "Methinks it is like a weasel." *This*, of a creature that sucks the blood of its victim, but a second before he exclaims, "Now could I drink hot blood"! What wonder that, as the scene ends, a fear crosses his mind that, like Nero, he may murder his own mother! And this is the same man who besought the players to moderate all passion and repudiated in his interlude with Horatio the man who is passion's slave. The scene that opened with an appeal for temperance ends on the impulse to kill. *From art to murder!* As Romeo failed because he did not follow "utterly" the woman he loved, so Hamlet fails because he does not trust "utterly" the art he loves. He does not let the play speak for itself. Seldom has Shakespeare tied the end of a scene to its beginning more quietly, or more ironically and tragically. No, Hamlet's discourse on histrionic art—it has to be repeated—is no purple patch. It is the heart of the whole matter.

The King decides to send to England this madman who has threatened him—send him, as we learn later, to his death. Then, left alone, he turns from this preparation for a fresh murder to repent the murder that has rendered this further one necessary! And the incredible thing is that his words ring with sincerity. They are unquestionably an expression of genuine anguish at the farthest remove from hypocrisy. Angels, the sweet heavens, rain, snow, the newborn babe: every word, every metaphor, shows his longing for the miracle of rebirth. If the mere fragment, marred by interruptions, of *The Murder of Gonzago* which Hamlet allowed his uncle to witness—with a hurried summary of the rest—could produce this degree of repentance, what might the whole play, left to itself, have effected? Granted that open penitence and confession on Claudius' part would have been a miracle. Still, who was better fitted to perform that miracle than a man with the spiritual endowment of Hamlet, who better fitted to be the subject of it than a man as contrite as Claudius? Plainly Shakespeare put the play scene and the prayer scene side by side expressly to force us to ask that question. And no less plainly he framed the characters of the two men to suggest that, if Hamlet had managed his part better, that miracle I do not say would have taken place—it is the very nature of a miracle to be to the last degree improbable—but might have taken place. Even as it is, Claudius falls on his knees crying:

> Help, angels! Make assay . . .
> All may be well.

And it is at this moment that Hamlet, on his way to his mother's closet, enters.

Here is the perfect opportunity! Yet where is the man who would have Hamlet take it? Those who think he ought to kill the King no more have the courage of their convictions at this moment than Hamlet. His unwillingness to kill a defenseless man or a man in prayer everyone will understand and applaud. But if what really deters him goes no deeper than that, surely Hamlet would have killed the King when, if at all, he ought to have killed him: at the moment when the play was broken up. At bottom what deters him now is just what deterred him then: the fact that in his heart Hamlet does not believe in blood revenge in any circumstances. The excuse he offers for not seizing the present perfect opportunity proves this as nearly as anything of the kind can be proved. He says he would not send his enemy to heaven. He will wait until he can send him to hell. Dr. Johnson declared these words of Hamlet too terrible to be read or uttered. And all will agree to the extent of feeling that it was not the Hamlet we love and admire who uttered them. How then did Hamlet come to utter words that no one can believe Hamlet meant? How did his lips come to utter them? Who at one time or another has not assigned a worldly motive to a noble impulse? Then why not, in an extreme case, an infernal motive to a celestial impulse? The celestial impulse here is to save. Hence the expressed will to damn. Hamlet has a conscious belief that he ought to kill the King. He has an unconscious conviction that he ought not to. To hold the latter powerful conviction under the threshold, consciousness must invent a correspondingly powerful pretext for suppressing it. And that is exactly what Hamlet's consciousness does here and why we all feel that what he says is totally out of character. A man's consciousness is the merest surface of his self.

Meanwhile, Claudius cannot sustain the mood of repentance. Like Henry V before Agincourt, whose prayer of contrition was of no avail so long as

he retained the kingdom his father had stolen from Richard, Claudius feels
the redemptive forces powerless in the face

> Of those effects for which I did the murder,
> My crown, mine own ambition, and my queen,

and rising from his knees, he cries:

> My words fly up, my thoughts remain below.
> Words without thoughts never to heaven go.

It is as if the King were saying in so many words to his nephew: "You need
have had no scruples about my attitude. You were a fool to spare me." And
when, later in the play, he declares:

> No place, indeed, should murder sanctuarize;
> Revenge should have no bounds,

it is as if, in retrospect, he were deriding Hamlet for not having killed him.
If it may be phrased so oddly, it is like an *ex post facto* invitation to Hamlet
to *have* killed him!

## XII

The devils had their way in the play scene to a point where Hamlet was
ready to drink hot blood. The angels then had their moment when Hamlet
spared the King. It is the devils' turn again when the son enters his mother's
chamber—and the devils make the most of it.

If we wanted to be cynical, we might put it thus: this man who addressed
the players on the subject of temperance now comes to read a lecture to
his mother on self-control, and to make it the more impressive prefaces it
by an impulsive murder. It is the old story. Over and over, if in less extreme
degree, we have had this situation in Shakespeare. Who was Antonio, with
his argosies on seven seas, to take Shylock to task for love of money? Who
was Hal, fresh from Gadshill and the tavern, to lecture Falstaff on his wild
courses and low life? Who was Brutus, his hands still red with Caesar's
blood, to attack Cassius so savagely for accepting bribes? Who now is
Hamlet, just after thrusting his rapier through a curtain at a cry behind it,
to turn and lecture his mother for letting her blood get the better of her
judgment? *You are angry, Jove; therefore you are wrong.* It is not by
chance that a looking glass is the central symbol throughout this scene.

Because he shattered the glass he was holding up to the King in the play
scene, he attempts to hold up one to his mother now.

> Come, come, and sit you down. You shall not budge,

he cries to the woman to whom he has just said, would you were not my
mother!—

> You go not, till I set you up a glass
> Where you may see the inmost part of you.

But already, on entering the chamber, he has set up, unawares, the glass of
his own countenance wherein is reflected what at the moment is the inmost
part of him, the Nero impulse. His mother sees it and cries out:

> What wilt thou do? Thou wilt not murder me?
> Help, help, ho!

And the murder of Polonius follows.

We may say that the eavesdropper got what he deserved. We may say
that Hamlet thought it was the King. But how ignominious for the man
who over and over had repudiated rashness, to kill a man behind a curtain
without so much as drawing it aside to identify the victim! He might as
well have been blindfolded himself.

> What devil was't
> That thus hath cozen'd you at hoodman-blind?

His own words a few moments later to his mother! In condemning her he
is condemning himself. The touch is typical. The long passage from which
these lines are taken, in which he institutes an elaborate contrast between
the King and his father, is perhaps the most extended example of empathy
in the play. It is a tissue of ironies, practically every sentence in it containing some oblique reference to the speaker. The idealized picture of the
father and the debased portrait of the uncle, whatever incidental truth they
may have as applied to their ostensible subjects, are primarily nothing but
the divine and diabolic sides of Hamlet's own nature set over against each
other with preternatural insight and savage truth. Brothers! And the sin
which he chastizes in his mother is nothing but his own in reverse. Anger
and sensuality (plus the cruelty in which they both usually culminate) are
the two dominant animal passions in man, one generically masculine, the
other feminine. Thus each is an image of the other. When Hamlet sees his
mother descend into the second, it is a picture of himself descending into
the first. He tears himself to tatters in an impotent fury over the senseless-
ness of the deed he has just committed, the rashness with which he has
abdicated the throne of self-control.

> A king of shreds and patches!

he cries at the culmination of his tirade. Exactly! It is just the sort of king
over himself he is being at the moment. And, pat, on the note of disintegration, the Ghost enters, as if at a cue.

In contrast with his visitation on the platform, the Ghost utters but onc brief speech and seems more concerned with Gertrude than with Claudius. On his withdrawal, as if he had drained off the poison with him, an interlude of exquisite tenderness follows as Hamlet says "good-night" to his mother. But unluckily he turns back for "one word more" and falls into a further savage denunciation of his uncle, calling him, in their Elizabethan equivalents, a toad and an old tomcat. "At the end of the scene," says Dr. Joseph Quincy Adams,

Hamlet grasps the body of Polonius, and starts out with the words: 'I'll lug the guts into the neighbor room.' Yet some persons, in their effort to explain the play say that Hamlet failed to take revenge on Claudius because he had such a delicate, sensitive, almost sentimental nature, that he could not bear the thought of shedding blood. The line just quoted shows that whatever else Hamlet may be, he was not a sentimentalist. As an experienced soldier he was accustomed to bloodshed; he had no compunctions at sending Rosencrantz and Guildenstern to their death; and he did not—nor did the dramatist and his audiences—live in an age when sentimentality of this kind flourished.

Whatever may be true of the age and the audience, what ground is there for implying that Shakespeare considered aversion to the thought of shedding blood sentimental? The Hamlet who made the remark about the guts is a different being from the one who had just said to his mother, of her cleft heart,

> O, throw away the worser part of it,
> And live the purer with the other half,

as different as are those worser and purer halves of his mother. It was the brutal, not the pure Hamlet of the two that was nearer sentimentality.

## XIII

Up to the play scene, the opposing natures in Hamlet are in something like equipoise. With the play, blood gains the upper hand and confirms its victory in the murder of Polonius. From that point on, Hamlet gives the impression of a man whose will has abdicated in favor of fate. There are those who describe his indubitably changed attitude as a new "air of self-possession."* It would be nearer the mark to call it the calmness of desper-

* "Hamlet returns from his voyage a changed man, with an air of self-possession greater than at any other time of the play. We are not told why; but we may fancy, if we like, that the seas have helped to expel the 'something-settled matter in his heart,' or that he has gained confidence from the hoisting of Rosencrantz and Guildenstern with their own petar, or that simply his 'cause of distemper' is wearing off." (See Dover Wilson, *What Happens in Hamlet*, p. 266.)

"From this time on Hamlet is increasingly better. He begins to display more interest in life, he takes on a more hopeful attitude towards the world, his thinking loses much of its morbid quality, and his confidence in human nature is in part restored. . . . All these things indicate that the dark cloud of melancholia which we saw descend upon him at the beginning of the play is rapidly lifting." (See *Hamlet*, edited by Joseph Quincy Adams [Boston, 1929], p. 288.)

ation, though it is far from being all calmness. The fourth and fifth acts exhibit Hamlet's gradual engulfment under the ancestral tide. In the lines to Horatio he had commended the commingling of blood and judgment. Now, in the Fortinbras soliloquy, his emotions fairly whip his reason toward bloodshed, he speaks of "excitements of my reason and my blood," and ends in an utter confusion of the two:

> My thoughts be bloody, or be nothing worth!

Irresistible forces from underneath are usurping the name of reason.

The metaphor Shakespeare uses for this upsurge of racial emotion is *water*—the oldest and most universal symbol for the unconscious. Land emerged from the sea; higher forms, via the amphibian, from the ocean; the child from the womb. How natural that recession into or under water should represent atavism. Over and over Shakespeare so uses it in the last two acts of *Hamlet*. The first two acts were the camel—they treated of Hamlet's burden. The third was the weasel—it was dedicated to hot blood. The last two are the whale—they tell how Hamlet was swallowed by the "monster" of the unconscious. "Very like a whale." And Hamlet is not the only one who is so swallowed.

Take Laertes. At his father's death he is suddenly infected with an exaggerated devotion to his memory that is like a parody of Hamlet's idealization of his father. Like a wolf with the pack at its back, he rushes in with the rabble to demand revenge. How does Shakespeare express this piling-up of retrogressive forces? In terms of water:

> The ocean, overpeering of his list,
> Eats not the flats with more impetuous haste
> Than young Laertes, in a riotous head,
> O'erbears your officers.

Or Ophelia. The past, in another fashion, floods into her bewildered brain, sings on her lips, brings tears to the eyes of all who see or hear her, and ends by pulling her down to death under water, "muddy death." Did she bend down to the brook, or did the brook rise up to take her to itself? Why ask? It is enough that she had become

> a creature native and indued
> Unto that element.

And to the refrain, "drown'd, drown'd," Laertes exclaims:

> Too much of water hast thou, poor Ophelia,
> And therefore I forbid my tears.

Ophelia's death is an allegory of Hamlet's. How fitting, when it was his act that dragged her down to it!

And Hamlet himself. When he is once more set naked on Claudius' kingdom, out of what element is it that he emerges? Water—the sea. After an encounter with pirates.

But more interesting than any of these are the gravediggers. Between the account of Ophelia's death and the entrance of her funeral procession, the demands of both psychology and the theater call for an easing of the dramatic tension, and we have it in the churchyard scene. The conversation of the clowns before the entrance of Hamlet and Horatio seems, in particular, to be pure comic relief. But beware of Shakespeare on such occasions! Unless all precedents fail, it is precisely in this interlude that we may expect some secret comment by the poet on his play. There could be no more appropriate place in which to bury it. It is like the garden scene in *Richard II*, and here, as there, the poet makes a delver in the earth, but of a very different sort, his near-mouthpiece. ("Come, my spade. There is no ancient gentlemen but gardeners, ditchers, and grave-makers; they hold up Adam's profession.")

It was not of earth, however, but of water, that the two clowns were speaking a moment before. The lines are familiar, but their high metaphysical import can easily be missed:

FIRST CLO.:  For here lies the point: if I drown myself wittingly, it argues an act: and an act hath three branches; it is, to act, to do, and to perform: argal, she drowned herself wittingly.

SECOND CLO.: Nay, but here you, goodman delver,—

FIRST CLO.:  Give me leave. Here lies the water; good: here stands the man; good: if the man go to this water, and drown himself, it is, will he, nill he, he goes,—mark you that? but if the water come to him, and drown him, he drowns not himself: argal, he that is not guilty of his own death shortens not his own life.

The pertinence of this to Ophelia's death and the question of her burial is obvious. But how about its pertinence to Hamlet? Read it alongside the apology to Laertes and behold! it is the same speech translated from the abstract into the concrete with "water" substituted for "madness." Not she, but the water, did the drowning; not he, but his "madness," did the killing. Simply two different terms for the unconscious. What a tribute by Shakespeare to this witty old clown to identify his wisdom, which he had, as it were, dug out of the earth, with what is perhaps the deepest insight into his own trouble attained by the philosophic Prince in the course of his entire role! Here, once more, is the "democracy" of Shakespeare, the kind of human "equality" in which he believed.

Hamlet and Horatio enter the churchyard, and in their conversation about skulls and death we have a sort of psychological grave-digging to match the earthy one. Hamlet does not know that the grave the clowns are digging is for the girl he has driven to death. The funeral procession enters and Laertes reveals the truth. The leaping in the grave follows, in which the two men out-herod Herod and each other in their rant. That Hamlet should act like Laertes! The symbolism is the same as before, except that the element to which he now reverts is earth rather than water. Unawares, Hamlet and Laertes are rehearsing the end of the play.

> This is mere madness,

cries the Queen, and with keen insight into her son's divided self concludes:

> And thus a while the fit will work on him;
> Anon, as patient as the female dove,
> When that her golden couplets are disclos'd,
> His silence will sit drooping.

If the last act of *Hamlet* were given a title, it should be "The Graveyard." This scene is a kind of overture to it.

## XIV

At the beginning of the next scene Hamlet and Horatio enter in the middle of a conversation:

> HAM.: Sir, in my heart there was a kind of fighting
> That would not let me sleep; methought I lay
> Worse than the mutines in the bilboes. Rashly,
> And prais'd be rashness for it, let us know,
> Our indiscretion sometimes serves us well
> When our deep plots do pall; and that should teach us
> There's a divinity that shapes our ends,
> Rough-hew them how we will.

It would be interesting to know how many times that last line-and-a-half has been quoted as Shakespeare's own religious wisdom by persons who never read or never noticed the apostrophe to rashness and indiscretion that precedes it or the account of the callous and superfluous murder, of which it is made the justification, that follows it. A rash deed may perhaps be forgiven. But how about a deliberate apotheosis of rashness? An identification of it with divinity! "Divinity of hell"—Iago's phrase—comes to mind. "When people get it into their heads that they are being especially favored by the Almighty," says Samuel Butler, "they had better as a general rule mind their $p$'s and $q$'s." Shakespeare, I take it, is saying much the same thing in a different tone. What a revolution in Hamlet's philosophy the lines register! How unobtrusively the Fortune whose instrument he once abhorred the very thought of becoming has been translated into the Divinity he is only too willing to have shape his ends!

The Osric scene, with the summons to the duel, comes next, as if to confirm the point in another key. Hamlet's contempt for this befeathered yes-man is measureless. "He did comply with his dug before he sucked it." "Thus has he . . . only got the tune of the time." But with what poor grace these thrusts come from one who has just uttered a general compliance with Fate and who is about to fall into the tune of the time in the matter of blood revenge! Disdain is self-condemnation. Unluckily, Hamlet did not live to cry with Beatrice: "Contempt, farewell!"

Only moments now remain. It is not the contest with Laertes that Hamlet dreads, but—Something. "But thou wouldst not think how ill all's here about my heart; but it is no matter." His good angel, through Horatio, would save him at long past the eleventh hour by bidding him heed this last intimation of his genius: "If your mind dislike any thing, obey it." This is no appeal to indiscretion. Here *was* the Divinity he should have let shape his ends. But it is like Caesar disregarding the Soothsayer. The man is doomed.

> HAM.: Not a whit, we defy augury; there's a special providence in the fall of a sparrow. If it be now, 'tis not to come; if it be not to come, it will be now; if it be not now, yet it will come: the readiness is all. Since no man has aught of what he leaves, what is't to leave betimes? Let be.

There was an earlier character in Shakespeare who spoke in the same vein —almost to the very tone and words:

> By my troth, I care not; a man can die but once; we owe God a death. I'll ne'er bear a base mind: an't be my destiny, so; an't be not, so. No man's too good to serve 's prince; and let it go which way it will, he that dies this year is quit for the next.

The parallel is startling. It is as if Shakespeare were sitting right beside us, telling us, in so many words, what he thought of Hamlet's speech to Horatio on the defiance of augury.

For who spoke those words?

Feeble. Yes, Feeble! the final and feeblest among that band of recruits in *Henry IV* of which Mouldy, Shadow, Wart, and Bullcalf were the more bellicose and terrible members—Falstaff's "most forcible Feeble." Thus does Shakespeare place the indelible stamp of feebleness on Hamlet's philosophy of fate. (By which I do not imply for a moment that he ever consciously connected the two passages. "The one word that explains the

Shakespeare miracle," said Thoreau, "is unconsciousness." Here, perhaps, is an instance of what he meant.)

But we need not appeal to Feeble. Anyone can confirm Hamlet's reaction. In proportion as our will declines, our belief in destiny mounts. When we are compelled to confront the consequence of some weak or bad act of our own, the easiest way to escape a sense of sin is to put the blame on fate or the stars, or, as we are more likely to do today, on heredity, environment, our bringing up, or just "tough luck." Iago and Edmund, it will be remembered, had some sensible things to say under this head for all their villainy.

Hamlet's fears are strong enough in themselves to bring their own fulfilment, and the end rapidly approaches. The King—to go back for a moment—frightened at the news of Hamlet's return to Denmark, has concocted his plot for the duel.

> ... with ease
> Or with a little shuffling,

he tells Laertes,

> you may choose
> A sword unbated, and, in a pass of practice
> Requite him for your father.

What worlds away from his words in the prayer scene!—

> But 'tis not so above;
> There is no shuffling, there the action lies
> In his true nature, and we ourselves compell'd
> Even to the teeth and forehead of our faults
> To give in evidence.

So in one word, *shuffling*, does Shakespeare make Claudius pass judgment in advance on his own act of treachery.

Just before the duel, Claudius puts Laertes' hand in Hamlet's, and Hamlet, in words that ring with sincerity, begs Laertes' pardon for the wrong he has done him, attributing it to the distraction from which he suffers. Laertes, about to do a dastardly deed, is embarrassed by Hamlet's generosity of tone, and, as men are prone to do in such circumstances, retreats into words, speaking of his honor (twice in three lines), of his name, of peace, of love. The foils are brought, this man of honor chooses the unbated poisoned rapier, and the play begins.

Hamlet scores two hits. Gertrude drinks the poisoned liquor. The passing is resumed. Laertes wounds Hamlet. Hamlet, aroused and guessing the truth at last, forces Laertes to exchange rapiers and wounds him. The

Queen falls. Laertes confesses his treachery. Gertrude, crying that she is poisoned, dies. Hamlet orders the door locked, as Laertes, near his end, tells with what the rapier is anointed and implicates the King.

> The point envenom'd too!

cries Hamlet,

> Then, venom, to thy work!

and runs the King through with his sword, and for full measure tries to force the dregs of the poisoned cup on him as he expires. (Strangely, it remains for the dying Cleopatra, not yet created, to make Shakespeare's profoundest comment on this deed.)

## XV

At last Hamlet has killed the King.
*But has he?*
When we look back, everything converges to answer that question with those two words of the Prince's own: "Never Hamlet."

> Never Hamlet!
> If Hamlet from himself be ta'en away.

But who, then, did kill the King, if not Hamlet?

Why! his rashness, his indiscretion, the divinity "of hell" that shaped his end, fortune, fate, "this water," the Devil. Shakespeare has been at pains to supply an abundance of answers, as if to show how important he considered the question.

It is just as it was with Romeo in the two duels in *Romeo and Juliet.* From the viewpoint of drama we have only approval for Hamlet's conduct in this scene, his sending to death the two plotters against his own life. What else could he have done? Was he not acting in self-defense? But at the elevation of poetry, from which we see not just this scene but the action in its entirety, it is another matter. As Romeo descended to the level of Mercutio in killing Tybalt, Hal to the level of his father in invading France, Brutus to the level of Cassius in murdering Caesar, so Hamlet here finally descends to the level of Laertes. With the rapiers, he once for all exchanges fairness for venom. This duel, like so many duels in literature,* is symbolic, condensing into a sudden image the meaning of the play. Under a provocation that, this time, seems like necessity, Hamlet repeats the pattern he cut out for himself at the crisis in the play scene: he converts art—in this case the art of fencing—into death. It is now too

---

* Examples are the duels in Turgenev's *Fathers and Sons,* Tolstoy's *War and Peace,* Dostoevsky's *The Brothers Karamazov,* and Chekhov's *The Duel.*

late to blame him. Hamlet's mistake, like those of the other characters just mentioned, was made far back, while he was still free. From the moment when, trembling with suppressed excitement, he interrupted *The Murder of Gonzago* by crying out:

> He poisons him i' the garden for's estate,

to his final

> Then, venom, to thy work!

an unbroken chain of reflex actions—of which the killing of Polonius and the sending of Rosencrantz and Guildenstern to their doom are the most conspicuous—all tend to one conclusion: that the killing of the King was as purely an instinctive act as is that by which a man draws back his hand from fire.

> The lion dying thrusteth forth his paw.

Hamlet's deed was like that. It was not divinity shaping man's end; it was man, under the compulsion of circumstance, imitating the action of the tiger. And the thrill we get in the theater as the King falls—from which not a single spectator, I believe, is exempt—is not a celestial one. We take the deed *there* as a noble act finally accomplished. It is only afterward, when we recollect it in tranquillity, that we recognize its senseless and fatalistic character. Indeed, in spite of differences, the situation resembles the one where Richard II runs amuck and kills the assistants of Exton. It was desperation, not bravery, that prompted Richard's act. A second later, Exton in turn strikes him down, only to realize the next second what he has done and to wish it undone:

> For now the devil, that told me I did well,
> Says that this deed is chronicled in hell.

It is not at the moment of action, but afterward, that we see. And that can be as true of the theater as of life.

But we left the action at its climax.

Laertes begs Hamlet's forgiveness and follows the King. Hamlet, as if visited by his own genius at the end, speaks to those around him as if they were gathered in a theater as "audience to this act," prevents Horatio from drinking the last drops of the poisoned liquor, and cries to his friend in words the whole world knows by heart:

> Absent thee from felicity awhile,
> And in this harsh world draw thy breath in pain,
> To tell my story.

Martial music is heard in the distance, and a salute. The conquering Fortinbras has come from Poland, and Hamlet has just enough breath left to
give him his dying voice as his successor. What irony! Like Henry V's,
all the Elder Hamlet's conquests have been for nothing—for less than
nothing. Fortinbras, his former enemy, is to inherit the kingdom! Such is
the end to which the Ghost's thirst for vengeance has led.

For Hamlet "the rest is silence." The tragedy is summed up in the contrast between those four mysterious words and Horatio's

> Good-night, sweet prince,
> And flights of angels sing thee to thy rest!

Fortinbras, who has now entered, gazes around him as on a battlefield:

> This quarry cries on havoc. O proud death!
> What feast is toward in thine eternal cell,
> That thou so many princes at a shot
> So bloodily hast struck?

And Horatio promises to tell, in explanation,

> Of carnal, bloody, and unnatural acts,
> Of accidental judgements, casual slaughters,
> Of deaths put on by cunning and forc'd cause,
> And, in this upshot, purposes mistook
> Fall'n on the inventors' heads.

The Ghost's words sounded eloquent and noble when he was clamoring
for revenge. This is their harvest.

The dead Hamlet is borne out "like a soldier" and the last rites over his
body are to be the rites of war. The final word of the text is "shoot." The
last sounds we hear are a dead march and the reverberations of ordnance
being shot off. The end crowns the whole. The sarcasm of fate could go
no further. Hamlet, who aspired to nobler things, is treated at death as if
he were the mere image of his father: a warrior. Shakespeare knew what
he was about in making the conclusion of his play martial. Its theme has
been war as well as revenge. It is the story of the Minotaur over again,
of that monster who from the beginning of human strife has exacted his
annual tribute of youth. No sacrifice ever offered to it was more precious
than Hamlet. But he was not the last.

If ever a play seems expressly written for the twentieth century, it is
*Hamlet*. It should be unnecessary to underscore its pertinence to an age in
which, twice within three decades, the older generation has called on the
younger generation to settle a quarrel with the making of which it had

nothing to do. So taken, *Hamlet* is an allegory of our time. Imagination or violence, Shakespeare seems to say, there is no other alternative. They are the two forces that exact obedience, the one freely, the other under compulsion. Art or war: it is the only choice humanity ever had or ever will have. Unless the first is resorted to while we are free, the other has to be resorted to under the pressure of events. Hamlet made the right choice, but then, at the moment of triumph, converted an instrument of regeneration into an instrument of revenge. Made for heaven, he was tempted by hell—and fell.

## XVI

The prime requisite for an understanding of *Hamlet* is a belief in ghosts. The common reader who has that will come nearer its heart than the most learned man who lacks it—just as a youth of seventeen who is in love is better fitted to comprehend the *Divine Comedy* than a scholar who has spent a lifetime on it but who has never shared the experience on which it is based. If "a belief in ghosts" sounds too old-fashioned or superstitious, call it, more pedantically, a belief in the autonomous character of the unconscious. The two are the same.

Dover Wilson has written of the belief in spirits of Catholics and Protestants in Shakespeare's day.* Catholics, he tells us, held that ghosts came from Purgatory and were actually souls of the departed. Protestants thought they came from hell (or rarely from heaven) and were devils (or angels) who had assumed the shape and appearance of the dead.

I once asked a young girl (barely over the border of childhood) to whom I had read *Hamlet*, whether she thought the Ghost was Hamlet's father or the devil. I like to get the fresh reaction of innocence to a masterpiece, uncontaminated by traditional critical opinion. "I don't see that it makes any difference," she said, "I should think it would be just the same." "Just the same?" I inquired, arrested. "Well," she explained, "I should think that whoever told you to kill somebody was the devil." *Just the same:* in a flash those three words show that the Catholic and Protestant views that Wilson discriminates are really one. The Father, in so far as he represents authority and force, *is* the Devil, a power utterly transcending anything human in any common meaning of that term. Shakespeare here, as usual, is a harmonizer of opposites.

But it is not just Shakespeare and childhood who agree. The poets have always seen that the supreme question for humanity is the existence of the

---

* What he writes is interesting and important. Only one wishes he would not speak of Elizabethan ghosts. It sounds like talking of a *fin de siècle* phantom or a mid-Victorian devil. Ghosts and devils, like poets and angels, are all contemporaries. They belong to no particular century.

gods—and devils. Their existence and their incidence in human affairs. It is startling to compare one or two of their utterances with Shakespeare's.

Go back to Aeschylus, the first of the supreme Greek dramatists. Clytemnestra is speaking of her slaying of her husband, Agamemnon:

> And criest thou still this deed hath been
> My work? Nay, gaze, and have no thought
> That this is Agamemnon's Queen.
> 'Tis He, 'tis He, hath round him wrought
> This phantom of the dead man's wife;
> He, the Old Wrath, the Driver of Men Astray,
> Pursuer of Atreus for the feast defiled;
> To assoil an ancient debt he hath paid this life;
> A warrior and a crowned King this day
> Atones for a slain child.

Or come down, past Shakespeare, almost to our own day, to Dostoevsky. Raskolnikov is speaking of the murder of the Old Pawnbroker:

> Did I murder the old woman? I murdered myself, not her! I crushed myself once for all, for ever. . . . But it was the devil that killed that old woman, not I.

And then go back to Shakespeare, to Hamlet. He is apologizing for the slaying of Polonius:

> Was't Hamlet wronged Laertes? Never Hamlet!
> If Hamlet from himself be ta'en away,
> And when he's not himself does wrong Laertes,
> Then Hamlet does it not, Hamlet denies it.
> Who does it then? His madness. If't be so,
> Hamlet is of the faction that is wrong'd;
> His madness is poor Hamlet's enemy.

Or to the First Gravedigger:

> But if the water come to him, and drown him, he drowns not himself.

The Old Wrath, the Devil, Madness, the Water, Whoever Tells You To Kill: what difference does the terminology make? Each of these words or phrases is just another name for the infernal forces which, unless warded off by an eternal vigilance, rush in at the slightest abdication of his own freedom, to possess man. (To the celestial forces that can take possession of him Shakespeare was to turn his attention more and more in the plays that follow *Hamlet*.) Perhaps the profoundest and certainly the most detailed analysis of this idea in modern literature is *The Possessed* of Dostoevsky, or *The Devils*, as the title of the novel should properly be translated. But probably Orestes from ancient literature, and Ivan Karamazov from recent, are the two most interesting single figures to place beside Hamlet. Orestes murdered his mother, went mad, and was pursued by the Furies. Hamlet was visited by his Father, played with murderous thoughts, and committed irresponsible acts. Ivan Karamazov played with murderous thoughts, was visited by the Devil, and went insane. "God will conquer!" cried Alyosha Karamazov in the critical hour when his brother's mind hung in the balance, "he will rise up in the light of truth, or . . . he'll perish in hate, revenging on himself and on everyone his having served the cause he does not believe in." So with Hamlet. He is that second alternative. God did not conquer, and Hamlet wreaked revenge on himself and on everyone for having served the cause he did not believe in, the cause of blood revenge.

In *War and Peace*, Tolstoy gives us the same situation with the other outcome. Pierre, like Brutus, conceives it to be his duty to kill a tyrant: Napoleon. Like Hamlet, he wanders about in a daze. "He was suffering the anguish men suffer," says Tolstoy, "when they persist in undertaking a task impossible for them—not from its inherent difficulties, but from its incompatibility with their own nature." But at the critical moment there is a child in a burning building. Pierre dashes in to save her and in doing so saves himself. He is purged from his mad resolve. Nor is it just the heroism of the act that does it. It is its symbolism no less. In saving the actual child from the literal fire, he saves his own innocence, the child within himself, from the criminal fire that threatens to consume him. Imagination triumphs over force.

It is interesting to speculate on what might have occurred if some happy chance or good angel had intervened in Hamlet's case as it did in Pierre's. Suppose for a moment that Hamlet had let *The Murder of Gonzago* take its unhindered way, and imagine further that the miracle happened: that Claudius repented and surrendered the throne to Hamlet. What might have followed?

Such conjectures are idle enough, and I should not be recording any of mine here if by chance I had not discovered that one of Shakespeare's own contemporaries, a man who had seen and perhaps known him in the flesh, had cherished an idea curiously similar to one of my own, not precisely about Hamlet, to be sure, but about what I may call the Hamletian Shakespeare.

Suppose Hamlet had taken over the throne of Denmark. The Prince as King: is it hard to conceive him in that role? Fortinbras at any rate did not think so:

For he was likely, had he been put on,
To have prov'd most royally.

One thing certainly we can count on: he would have made a most unconventional monarch. He would have been just about everything the rest of
Shakespeare's kings were not.

In the first place, he had what ought to be the prime negative requisite for those in high position the world over, what only Henry VI of
Shakespeare's kings in the History Plays possessed: no love of power. It is
precisely because those who are greedy for power so often get it that
power is so often administered in the interest of greed. Except for a couple
of passages near the end of the play that are mere rationalizations of his
hatred of his uncle, there is nothing to indicate that Claudius' usurpation
of the throne, as such, ever caused Hamlet so much as one wakeful night.
He was interested in higher things than governing—and for that very
reason was fitted to govern. Again, with that same exception of Henry VI,
all Shakespeare's kings welcomed, by daylight at least, the ceremonies of
royalty. They enjoyed being lifted by "degree" above their natural station. Hamlet disdained all such trappings and went to the other extreme
of debasing himself from Prince to madman. He practiced to the point of
perversion by daylight what Henry V only soliloquized about by night.

Secondly: Hamlet had the love and confidence of the people. Twice
Claudius refers to this:

> Yet must we not put the strong law on him:
> He's loved of the distracted multitude,

and

> The other motive,
> Why to a public count I might not go,
> Is the great love the general gender bear him,
> Who, dipping all his faults in their affection,
> Would, like the spring that turneth wood to stone,
> Convert his gyves to graces.

The History Plays discriminated the commons as a group of individuals,
from the mob as a pack of wolves. So here. The love of the people for
Hamlet is thrown in contrast with the backing by the rabble of Laertes, a
love that aroused the same jealousy in Claudius as a similar affection for
Rosalind—that feminine Hamlet over whom the cloud never fell—did in
the Duke in *As You Like It*.

Thirdly: Hamlet had the creative instinct and capacity to alter the royal
occupation from what it always has been, war, to what it ought to be,
art: not "art" as amusement or distraction, but art in its deepest and most

religious sense. "Empire against art," said Blake, putting it in three words. If a Falstaffian Hal could have taught England to play in the common acceptation of the term, Hamlet could have taught Denmark to play in a deeper creative sense.

What Hamlet's succession might have meant may be seen by asking: What if, on the death of Elizabeth, not James of Scotland but William of Stratford had inherited the throne! That would have been England falling before William the Conqueror indeed. And it did so fall in the sense that, ever since, Shakespeare has been England's imaginative king, who has taught more men and women to play perhaps than any other man in the history of the world. But if the England of his own day could have crowned him more specifically, by following his spirit, it might have found its way between the Scylla of a decadent Renaissance and the Charybdis of a puritanical reformation and revolution. It might have substituted freedom and imagination for luxury and dogma. And so might Denmark have achieved a similar consummation under Hamlet, even if he had worn no crown, instead of condemning itself, as all the kingdoms of the world have condemned themselves in the past, to a perpetual oscillation between the softness of a Claudius and the hardness of a Fortinbras.

Browsing one day among Elizabethan allusions to Shakespeare, I ran on these lines of John Davies of Hereford:

> *To our English Terence, Mr. Will Shake-speare*
> Some say (good Will) which I, in sport, do sing
> Had'st thou not plaid some kingly parts in sport,
> Thou hadst been a companion for a *king:*
> And beene a king among the meaner sort.
> Some others raile; but, raile as they think fit,
> Thou hast no rayling, but a reigning wit:
>> And honesty thou sow'st, which they do reape:
>> So to increase their stocke which they do keepe.

Shakespeare—so John Davies of Hereford believed—was fit to be a king of the common people. He still is. He is an unfallen Hamlet.

# Index